A NEW HISTORY OF
CLASSICAL RHETORIC

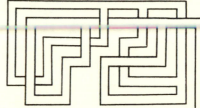

A NEW
HISTORY OF
CLASSICAL RHETORIC

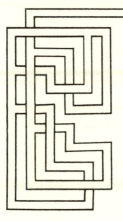

GEORGE A. KENNEDY

AN EXTENSIVE REVISION AND
ABRIDGMENT OF

The Art of Persuasion in Greece

*The Art of Rhetoric in the
Roman World*

AND

*Greek Rhetoric under
Christian Emperors*

WITH ADDITIONAL DISCUSSION
OF LATE LATIN RHETORIC

PRINCETON UNIVERSITY PRESS
PRINCETON, NEW JERSEY

Library of Congress Cataloging-in-Publication Data

Kennedy, George Alexander, 1928–
A new history of classical rhetoric / George A. Kennedy.
p. cm.
"An extensive revision and abridgment of The art of
persuasion in Greece, The art of rhetoric in the Roman world,
and Greek rhetoric under Christian emperors,
with additional discussion of Late Latin rhetoric."
Includes bibliographical references and index.
ISBN 0-691-03443-5 (alk. paper) — ISBN 0-691-00059-X (pbk. : alk. paper)
1. Rhetoric, Ancient. 2. Speeches, addresses, etc.,
Greek—History and criticism. 3. Speeches, addresses, etc.,
Latin—History and criticism. 4. Persuasion (Rhetoric)
5. Oratory, Ancient. I. Kennedy, George Alexander, 1928–
Art of persuasion in Greece. II. Kennedy, George Alexander,
1928– Art of rhetoric in the Roman world.
III. Kennedy, George Alexander, 1928– Greek
rhetoric under Christian emperors. IV. Title.
PA3038.K46 1994
808'.04281—dc20   94-11249

TO MY GRANDDAUGHTER,
AMY RUTH MORTON

Contents

CONTENTS

CHAPTER TWELVE

Christianity and Classical Rhetoric

CHAPTER THIRTEEN

The Survival of Classical Rhetoric from Late Antiquity to the Middle Ages

This book is a revised history of rhetoric as that term was usually understood throughout classical antiquity: the art of persuasion by words or the
art of civic discourse, taught and practiced in schools and applied in public
address. It includes an account of rhetorical features of early Greek literature that anticipated the formulation of "metarhetoric," or a theory of rhetoric, in the fifth and fourth centuries B.C., of the development of that theory
throughout the Greco-Roman period, of the teaching of literary and oral
composition in schools, and of Greek and Latin oratory as the primary rhetorical genre. The influence of rhetoric on literature other than oratory is
only touched upon in passing. Since the formal disciplines of rhetoric and
philosophy constantly interact, something is necessarily said about the history of ancient philosophy and its quarrel with, or acceptance of, rhetoric.
Because the sophists of the Roman Empire were among the leading defend-
ers of pagan religion, and because Christians borrowed many features of
classical rhetoric for their own writing and preaching, later chapters of the
book discuss the relationship of classical rhetoric to religion.

There is a sense in which a history of rhetoric might be thought of as a
history of the values of a culture and how these were taught or imposed
upon the society. Such a history would trace the formation and expression
of ideologies and power structures and the uses of propaganda in the history
of the culture. It would necessarily range widely, not only discussing the
educational system, oratory, philosophy, religion, and literature of the culture, but also dealing with its art, architecture, city planning, political and
economic institutions, class structure, gender relations, dress, food, and virtually everything that created and expressed what the culture was. This
book does not attempt that formidable task, impossible in one book unless
limited to a short historical period. It does, however, provide an account of
one discipline that was a basic tool of power and cultural integrity in antiquity, and it also describes in some detail the system of classical rhetoric that
continued to be studied and adapted, in a variety of ways, throughout the
Middle Ages, the Renaissance, and the early modern period and that is again
being studied widely today to gain understanding of rhetoric as a phenomenon of human life, language, and history.

Thirty years have passed since the publication of *The Art of Persuasion in
Greece*. Both my own studies and the research of others have required significant revision of the account given there. Material from *The Art of Rhetoric
in the Roman World* and *Greek Rhetoric under Christian Emperors* has required less change, but has here been shortened, rearranged, and somewhat
revised. In writing now primarily for students, I have explained some fea-

tures of ancient society more fully than scholars require, have eliminated much of the scholarly apparatus and bibliographical notes, for which the reader can consult the original volumes, and have added references to books and articles published since the date of my original works.

I am indebted to my colleague, Cecil W. Wooten, for many helpful suggestions and encouragement, and to Carol Roberts for her careful work as copy editor for Princeton University Press.

Chapel Hill
August 1993

A NEW HISTORY OF
CLASSICAL RHETORIC

Introduction: The Nature of Rhetoric

The English word "rhetoric" is derived from Greek *rhētorikē*, which apparently came into use in the circle of Socrates in the fifth century and first appears in Plato's dialogue *Gorgias*, probably written about 385 B.C. but set dramatically a generation earlier. *Rhētorikē* in Greek specifically denotes the civic art of public speaking as it developed in deliberative assemblies, law courts, and other formal occasions under constitutional government in the Greek cities, especially the Athenian democracy. As such, it is a specific cultural subset of a more general concept of the power of words and their potential to affect a situation in which they are used or received. Ultimately, what we call "rhetoric" can be traced back to the natural instinct to survive and to control our environment and influence the actions of others in what seems the best interest of ourselves, our families, our social and political groups, and our descendants. This can be done by direct action—force, threats, bribes, for example—or it can be done by the use of "signs," of which the most important are words in speech or writing. Some concept of rhetoric, under different names, can be found in many ancient societies. In Egypt and China, for example, as in Greece, practical handbooks were written to advise the reader how to become an effective speaker.

Classical writers regarded rhetoric as having been "invented," or more accurately, "discovered," in the fifth century B.C. in the democracies of Syracuse and Athens. What they mean by this is that then, for the first time in Europe, attempts were made to describe the features of an effective speech and to teach someone how to plan and deliver one. Under democracies citizens were expected to participate in political debate, and they were expected to speak on their own behalf in courts of law. A theory of public speaking evolved, which developed an extensive technical vocabulary to describe features of argument, arrangement, style, and delivery. In recent years, the term "metarhetoric" has been coined to describe a theory or art of rhetoric in contrast to the practice or application of the art in a particular discourse. The first teachers of rhetoric were the itinerent lecturers of fifth-century Greece known as "sophists," to be discussed in the next chapter; beginning with Isocrates in the fourth century, regular schools of rhetoric became common, and throughout the Greco-Roman period the study of rhetoric was a regular part of the formal education of young men.

Classical rhetoricians—that is, teachers of rhetoric—recognized that many features of their subject could be found in Greek literature before the "invention" of rhetoric as an academic discipline, and they frequently used rhetorical concepts in literary criticism. Conversely, the teaching of rhetoric in the schools, ostensibly concerned primarily with training in public address, had a significant effect on written composition, and thus on literature. All literature is "rhetorical" in the sense that its function is to affect a reader in some way—"to teach and to please," as the Roman poet Horace and many other critics put it—but beginning in the last three centuries B.C., much Greek and Latin literature is overtly rhetorical in that it was composed with a knowledge of classical rhetorical theory and shows its influence.

In the third chapter of his lectures *On Rhetoric*, Aristotle distinguished three "species" of rhetoric. An audience, he says, is either a judge or not a judge of what is being said. By this he means that an audience either is or is not being asked to make a specific decision on an issue presented to it. If the audience is a judge, it is either judging events of the past, as in a court of law, in which case the speech is classified as "judicial," or it is judging what action to take in the future, in which case the speech is "deliberative." If the audience is not being asked to take a specific action, Aristotle calls the speech "epideictic" (i.e., "demonstrative"). What he has in mind are speeches on ceremonial occasions, such as public festivals or funerals, which speeches he characterizes as aimed at praise or blame. These three categories—judicial, deliberative, epideictic—remained fundamental throughout the history of classical rhetoric and are still useful in categorizing forms of discourse today. The concept of epideictic rhetoric, however, needs to be broadened beyond Aristotle's definition. In later antiquity, some rhetoricians included within it all poetry and prose. Perhaps epideictic rhetoric is best regarded as any discourse that does not aim at a specific action but is intended to influence the values and beliefs of the audience.

In its fully developed form, as seen for example in writings of Cicero in the first century B.C. and of Quintilian a century later, classical rhetorical teaching consisted of five parts that parallel the act of planning and delivering a speech. Since a knowledge of how to speak in a law court was probably the skill most needed by most students, classical rhetorical theory primarily focused on judicial rhetoric. Rhetoricians, however, usually also gave some attention to deliberative and epideictic forms, and from the time of the Roman Empire some treatises describe epideictic forms in considerable detail.

The first of the five parts of classical rhetoric is "invention" (Gk. *heuresis*, Lat. *inventio*). This is concerned with thinking out the subject matter: with identifying the question at issue, which is called the *stasis* of the speech, and the available means of persuading the audience to accept the speaker's position. The means of persuasion include, first, direct evidence, such as witnesses and contracts, which the speaker "uses" but does not "invent"; second, "artistic" means of persuasion, which include presentation of the speaker's character (*ēthos*) as trustworthy, logical argument (*logos*) that may convince the audience, and the *pathos* or emotion that the speaker can awaken in the audience. The artistic means of persuasion utilize "topics" (Gk. *topoi*, Lat. *loci*), which are ethical or political premises on which an argument can be built or are logical strategies, such as arguing from cause to effect. A speaker can also use topics, many of which became traditional, to gain the trust or the interest of the audience. The importance of the case can be stressed, not only for the speaker, but as a precedent for future decisions or for its effect on society.

The second part of classical rhetoric is "arrangement" (Gk. *taxis*, Lat. *dispositio*). "Arrangement" means the organization of a speech into parts, though the order in which arguments are presented, whether the strongest first or toward a climax, is sometimes discussed. Rhetoricians found it difficult to separate discussion of arrangement from discussion of invention and often merged the two into an account of the inventional features of each part of a speech. The basic divisions recognized by the handbooks and applying best to judicial oratory are (1) introduction, or prooemium, (Gk. *prooimion*, Lat. *exordium*); (2) narration (Gk. *diēgēsis*, Lat. *narratio*), the exposition of the background and factual details; (3) proof (Gk. *pistis*, Lat. *probatio*); and (4) conclusion, or epilogue, (Gk. *epilogos*, Lat. *peroratio*). Each part has its own function and characteristics: the prooemium, for example, aims at securing the interest and good will of the audience; the narration should be clear, brief, and persuasive; the proof supplies logical arguments in support of the speaker's position and also seeks to refute objections that might be made against it; the epilogue is often divided into a recapitulation and an emotional appeal to the audience. Some rhetoricians added other parts. At the beginning of the proof often a "proposition" and a "distribution" of headings is discussed. Sometimes there is what is called a "digression" or "excursus," which is not so much a true digression as a discussion of some related matter that may affect the outcome or a description of the moral character, whether favorable or unfavorable, of those involved in the case. Deliberative speeches usually have a prooemium, proof, and epilogue and can often omit a narration. Epideictic speeches have a structure of their own; for example a speech in praise of someone may take up the "topics" of his or her country, ancestry, education, character, and conduct.

Once the speaker has planned "what" to say and the order in which to say it, the third task is to decide "how" to say it, that is how to embody it in words and sentences. This is "style" (Gk. *lexis*, Lat. *elocutio*). It is characteristic of classical rhetoric to regard style as a deliberate process of casting subject into language; the same ideas can be expressed in different words with different effect. There are two parts to style: "diction," or the choice of words; and "composition," the putting of words together into sentences, which includes periodic structure, prose rhythm, and figures of speech. Discussion of style is usually organized around the concept of four "virtues" (*aretai*) that were first defined by Aristotle's student Theophrastus: correctness (of grammar and usage), clarity, ornamentation, and propriety. Ornamentation includes "tropes," literally "turnings" or substitutions of one term for another as in metaphor; figures of speech, or changes in the sound or arrangement of a sequence of words, such as anaphora or asyndeton; and figures of thought, in which a statement is recast to stress it or achieve audience contact, as in the rhetorical question. Styles were often classified into types or "characters," of which the best known categorization is the threefold division into "grand," "middle," and "plain."

Invention, arrangement, and style are the three most important parts of classical rhetoric, applicable equally to public speaking and written composition. The earliest recognition of them as three separate actions seems to be in Isocrates' speech *Against the Sophists* (section 16), written about 390 B.C. Aristotle discusses all three subjects in his lectures *On Rhetoric*, which in its present form dates from around 335 B.C., but in the first chapter of book 3 he suggests that a fourth part might be added, "delivery." By the first century B.C. in fact two more parts had been added. Fourth in the usual sequence comes "memory." Once a speech was planned and written out, the student of rhetoric was expected to memorize it word for word for oral delivery. A mnemonic system of backgrounds and images had been developed for this purpose.[1] The best ancient discussion is found in the third book of the *Rhetoric for Herennius*, written in the early first century B.C. Fifth and last came "delivery," as Aristotle had proposed. This is divided into control of the voice—volume, pitch, and so on—and gesture, which includes effective control of the eyes and limbs. The best ancient discussion is found in Quintilian's *Education of the Orator*, book 11.

Classical metarhetoric, as set out in Greek and Latin handbooks from the fourth century B.C. to the end of antiquity, was a standard body of knowledge. Once fully developed, it remained unaltered in its essential features, though constantly revised and often made more detailed by teachers who sought some originality. Was the teaching of rhetoric ever called into question in antiquity? The answer is "yes." Just as today "rhetoric" in popular usage can have negative connotations as deceitful or empty, so it was viewed with hostility or suspicion by some in classical times.

The earliest context in which this criticism explicitly appears is the *Clouds* of Aristophanes, a comic play originally staged in 423 B.C. at the height of the activity of the older sophists.[2] The play includes a debate (lines

---

[1] The beginnings of the mnemonic system were traditionally attributed to the sixth-century B.C. Greek poet Simonides (Cicero, *On the Orator* 2.360); that some techniques were known in the fifth century can be seen in *Dissoi Logoi* 9 (Sprague, *The Older Sophists*, 292–93).

[2] The text we have is a revision by the poet made a few years later.

889–1104) between "Just Speech" and "Injust Speech," in which injustice acknowledges itself the "weaker" but triumphs by verbal trickery over
justice, the "stronger." In Plato's *Apology* (18b8) Socrates, imagined as
speaking at his trial in 399 B.C., says he is accused of "making the weaker
argument the stronger." Aristotle (*On Rhetoric* 2.24.11) identifies "making
the weaker cause the stronger" with the use of argument from probability as
described in fifth-century rhetorical handbooks and says the phrase was
used against the sophist Protagoras. The phrase reflects the frustration of
those unskilled in the new techniques of debate when traditional ideas of
morality and truth were undermined by verbal argument and paradoxical
views that seemed wrong to common sense were seemingly demonstrated.
Examples might include not only the comic debate in the *Clouds* but
Zeno's argument that Achilles could never overtake a tortoise in a race or
the argument attributed to Lysias in Plato's *Phaedrus* that it is better to
accept as lover a person who does not love you than one who does. To make
the weaker argument the stronger can certainly be open to moral objections,
but historically the discovery in the fifth century of the possibilities of logical argument, and thus the willingness to ask new questions, proved fundamental to scientific progress and social and political change. That the earth
is round and circles the sun had long seemed absurd to most people, and to
argue that blacks should be equal to whites had long seemed to many the
"weaker cause."

The most important and most influential of the critics of rhetoric was
Plato, especially in the dialogue *Gorgias*.[3] The word *rhētōr* in Greek means
a public speaker, but it often had the more dubious connotation of a "politician"; the abstraction *rhētorikē* could then be represented as the morally
dubious technique of contemporary politicians in contast to the nobler
study of philosophy with its basis in "truth." Socrates in the *Gorgias* certainly criticizes fifth-century political orators as having corrupted the people, but his criticism is more immediately addressed to Gorgias and Gorgias'
follower Polus for teaching a form of flattery and for their ignorance of the
subjects on which they spoke. Gorgias was one of several traveling lecturers,
called "sophists" (literally "wise men"), who sought to teach techniques of
success in civic life, including what came to be called rhetoric. The sophists
as a group were philosophical relativists, skeptical about the possibility of
knowledge of universal truth. The earliest of the sophists, Protagoras, had
begun a treatise with the famous words "Man is the measure of all things, of
things that are in so far as they are and of things that are not in so far as they

---

[3] Schiappa, in "Did Plato Coin *Rhētorikē*?" has argued that Plato actually coined the word
rhētorikē, which does not occur in any earlier text, but the dramatic date of the dialogue is in
the late fifth century, and both Gorgias and Polus are represented there as accepting the term
without objection.

are not."[4] One of the surviving works of Gorgias, entitled *On Nature*, argues in outline form that nothing exists, that if it does exist it cannot be known, and that if it could be known knowledge could not be communicated by one person to another.[5] The consequence of this position is that the value of opinions about what is true, right, or just should be judged from the circumstances as understood by individuals at a particular time; courses of practical action can best be determined by considering the advantages of the alternatives. This opens up a place for rhetoric in debate and a need to argue both sides of an issue as persuasively as possible, but it also opens up a place for skill in "making the weaker the stronger cause." Socrates in the *Gorgias*, and elsewhere in Plato's dialogues, contends that there is such a thing as absolute truth and universal principles of right and wrong. In the *Gorgias* (463a–b) he describes rhetoric as a form of flattery and a sham counterpart of justice. But in a later dialogue, *Phaedrus*, Socrates is made to describe a valid, philosophical rhetoric that would be based on a knowledge of truth, of logical method, and of the psychology of the audience. As we shall see, Isocrates and others attempted to answer Plato's objections, and Aristotle eventually provided the best solution to the argument by showing that rhetoric, like dialectic, is a morally neutral art, which can argue both sides of an issue but which draws on knowledge from other disciplines in the interests of determining what is advantageous, just, or honorable and employs a distinct method of its own.

Although criticisms of rhetoric were occasionally voiced by others in the fourth and third centuries B.C., the utility of the study of rhetoric for civic life and for writing became generally recognized. The question was, however, reopened in the middle of the second century B.C. by teachers of philosophy, who seem to have been threatened by the number of students flocking to rhetoricians for advanced study rather than to the philosophical schools, traditionally the source of higher education in antiquity. These students included Romans interested in acquiring a knowledge of Greek culture. Cicero (*On the Orator* 1.46) says that the philosophers in Athens in the late second century B.C. "all with one voice drove the orator from the government of states, excluded him from all learning and knowledge of greater things, and pushed down and locked him up in courts of justice and insignificant disputes as though in a mill." Cicero's dialogue *On the Orator*, written in the middle of the first century B.C., is an eloquent and thoughtful response to criticisms of rhetoric, which are blamed in the first instance on Socrates' division between tongue and brain (3.61). In books 1 and 3, Crassus, the character in the dialogue with whom Cicero clearly most identified,

---

[4] For discussion of this statement as well as "making the weaker the strong cause" as applied to Protagoras, see Schiappa, *Protagoras and Logos*, 103–33.

[5] For English translations of the surviving writings of the sophists, see Sprague, *The Older Sophists*.

describes an ideal orator trained in rhetoric, philosophy, law, history, and all knowledge. Such an orator should be morally good and an active participant in public life. The more practical process of rhetoric is substituted for the more theoretical goal of philosophy, but with a deeper basis of knowledge than could be derived solely from the study of rhetorical rules.

Hostility between rhetoric and philosophy existed throughout the period of the Roman Empire. The problem was acerbated by Stoic and Cynic philosophers who criticized the emperors as autocratic. The emperor Domitian, toward the end of the first century after Christ, expelled philosophers from Rome, and the rhetorician Quintilian, who enjoyed Domitian's patronage, scorned them as antisocial dissidents. The emperor Marcus Aurelius in the second century had studied with the rhetorician Fronto but increasingly turned to the attractions of philosophy. That Plato's criticisms of rhetoric were still regarded as forceful is seen in the fact that Aelius Aristides in the mid–second century composed an extended reply to Plato entitled *In Defense of Oratory*. Later in the century the skeptical philosopher Sextus Empiricus in *Against the Rhetoricians* dismissed the study of rhetoric as a waste of time. Rhetoric was a problem for early Christian thinkers. Saint Paul in first Corinthians (2:4) rejects the "wisdom of this world": "My speech and my proclamation are not in persuasive words of wisdom, but in demonstration of the Spirit and power, in order that your faith may not be in the wisdom of men but in the power of God." Radical early Christians often scorned rhetoric as worldly, but Paul was, within his own faith, a skilled rhetorician, and the Apologists of the second century found traditional rhetorical skills useful in presenting the new faith to larger audiences. With the toleration and official establishment of Christianity in the fourth century, Christian leaders show a greater openness to the study of rhetoric. Saint Augustine began his career as a teacher of rhetoric; though he abandoned that on his conversion, he eventually worked out a synthesis of the place of rhetoric in interpretation of the Bible and in preaching as described in *On Christian Doctrine*.

Some modern readers sympathize with philosophy in its dispute with rhetoric. In the former discipline they see devotion to truth, intellectual honesty, depth of perception, consistency, and sincerity; in the later, verbal dexterity, empty pomposity, triviality, moral ambivalence, and a desire to achieve self-interest by any means. The picture is not quite so clear cut. Rhetorical theorists such as Aristotle, Cicero, and Quintilian are not unscrupulous tricksters with words. Furthermore, rhetoric was at times a greater liberalizing force in ancient intellectual life than was philosophy, which tended to become dogmatic. The basic principle of humane law—that anyone, however clear the evidence on the other side seems to be, has a right to present a case in the best light possible—is an inheritance from Greek justice and Roman law. Political debaters under democracy in Greece and republican government in Rome recognized the need to entertain opposing views when expressed with rhetorical effectiveness. Finally, linguistic, philosophical, and critical studies in the twentieth century have pointed to the conclusion that there is no such a thing as nonrhetorical discourse; even ostensibly objective scientific and philosophical writing contains social and political assumptions that may be questioned and uses rhetorical techniques that carry ethical and emotional connotations to argue its case. In the first chapter of *On Rhetoric* Aristotle presents reasons for concluding that rhetoric is useful; we can go beyond that to say it is necessary and inevitable. In speaking, writing, hearing, and reading, we are better off if we understand the process.

Persuasion in Greek Literature
before 400 B.C.

As part of the research that led to his lectures *On Rhetoric*, Aristotle compiled a work called *Synagōgē Technōn*, a survey of the history of rhetoric in Greece before his time with a collection (*synagōgē*) of material from the handbooks (*technai*) that were available to him. This work has not survived, but we have reports of its contents by later writers.[1] Cicero, for example, reports (*Brutus* 46–48) that Aristotle identified the "inventors" of rhetoric as Corax and Tisias in Sicily in the second quarter of the fifth century. According to this story, versions of which are repeated by others, as a result of the overthrow of tyranny and the establishment of democracy in Syracuse there was much litigation over the ownership of private property; Corax and Tisias "wrote 'an Art' and 'precepts'; for before that time no one was accustomed to speak by method or art, though they did so carefully and in an orderly way." Cicero may have been writing from secondhand information or memory and may not accurately report what Aristotle said, and, as will be explained in the next chapter, it is likely that Corax and Tisias are actually the same person. However, the passage, taken together with later accounts, does seem to indicate that Aristotle associated attempts to describe a technique of public speaking with the emergence of democracy and thought that features of what was called rhetoric in his time could be found in fifth-century handbooks and speeches and existed still earlier in careful and orderly composition of speeches intended to persuade, though not codified as a method. That this may have been his view is supported by his habit of quoting in his extant work *On Rhetoric* examples of techniques from Greek literature as early as the Homeric epics.

Before attempts to provide a method of public speaking and to write handbooks of civic rhetoric, there certainly existed in Greece some conception of rhetoric in a more general sense. The common title for an early handbook was *technē logōn*, "Art of Speech," and the Greek word *logos* can be taken as the genus of which civic rhetoric was a species. *Logos* has many meanings through the long history of the Greek language; it is anything that is "said," but that can be a word, a sentence, part of a speech or of a written work, or a whole speech. It connotes the content rather than the style (which would be *lexis*) and often implies logical reasoning. Thus it can also mean "argument" and "reason," and that can be further extended to mean

---

[1] The evidence is collected in Radermacher, *Artium Scriptores*, 11–35.

11

"order" as perceived in the world or as given to it by some divine creator. *Logos* as a metaphysical principle appears in early Greek philosophy and in Plato; it was taken up by the Stoics and then by early Christians, as in the opening verses of the Gospel according to Saint John, "In the beginning was the Word," where it refers to God's plan and thus to Christ. *Logos* is thus a very broad concept.

Unlike "rhetoric," with its sometimes negative connotations, *logos* was consistently regarded as a positive factor in human life, and teachers of rhetoric often celebrated it. In his *Encomium of Helen* (section 8), the sophist Gorgias says "*Logos* is a powerful lord that with the smallest and most invisible body accomplishes most godlike works. It can banish fear and remove grief and instill pleasure and enhance pity." Somewhat later, Isocrates wrote what amounts to a prose hymn to *logos* (*Nicocles* 5–9, repeated in *Antidosis* 253–57; cf. also *Panegyricus* 47–50):

> In most of our abilities we differ not at all from the other animals; we are in fact behind many in swiftness and strength and other resources, but because there is inborn in us an instinct *to persuade* each other and to make clear to each other whatever we wish, we not only have escaped from living as brutes, but also by coming together have founded cities and set up laws and invented arts; and *logos* has helped us attain practically all of the things we have devised. For it is *this* that has made laws about justice and injustice and honor and disgrace, without which provisions we should not be able to live together. By *this* we refute the wicked and praise the good. Through *this* we educate the ignorant and test the wise; for we regard the ability to speak properly as the best sign of intelligence, and truthful, legal, and just *logos* is the image of a good and trustworthy soul. With *this* we contest about disputes and investigate what is unknown; for the same arguments by which we persuade others while speaking privately, we use in public councils, and we call rhetorical (*rhētorikoi*) those who are able to speak in a crowd, and we think good advisers are those who dispute best about problems among themselves. If I must sum up about this power (*dynamis*), we shall find that nothing done with intelligence is done without speech, but *logos* is the marshal of all actions and thoughts, and those most use it who have the greatest wisdom.

There are several interesting features in this passage. *Logos* is a *dynamis*, a power or faculty, the same word that Aristotle later uses in his definition of rhetoric (1.2.1); it is an innate instinct "to persuade"; in political life it is seen in persons called *rhētorikoi*, those with the skills of rhetoric. "Rhetoric" is thus that form of *logos* found in civic discourse.

Before the word "rhetoric" came into use in Greek, its closest equivalent was *peithō*, "persuasion," the power in *logos*. In early Greece Peitho was regarded as a goddess. In Hesiod's *Theogony* (349) she is a primordial being, daughter of Ocean and Thethys; more commonly in early Greek poetry and vase painting, she is a daughter of Aphrodite and thus associated with the appeal of sex. By the fifth century, however, Peitho is associated with political contexts, thus foreshadowing rhetoric. Herodotus (8.111) reports that early in the century Themistocles told the Andrians that the Athenians came to them with two great goddesses, Peitho and Anangke: speech to persuade them to act in their own best interests and the use of force to constrain them if necessary. In midcentury the dramatist Eupolis (fr. 94.5) wrote that Peitho sat on Pericles' lips, referring to his power to persuade the citizens. The first explicit identification of Peitho with rhetoric comes in Plato's *Gorgias* (453a2), where Socrates attributes to Gorgias, and the sophist accepts, the definition of rhetoric as *peithous dēmiourgos*, "the worker of peitho." This may well be a genuine definition by Gorgias of the art he taught, since it is very much in his style.

Greek literature—especially epic, drama, and historiography—make much greater use of formal speeches than is usually found in modern literature. Speech in the Greek epic, which describes a society without the use of writing, is a form of inspiration and gift of the gods.[2] But it is also something that can be taught: Phoenix has "taught" Achilles to be a "speaker (*rhētēr* = *rhētōr*) of words and doer of deeds" (*Iliad* 9.442). Probably the teaching involved listening to older speakers and, like an oral bard, acquiring formulas, themes, maxims, and stock topics, such as myths, historical examples, and proverbs, which are the ancestors of the commonplaces of later oratory. Heroic orators are performers who engage in formal speech acts that generally fall into the genres of commanding, rebuking, or remembering the past.[3] Oratory in the Homeric poems is represented as extemporaneous and as fitted together out of words or groups of words. The common soldier Thersites knows many words in his mind, but they are disordered and he is unpersuasive (*Iliad* 2.213), while Achilles is ready and cunning of speech (22.281).[4] No attempt is made to represent differences in diction or composition by different speakers (nor is this done elsewhere in Greek literature except in comedy and in some of the Platonic dialogues), but speakers are described as differing in fluency: Menelaus spoke fluently, but with few words; Odysseus was unprepossessing in stance, but when he spoke his words flew like flakes of snow (3.209–24). Nestor's voice flowed from his mouth "sweeter than honey" (1.249), and he often seems verbose. Later writers (e.g., Aulus Gellius 6.14.7) regarded Menelaus as an exemplar of the grand style, Nestor of the middle style, and Odysseus of the grand style.

The three speeches addressed to Achilles in *Iliad* 9 to persuade him to

---

[2] See Solmsen, "Gift of Speech."
[3] See Martin, *Language of Heroes*, 43–88.
[4] On the rhetoric of Achilles, see Martin, *Language of Heroes*, 146–205.

return to battle make interesting examples of heroic oratory and show the use of different kinds of argument. Odysseus, for example, gives a well-arranged speech (9.225–306): first he provides a prooemium, in which he seeks Achilles' goodwill by thanking him for his hospitality; then he states his proposition (228–31), that the Greek ships will be destroyed unless Achilles returns to defend them; there follows a brief narration of how the situation developed (232–46), leading to a specific demand that Achilles return (247–48); in the proof (249–306), Odysseus cites four reasons why Achilles should return. The first is "ethical," that is, an appeal to character: Achilles will regret it later if he fails to help the Greeks now. The second is an appeal to external authority: return will be consistent with the advice of Achilles' father. The third might be called "nonartistic," a list of specific rewards Agamemnon has offered Achilles if he will return (gold, the girl Briseis, etc.), plus other prizes he will get when Troy is captured. The last argument, functioning as an epilogue, is emotional: Hector is said to be boasting that no one is his equal, a slur on Achilles, who should return to kill him.

The earliest scene in Greek literature approximating a court trial is the dispute between Apollo and Hermes in the "Homeric" *Hymn to Hermes* (235–502), probably composed in the sixth century B.C. Hermes, though only one day old, has stolen Apollo's cattle. When accused by Apollo he responds that he knows nothing about the cattle and employs what is apparently the earliest specific example of argument from probability (*eikos*) in Greek: is he, a baby, "like" (*eoika*) a cattle thief? (265); that is, is it "probable" that he could have stolen cattle? He is willing to take an "exculpatory oath," which is a common feature of early Greek legal procedure and should settle the matter. But Apollo is not satisfied and drags Hermes off to appear before Zeus as judge. Apollo and Hermes deliver speeches; Apollo has evidence in the cows' tracks and a witness in an old farmer, whom Hermes in the best classical style has tried to bribe, but Apollo does not develop any arguments from his evidence. Hermes tries to awaken the judge's sympathy and again offers to swear an oath. Zeus orders Hermes to show Apollo where he has hidden the cattle.

A further stage in the development of legal procedure and rhetoric is found in the trial scene in Aeschyus' *Eumenides*, the third play in the tragic trilogy *Oresteia* produced in 458 B.C. Orestes is accused by the Furies of murdering his mother, Clytemnestra, who had earlier killed his father, Agamemnon, and the question is Orestes' right to take revenge. The story is often used by later rhetoricians to illustrate forms of argument. There is first (397–489) a preliminary hearing, as usual in Greek courts, in which the goddess Athena as judge hears and examines the charge of the prosecution and then examines Orestes, who has refused to swear an exculpatory oath (429). She inquires about Orestes' descent, nationality, actions, and proposed defense, to which he replies in something close to a set speech. Athena determines that the charge is actionable and turns the trial over to a jury, which is the chorus in the play. The formal trial begins at line 566. Orestes cannot well argue that he did not actually kill his mother—what later rhetoricians will describe as stasis of fact—but he can and does argue that he did so justly (stasis of quality), and he can transfer the responsibility for his action to the god Apollo, who is present to support him and has urged him on. Apollo in turn testifies that Zeus had approved. The prosecutors object that this is inconsistent with what is known of Zeus, citing the fact that Zeus had bound his own father, Cronos, and thus accords no special honor to a father over a mother. The argument is inherently one of probability, though that term does not appear, and since it is based on the use of an example the argument is inductive: what Zeus did on one occasion is regarded as a sign of his general attitude. Apollo responds that the example is not applicable: bonds may be loosed, but death cannot be undone. He then argues that a mother is not the true parent of a child, only the "nurse of the newly planted embryo" (658–59). The "sign" of this—the technical word *tekmērion* is used (662)—is that there can be fatherhood and no mother: an example is the judge, Athena herself, who sprang from Zeus' head without a mother. The heart of the matter is the definition of a parent, and in this rather outrageous argument Apollo is seen anticipating something like the verbal trickery of the sophists: what might be called the weaker is made the stronger cause. Athena, however, accepts the argument. She proclaims herself always for the male; if a wife has killed a husband, his death means more to Athena than the revenge of a son on his mother; if the votes of the jury are equal, she will cast a deciding vote to acquit Orestes (734–43). And so it happens.

The fifth century B.C. was the period of the emergence of radical democracy in Athens. Although older procedures were continued in homicide cases, most criminal and civil suits were now tried in courts with very large juries—a minimum of 201 members and sometimes many more—chosen by lot from among the male citizens. Prosecutors and defendants were ordinarily expected to speak on their own behalf, but if physically incapacitated or not citizens they could be represented by someone else, and women had to be represented in court by a male relative. There were no professional lawyers in Greece. There was no public prosecutor either; even in the case of criminal trials, prosecution had to be initiated by someone with a personal interest in the case. Although there were clerks and attendants, there was no judge to interpret the law, charge juries, and impose rules of relevance. The jury *was* the judge and judged both law and fact; there was no appeal from their decision, though cases could be reopened if there was new evidence. Testimony of witnesses was taken down in writing in advance of the trial and read out by the clerk; there was little opportunity for cross-

15

examination, though the litigants could ask each other direct questions. Trials had to be completed in one day; each side was allotted a maximum amount of time, which was measured by a water clock. The jury voted by secret ballot: a white (for innocent) or black (for guilty) pebble was cast into an urn by each juror at the conclusion of a trial.

Because of the need to address a large jury and the limited amount of time available to each side, the presentation of a case consisted of formal speeches by each side. These speeches had to be well organized to be effective, and the circumstances as a whole required that anyone involved with the law be able to plan and deliver a good speech. These are the conditions that led to the writing of handbooks of judicial rhetoric, which litigants could use in preparing speeches. One other option, however, emerged in the late fifth century and was common in the fourth. Someone who had to speak in court and was unsure of his ability to do so could hire a speech-writer (*logographos*) to write a speech for him, which he then memorized and delivered as best he could. A number of such speeches have been preserved, the work of Antiphon, Lysias, Isaeus, Isocrates, Demosthenes, Hyperides, and others. A skilled logographer tried to present the character of the client in the most favorable way and also supply the arguments available to support the case.

The government of Athens was largely administered by officials elected by lot for terms of a year at a time, which was regarded as the most democratic method. Legislative power lay with an assembly (*ecclēsia*) of all adult male citizens, meeting regularly. Several thousand were often in attendance. There was also a smaller council (*boulē*), chosen by lot, that responded to emergencies and prepared the agenda of the assembly. Although anyone who wished could speak in a meeting of the assembly, the leadership role was taken by individual *rhētores*, "political speakers." These speakers represented the views of shifting factions within the state and varying degrees of democratic or oligarchic ideology; there were, however, no organized political parties. Some of the *rhētores* were persons of great vision and integrity; others, often labeled "demagogues," sought power, wealth, and influence for themselves. Athenian politics was very volatile, and the city was easily led into rash actions by the enthusiasms of a mob. The American Founding Fathers—Adams, Jefferson, Madison, and others—deeply distrusted radical democracy as seen in Athens and were determined to avoid its excesses in creating the United States Constitution.

Athens faced great challenges in the fifth century: during the first quarter of the century there was the threat of domination by Persia and the invasion of Greece by Darius and Xerxes, eventually defeated by the alliance of Athens and Sparta. This was followed in midcentury by the development of an empire on the part of Athens, ostensibly in defence against Persia but bringing both political and economic control of the region into Athenian hands. During the last third of the century Athens was engaged in a bitter struggle with Sparta, the Peloponnesian War, which Athens eventually lost. After a short period of oligarchic government—the rule of the "Thirty Tyrants" in 404 B.C.—Athenian democracy was reestablished and continued in the fourth century. Aristotle's *Constitution of the Athenians* describes the government of that time in detail. Intense political debate was engendered by the crises of the fifth and fourth centuries and is the context in which deliberative oratory evolved into a high art.

The fifth century was also the great age of Greek drama, when tragedies of Aeschylus, Sophocles, and Euripides and comedies of Aristophanes were first presented in the theater. Speeches in Greek drama share many of the features of invention and style of contemporary Greek oratory and are thus evidence for the developing uses of rhetoric. The fifth century was also the high point of Greek art—itself a form of rhetoric in its assertion of the glory of Athens and its religious traditions as seen, for example, in the sculptures of the Parthenon—and it was the time when the sophists stepped into this exciting environment to make their own distinctive contribution to thought and expression.

Sophists were largely foreigners but immediately attracted Athenian followers and imitators. Perhaps the best picture of the sophists as a group emerges in Plato's dialogue *Protagoras*, in which Protagoras of Abdera, Prodicus of Cos, and Hippias of Elis are dramatized in conversation with Socrates. Protagoras (319a) claims to know the art of politics and how to make men good citizens. His techniques of teaching are primarily two: he is willing to engage in a dialectic of question and answer or to expound ideas in an extended speech (320a). According to Cicero (*Brutus* 46), reporting Aristotle's *Synagōgē* as mentioned earlier, Protagoras wrote a collection of "topics" that exemplified general lines of argument and could be imitated and adapted by others, and a book of *Contradictory Arguments* is attributed to him by Diogenes Laertius (3.37). Protagoras was, Diogenes says (9.52), "the first to distinguish the tenses of the verb, to expound the importance of the 'right moment' (*kairos*), to conduct debates, and to introduce disputants to the tricks of argument."[5] As noted earlier, Aristotle mentions him as a speaker who made the "weaker cause the stronger." An anonymous treatise of the late fifth century entitled *Dissoi Logoi*, or "Two-Fold Arguments," provides good examples of how to argue on both sides of a issue: that something is good or bad, honorable or disgraceful, just or unjust, true or false, and so on.[6]

The sophist we know best, and a major figure in the early development of rhetoric in Greece, was Gorgias, who first came to Athens on an embassy

[5] Cf. Sprague, *The Older Sophists*, 4–5.
[6] For translation, see Sprague, *The Older Sophists*, 279–93.

from his native city of Leontini in Sicily in 427 B.C. The source of this information is the historian Didorus Siculus (12.53), who goes on to say, "When
he had arrived in Athens and been brought before the people, he addressed
the Athenians on the subject of an alliance, and by the novelty of his style
he amazed [them]. . . . He was the first to use extravagant figures of speech
marked by deliberate art: antithesis and clauses of exactly or approximately
equal length and rhythm and others of such a sort, which at the time were
thought worthy of acceptance because of the strangeness of the method,
but now seem tiresome and often appear ridiculous and excessively con-
trived."[7] Gorgias is reported to have been a student of the philosopher Empedocles, who had also been active in the democratic revolution in Sicily in
the second quarter of the fifth century and acquired a reputation there as a
fine orator (Quintilian 3.1.8; Diogenes Laertius 7.57–58). Diogenes says
that in his (now lost) dialogue *The Sophist*, Aristotle had said that "Empedocles was the first to discover rhetoric," that in his dialogue *On the Poets*
(also now lost) he described Empedocles as skilled in diction and inclined to
use metaphors and other effective poetic devices, and that Gorgias claimed
to have been present on an occasion when Empedocles "played the wiz-
ard."[8] This seems inconsistent with Aristotle's description elsewhere of
Corax or Tisias as "inventor" of rhetoric, but perhaps Aristotle recognized
two separate traditions as developing in the first half of the fifth century.
One, traced to Corax or Tisias, would be the composition of rhetorical
handbooks, including examples of argument from probability; the other
would be the development of a poetic style in speech and written prose,
traced back through Gorgias to Empedocles. In discussing the origins of
artistic prose at the beginning of book 3 of *On Rhetoric*, Aristotle gives
Gorgias as an example, not as its inventor, and in his treatise *On Sophistical
Refutations* (183b31) he begins a brief survey of the development of rhetoric with Tisias "after the first [inventors]." These predecessors may well be
the same persons referred to in the quotation by Cicero at the beginning of
this chapter, those who spoke carefully and in an orderly way but not by
"method," and they probably should be thought to include Empedocles.
We know Empedocles' own writings only from portions of his philosophical
poems, but some similarities to the style and arguments of Gorgias can be
detected in them. Gorgianic figures are, in fact, a feature of the efforts of
philosophers in the fifth century to create a new form of discourse for their
speculations and can be observed in varying degrees in the fragmentary
prose works of Anaxagoras, Heraclitus, and Democritus as well as in the
poetry of Parmenides and Empedocles. Gorgias' originality was the application of this style to the forms of civic oratory.

[7] Cf. Sprague, *The Older Sophists*, 32–33.
[8] Cf. the remarks of Gorgias in the magical qualities of speech in *Encomium of Helen* 10.

The passage in *On Sophistical Refutations* continues (184a) with criticism of sophists like Gorgias who "gave their students speeches to learn by heart, either 'rhetorical' speeches or those consisting of questions [and answers], in which they thought the arguments of each side occurred. Thus their teaching was quick but not a matter of art; for they supposed they could educate by giving not a *technē* ('art') but the results of *technē*, as if one could say he would transmit knowledge about preventing foot pain and then did not teach shoe-making or where to get such things, but provided many kinds of all sorts of shoes; for he has met a practical need but not imparted a *technē*." It thus seems possible to distinguish two traditions in the development of rhetoric in the fifth century: one is the tradition of the sophists, who taught mainly by example and imitation, not by providing precepts and rules, and whose epideictic speeches exemplified methods of inquiry but often dealt with issues of some philosophical significance; the other is the more pedestrian, less philosophical tradition of the handbook. As we shall see in the next chapter, the latter were simple outlines of the conventional parts of a speech with examples of what might be said in each part. Neither handbook writers nor sophists seem to have discussed rhetoric in abstract terms nor attempted to define it and identify its parts, as do later writers. In Plato's *Gorgias* the sophist himself and his follower Polus are represented as very inept at describing what they do, more inclined to praise the importance of their art than to define it, and easily trapped in Socrates' arguments against rhetoric. The original sophists do not seem to have written handbooks; when later writers refer to their *technē* this does not mean a written rule-based handbook but speeches that are examples of their technique. The two traditions, however, come together in the early fourth century in the school of Isocrates; much of his instruction took the form of speeches he wrote for students to study and imitate, but he claims also (e.g., *Against the Sophists* 16–18) to have provided detailed precepts about rhetorical composition.

The direct evidence for Gorgias' thought and style is largely dependent on four texts: a paraphrase of his treatise *On Nature*, quoted in two later Greek philosophical works; a portion of a funeral oration, quoted by Dionysius of Halicarnassus at the beginning of his essay *On Demosthenes*; and two rather short speeches preserved in Byzantine manuscripts, the *Defense of Palamedes* and the *Encomium of Helen*.[9] *On Nature*, subtitled *On the Non-Existent*, argues by a process of definition and division of the propositions that nothing exists (that is, that the real world is an illusion); that if it does exist it cannot be comprehended by human beings; and that if it could be comprehended knowledge of whatever exists cannot be communicated

---

[9] Translations by George Kennedy in Sprague, *The Older Sophists*, 30–67, with a revised version of the *Encomium* in Kennedy, *Aristotle*, 283–88.

from one person to another. Since the text is only a paraphrase or outline of the argument, it does not provide good evidence for the original verbal style, but it is the major evidence that, unless this is simply to be regarded as a verbal exercise, Gorgias was interested in philosophical questions and that his epistemological position, like that of Protagoras and in sharp contrast to the later views of Plato, was skeptical or at least relativistic. Even if the work was primarily a logical exercise, it shows Gorgias' willingness to question common beliefs and play with paradoxical themes. Aristotle apparently took Gorgias' argument seriously, for he is said by Diogenes Laertius (5.25) to have written a reply. Scholarship on Gorgias has much debated the degree to which he should be regarded as a serious philosopher;[10] there was, however, no sharp division between philosophy and rhetoric in the fifth century and all sophists explored the themes of truth and opinion, nature and convention, and language and reality. Gorgias, in common with others, was probably content to encourage debate and suspend final judgment. This is even the position of Socrates as seen in the early dialogues of Plato.

The three other texts show that Gorgias used somewhat different, although always exaggerated, self-consciously artistic styles in different genres.[11] The surviving piece of his funeral oration differs from other early examples of that genre chiefly in its exaggerated use of antithesis. The *Defense of Palamedes* (Odysseus charged Palamedes with treason in the Trojan War) provides a model of topics in judicial oratory, but in a more poetic style than would be used in a Greek court. The *Encomium of Helen*, most famous of Gorgias' surviving works and most poetic in style, seeks to show that she was morally blameless in leaving her husband, Menelaus, and eloping with Paris—the incident that precipitated the Trojan war. At the end of the speech Gorgias claims to have removed a woman's disgrace, provided a logical argument, corrected injustice and ignorance, and composed a *paignion*, or playful exercise, suggesting that the speech should be both taken seriously and not seriously at the same time. This ambivalence and refusal of closure, highly annoying to conservative Greeks of the time, was characteristic of the sophists and of Socrates as well and has considerable appeal to some modern critics.

The *Encomium of Helen* is divided into prooemium, narration, proof, and epilogue; there is little use of metaphor, but there is constant use of other poetic devices that came to be called "Gorgianic figures." These include phrases or clauses with contrasting thought (antithesis), often of equal length (parison); rhyme at the ends of clauses (homoeoteleuton); and a fondness for sound play of all sorts (paronomasia). The speech also provides a model form of argument. Gorgias proposes that Helen must have gone off

---

[10] See, e.g., Untersteiner, *The Sophists*, 140–74, and de Romilly, *Magic and Rhetoric*, 3–22; there is a good summary in Consigny, "Styles of Gorgias."

[11] See Consigny, "Styles of Gorgias."

with Paris for one of four reasons: by fate and the will of the gods; because she was taken by force; because she was persuaded by speech, or because she was overcome by love. In each case he seeks to show that she was blameless. Isocrates later wrote another "encomium" of Helen. In the introduction he criticizes Gorgias' speech on the ground that it is not truly an encomium: it defends Helen against charges but does not then go on to praise her in a positive way, as Isocrates seeks to do. The most famous passage in Gorgias' *Encomium* is that referred to at the beginning of this chapter in which Gorgias celebrates the power of *logos*, which he compares to the effect of drugs on the body. *Logos* can exercise this power because human beings lack knowledge and must rely on opinion. Examples are cited from scientific writings that make incredible things seem true, from political debate, and from philosophical disputation.

The great political leaders of Athens in the fifth century were Themistocles, Aristides, Pericles, Nicias, Cleon, and others, of whom Pericles (c. 495–429 B.C.) was the most successful and admired. These leaders spoke to the people regularly, and much of their influence came from their rhetorical abilities. Their speeches, however, were not written down, and thus no examples of them can be studied. What we have instead are versions of speeches attributed to them by writers of the history of the period. The most important of the sources is Thucydides, who wrote a history of the Peloponnesian War from 430 to 406. He had heard some of the speeches of Pericles and other leaders but sometimes had to rely on reports of speeches he had not personally heard (he was exiled from Athens for twenty years during the middle of the war because he was blamed for a military defeat). He claims (1.22) to have reconstructed speeches on the basis of *ta deonta*. Exactly what this means has been much debated, but it seems to refer to what was "needed" on the occasion; thus he may be assumed to have assessed the challenge facing the speaker to persuade an audience to some particular action or belief and then to have created a speech to meet that need in the light of what he knew of the contents and of the result of the debate. He often provides speeches on both sides of an issue, but the speeches are very compressed, probably much shorter than what was actually said. Yet they seem to illustrate well the kinds of arguments used in the fifth century, including techniques of the sophists, and are valuable evidence for the development of Greek political rhetoric.

The most famous of the speeches in Thucydides' *History* is the *Epitaphios*, or "Funeral Oration," attributed to Pericles at the ceremony in Athens for those who died in the first year of the Peloponnesian War (2. 35–46). Pericles apparently used the occasion of the speech to set out the cultural ideals that made Athens great in the fifth century: patriotism, freedom under the law, self-confidence, versatility, and reliance on public debate to determine policy. In a famous passage he is made to say, "We culti-

21

vate refinement without extravagance and knowledge without effeminacy;[12] wealth we employ more for use than for show, and place the real disgrace of poverty not in owning to the fact but in declining the struggle against it. . . . In short, I say that as a city we are the school of Greece." The greatness of Athens provides justification for the patriotism of those who have died and those who will in the future sacrifice their lives in its service. Pericles is made to set out his ideals as though they were completely attained, but we know that they were not, and the account of the effect of the plague that follows immediately in Thucydides' narrative shows his own recognition of how fragile Athenian values were in actuality.

Thucydides' version of the "Funeral Oration" reveals a number of characteristics of epideictic oratory.[13] A speaker on a ceremonial occasion is faced with the challenge of trying to say something original and significant rather than to present a series of platitudes. But there are also audience expectations of what is traditionally appropriate, which a speaker should respect. From other funeral orations, such as that by Lysias, we know what the Athenians regarded as appropriate topics: the speaker should acknowledge that his words will be inadequate to the occasion; he should praise the ancestors of those who have died by reviewing great moments in the past history of the city; he should offer some consolation to those who are left behind; and so on. Pericles is shown as touching on these traditional topics while avoiding a trite and obvious arrangement of material. It is also characteristic of epideictic rhetoric that it glosses over historical realities and amplifies its praise of those involved. In later epideictic speeches, such as those addressed to Roman emperors, this clearly involves flattery, but by holding out an ideal as something real the speaker hopes to make it true in the future belief or actions of the addressee and the audience. The basic function of epideictic oratory is to enhance belief in certain moral and civic values and thus to increase social bonding and the solidarity of the cultural group.

Of the political debates in Thucydides' *History*, one of the most interesting is that between Cleon and Diodotus (3. 37–48). The city of Mytilene had revolted from Athenian domination in 428 B.C. Athens forcibly recovered it, and the assembly voted to put all the male Mytileneans to death, both those who had led the revolution and those who opposed it, and to sell the women and children into slavery, making the city an example for any others that might be inclined to revolt. By the next day there was a reaction in Athens against this cruel decision, and a second meeting of the assembly was held to reconsider it. Cleon, who supported the more severe punish-

---

[12] In the Greek this phrase employs the Gorgianic figures of isocolon and homoeoteleuton. Since the speech was given three years before the arrival of Gorgias in Athens, we should probably attribute the use of these figures to Thucydides rather than to Pericles.

[13] The most detailed discussion of the speech and its cultural context is now that by Loraux, *The Invention of Athens.*

ment, argues that it is not only "just" but "expedient" in that it will avoid future revolts. Diodotus, in opposition, might have been expected to stress the argument from justice and mercy; instead, however, he argues primarily on the basis of what is in the best interests of Athens, in this case to spare those who were Athens' friends and thus to encourage such factions elsewhere. He also argues against the utility of the death penality, the earliest example of this topic, which continues as a subject of debate today. The assembly voted in favor of Diodotus' position, though by a narrow margin. The two speeches are unusually clear examples of the topics of justice and expediency and deserve to be read as background for Aristotle's discussion of the species of rhetoric (*On Rhetoric* 1.3).

Another famous example of opposing arguments found in Thucydides' *History*—this time on the conflict of "might" versus "right"—is the "Melian Dialogue" (5.87–111). Thucydides' work as a whole, both in the speeches and in some of his own reflexions on events,[14] brings into very sharp focus the basic issues underlying political debate: democracy versus oligarchy; freedom versus slavery; national self-interest versus justice; independence versus empire; faction versus unity; enlightened leadership vs. personal political ambition. His unflinching gaze on the events of his own time, unaffected by religious superstition or a desire to please his audience, surely in part reflects the power of his own mind to comprehend abstract forces, but the presence of similar ideas in writings of others and in conversations attributed by Plato and Xenophon to Socrates also suggests that in the second half of the fifth century moral and political concepts were being confronted and defined in ways not previously known. At least among intellectual leaders a new ability in abstract thought or theory was being cultivated. Sophists contributed to this development, as did philosophers and others engaged in what we may call science; the late fifth century was also the time of Democritus, who developed an atomic theory in physics, and of the school of Hippocrates, which made significant advances in medicine, based on careful observation of symptoms and logical reasoning from cause to effect.

We do have three speeches by one political speaker of the late fifth century, Antiphon, but they are speeches written for delivery in the law courts and are thus examples of his activities as a logographer.[15] Thucydides (8.68) describes Antiphon as "the one man most able to help those who consulted him about speaking in a court of law or the assembly." Among the works of Antiphon are also preserved three *Tetralogies*, two speeches for the prosecu-

[14] E.g., his "estimate" of Pericles in 2.65 and his analysis of revolution in 3.82.

[15] Antiphon "the Orator" has often been distinguished from Antiphon "the Sophist," author of *On Truth* and *On Concord*, some portions of which survive. J. S. Morrison in Sprague, *The Older Sophists*, 106–240, argues that they are the same person and provides translations of everything attributed to an Antiphon. For translations of the speeches, see also Maidment in the first volume of the Loeb Classical Library *Minor Attic Orators*.

tion and two for the defense in each of three imaginary cases. It is doubtful whether these are actually works by Antiphon: though they have been dated as early as the 440s, recent research suggests that they may have been written in the fourth century, since they seem to reflect legal arguments current at a time after Antiphon's death.[16] Nevertheless, they remain interesting models of what could be said on two sides of an issue in different kinds of trials and of the relatively low value the Greeks put on direct evidence.

Public address in Greece was almost exclusively a male function. Women did not study in rhetorical schools, nor did they speak in law courts and assemblies. Some probably acquired an understanding of rhetoric from written texts and from hearing ceremonial oratory. That Greeks regarded women as capable of eloquence is clear from Greek epic and tragedy, which includes speeches assigned to women of the heroic past, and from comedies of Aristophanes, especially *Lysistrata*, in which woman are imagined as speakers in contemporary Athens. Two queens named Artemisia ruled Greek states in Asia Minor in the classical period and must have had some occasion to speak in public. The earlier of these commanded her own forces in the army of Xerxes when he invaded Greece in 480 B.C. Herodotus attributes two short speeches to her (8.68 and 102). A second Artemisia succeeded her husband as queen in Caria from 353 to 352. In his memory she built the Mausoleum, one of the "seven wonders" of the ancient world, and sponsored a rhetorical contest, in which the leading sophists of the time participated (Aulus Gellius 10.18). In Rome, women were less secluded than in Greece, sometimes exercised great influence through husbands and sons, and spoke in public on rare occasions. According to Quintilian (1.1.6), a speech by Hortensia, daughter of the great orator Hortensius, addressed to Caesar, Pompey, and Crassus, was still read a century later, "and not only as an honor to her sex."

Although Greek literature from the earliest times was "rhetorical" and illustrates techniques that were eventually defined and described, the fifth century was a crucial time in the emergence of a consciousness of rhetoric on the part of speakers and audiences. In *The Art of Persuasion in Greece* (pp. 30–35) four "signs" of this heightened conciousness were identified and seem worth summarizing here; all have been touched upon earlier. The first three are factors in the early development of three of the five parts of rhetoric identified in chapter one: invention, arrangement, and style. The first is the growing interest in forms of proof and argument.[17] They include, of course, great reliance on argument from probablity, based on the assumption of universal characteristics of human nature. These arguments not only can be found in the political discourse of the fifth century but are often used

[16] Cf. Carawan, "The *Tetralogies*."
[17] See Solmsen, *Intellectual Experiments*.

in drama as well. To take one example, in Sophocles' *Oedipus the King* (probably produced about 429 B.C.), Creon seeks to prove that he has no motive to replace Oedipus as king (lines 583–615): Is it probable that he would plot against the king when he now enjoys all the benefits without any of the cares of office? A certain standard of human nature is accepted, and the proposed action is compared to it. Similar arguments are found elsewhere, for example, in Euripides' *Hippolytus* 983–1035. As specious as such arguments may seem today, we have little choice but to believe that they appealed to the Greeks, not only as signs of mental cleverness but as potentially persuasive, depending on what probabilities might be advanced against them.

A second sign of rhetorical consciousness was awareness of the possibilities of artistic unity in speeches and the advantages of dividing them into logical parts. Instances can, as noted earlier, be found as early as the speeches in the Homeric poems, but by the late fifth century the technique was being taught in rhetorical handbooks and exemplified in sophist speeches, such as Gorgias' *Encomium of Helen*.

A third sign of rhetorical consciousness is experiment in rhetorical style, applied now to prose as well as to poetry, and the beginnings of attempts to describe different styles. Gorgias' use of poetic devices in prose is the most obvious example of experimentation, but there were others. The sophist Thrasymachus is said by Aristotle (*On Rhetoric* 3.8.4) to have begun the use in prose of the paean (a succession of three short syllables and one long at the end of clauses or sentences); Aristotle regarded this as the most appropriate rhythmical unit in artistic prose. In fact it is not very common in Greek, and the importance of Thrasymachus is primarily his apparent consciousness of prose rhythm, which became traditional in Greek and Latin. Another feature of fifth-century style, seen in Gorgias but more generally common in fifth-century Greek, is a marked love of antithesis, that is, of a balanced contrast of words or ideas. When Plato in the *Protagoras* or *Symposium* seeks to imitate the style of sophists, he frequently employs antithesis, and it is a feature of the style of early plays of Sophocles and Euripides and of the prose of Antiphon and Thucydides. Its frequency in the speeches in the early books of Thucydides probably represents the actual style of the speakers.[18] The potential for antithesis is, however, deeply engrained in the Greek mind, as is evident from the constant use of the grammatical construction *men ... de* ("one the one hand, ... but on the other ..."), from the fondness of the Greeks for contrasting figures like Prometheus and Epimetheus, and from the symmetry favored by Greek artists, most notably in architectural pediments. Antithesis as a stylistic device is a counterpart to

[18] See Finley, "The Origins of Thucydides' Style," 82–84.

argument on two sides of an issue as practiced by sophists or as seen in the debates in drama and in Thucydides' *History*.

Styles were also being described for the first time. An awareness of different rhetorical and literary styles seems innate in any highly developed culture, though classification and description of the possible styles only slowly develop. The description of the speaking styles of Menelaus, Odysseus, and Nestor in the *Iliad* already shows such awareness. The earliest extant passage to discuss differences in style is found in Aristophanes' *Frogs*, produced in 405 B.C., where Aeschylus and Euripides are represented as criticizing each other's style and defending their own (lines 830–1431). Aeschylus defends his use of elevated diction, which Euripides attacks as pompous and swollen; Euripides' style is criticized by Aeschylus as thin and pedestrian and defended by Euripides as simple and natural. Lines from their plays are weighed on a scale, with the result that Aeschylus' heavy style seems always to win. Thus, by the late fifth century metaphors were being used to describe style in physical or physiological terms, and a concept of a grand style and a plain style was evolving. In the fourth century these are identified with a written and a spoken style, respectively, by Isocrates and Alcidamas and as discussed in the twelfth chapter of the third book of Aristotle's *On Rhetoric*. As we shall see, Theophrastus then added the concept of a mean or middle style, leading to the three genera of style as understood by Cicero and other later writers.[19]

The fourth sign of rhetorical consciousness is the beginning of the science of philology and grammar. Until the fifth century, Greeks had felt no need to describe their own language, which young people learned directly by imitation of elders and without any codification of rules. Several of the sophists, however, engaged in linguistic studies: Protagoras' work on the gender of nouns and the mood of verbs has been mentioned earlier; he also compiled an *Orthoepeia*, which appears to have been a list of "proper" words as distinct from metaphors. Prodicus of Ceos studied definitions. An interest in etymologies is evident from Plato's *Cratylus*, set dramatically in the fifth century. Apparently at least two schools existed, one insisting that language is a matter of conventional or arbitrary usage, another that there is some natural root meaning in the sound of words. Debate over the comparative claims of nature (*physis*) versus custom or convention (*nomos*) is often taken as characteristic of the time, not only in discussion of language but on ethical and political issues as well.

An important factor in the development of rhetoric in Greece, only recently recognized, is the increased use of writing beginning in the second half of the fifth century. Forms of syllabic writing, called "Linear A and B," had been used for administrative and commercial records in Greece in the

---

[19] On the development of stylistic theory, see O'Sullivan, *Alcidamas, Aristophanes*.

second millennium, but literacy was lost in the "Dark Ages" after 1100 B.C. A form of the Phoenician alphabet was then introduced about the eighth century, again at first for practical purposes. The Homeric epics and other early Greek literature are the result of an oral tradition of recomposition in performance by illiterate bards; written texts of Greek poetry probably first came into existence in the seventh century. By 500 B.C. poets, philosophers, and others were composing in writing, but "publication" continued to take the form of oral presentation of their works. Elementary schools to teach reading and writing probably came into existence in the sixth century; by the fifth century literacy was common throughout the Greek-speaking world. A reading public then emerged for the first time, and copies of books, in the form of handwritten papyrus scrolls, could be purchased relatively cheaply.[20] Although rhetoric was the art of oral discourse, the description of rhetorical techniques and the teaching of rhetoric required reliance on writing. It made possible the handbooks of judicial rhetoric and the written versions of epideictic speeches of sophists. In Plato's *Phaedrus* a young man has been listening to a sophistic speech by Lysias, has secured a written copy of it to study, and reads the speech to Socrates. Socrates himself wrote nothing; Plato adopted the dialogue form as a written version of oral discussion and consistently shows ambivalence if not hostility to reliance on written texts for the authoritative exposition of philosophy. In the myth of Theuth at the end of the *Phaedrus*, he makes Socrates argue that writing is destructive of memory and written texts are inadequate in that they cannot "answer" questions put to them.[21] The sophist Alcidamas wrote a short work *Against Those Writing Written Texts*, which also opposes the increased reliance on writing.[22] Opposition to writing is, however, one of the best signs that it was gaining ground in the culture.

Increased use of writing in the fifth century probably resulted from practical needs, such as communication over the distances of the far-flung Athenian empire, keeping administrative records, and note taking by those with scholarly interests in geography, history, medicine, and other subjects. The effect of this "literate revolution"[23] of the late fifth and fourth century, however, was to facilitate the working out of complex, abstract thought; the coinage of a technical vocabulary to describe phenomena, including that of speech; rewriting and revision as a regular part of composition, and probably also the development of the periodic style, that is, writing in long, complex sentences not easily understood when first heard. These are all characteris-

---

[20] See, e.g., Plato, *Apology* 26d–e.

[21] For an interesting "deconstruction" of Plato's position, arguing for the priority of writing over speaking, see Derrida, "Plato's Pharmacy."

[22] Translation in Matson et al., *Readings from Classical Rhetoric*, 38–42.

[23] See Havelock, *The Literate Revolution*, and Cole, *Origins of Rhetoric*.

tics of the great "speeches" of Isocrates, which were the result of painstaking revision and published as written pamphlets rather than delivered orally. Demosthenes and other orators began to publish revised, written versions of their speeches to reach a wider audience. Aristotle, in contrast to Socrates and Plato, relied heavily on writing. His research involved extensive collection of written evidence, and his lectures were apparently written out in advance of delivery. Texts could now be consulted, studied, reread, and criticized. The concept of a "topic" in rhetoric may owe its origin to writing; *topos* literally means "place," and a "topic" may originally have been the place in a handbook or other written work from which the idea, argument, or form of expression could be borrowed.[24]

The increased use of writing in classical Greece has been regarded as a technological innovation comparable in significance to the invention of printing in the fifteenth century and the introduction of the computer in the twentieth century.[25] All three affect in subtle ways the view of reality, ideas, and language. We should not, however, exaggerate the influence of writing in the history of rhetoric; it was an important tool for developing rhetorical theory in treatises and handbooks and for studying rhetorical models to be imitated. But the objective of the study of rhetoric in the classical period was primarily the ability to speak in public, including extempore speaking; only secondarily did instruction in rhetoric take on the goal of teaching students how to compose or analyze written texts. This *letteraturizzazione*, or "application of rhetoric to written composition," is largely a phenomenon of periods in which opportunities for civic oratory were reduced, often with the loss of the freedom of speech that characterized Greek democracies and the Roman republic. Since schools of rhetoric were the only common form of secondary education in the classical world, they prepared both speakers and writers, and their influence is often seen in literature, especially in the time of the Roman Empire. Even so, classical society remained highly oral; throughout antiquity it was customary for written works to be read aloud, even when read privately by one individual. Readers had an "ear" as well as an "eye" for texts, and the sound of the spoken word remained an important feature of written works to a degree not always appreciated today.

The previous chapter noted the existence in antiquity of hostility to rhetoric. Rhetoric was, from the beginning, controversial. The question has recently been raised "What was the rhetoric of rhetoric?"[26] That is, what means did sophists and teachers of rhetoric use to persuade their contempo-

---

[24] See Cole, *Origins of Rhetoric*, 88–89.

[25] See Ong, *Orality and Literacy*.

[26] See Cahn, "The Rhetoric of Rhetoric." He identifies six tropes of "disciplinary self-constitution," which he calls artist, language, *kairos*, *technē*, *natura*, and *ars est artem celare* ("art is to disguise art").

raries that the art deserved serious study? How did they succeed in establishing a discipline that prevailed for centuries? Several strategies are evident. One was to stress the usefulness of the skills they could impart. Even Aristotle, in the first chapter of his treatise where he seems to be addressing students of philosophy, is at pains to explain how rhetoric is useful. Students probably did learn to be better speakers by studying rhetoric, but the results were unpredictable and the rhetoric of rhetoric regularly involved appeal to a higher vision. Rhetoric could be regarded as a natural force, *the* distinctive human faculty, as Isocrates claimed, or even something divine, as Gorgias suggested in his *Encomium of Helen*. Isocrates also identified it as dealing not with humdrum details of everyday business but with the great questions of national identity and human life. The question of whether or not rhetoric was an art, as in the argument between Socrates and Gorgias, was important because if rhetoric was an art it could claim to have method and theory to be learned from its teachers. It could claim a place among other systematic disciplines; analogies between rhetoric and medicine as curative arts are frequent. The eloquent orator then becomes a civic ideal, the master artist of civic life. He alone is in full control of language, which serves to authorize his art and his personal claims. But knowledge of rule is not enough: the orator must grasp *kairos*, that sense of the opportune, when to say what. He is most effective when he is able to disguise the techniques he uses. All of these qualities helped to create a mystique that had much to do with establishing a high place for rhetoric in the scheme of human affairs, and with it high status for its teachers and practitioners. The process was complete and ready to survive the collapse of democracy when philosophers, especially Aristotle and his student Theophrastus, lent their authority to the study of rhetoric as a serious academic discipline.

Greek Rhetorical Theory from Corax to Aristotle

The comparative chronology of the major figures to be discussed in this chapter is as follows: Gorgias lived to be at least 105 years old (he may have been born around 480 or 475 and survived until about 375 or 370 B.C.) Socrates lived from 469 to 399; Isocrates from 436 to 338; Plato from about 429 to 347; Aristotle from 384 to 322.

Plato's *Phaedrus* includes a passage (266d1–67d9) that appears to be an account of handbooks of rhetoric as known in the late fifth century. At this point in the dialogue Socrates has just given a description of dialectic as a process of logical definition and division of a subject and then asks if that is the art Thrasymachus and others use to become skilled in speaking. Phaedrus thinks it is not and says that the nature of rhetoric seems still to be elusive. The discussion continues:

> *Socrates*: What do you mean? Could there somehow be some fine thing that they (the sophists) leave out and yet is a matter of art? If there is, it deserves all due honor by you and me and we should say what really belongs to rhetoric and has been left out.
>
> *Phaedrus*: There are perhaps very many other things, Socrates—those in the books that have been written about the art of speech (*logōn technē*).
>
> *Socrates*: You did well to remind me. As I recall there is first the matter that a prooemium should be spoken at the beginning of a speech. That is what you were referring to, wasn't it, the niceties of the art?
>
> *Phaedrus*: Yes.
>
> *Socrates*: Second, there should be a narration (*diēgēsis*) and witnesses to it; third, proof from signs; fourth, probabilities; the man from Byzantium, an admirable adorner of speech, includes in speeches, I think, a proof and a supplementary proof.
>
> *Phaedrus*: You mean the worthy Theodorus?
>
> *Socrates*: Who else? And [he says] that one should create a refutation and supplementary refutation, both in prosecution and defense. But we are failing to include that very fine person Evenus of Paros, who first discovered insinuation and indirect praise—some say that he also composed examples of indirect praise in meter so that they could be remembered better—for he was a clever man. Shall we leave Tisias and Gorgias to their slumbers? They saw that probabilities are more hon-

ored than truth, and they make small things seem great and great
things small by the strength of words, and new things old and the oppo
site new, and they discovered both brevity of speech and unlimited
length on all subjects. Once, when Prodicus heard of this from me he
broke into laughter, and said he alone had discovered the art speeches
needed; they should be neither long nor short but of due measure.

Phaedrus: Very wisely said, Prodicus.

Socrates: Shouldn't we mention Hippias? For I think that visitor from Elis
would also agree with him.

Phaedrus: Of course.

Socrates: And what shall we say about those "museums" of words of
Polus—his diplasiology and gnomonology and eikonology[1]—and the
collection of nouns that Licymnius gave him for creating fine diction?

Phaedrus: Wasn't there something of this sort by Protagoras, Socrates?

Socrates: His *Orthoepeia*,[2] my boy, and many other fine things. The ability
of Thrasymachus in words that awaken pity for old age and poverty
seems to me to have gained him victory in the art, and the man has
been wonderful at first moving the masses to anger and then when they
were angered charming them out of it "by magic," as he said. He is the
best both at attacking and answering attacks of almost any sort. But the
end of speeches seems a subject agreed upon by all in common, though
some give it the name "recapitulation" and others call it something
else.

Phaedrus: You mean reminding the audience at the end about what has
been said by summarizing each heading?

Socrates That's what I mean, and anything else you can say about the art
of speech.

Phaedrus: Little things, not worth mentioning.

What is under discussion are "books" available in the late fifth century:
some seem to be chiefly examples of rhetorical techniques taught by famous
sophists—Protagoras, Gorgias, Prodicus, and Hippias—others are rhetorical
handbooks by minor figures, including Tisias, Theodorus, and Polus. Socrates starts with the prooemium and moves through the traditional parts of
a judicial speech: narration, proof (with a number of subdivisions), and finally epilogue. This probably reflects the order of topics in some handbook
such as that by Theodorus, which is later followed by most writers on the
subject. Between proof and epilogue Socrates inserts mention of books that

---

[1] "Diplasiology" means "doubling" words; the Neoplatonic commentator Hermeias understood the term literally, as in "Alas, alas"; modern scholars tend to think words compounded of
two roots are referred to; see Radermacher, *Artium Scriptores*, 114. A gnomonology would be a
collection of wise sayings, an eikonology a collection of similes.

[2] "Proper meanings."

provide examples of various kinds of diction and thus relate to style. Aristotle criticizes writers of handbooks in the first chapter of *On Rhetoric*, first (1.1.4) for neglecting logical argument and concentrating on ways to arouse emotion, and then (1.1.9) for their concern only with "external" matters, such as defining the parts of an oration and what should be included in each, things which aim at putting the audience in a certain frame of mind rather than proving something. He adds that the handbook writers are interested only in judicial oratory, where he admits there is more of a need to awaken the jury's interest and goodwill than there is in addressing an assembly on a subject of public concern. Elsewhere, however, he seems to acknowledge that the early handbooks did include attention to certain kinds of argument. The "Art of Corax," he says (2.24.11) is based on the fallacious argument that what is contrary to probability is also probable: "for example, if a weak man were charged with assault, he should be acquitted as not being a likely suspect for the charge. . . . And if he is a likely suspect, for example if he is strong, [he should be acquitted] for the very reason that it was going to seem probable." Plato cites this same argument (*Phaedrus* 273a–b), attributing it to Tisias. Aristotle also instances a form of argument from probability based on what it would have been a mistake for someone to do as "the whole art before Theodorus" (2.23.28) and, like Plato, attributes to Theodorus multiple divisions of parts of an oration (3.13.5). To judge from Cicero's summary of the *Synagōgē* (*Brutus* 48), Aristotle there described Theodorus as "subtle in art but dry in speech."

In this passage three different strands in the early history of rhetoric seem to be interwoven. Although Plato's sources are published "books," no one book contained the whole picture that Socrates constructs. One strand can be clearly isolated: the lexicographical works attributed to Protagoras, Polus, and Licymnius, which taken together apparently catalogued different types of diction on the basis of meaning or form and provided lists of examples.

A second strand seems to be inventional or stylistic usages to be found in writings of Evenus, Gorgias, and Thrasymachus. Rather little is known about Evenus.[3] He seems to have been a sophist who charged high fees and had his students memorize stock phrases, including passages that exemplified indirect ways of praising or blaming someone. Probably these were written down in a small book of which Plato had some knowledge. As for Gorgias, on the basis of what was said in chapter 2 we can be reasonably confident that he did not write a handbook of precepts for rhetoric, and references to his "art" should be taken to mean the rhetorical techniques of his epideictic speeches, which others learned by imitation. Thrasymachus was a politician and sophist and is Socrates' opponent in the first book of the

---

[3] For the testimonia, see Radermacher, *Artium Scriptores*, 127–28.

Republic, where he argues that justice is the power of the stronger. Socrates (*Phaedrus* 271a4–8) refers to him as having published a handbook, which some later writers also mention.[4] Aristotle says (*On Rhetoric* 3.1.7) that Thrasymachus "tried to say something about rhetorical delivery" in his *Eleioi*, or "Emotional Appeals." This is perhaps what Socrates is referring to, and from Plato and Aristotle taken together that work would seem to have offered some precepts as well as examples of pathetical expressions, which Thrasymachus also employed in speeches.

These first two strands woven into Plato's account do not specifically apply to any one species of rhetoric; study of diction and emotional appeal would be equally useful for deliberative, epideictic, or judicial oratory.

What remains is the handbook that outlined the form and content of a judicial speech, seen in the structure Plato seems to follow and in Aristotle's reference to the exclusive concern of handbook writers with judicial oratory.[5] Clearly we can attribute to Theodorus a handbook that included division of the basic parts into several subparts, as mentioned by both Plato and Aristotle. Theodorus would seem to be a contemporary of Socrates who had come from Byzantium, settled in Athens, and had "followers" there.[6]

The only surviving handbooks of rhetoric from the classical period in Greece are Aristotle's famous treatise—which indeed is something more than a handbook but includes portions in which specific precepts are offered and in the second half of book 3 provides an account of the parts of the oration that clearly owes something to earlier works—and the *Rhetoric for Alexander*, probably by Anaximenes of Lampsacus, who was a contemporary of Aristotle. A prefatory letter, added to the latter work at a later time, credits its sources on rhetorical doctrine as "Corax" and Aristotle's *Theodectea*. We saw in chapter 1 that Aristotle's *Synagōgē* was understood by later writers to have traced the history of one strand of rhetorical instruction from Corax and Tisias in Sicily in the second quarter of the fifth century. The conclusion of twentieth-century scholars has been that the writing of handbooks of judicial rhetoric began with Corax or Tisias and was continued by Theodorus and others; that the handbooks were arranged by the parts of an oration, giving advice as to what should be treated in each part; and that the discussion of proof was primarily, perhaps exclusively, devoted

[4] Cf. Radermacher, *Artium Scriptores*, 70–76.

[5] Cole, in *Origins of Rhetoric*, 130–32, argues that the organization of the discussion in the *Phaedrus* by the parts of the judicial oration does not reflect the structure of earlier handbooks but is a pattern imposed by Plato on the material. This is part of Cole's program of denying any real development of rhetoric in Greece before Plato and is not consistent with the evidence or the judgment of most scholars.

[6] Aristotle, in *On Rhetoric* 3.13.5, speaks of his followers or school.

to the use of argument from probability.[7] This tradition now probably needs to be modified in a number of ways.

First, we should admit that we know very little about the form and content of fifth-century handbooks. Among the sources that have been used are a collection of "prolegomena," introductions to the study of rhetoric composed in late antiquity that describe in some detail the activities of Corax and Tisias, though inconsistently when compared both to earlier evidence and to each other.[8] Some of what they say goes back to Aristotle's *Synagōgē*, some to other sources. According to one story, Tisias was a pupil of Corax and refused to pay for his instruction. Upon being dragged into court, he argued that if he won the dispute he need not pay, by that decision; if he lost, however, payment would be unjust, since what he learned would be proved worthless. Corax replied by reversing the argument. The court turned them both out with the epigram "a bad egg from a bad crow." The word for "crow" in Greek is *corax*. That is an unusual name for a Greek but might be a nickname, derived from an impression of his tiresome "cawing" in his speeches.[9] It has recently been plausibly suggested that Corax and Tisias are one and the same person, Tisias the Crow.[10] This would explain why the example of argument from probability that Plato attributes to Tisias is attributed by Aristotle to Corax and why writers of the Roman period sometimes say that Aristotle identified Corax as the "inventor" of rhetoric and at other times identify Tisias as such. Perhaps what Aristotle said in the *Synagōgē* was something like "Corax, as Tisias was called." What Plato actually makes Socrates say in the reference to Tisias in *Phaedrus* 273c8 is "It was a wonderously hidden art that Tisias or another seems to have discovered, *whoever he really is and whatever he likes to be called!*" Plato and Aristotle are the only writers who might reasonably be assumed to refer to Tisias the Crow with some knowledge of what he taught, and they agree that what he taught was the use of argument from probability, or at least a certain form of argument from probability that could be used on opposite sides of the same case. And they attribute nothing else to him. Cicero says (*On Invention* 2.6) that after Aristotle wrote his *Synagōgē* everyone consulted it rather than the original handbooks, which were soon lost.

We should probably assume that the early written handbooks were largely made up of illustrative examples, arranged by the parts of the oration in which they might be used, thus resembling to a degree the collections of commonplaces and other passages for imitation made by Protagoras or

---

[7] This traditional view owes much to its clear formulation in Navarre's *Essai sur la rhétorique grecque* of 1900.

[8] Prolegomena are discussed in chapter ten below.

[9] Cf. Pindar, *Olympian* 2.86:88, comparing other poets to crows cawing against the eagle of Zeus.

[10] Cf. Cole, "Who Was Corax?"

Thrasymachus and the *Dissoi Logoi* or the *Tetralogies* attributed to Antiphon, mentioned in the last chapter. But some introductory discussion may have been included, and some specific precepts for each of the parts of the oration probably should be envisioned: something like, "In the prooemium you should gain the goodwill and attention of the audience. You can, for example, say. . . ."

Plato's *Gorgias*

The sophist Gorgias has been repeatedly mentioned earlier in this book and is clearly an important figure in the early history of rhetoric. As the passage quoted in chapter 2 from Aristotle (*On Sophistical Refutations* 184a) shows, Gorgias was unsystematic in his teaching; that is, he did not lecture on rhetoric or write a handbook of rhetorical rules. Instead, his concept of rhetoric was embodied in epideictic speeches, such as his *Encomium of Helen* with its four parts of prooemium, narration, proof, and epilogue; its logical division of the subject; its discussion of the power of *logos*; and its use of poetic figures of speech. These techniques were imitated by others, but we cannot say with confidence that Gorgias' students delivered speeches that he then criticized to help them improve their skills. References by other writers to Gorgias' views on rhetoric are probably drawn from passages in his speeches in which he spoke about his art, or possibly to things he said in conversation with others. Examples include the definition of rhetoric (or perhaps of *logos*) as "worker of persuasion" (Plato, *Gorgias* 453a2) and the statement by a character in Plato's *Philebus* (58a8–b2) that he had often heard Gorgias say that the art of persuasion differed from other arts in that all things are made its slaves of their own will and not by force and that it was by far the greatest of all arts. A concept of *kairos* is also attributed to Gorgias. *Kairos* means the opportune moment, the right time to say or do the right thing. It was widely recognized by rhetoricians that knowing the rules was not much help unless one knew how and when to apply them. In his essay *On Literary Composition* (12) Dionysius of Halicarnassus discusses the problem and says that no orator or philosopher had succeeded in defining an art of *kairos*, "not even Gorgias of Leontini, who though first to try to write about it wrote nothing worth mentioning."

In Plato's *Gorgias* Socrates visits a house in Athens where Gorgias is staying.[11] The dialogue is divided into three parts: in the first, Socrates interrogates Gorgias about rhetoric; in the second Gorgias is largely replaced by his follower Polus; in the third Socrates enters into debate with Callicles about justice. There is a dramatic heightening of tension in that Gorgias is represented as a somewhat amiable, if pompous, defender of his art and is treated

---

[11] Dodds' *Gorgias* is the best commentary on the dialogue; for discussion, see also Guthrie, *History of Greek Philosophy*, vol. 4, 284–312.

with courtesy by Socrates; Polus is a rash young enthusiast for the new rhetoric, with whom Socrates is rather caustic; and Callicles is a very hard-headed, politically ambitious young man, whose obsession with achieving success at any cost awakens deep moral objections on the part of Socrates. The overall theme of the dialogue is the question of how one should live one's life, whether in accord with virtue or in pursuit of power, but rhetoric as a tool to success is a major issue in the discussion. Several of Plato's dialogues, the *Protagoras* for example, are "aporetic"; that is, no agreement is reached about the issues discussed, and Socrates himself is shown as dissatisfied with the discussion. The *Gorgias* is "dogmatic" in the sense that Socrates is shown as firm in his beliefs, but it is aporetic in the sense that he cannot be said to successfully convert Gorgias, Polus, and Callicles to full understanding or acceptance of his views. They do not refute Socrates' arguments, but his standards of knowledge and justice seem to them unrealistic. The dialogue leaves the reader with a sense of the gap between philosophy and the everyday world. The philosophical issues of the *Gorgias* are resumed and more thoroughly discussed in the *Republic, Phaedrus,* and later dialogues.

Consistent with what we know of him from other sources, Gorgias appears in the dialogue as having no highly developed theory of rhetoric and as not having thought much about defining and describing it in abstract terms. Plato does not allow Gorgias to offer any real defense of his belief that rhetoric is an art and shows him making several tactical mistakes in argument. For example, he is led by Socrates to claim that rhetoric is "knowledge about words" (449d8–9). When Socrates asks if that includes knowledge of words that explain to the ill how to get well, Gorgias says "no." Logically he should have said "yes," since subsequently (456b) he describes how he has accompanied his brother, a doctor, on his rounds and used rhetoric to persuade patients to undergo treatment. Under Socrates' questioning Gorgias limits the use of rhetoric to persuasion in law courts, councils, assemblies, and other public meetings (452e). He then casually adds (454b7) that it deals with justice and injustice, a tactical mistake and not likely to have been the view of the historical Gorgias, who surely believed that his art applied to any topic. He also grants (454e8) that rhetoric produces belief, not knowledge. This is consistent with Gorgias' statements in the *Encomium of Helen* and with the skepticism of his treatise *On Nature,* but it opens up the opportunity for Socrates to deny that rhetoric is an art since it is not a form of knowledge of any particular subject. Socrates' absolutist theory of knowledge leads to what might be called the fallacy of the expert: he ironically claims (455b) that if an assembly is debating whether to build a city wall, the rhetor will keep silent and the architect will give advice. Plato does not allow Gorgias to point out that one and the same person needs knowledge of the subject and a knowledge of how to communicate that knowledge. Gorgias is represented as not regarding knowledge as very important and casually claims (460a) that if one of his students lacks knowledge of a subject he will teach it to him. Plato is more fair to Gorgias when the latter distinguishes between rhetoric as an amoral force and the morality of the orator (456c7–57c3). It is not fair, in Gorgias' view, to blame the teacher if the pupil makes an unjust use of his art. Socrates asserts, however, that since it has been agreed that rhetoric deals with justice, it is inconsistent to say that the orator might use rhetoric for unjust purposes (460e–61b2).

Meanwhile, Polus[12] has become increasingly impatient with what he regards as Gorgias' attempts to be polite to Socrates and thus with his mentor's unwillingness to insist on his knowledge and ability to teach it to others. He takes up the discussion and demands to know what Socrates thinks rhetoric is. This produces the most famous passage in the dialogue (462b–66a), in which Socrates describes rhetoric as a form of flattery and a counterpart to cookery. The passage has sometimes been taken as a seriously intended definition of rhetoric,[13] and certainly Plato was hostile to the political rhetoric of his time; but Socrates, in response to Polus, deliberately takes an extreme view for purposes of discussion. He delights in ironic dialogue. The truth will lie somewhere between the positions of Socrates and those of his opponents; the *Phaedrus* will show that there can be an art of rhetoric if properly understood.

Here in *Gorgias* Socrates denies that rhetoric is a *technē* or art based on a form of knowledge; it is instead an *empeiria*, something acquired by experience, or a *tribē*, a "knack," and one of four forms of flattery that Socrates identifies. Each is a reflection of a true art. There are two categories of arts, Socrates explains, those that work on the soul, here called politics, and those that affect the body. Each category is then divided into two, depending on whether it establishes a good condition of soul or body or whether it corrects some deficiency. *Legislation* establishes the correct conditions in the state and the individual; *justice*, meaning punishment for violating written or unwritten law, corrects faults; *gymnastics* establishes healthy conditions of the body; *medicine* corrects unhealthy conditions. Each of the four forms of flattery is an *antistrophos*, or counterpart, to one of the true arts. (Aristotle will use a form of the same word to describe rhetoric as a counterpart to dialectic in the first sentence of *On Rhetoric*.) *Sophistic* is defined as the counterpart to legislation and establishes pleasant but false principles in the soul; *rhetoric* tries to correct departure from these norms; similarly, *cosmetics* produces a false impression of healthiness in the body and (gourmet)

---

[12] "Polus" was apparently the name of a real person. It means "colt," and Plato takes advantage of this in characterizing him as young and impetuous.

[13] Quintilian 2.15.24–28 refers to this view and seeks to refute it.

cookery corresponds to medicine, making food taste better but not correct-
ing illness. In addition to the correlation of each of the sham arts with a true
art, there is an analogy between those that are normative and those that are
corrective. Thus rhetoric, as a sham art of the soul, corresponds on the one
hand to justice and on the other hand to cookery as imitating a corrective
art.

A person who has done wrong, Socrates tells Polus (480d), will only become worse by use of rhetoric in self-defense; instead, one should use rhetoric to make one's crime clear to judges, to secure punishment, and to rid
oneself of evil. Although this logically follows from Socrates' position, it is
hardly a serious suggestion and is surely intended to startle Polus into thinking about the subject. Toward the end of the *Gorgias* some possibility of a
just and valid use of rhetoric is briefly considered. Callicles has observed
(503a3) that some orators speak with a concern for the citizens, and rather
surprisingly Socrates agrees. There is, he says, the rhetoric that is a form of
flattery and shamelessly seeks to move a crowd, but there is at least potentially another kind of rhetoric,

> "and this other is beautiful, making provision that the souls of citizens be
> the best possible, striving to say what is best, whether this is more pleas-
> ant or more unpleasant to the audience. But you have never seen this
> rhetoric. Or if you are able to name any such orator, why have you not told
> me who he is? (503a–b). . . . Will not that orator, artist and good man
> that he is, look to justice and temperance? And will he not apply his words
> to the souls of those to whom he speaks, and his actions too, and . . . will
> he not do it with his mind always on this purpose: how justice may come
> into being in the souls of his citizens and how injustice may be removed,
> and how temperance may be engendered and intemperance removed,
> and every other virtue be brought in and vice depart?" (504e)

It is this possibility that opens the way for discussion of a philosophically
valid rhetoric in the *Phaedrus*. Socrates' conclusion in the *Gorgias* is that
flattery of all sorts should be avoided; rhetoric, which Socrates has now tacitly recognized as a possibly legitimate art, should be used only for the sake
of justice (527c3–4). The importance of the dialogue is that for the first
time it poses in detail the question of the morality of rhetoric in society and
for the first time emphasizes the need for knowledge as the basis of communication. Its main weakness is its failure to distinguish those arts, like politics, that have a specific subject matter from those, like rhetoric, that are
faculties applicable to many subjects. That distinction will be made clear for
the first time by Aristotle. The sophists were not immoral figures seeking
personal power, but their enthusiasm for rhetoric ran the risk of encouraging opportunism. Plato's integration of the intellectual, moral, and rhetorical qualities of the orator into the whole man avoids that risk, but at the cost

of practical effectiveness. Socrates was executed on a charge of which he was innocent, whereas rhetoric might have secured his acquittal at the cost of some flattery of the jury. The rhetoric Socrates seeks is an ideal, beyond the possibilities of the Greek or the modern city. Plato's recognition of this is shown in the *Republic*, which takes up many of the moral concepts of the *Gorgias* but finds it necessary to imagine an ideal state in order to find justice.[14]

Plato's *Phaedrus*

Phaedrus, written perhaps ten years after *Gorgias*, is divided into two parts, which correspond to the two methods of rhetorical instruction current in fifth-century Greece.[15] The first half includes a set of three epideictic speeches similar to those composed by sophists; at Stephanus[16] page 257b7 begins a theoretical discussion analogous to a rhetorical handbook, which touches, often critically, on such topics as the definition of rhetoric, its parts, and forms of argument. The dialogue is an artistic unity, but there has never been agreement about how to describe its subject in a few words. Much of it deals with rhetoric, but there is also discussion of several basic Platonic doctrines, including love, inspiration, and the nature of the soul. Plato's view of rhetoric here is that it cannot be divided from its substance: a speech must be about something and it is that something that matters most. The thesis to be demonstrated should be morally valid and should mold the form of the speech. Plato chooses love as the subject of the three speeches in part one for a variety of reasons. First, it was a common rhetorical theme, found for example in Gorgias' *Encomium of Helen*; second, love exemplifies the fact that rhetoric involves the souls of the speaker and the hearer. The orator who pleads the cause of the nonlover, as is done in the first two speeches, is directly harming both himself and the person addressed. Moreover, the choice of subject allows a contrast between sincere love and a cynical use of rhetoric as a cold exercise of technique in violence to human feelings. Finally, Plato regards true rhetoric as best exemplified in the dialectic with which the philosopher persuades and ennobles the soul of his beloved.[17]

The dialogue begins with an elaborate introduction, unusual in Plato's

[14] Portions of this discussion are adapted from Kennedy, *Classical Rhetoric*, 45–52.

[15] There is an extensive bibliography on the dialogue. Notable among more recent discussions are Guthrie, *History of Greek Philosophy*, vol. 4, 396–433, and Ferrari, *Listening to the Cicadas*.

[16] References to passages in Plato's dialogues are traditionally based on page numbers in the edition of Henri Estienne, Geneva 1578; these numbers are usually printed in the margin of modern editions and translations.

[17] The association of rhetoric and love is also a theme of the speeches in Plato's *Symposium*.

works in that it shows Socrates out of his usual environment in the city and places him and Phaedrus alone in a romantic natural setting. The first half of the dialogue can be read as an attempted erotic and intellectual seduction, a seduction of Socrates by Phaedrus to the beauty of rhetoric and of Phaedrus by Socrates to the truth of philosophy. The playful mood of the introduction disguises serious intent; even the first line, "Dear Phaedrus, where are you going and where are you coming from?" can be interpreted at two levels of meaning, and issues important for the thought of the dialogue are lightly touched upon: writing, for example, the name Pharmaceia,[18] and the interpretation of myth.

Phaedrus has been studying a written copy of a sophistic speech by Lysias, which he much admires, and is finally persuaded to read it aloud to Socrates. Lysias is otherwise known to us as a writer of speeches for serious occasions, but he probably sometimes played with sophistic forms. This speech, however, is almost certainly by Plato, who clearly enjoyed showing his rhetorical virtuosity by imitating the style of other writers or speakers. Other striking examples are the long speech by Protagoras in the dialogue bearing his name and the six speeches, also on love, attributed to well-known friends of Socrates in the *Symposium*. The speech Phaedrus reads argues that a young man should accept as his lover an older man who does not love him in preference to one who does. Homosexual relationships between men and adolescent boys were a common feature of upper-class society in classical Greece, often regarded as part of the boy's education and resulting not so much from sexual orientation as from the segregation of the sexes and from the cult of the male body in Greek athletics. The argument can, however, easily be recast in heterosexual terms: an intimate relationship without emotional involvement is preferable in that neither partner makes excessive demands on the other and neither is hurt when the relationship ends. Socrates at first claims to be quite overcome by the beautiful language of the speech Phaedrus reads but then points out what seem to him its flaws in invention and arrangement. He is finally persuaded to try his skill at giving a better speech.

Socrates' first speech is a technical improvement over that of Lysias in terms of the rhetorical theory that was being developed in fifth-century Greece. There is a prooemium (237a7ff.), a narration (237b2ff.), a proof (237b7ff.), and an epilogue (241c6ff.). It has a more logical development, beginning with a definition of love (237d1ff.) and moving on to a consideration of relative advantages and disadvantages in the proposed relationship. The proof is largely indirect: the disadvantages of accepting the lover are demonstrated under such headings as intellectual, physical, and economic.

---

[18] The name of this nymph is one of several terms in the dialogue that provide an opening for the deconstructive reading given it by Derrida in his "Plato's Pharmacy."

Socrates veils his head while giving the speech, thus implying his feeling of guilt at doing something immoral, when he has finished he attempts to leave but is stopped by his *daimōn*, that inner spirit that sometimes speaks to him when he is about to do something wrong (cf. *Apology* 31c9ff.). The speech he has given, he says, is "dreadful, dreadful" (242d4); love is a god, or something divine, but the two speeches have spoken of him as something evil. This must be redressed in a palinode like that by the early poet Stesichorus, who was struck blind when defaming Helen and regained his sight when he recanted. In fact, Socrates' speech is worse than Lysias' speech for the very reason that it is a rhetorical improvement over it.

Socrates then delivers a much longer speech in favor of the older lover, demonstrating the nature of the soul and of love at considerable length by use of a myth: the flight of the immortal soul upward, imagined as a charioteer seeking to govern two winged horses, one inclined to pull it downward to earthly lust, one upward to heavenly contemplation. Platonic metaphysics, including the theory of forms, the doctrine of imitation, and the concept of "Platonic" love, are here cast in highly poetic language, giving visual specificity to philosophical abstractions.[19] The passage has been admired by many readers over the centuries; even if one rejects its philosophical views, it can be appreciated as literary art. Plato, for all his ambivalence about rhetoric, and for all his apparent rejection of poetry in the *Republic*, was an accomplished rhetorician and prose poet. His rhetorical skill throughout the dialogues has indeed made him one of the most dangerous writers in human history, responsible for much of the dogmatism, intolerance, and ideological oppression that has characterized Western history. But the dialogues can, and probably should, be read in a nondogmatic way as an exploration of important issues in philosophy and human life that invite ongoing debate rather than blind acceptance. Indeed, they were so read by Plato's associates, including Aristotle, in the Academy, the school Plato founded in Athens after the death of Socrates.

After Socrates' second speech the style of the *Phaedrus* changes from rhetorical exposition to dialectical analysis of rhetoric. The question of the legitimate use of writing is raised initially (257c–58e) and will recur to frame the dialogue at the end. As noted in chapter 2, this was an important contemporary issue in Greek society, since reliance on written texts was increasing in the late fifth century and was affecting thinking and composition in a variety of ways. Here at the beginning of the discussion Socrates only notes

---

[19] It is unlikely that the historical Socrates held the beliefs given him here. By the time he wrote the *Phaedrus* Plato had gone beyond the questioning characteristic of Socrates to the development of his own idealistic philosophy. The problem of what in Plato's writings represents the genuine thought of Socrates is a vexing one, known as "the Socratic question." In general, earlier dialogues, such as *Protagoras*, are probably closer to Socratic thought than are either *Gorgias* or *Phaedrus*.

that both speaking and writing can be done well or badly. He then discusses what the standards should be (259e–74b). The good orator cannot be content with knowing what *seems* to be true; he needs to know what *is* true. Is this knowledge adequate, or is more involved if rhetoric is to be an art in its own right? Socrates offers a preliminary definition of rhetoric as "a kind of leading the soul (*psychagōgia*) by means of words, not only in law courts and any other public assemblies, but in private encounters" (261a7–9). Although Plato, Aristotle, and their successors usually treat rhetoric as a feature of public address, Plato here recognizes that there is a more general phenomenon of rhetoric in all human communication. Socrates then stresses the need for logical structure in a speech, which structure will result from definition of the subject and division of it into headings (263b6–9) and will be evident in the total unity of the parts: "Every speech should cohere like a living thing having its own body so that nothing is lacking head and foot, but should have a middle and extremities fitting each other and written into the whole" (264c2–5).

There follows the review of books on rhetoric, quoted at the beginning of this chapter. Their authors, Socrates says, deal only with preliminaries and lack needed knowledge of logical proof, and they leave it up to the student to discover how to achieve unity (269b–c). Anyone who writes an art of rhetoric should describe the soul, how it affects, or is affected by, others, and how the speaker should fit each kind of speech to each state of the soul (271a4–b5). There is then a return to the speaker's need for knowledge. The example of argument from probability attributed by Aristotle to Corax and quoted earlier in this chapter is cited here and attributed to Tisias, with the conclusion that probability can only be known when tested against knowledge of truth (273d–e). There follows the tale of Theuth and Thamus, in which Socrates returns to the issue of writing, arguing that it encourages forgetfulness, that it can fall into the hands of those who do not understand it and cannot answer questions or answer back, and that it is an illegitimate brother of true, oral discourse. If one who knows truth and beauty uses writing, it will be only as a kind of plaything for his own amusement. This passage has been used by Derrida as a classic text in the debate over "logocentricity" that has emerged in late-twentieth-century critical discussions, the view that spoken language has some direct access to reality lacking in writing.[20]

A philosophically valid art of rhetoric as outlined in the *Phaedrus* may be summarized as follows: a speaker should have good knowledge of the subject discussed, a good understanding of logical proof, and a knowledge of human psychology that makes it possible for arguments to be adapted to an audience.[21] The goal of persuasion should, of course, be virtuous action,

[20] Derrida, "Plato's Pharmacy."
[21] The doctrine is well summarized in one long sentence in 277b5–c6.

justice, and belief in the truth. These demands become the basis for Aristotle's theory of rhetoric, though Aristotle adapts them to practical realities to a greater extent than Plato seems to allow. Plato's requirement of the speaker's knowledge of audience psychology is an important addition, taken up by Aristotle in book 2 of *On Rhetoric*. In public address, it is complicated by the presence in many audiences of people with diverse values and interests. Plato does not make much allowance for this situation; Aristotle tries to cope with it by looking at audiences in terms of groups of people with the same age or status.

At the end of the *Phaedrus* Socrates speaks of young Isocrates as one who, because of his noble character and interest in philosophy, may achieve great distinction in rhetoric. It is difficult to know how to take this reference, which is the only mention of Isocrates by name in Plato's writings. Is it a genuine hope of the historical Socrates? A complement by Plato to a famous contemporary? Or should it be read ironically as suggesting Plato's disappointment at the direction Isocrates' career had taken him? Isocrates is certainly an important figure in the history of Greek rhetoric, and we need now to consider his contributions.

Isocrates

Isocrates was a few years older than Plato; he is said to have studied with Prodicus, Gorgias, and others, and he certainly knew Socrates.[22] After his family's property was lost in the Peloponnesian War, he became a logographer, writing speeches for others to deliver in the law courts. Six of these survive. About 390 B.C. he opened a school in Athens, where over the next forty years he taught a large number of young men; among his students several became prominent political leaders or writers. *Against the Sophists*, a speech he wrote about the time of the opening of his school but which is only partially preserved, gives a picture of what he had in mind to do there and can be complemented by his later account in *Antidosis*. Isocrates himself has often been thought of as a sophist: he resembles the sophists in accepting payment for teaching,[23] in offering instruction in the skills needed for success in public life, and in writing speeches that were models for imitation by others. He is, however, at pains to distinguish himself from sophists and indeed from any other educators of the time. He claims to teach philosophy, and he never refers to his art as *rhētorikē*, always as an art of *logos*, but he means by that the art of political discourse on important

---

[22] The sources on Isocrates' life are the essay *Isocrates* by Dionysius of Halicarnassus, the account of him in *Lives of the Ten Orators* (preserved with the works of Plutarch), and some references in his own writings. The best translation of Isocrates' works is that in the Loeb Classical Library, vols. 1–2 by Norlin, vol. 3 by VanHook.

[23] Perhaps only from foreign students; cf. *Antidosis* 39.

subjects. He never mentions Plato by name, but it is easy to regard his writings as in some sense a response to Socratic and Platonic criticism of rhetoric as found in the *Gorgias*. That dialogue objects to rhetoric as lacking any distinct subject matter, thus not a form of knowledge; Isocrates sought to provide an appropriate subject matter and teach knowledge of it. The subject he came to favor was Panhellenism, the cultural unity of all Greeks and the development of international policy to preserve and enhance it. The form of exposition he chose was the writing of elaborately polished discourses, epideictic in style though sometimes cast in the genres of deliberative or judicial speeches or as letters, which were studied by his students as models of composition and were published as pamphlets to be read by the public.

In *Against the Sophists* Isocrates first (1–8) attacks the pretension of sophists—none are specifically named—who arrogantly claim to impart to students all that they need to know to be happy, successful, and prosperous. These teachers are eager for money, distrustful of their own students, and lacking in any knowledge of what they pretend to teach. A second group attacked (9–14) are those who claim to teach *politikoi logoi*, political oratory. They pay no attention to ability or experience and teach some inflexible rules, without any consideration of how these are to be applied in an appropriate way: "speeches are good only if they have a share in what is opportune (*kairos*), appropriateness of style, and originality." Isocrates then outlines his view of teaching. First, the student must have some native ability. Education can improve this, for example by showing students where to turn for topics of argument and by encouraging self-improvement. The following passage (16–18) is the most specific account Isocrates gives of his proposed methods:

> Since I have gone this far I want to speak more clearly about these matters. I say that to grasp a *knowledge* of the *ideas* from which we speak and compose all speeches is not very difficult if one gives himself over, not to those making easy promises, but to those knowing something about it; but what one should *choose* from among these for each subject and join to each other and *arrange* deftly, and further not to make a slip about the *right moments* to use them, but *to adorn* the whole speech *appropriately* with *striking thoughts* and to speak with rhythmical and musical words, these things need much study and seem to be the work of a manly and original soul,[24] and the student should, in addition to having the necessary *natural ability*, *learn* the *forms* of speech and be *practiced* in their use, and the teacher, for his part, should *go over these matters* so *carefully* as to leave out nothing that can be taught and otherwise should himself pro-

---

[24] Plato seems to have been struck by this phrase and makes Socrates echo it, rather ironically, in *Gorgias* 463a7.

vide such an *example* that those who are being formed and are able to *imitate* him will, from the start, shine in their speaking in a more flowery and graceful way than others. When all of these things combine, those engaged in *philosophical study* will achieve complete success; but in so far as any of the things mentioned are left out, necessarily the disciples will be worse off.

This passage shows Isocrates' awareness of a number of features that become standard in later rhetorical theory. Rhetorical ability is a form of *knowledge*. The Greek word here, *epistēmē*, is used by Plato to mean "full and certain knowledge of truth"; Socrates in the *Gorgias* denies that it is applicable to rhetoric as currently practiced. For Isocrates this is to be knowledge of what he calls "ideas"; Aristotle will use a related word (*idia*) to describe the propositions or topics of politics and ethics that are used by a speaker. Knowledge of these matters can come from reading or from discussion by a teacher, but the student must choose from the available topics in composing a speech. Up to this point Isocrates is discussing what comes to be known in rhetorical theory as invention. He then moves on to arrangement: the student needs to learn how to *arrange* the ideas and seize the right moment (*kairos*) for employing them. Third, Isocrates touches on style. This is the earliest passage in Greek that seems to show awareness of invention, arrangement, and style as three parts of rhetoric. The student needs to be able to *adorn* a speech *appropriately*. Ornamentation and propriety will be defined by later teachers as two of the "virtues" of good style. The word translated as "striking thoughts" is *enthymēmata*, "enthymemes," which will be adopted by Aristotle to mean a rhetorical syllogism. Here Isocrates seems to use it in more of a stylistic than a logical sense; perhaps it refers to the amplification of the ideas as they are found in the large periodic sentences of Isocrates' own writing.

From the elements of rhetoric Isocrates then turns to educational method. Here, as elsewhere, he emphasizes that a student must have some natural ability. That can be improved by *learning* and by *practice*. By *forms of speech* Isocrates may mean the various rhetorical genres such as he practiced himself: panegyric, encomium, apology, and epistle. The passage seems to imply that Isocrates expected to provide some systematic discussion of rhetoric, probably in lectures: *go over these matters . . . carefully*. Possibly, however, this took the form of a critique of a written speech in which he pointed out its use of invention, arrangement, and style. He himself will provide *examples* for *imitation*. This, indeed, seems to have been his major activity. He consulted his more advanced students as he revised his own writings and invited their criticism (cf. *Panathenaicus* 200), and his students wrote speeches, which he criticized and helped them improve. At the end of the passage Isocrates refers to his students as engaged in *philo-*

sophical study, a phrase that perhaps somewhat jarred on the ears of Plato. Isocrates separates himself from sophists, but what he teaches is *sophia*, wisdom in a practical sense, what Aristotle will term *phronēsis*.

From this point *Against the Sophists* continues (19–20) with an attack on the writers of rhetorical handbooks "who lived before our time" and who professed to teach how to conduct lawsuits. These are the worst of those he singles out for criticism, mere teachers of meddlesomeness and greed. Isocrates does not think there is an art that can teach self-control and justice to those who do not have it; he does think that study of political discourse can help to stimulate and form virtue (21). The speech then breaks off at the point where Isocrates is going to explain his meaning more fully. It leaves the impression that there were in early-fourth-century Athens many teachers—far more than we can now identify—who offered instruction in verbal skills, often of a very superficial sort. Plato could not refer to them in dialogues set dramatically in the lifetime of Socrates, but their existence may be one reason for the sharpness of his criticism of the teaching of rhetoric. It is likely that he lumped Isocrates with them: thus the reference to "young Isocrates" at the end of *Gorgias* may well be ironic.

About 354 B.C., when he was eighty-two years old, Isocrates became painfully aware that there was hostility to him in Athens based on a perception that he had become rich and on misunderstanding of what went on in his school. This led him to write *Antidosis*, a long speech in defense of his life and work. The speech is an "apology"; Isocrates imagines himself on trial for his life, like Socrates, accused of "making the weaker cause the stronger" (15) and corrupting the young (30), and the speech has many allusions to Plato's *Apology of Socrates*. Isocrates quotes portions of his own speeches as witnesses of his devotion to truth, to country, and to high moral standards. He supplies less detail about his school than we would like but does say (87) that students remained with him for three or four years and names some of them (93). His best-known student was Timotheus, who became an important general in the second quarter of the fourth century, but Timotheus had been somewhat discredited and Isocrates has to supply a defense of him (101–39). Timotheus was brilliant, but perceived as cold and arrogant. There is an interesting passage in which Isocrates tells how he had tried to get Timotheus to improve his relations with the public. He grants that political leaders should say what is true and just, "yet they must at the same time not neglect to study and consider well how in everything they say and do they may convince the people of their graciousness and human sympathy" (132). This clearly represents a practical compromise from Socratic standards of rhetoric. Isocrates has sometimes been regarded as the father of liberal education: he offers (167–88; 261–69) a defense of a program of studies that are not immediately practical, or will not lead to careers for all individuals, but will train the mind. Training of the mind he calls "philosophy," and says it is a "counterpart" to gymnastics, or training of the body; ~~each involves parallel forms of instruction, exercise, and other studies~~ (181).[25] In sections 253–57 he repeats the passage quoted in chapter 2 celebrating the centrality of speech in human life. Returning to the benefits of liberal education, he warns the young against giving too much time to philosophical subtleties, and he ridicules the theories of pre-Socratic philosophers, including Empedocles and Parmenides, and Gorgias' attempt to prove that nothing exists (268–69). Though Plato is not named, this is surely criticism of the epistemological and ontological interests of the Academy as a waste of time.

Toward the end of the speech (274–78) Isocrates, late in his career, sets out his philosophy of rhetorical education:

> I think that there never was and is not now an art that could instill virtue and justice in those of a depraved nature and that those who make promises on that score will grow weary and cease their idle talk before discovering any such thing; but I do think that people can become better and worthier if they are ambitious about speaking well, and if they are enamored with being able to persuade their hearers, and if, in addition, they set their hearts on the gain to be had, not gain as named by the ignorant, but what truly has this meaning. And how this is so, I think to make clear immediately.
>
> First, it is not possible that a person choosing to speak or write speeches worthy of praise and honor will support unjust or petty causes or those concerned with private contracts; rather he will choose great and beautiful and humane subjects and those concerned with issues of common interest; for if he does not find such he will accomplish nothing to his purpose. Second, from among deeds pertaining to his hypothesis he will choose those that are most fitting and most advantageous, and accustoming himself to contemplate and judge examples of this sort, he will feel their influence not only in regard to the speech at hand but also in other actions, so that speaking and thinking well will come to be an attribute of those who are philosophically and ambitiously disposed. And one who wishes to persuade others will not be negligent of his own virtue, but will pay special attention to it that he may get the finest reputation among his fellow-citizens. Who does not know that words seem more true when spoken by those who lead good lives than by those whose lives have been criticized and that proofs based on a person's life have greater power than those provided by speech? Thus, the stronger a person desires to persuade hearers, the more he will work to be honorable and good and to have a good reputation among the citizens.

[25] The opening sections of Isocrates' *Panegyricus* contain an elaborate comparison of oratory and athletics as contests.

Here Isocrates is arguing for a kind of behavioral conditioning. Get students to practice themes about patriotism and virtue, about justice and temperance and courage and wisdom; have them study examples from history and choose from among these examples to illustrate their arguments. Encourage their ambitions to be great speakers. Their own characters will thereby be molded, and not only will they apply the lessons they learn in their speeches, but they will try to live up to these standards, knowing that their effectiveness with an audience will result in large part from the audience's trust in their character. The more ambitious they are, the more virtuous they will become. Character (*ēthos*) is an important factor in rhetoric, sometimes the most important. Aristotle, Cicero, and Quintilian will discuss its role. Isocrates' program of moral improvement by reading and writing about virtue has been a traditional part of western education. It does not always succeed, and the question of whether and how virtue can be taught, discussed by Plato in *Protagoras*, continues to be debated today.

There are references in later writers to Isocrates' *technē*.[26] Some may be references to the "art" found in his published speeches, but others are references to a handbook. The young Cicero could not find a copy but knew of "precepts" taught by Isocrates' students (*On Invention* 2.7). He later refers to discussion of Isocrates in Aristotle's *Synagōgē* (*Brutus* 48), which may thus be one source. An anonymous biography of Isocrates quotes Aristotle as saying in the *Synagōgē* that Isocrates wrote a rhetoric handbook but later destroyed it himself.[27] Quintilian knew of a handbook attributed to Isocrates but was not sure it was genuine (2.15.4). He says Isocrates was the first to regard rhetoric as a *dynamis*, "power, faculty," which is the definition given in *Against the Sophists*, quoted earlier, and that he defined rhetoric as *peithous dēmiourgos*, "worker of persuasion," the definition we have seen attributed by Plato to Gorgias. Elsewhere Quintilian says that Isocrates thought praise and blame were present in every form of oratory (3.4.11) and that the followers of Isocrates require the narration in a speech to be clear, brief, and probable (4.2.31), adding that Aristotle is referring to Isocrates when he objects to the requirement of brevity (*On Rhetoric* 3.16.4).[28] Syrianus, a rhetorician of the fifth century after Christ, claims knowledge of a discussion of style in a "private *technē*" of Isocrates,[29] which could be some kind of manual for his students or could mean his oral instruction as recorded by students. According to Syrianus, Isocrates emphasized purity of diction, the avoidance of hiatus,[30] and the careful use of correlative conjunc-

---

[26] They were collected by Radermacher, in *Artium Scriptores*, 153–63.

[27] Radermacher, *Artium Scriptores*, 155.

[28] Aristotle actually objects to a requirement of rapidity, not brevity.

[29] Cf. Radermacher, *Artium Scriptores*, 157–58.

[30] Hiatus is the "clash" resulting from beginning a word with a vowel or diphthong when the previous word ends in a vowel.

tions. These are all characteristics of Isocrates' prose style in his published speeches.

Modern scholars often distinguish an Isocratean tradition in classical rhetoric, contrasted with an Aristotelian tradition.[31] So understood, the Isocratean tradition emphasizes written rather than spoken discourse, epideictic rather than deliberative or judicial speech, style rather than argument, amplification and smoothness rather than forcefulness. The distinction specifically derives from a passage in Cicero's On Invention (2.8), which speaks of two "families" of teachers in the period after Isocrates and Aristotle, one primarily interested in philosophy but giving some attention to rhetoric, the other entirely devoted to interest in speech. Cicero says, however, that the two traditions have come together, and it was one of his great missions in On the Orator to encourage such a union. Quintilian (3.1.13) speaks of "diverse paths" in the two centuries from Aristotle to Hermagoras but seems to have in mind Peripatetic successors of Aristotle, Isocrateans, and others, of whom he mentions Theodectes. If the term is taken in a very general sense, the Isocratean tradition could be said to have been revived in the second century after Christ in the movement known as "the Second Sophistic," exemplifed especially by Aelius Aristides. These later sophists share Isocrates' predilection for epideictic rhetoric, amplification, and smoothness. But the orators and rhetoricians of the Second Sophistic would not have acknowledged Isocrates as their only model; they sought rather to attain the purity and clarity of Attic prose of the fourth century B.C. and found models in Plato, Xenophon, Demosthenes, and others, as well as in Isocrates.

The Rhetoric for Alexander

Two systematic works on rhetoric survive from fourth-century Greece. The more famous is Aristotle's treatise On Rhetoric, probably put in its present form about 335 B.C. The other, probably a more typical handbook of the time, is called the Rhetoric for Alexander.[32] It takes its title from an introductory letter purporting to be by Aristotle addressing Alexander the Great, which resulted in the work's being preserved with the writings of Aristotle. This dedicatory letter is regarded by all modern scholars as a forgery; spurious letters carrying the names of Plato, Demosthenes, Aeschines, and others also exist, though why such things were written is not well understood. From an historical reference in chapter 8, it seems that the Rhetoric

---

[31] Cf. esp. Solmsen, "The Aristotelian Tradition."

[32] There is a translation by Rackham in the second volume of the Loeb Classical Library edition of Aristotle's Problems. The best text is that of Fuhrmann, Anaximenis Ars Rhetorica. There has been relatively little scholarship on the treatise since that noted in my Art of Persuasion in Greece.

for Alexander was written after 341 B.C., and the existence of a papyrus fragment (Hibeh Papyrus 26), which can be dated to the fourth century, suggests that it was written shortly after that date, making it contemporary with
Aristotle's *On Rhetoric*. The original author may have been Anaximenes of
Lampsacus, who, like Aristotle, was a teacher of Alexander, but the identification is based only on a passage in Quintilian (3.4.9), where it is said that
Anaximenes identified seven species of oratory: hortatory, dissuasive, laudatory, invective, accusatory, defensive, and investigatory. This is stated in the
second sentence of the treatise and is the basis of discussion of what follows;
the first sentence also introduces the Aristotelian classification of three genera, but that is not otherwise employed and, coming immediately after the
spurious introductory letter, may well be a small change made by the author
of that letter. The end of the introductory letter identifies two sources on
which the forger claims the treatise was partly based: Aristotle's *Theodectea*,
to be discussed below, and the *technē* of Corax. The reference to the *Theodectea* may result from awareness of some similarities to Aristotle's extant
treatise *On Rhetoric*; the reference to the problematic figure of Corax probably only connects the treatise to the handbook tradition that was regarded
as beginning with Corax.

Anaximenes, if he was the author, made no direct use of Aristotle's major
treatise, for he has nothing to say about Aristotle's most characteristic and
original theories and does not use his terminology; the three Aristotelian
means of persuasion, the three kinds of rhetoric, and the theories of the
enthymeme, example, and metaphor are all ignored. There is nothing corresponding to Aristotle's important account of emotions and character in
book 2. The word *rhētorikē* never occurs in the treatise, only in the title,
which is probably a later addition, and no definition of the art is offered. On
the other hand, there is a parallelism of structure between *On Rhetoric* and
the *Rhetoric for Alexander*. Chapters 1 to 5 of the latter deal with arguments
specific to each of the species of rhetoric and correspond roughly to the first
book of Aristotle's work. Chapters 6 to 22 deal with what are called *chrēseis*,
literally "uses," which resemble what Aristotle calls topics in the later part
of his second book; chapters 23 to 28 discuss style, corresponding to the first
half of Aristotle's third book; and chapters 29 to 37 discuss arrangement,
treated by Aristotle in the second half of his third book. The similarities
combined with the differences between the two works suggest that Aristotle
did not originate the overall structure of his treatise but is following an order
of subjects that was commonly used in handbooks in the second half of the
fourth century.

There are some similarities between the *Rhetoric for Alexander* and precepts on style attributed to the Isocratean *technē* as discussed above. These
include the demand in chapter 25 that conjunctions should be carefully
correlated and hiatus should be avoided, and the requirement in chapter 30

that a narration should be clear, brief, and probable. But if the treatise came out of the Isocratean school, it is strange that Isocrates is never mentioned or quoted and direct indebtedness to Isocrates is as tenuous as it is to Aristotle. In chapter 28 the author stresses the importance of a speaker's reputation for success in oratory, a view shared by Isocrates, but also puts great emphasis on observing the rules found throughout the treatise if a speaker hopes to succeed. This is not at all the view of Isocrates; it reflects the attitude of those pedestrian teachers of rhetoric whom he criticizes for arrogantly claiming to know all there is to know about the subject. The author does not quote examples from speeches to illustrate his precepts; though his rules were probably based in a general way on observation of techniques in use, he presents them as a system to which speakers should conform. The treatise seems to have been little known subsequently and made no original contribution to the development of a theory of rhetoric, nor to the development of rhetorical terminology. Its importance is simply as an example of a handbook of the time and for its description of techniques that can be found in fourth-century speeches. Orators of the time may not have known this particular work, but they probably knew something like it.

Aristotle

Aristotle came from a Greek family that had settled in the colony of Stagira on the borders of Macedon. His father was personal physician to the Macedonian king, and he himself had connections with the Macedonian rulers throughout his life. Since this was the period in which Macedon, under Philip II, became a major threat to the independence of the Greek city-states, eventually defeating them at the Battle of Chaeronea in 338 B.C., Aristotle was viewed with some suspicion in Athens, yet he regarded Athens as the cultural center of the Greek-speaking world and devoted considerable study to Athenian institutions. This includes drama, government, and political rhetoric, which flourished there more than in any other city.

In 367, at the age of seventeen, Aristotle went to Athens to study at Plato's Academy and remained there for twenty years. Plato was away in Sicily during the first three years of Aristotle's residence, and this lack of personal contact may have given Aristotle more opportunity to develop his own approach to philosophy than might otherwise have been the case. He was greatly indebted to Plato in many ways, expressed his personal affection for him, and viewed Plato as having defined many important issues of philosophy, but these two great thinkers saw the world very differently. Aristotle had a deep interest in natural science, perhaps derived from his father, which led him to research in biology, a subject of little interest to Plato but which helped form Aristotle's approach to ethics, politics, poetics, and rhetoric. He characteristically views the latter subjects as social phenomena that, like living organisms, develop natural potentialities into fully actualized forms. He had rather little interest in religion, little sympathy with Plato's mystical cast of mind, and serious doubts about, ending in complete rejection of, Plato's theory of transcendent forms. Plato, whether or not he can be said to be a dogmatist, was certainly at heart an idealist, deeply distrustful of sensory perceptions; Aristotle was a realist, far more pragmatic, fascinated with the complexity of nature and human life. Both shared, in differing ways, a commitment to the search for knowledge and understanding and also a strong motivation to discover and teach the moral basis on which social stability and human well-being could be best achieved.

During the second decade of his period in the Academy, Aristotle began the studies that eventually led to his works on logic and dialectic. He was the first person in history to develop an account of formal logic, including the theory of the syllogism, given its full statement in the *Analytics*; Aristotelian logic remained fundamental for philosophical studies until the modern period. The application of logic to philosophical questions is known as dialectic, which Aristotle describes in the treatise called *Topics*. Dialectic was also a form of exercise that trained students in method by requiring argument on two sides of a issue. As it was practiced in philosophical schools, a student proposed a thesis, for example, "pleasure is the only good"; a second student then sought to refute the thesis by asking a series of questions that could be answered "yes" or "no" and by offering definitions and divisions of the subject based on what was commonly believed or on propositions asserted by recognized authorities. "Topics" are the logical strategies employed in dialectic and are useful in rhetoric as well; Aristotle describes twenty-eight rhetorical topics in book 2, chapter 23 of *On Rhetoric*.

Even earlier Aristotle had begun to write and publish dialogues on philosophical subjects, exploring some of the same subjects found in Platonic dialogues. A dialogue as written by Plato or Aristotle can be thought of as a literary and dramatic presentation of a dialectical disputation. The elegance of the style of Aristotle's dialogues is praised by later Greek and Roman writers who knew them, but none of the dialogues has survived. According to Cicero (*Letters to Atticus* 13.19.4), Aristotle described himself as present at his dialogues, but perhaps he took no leading part in the discussion.

One dialogue, perhaps the earliest, was entitled *Gryllus*, and according to Quintilian (2.17.14) Aristotle there introduced some "subtle" arguments, for the sake of discussion, against the view that rhetoric is an art, arguments Quintilian regarded as inconsistent with Aristotle's later treatment of rhetoric.[33] The *Gryllus* clearly had some relationship to Plato's *Gorgias* and prob-

---

[33] The title comes from the name of Xenophon's son, who died in 362. Diogenes Laertius (2.55) says that Gryllus was the subject of encomia after his death; Aristotle may have begun the dialogue with reference to these and then led into the question of art.

ably tried to move discussion beyond the point it is left in that dialogue. The real opponent, even if not directly attacked, may have been Isocrates. Whether at this time or somewhat later, a pupil of Isocrates named Cephisodorus wrote an attack on the views of rhetoric advanced by both Plato and Aristotle.[34]

In the mid 350s Aristotle began offering a course of lectures on rhetoric. According to Cicero (*On the Orator* 3.141), he parodied a verse from Euripides' *Philoctetes*, saying "it is shameful to keep silent and allow Isocrates to teach." Apparently the course was taught in the afternoons, thus being a kind of extracurricular or public offering, accompanied by rhetorical exercises.[35] Probably Aristotle presented rhetoric as a popular "counterpart" to dialectic, which he was teaching students of philosophy at this time. His early lectures on rhetoric were probably the origin of some of the material to be found in *On Rhetoric* as later revised, for the work we have contains many references to orators active in this period. Chapters 5 to 15 of book 1 may be the "early core" of the treatise, deriving from this period.[36] These are the chapters in which Aristotle identifies the *idia*, or "specific" propositions of politics and ethics that become the basis for argument in the *eidē*, the three species of rhetoric: deliberative, epideictic, and judicial. This material can be regarded as answering the demand of Socrates in the *Gorgias* for some kind of specific knowledge if rhetoric is to be an art. Some of book 3 may also incorporate material from these early lectures; the reference to the actor Theodorus in 3.2.4 sounds as though he were still alive,[37] and it is difficult to see how Aristotle could have given popular lectures on rhetoric without discussing, as handbook writers regularly did, the parts of the oration, which is the subject of the second half of book 3. It is possible that the *Synagōgē*, to which frequent reference has been made, was a result of Aristotle's research in preparation for these early lectures, though that work may have been written when he returned to rhetoric later in his life.

About the time of Plato's death in 347 Aristotle left Athens and went to live in the Troad and then on the island of Lesbos, where he engaged chiefly in study of biology. In 343 Philip II invited Aristotle to come to Macedon and direct the education of the young prince Alexander. Alexander was about thirteen years old at the time, and it is likely that Aristotle taught him subjects regarded as appropriate for that stage in education and for an heir to a throne. These probably included literature, dialectic, some introduction to moral and political philosophy, and rhetoric. Alexander would need to acquire facility in speech himself and as a future ruler would equally need

[34] See Eusebius, *Praeparatio Evangelica* 14.6.9.
[35] See Philodemus 6, col. 48 (vol. 2, p. 50, in the edition of Sudhaus); Quintilian 3.1.14; Aulus Gellius 20.5.
[36] See Rist, *Mind of Aristotle*, 137–41.
[37] See Burkert, "Aristoteles im Theater."

to understand efforts of others to persuade him to some judgment or action. This teaching probably caused Aristotle to begin a revision of his own thinking about rhetoric. Isocrates at this time was cultivating favor with King Philip and doubtless not very happy to hear that Aristotle was teaching his son. He composed a letter to Alexander, enclosed in a letter to Philip, that begins rather defensively, implying that Alexander had probably heard criticism of Isocrates; pays respect to Alexander's unnamed teachers—he could hardly question Philip's judgment in choosing them—but warns against becoming fascinated by disputation for its own sake, which is probably a reference to Aristotelian dialectic; and ends by encouraging Alexander's interest in discourse (*logos*) as Isocrates defined it.

Aristotle's responsibility for Alexander only lasted for two or three years. In the early 330s he was perhaps living at his original home of Stagira, engaged in his own research, probably with some private students. Philip's defeat of Athens and its allies in 338 opened up the possibility for Aristotle to return there safely, which he did in 335. Instead of returning to the Academy, he opened his own school at the gymnasium of the Lyceum. In preparation for his return he seems to have revised his lectures on politics, poetics, and rhetoric, which would be appropriate subjects to attract students in Athens. The latest historical references in the treatise *On Rhetoric* date from this period.[38] Like the other surviving Aristotelian treatises, the work is basically the text of lectures to be given in his school, written in a highly compressed, nonliterary style; probably in lecturing he departed somewhat from the written text to explain points more fully, answered questions, and encouraged discussion. The text of the lectures was probably also available in the library of the school, where it could be studied by others. In 3.9.10 he refers to what he calls the *Theodectea*; later writers were somewhat uncertain whether this was a work by Aristotle or by Theodectes. Probably it was a collection of examples, with some discussion, of the rhetorical techniques of Aristotle's friend Theodectes, who was a sophist and dramatist of the time.

Book 3 of *On Rhetoric* was probably originally a separate work from books 1 and 2; that is, it was contained in a separate papyrus scroll. Throughout books 1 and 2 Aristotle seems to assume that rhetoric is entirely a matter of what is said. At the end of book 2 he refers to this as *dianoia*, "thought"— later writers will call it *heuresis*, "invention"—and then indicates he will turn to discussion of style and arrangement. The list of the works of Aristotle given by Diogenes Laertius (5.24) includes one on rhetoric in two books and a separate work, *On Style*, which may be our book 3. But the beginning of book 3 contains a summary of books 1 and 2, clearly linking it to what

---

[38] See Kennedy, *Aristotle*, 299–305.

preceeds. We cannot say with certainty whether the linking passages were the work of Aristotle or of a later Greek editor who sought to create a more comprehensive treatise.

On Rhetoric is a difficult work. It presents numerous specific problems of interpretation, for which modern commentaries and notes in translations supply some help.[39] There are, in addition, two general problems: one results from the inconsistency between what Aristotle says about rhetoric in the opening chapters and the treatment of the subject that follows, as well as from apparent inconsistency in the use of some key terms, especially *pistis*, *ēthos*, and *topos*. Most inconsistencies seem to result from the fact that *On Rhetoric* was written at different times and only partially revised to make a consistent whole. Moreover, various parts were apparently written with different audiences in mind: chapter 1 of book 1 takes a very austere, Platonic view of rhetoric and seems to be addressed to students of philosophy who have recently completed a course in dialectic; other parts (e.g., 1.9 and 15) provide practical precepts for speakers and read like a handbook in which consideration is given to techniques that will succeed and not to whether the use of the technique is morally justified.

This question of the moral stance of the treatise is at the heart of the second general problem in interpretation. In what is really a parenthetical remark in 1.1.12, Aristotle says one should not persuade what is debased (or morally wrong). In 1.2.7 he says that rhetoric "is a certain kind of off-shoot of dialectic and of ethical studies, which it is just to call politics." He occasionally refers to his *Politics* or *Ethics* as well as to some of his logical writings. In *Nicomachean Ethics* 1.2.4–6 he also calls rhetoric a subdivision of politics and in that work reveals his passionate feelings about the importance of justice, honorable dealings, and truth. In discussing rhetoric one might expect him to have much to say about the legitimate and illegitimate uses of rhetoric in society and about the duties of an orator, but he says virtually nothing beyond pointing out some sophistic fallacies. It is not even clear that he regards public debate and freedom of speech as essential for constitutional and orderly government. It is possible that Aristotle felt these issues had been adequately addressed in the *Gryllus* or in what he sometimes refers to as his "exoteric" discourses, in contrast to his specialized lectures. His definition of rhetoric (1.2.1) is "an ability in each case to see the available means of persuasion," and the sophistic tricks he sometimes lists are certainly "available"; the unanswered question is whether it is ever legitimate to use them. Doubtless Aristotle expected that moral issues

---

[39] In English there is the older commentary by Cope and Sandys and a commentary on books 1 and 2 by Grimaldi; Kennedy, *Aristotle*, provides introductions to the whole and to each chapter as well as running explanatory notes to the translation of the text.

about rhetoric would continue to be discussed, and one of the values of his treatise is that it supplies much material for such a discussion, without attempting an answer.

The most satisfactory response to the moral enigma of *On Rhetoric* is probably to recognize that it is a "formalist" treatise, largely an objective, nonjudgmental analysis of the forms that rhetoric took in his time and in this sense more like his scientific than his ethical writings. His dispassionate analysis of rhetorical techniques is thus analogous to his analysis of the forms of plants and animals in his biological works, or of constitutions, and even of poetry. In the *Poetics*, as in *On Rhetoric*, there are judgments of what is effective art but only a few observations that relate to the value of poetry in society—the most important is the identification in chapter 6 of *katharsis* as the goal of tragedy, but this tantalizing reference is given no explanation in the text. Most of the *Poetics* is devoted to a formal analysis of the parts and techniques of tragedy and epic. Similarly, throughout most of *On Rhetoric* Aristotle describes the "available means of persuasion," preserving objectivity and keeping an emotional distance from his subject as he might in dissecting an animal.

Although Aristotle does not explicitly divide the study of rhetoric into parts, as do later teachers, his treatise as a whole is divided into discussion of three of the traditional parts and includes some observations on a fourth. Books 1 and 2 discuss the content or thought of speeches, which later comes to be known as invention; book 3 begins with some remarks on delivery and then discusses style (3.2–12) and arrangement (3.13–19).

Aristotle begins book 1 by linking rhetoric to dialectic: both are methods, not substantive disciplines, and unlike specialized studies "both are concerned with such things as are, to a certain extent, within the knowledge of all people."[40] He criticizes previous handbooks for their neglect of logical argument and of speeches other than those in courts of law and justifies serious consideration of rhetoric as useful on several grounds: if judgments are not reached in the right way, truth and justice will be defeated; a good knowledge of the subject does not itself ensure that a speaker will be persuasive to a general audience, for skillful presentation is needed, based on assumptions shared by the audience; practice in arguing on either side of a question (as also in dialectic) helps to reveal the true state of the case and enables a speaker to refute an opponent; speech is a natural characteristic of human beings and a more appropriate way to resolve issues than is the use of force. Whatever Aristotle may have argued in *Gryllus*, *On Rhetoric* begins

---

[40] Aristotle fails to specify the differences between dialectic and rhetoric, apparently assuming the student understands them. The principle differences are that dialectic deals with general and abstract questions, rhetoric with specific cases and policies, and dialectic takes the form of question and answer, while rhetoric as viewed by Aristotle uses extended formal speeches.

with the confident assumption that rhetoric is an art, useful in society, capable of being described and practiced, morally neutral. It is a body of knowledge, derived from observation and experience, about how to persuade an audience; the subject matter, what is discussed in a speech, is provided by other studies, of which politics and ethics are the most important. As is true of other arts, rhetoric can be used for good or evil purposes. The rest of the treatise consists of a description of what this art is and of the knowledge needed by a speaker. Insofar as Aristotle is successful in his description of rhetoric as an art, he offers a response to Socrates' criticisms in *Gorgias*, and insofar as he is successful in showing that an understanding of logical argument, rather than nobility of sentiment and polish in style, is the most important element in persuasive speech, he offers a response to Isocrates.

Chapter 2 begins with the famous definition of rhetoric as "an ability, in each case, to see the available means of persuasion." "An ability to see" marks rhetoric as theory rather than practice, what has come to be called metarhetoric, though subsequently Aristotle often treats rhetoric as a matter of acutal speaking, or what he would call a "practical" art. The definition assumes but does not specify that rhetoric is a quality of speech, since the root of the word (*rhē-*) refers to speaking.[41] The definition is clarified by an earlier statement (1.1.14) that the function (*ergon*) of rhetoric is not to persuade but to see the *available* means of persuasion—a speech may be the best possible and still fail with an audience—and by a statement later in the chapter (1.2.12) that the function of rhetoric "is concerned with the sort of things we debate and for which we do not have other arts and among such listeners as are not able to see many things all together or to reason from a distant starting point." That is, it is concerned with issues debated in public before a popular audience, including of course a jury. "In each case" differentiates rhetoric from dialectic; rhetoric deals with particular issues involving specific persons and actions, what are later called "hypotheses," dialectic with universal or general questions.

The definition in chapter 2 is followed in the rest of that chapter and in chapter 3 by a series of divisions of the subject that are fundamental for classical rhetoric and appear, with minor variations, in many later discussions. The available means of persuasion in a particular case are either *nonartistic* or *artistic*. Nonartistic (or atechnic) means are forms of evidence, such as the testimony of witness and contracts, that the speaker uses but does not invent. They are discussed in detail in the last chapter of book 1. Artistic means of persuasion are three in number: the presentation of the *character* (ethos) of the speaker as trustworthy on the basis of what he says in the speech; the arousal of *emotion* (pathos) in the audience; the use of

---

[41] See Kennedy, *Aristotle*, 36–37 and 288–89.

argument (logos) that shows or seems to show something. These reflect Aristotle's assumption, stated in 1.3.1, that there are three major factors in a speech situation: speaker, subject (or speech), and audience. Logical argument is of two types: induction, which in rhetoric is the use of *examples* (paradigms) in which a speaker argues from one specific proposition to another with an implied generalization of their universal applicability; and deduction, which is the use of the rhetorical syllogism, called by Aristotle an *enthymeme* (1.2.8). A dialectical syllogism consists of a major premise, a minor premise, and a conclusion. The traditional example, though not cited by Aristotle, is "All men are mortal; Socrates is a man; therefore Socrates is mortal." The premises of an enthymeme are usually probable rather than certain, and one premise can often be assumed as known to the audience. An enthymeme thus often omits one premise and its common form is an assertion supported by a reason: "Socrates is mortal, for all men are," or "If Socrates is a man, he is mortal." Enthymemes are derived from what is regarded as probable (*eikos*) or from signs (*sēmeia*) (1.2.14–17). The propositions used in rhetorical arguments may be specific (*idia*), in which case they are borrowings from some body of popular knowledge, chiefly politics and ethics, or they are strategies of dialectic and rhetoric common to any subject, which Aristotle calls *topics*. As an example of the latter Aristotle cites argument from "the more and the less," which can be used, he says (1.2.21), in discussing questions of justice, physics, politics, and many other subjects.

Continuing his basic division of the subject in chapter 3 of book 1, Aristotle makes the distinction that later writers single out as his most distinctive contribution. There are three (and only three) species of rhetoric: judicial, deliberative, and epideictic. The distinction here is based on the function of the audience: an audience either is or is not a judge, and if it is a judge, it is asked to make a decision about either what has been done in the past or what should be done in the future. If judgment relates to the *past*, the decision is about what is *just* and the species of rhetoric is judicial; if judgment relates to the *future*, the decision is about what is in the *best interest* of the audience and the species is deliberative. If the audience is not making a practical decision in a law court or political assembly but is hearing a speech on some ceremonial occasion, the species is epideictic (literally, "demonstrative"), involves the question of what is *honorable*, and takes the form of either praise or blame. Aristotle elsewhere notes (2.18.1) that an audience of epideictic rhetoric may be judging a speaker's effectiveness in an oratorical contest. The rest of book 1 discusses specific propositions of politics and ethics as used in rhetoric, stressing that these should be more popular than philosophical, since the argument of a speech needs to build on what a general audience already believes. Propositions for deliberative rhetoric, which Aristotle regards as the highest form, are set out in chapters

4 to 8, for epideictic in chapter 9, and for judicial in chapters 10 to 15, including a final chapter on nonartistic means of persuasion.[42]

At the beginning of book 2 Aristotle returns to ethos and pathos as means of persuasion, then (2.2–11) analyzes a series of emotions—temporary states of mind that can be awakened or pacified—and a variety of character types based on age, class, wealth, and power (2.12–17), returning finally to further discussion of logical argument: examples, maxims, enthymemes, topics, fallacies, and refutations (2.19–26). Chapter 23 is the long list of "topics" in the sense of strategies of argument.

Book 3, after an introductory chapter noting the possible importance of delivery, discusses style and arrangement. He is at pains to distinguish poetic style from what is appropriate in oratory and prose. The virtue of prose style is to be clear and neither flat nor above the dignity of the subject but appropriate to it (3.2). The emphasis given to clarity is the stylistic counterpart to Aristotle's emphasis on logical proof in invention; the preference for a mean between extremes is characteristic of Aristotelian ethical thought. Among stylistic techniques discussed are simile (3.4), expansiveness (3.6), rhythm (3.8), periodic structure (3.9)—by which Aristotle does not mean long, complex sentences but short phrases that are parallel or contrasted—urbanity, and visualization (3.10–11). Metaphor is initially discussed in 3.2, where it is said to be the poetic device most useful in prose and to make what is said seem unusual, thus striking; discussion of it is resumed in 3.10–11. A final chapter (3.12) discusses the differences between oral and written styles.

In discussing arrangement Aristotle begins (3.13) by stating that the only necessary parts of an oration are statement of a proposition and proof, but he subsequently discusses prooemium (3.14–15), including how to meet a prejudicial attack; narration (3.16); proof (3.17–18), including direct interrogation of opponents in trials; and epilogue (3.19).

As seen in the passage from the *Phaedrus* on handbooks, quoted at the beginning of this chapter, some technical vocabulary for rhetoric had come into use in the fifth century. Aristotle adopted some of this and added other terms. Although some seem formidable in English, they were often easily understood by a Greek student. *Homoeoteleuton*, for example, simply means "having a similar ending." Many rhetorical terms are metaphors, including *metaphora* itself (literally, "a carrying over" or "transference"). They are either borrowed from another usage—"prooemium," for example, which originally meant the prelude to a song—or given a restricted meaning: Aristotle's most famous technical term, *enthymēma*, literally means something "held in the mind." Many of Aristotle's terms for aspects of invention,

---

[42] Aristotle did not divide the texts into chapters; chapter numbers, in most cases logical conveniences, were assigned to the text by George of Trebizond in the fifteenth century.

including "enthymeme," became part of the common rhetorical vocabulary of his successors, though often with slightly different meanings; some of the terms he uses to describe style—for example, "metaphor" and "period" (literally a "circular path")—were also accepted, but others, such as *ongkos*, ("expansiveness," literally "swelling") were not. He has no general term for a figure of speech, an important omission from the point of view of later rhetoricians.

The most problematic of Aristotle's rhetorical terms are *pistis*, "nonartistic proof," *ēthos*, *pathos*, *topos*, and "epideictic." The problem with *pistis* is that it can have at least three different meanings in the text: "proof," in the sense of logical demonstration; "proof" as a formal part of a speech; and "means of persuasion," including not only logical demonstration but the trustworthiness of character that a speaker can project and the emotion he conveys. The meaning has to be determined from the context. Aristotle's concept of nonartistic proof is limited to witnesses, documents, and evidence that could be introduced into a trial; there is need for a wider conception that would include such matters as the external authority that a speaker brings to a speech—a nonartistic form of ethos that a speaker uses but does not invent—or nonverbal means of persuasion accompanying speech—a loaded gun, for example.

Aristotle's initial definition of ethos (1.2.4) limits it to whatever is said in a speech that makes a speaker seem trustworthy, which is the view of it taken again in 1.9.1 and 2.1. The discussion of types of character in 2.12–17, however, seems to be concerned with how a speech should be adjusted to the characters of those in the audience, which is closer to Plato's requirement in the *Phaedrus* that a speaker should know the souls of his listeners. The discussion of the emotions in 2.2–11 is ostensibly a treatment of psychology, potentially useful in arousing or allaying emotions, but rather little is done to apply it to a rhetorical situation. Probably the chapters were written as a part of some other study and incorporated here with minor revisions. There seems to be need for a more general account of the role of character in oratory, including not only the character of the speaker and the audience but that of opponents, witnesses, and persons mentioned in a speech—all of which are to be found in orations of Lysias, Demosthenes, and other orators. Furthermore, the relationship of character to emotion would seem to need some fuller discussion. The accounts of rhetorical ethos and pathos found in the second book of Cicero's *On the Orator* and in the sixth book of Quintilian's *Education of the Orator* are more satisfactory from this point of view.[43]

The Aristotelian conception of a "topic" is also less than clear. Isocrates

---

[43] Aristotle's treatment of ethos and pathos are more fully discussed by Wisse, *Ethos and Pathos*, and Fortenbaugh, "Persuasion through Character."

had used the word *topos* to describe arguments about possibility and impossibility or arguments based on citation of an authority (*Helen* 4 and 38). Probably a "topic" was originally a "place" in a handbook or text that could be imitated and adapted to a new context by a speaker, thus a "commonplace."[44] In the second chapter of *On Rhetoric* Aristotle distinguishes between *idia*, propositions of politics and ethics with "specific" content or knowledge useful in each of the "species" of rhetoric, and *topoi*, strategies of argument useful in any discourse. The latter are discussed in his dialectical treatise, *Topics*, and in *On Rhetoric* 2.23. In 1.3.7–9 he identifies still another class of arguments, which he calls "commonalities" (*koina*): possible and impossible, past fact, future fact, and whether something is or is not important. In subsequent passages, however, Aristotle seems to refer to all three of these classes of argument as "topics."[45] In later Greek and Latin, in a philosophical context, including Cicero's *Topics* and Boethius' *On Topical Distinctions*, Greek *topos* and Latin *locus* usually mean dialectical topics or strategies. In rhetorical treatises, however, the word, like English "topic," is often given a wider variety of meanings: it includes commonplaces on human life and experience, stock descriptions, and also lists of possible things a speaker might discuss (see, for example, *Rhetoric for Herennius* 2.9).[46]

The Aristotelian conception of epideictic is derived from the uses of public address in the culture in which Aristotle lived and is too limited for general applicability. The principal category of public address in Greece that was neither deliberative nor judicial was ceremonial oratory at public festivals and funerals. In such speeches praise of a god, a man, or a city was the dominant theme. Aristotle recognized that such a speech might also be an invective, blaming rather than praising the subject. Most opportunities for this, however, fell within deliberative or judicial oratory—Demosthenes' speech *Against Midias*, for example—but Isocrates' *Against the Sophists*, though undelivered, could be cited. Praise is frequently introduced into deliberative and judicial speeches as well, and what Aristotle says about epideictic rhetoric could be useful to a speaker on such occasions. Most later Greek and Latin rhetoricians accept Aristotle's definition of epideictic, which they often call "panegyric" (in origin, a speech at a public assembly). In later antiquity, a large number of epideictic forms were practiced and are described in the treatises of Menander Rhetor. Modern rhetoricians usually prefer to think of epideictic rhetoric as a discourse in any literary genre that is not specifically deliberative or judicial and does not, therefore, urge

---

[44] See Cole, *Origins of Rhetoric*, 88–89.

[45] See 1.6.1; 1.15.19 and 22; 1.26.1; 2.22.13; 3.19.2.

[46] There is extensive scholarship on rhetorical topics; see, e.g., Conley, "Logical Hylomorphism"; Leff, "Topics of Argumentative Invention"; Nelson, "Topoi"; Ochs, "Formal Topics." There is a good summary in Blinn and Garrett, "Aristotelian *Topoi*."

specific action but serves to encourage belief, group solidarity, and acceptance of a system of values. Epideictic speech is thus of ideological importance. Its functions are more complex than Aristotle recognizes, for the ideals it describes are rarely actually attained; sometimes, praise can be ironic, a way of subtly identifying faults; more often a speaker confidently praises values in hopes that the audience will work to implement them. Isocrates seems to have realized this more clearly than did Aristotle, since it is characteristic both of his own orations and of his educational methods.

Although the theoretical structure of rhetoric as outlined in the first three chapters of On Rhetoric is fundamental to the subject as subsequently understood, and although some of Aristotle's terminology, including artistic and nonartistic means of persuasion, ethos and pathos, example and enthymeme, topic, and the three species of rhetoric came into common usage by rhetoricians, the specific content of Aristotle's discussion in book 1—the extended identification of the propositions of politics and ethics as used in rhetoric—never fully entered the tradition. This is equally true of his discussion of emotions and characters in chapters 2–17 of book 2; later writers discuss ethos and pathos but in rather different ways. The discussion of style that makes up the first half of book 3 should also be viewed as an interesting preliminary attempt to treat the subject systematically; it had influence on subsequent teaching primarily through the revisions made by Aristotle's student Theophrastus. Aristotle's treatment of style implies a distinction between diction, or word choice, and composition, or the combination of words into sentences, which became a standard feature of later accounts, but he never makes the distinction explicit. His emphasis on clarity as the one virtue of style (3.2) and on metaphor as the preferred stylistic device in prose (3.2 and 11) was neglected by most successors, though his discussion of periodic prose (3.9) was taken up by others, including Demetrius, and his interest in prose rhythm (3.8) was revived by Cicero and others.

Although Greek and Roman writers on rhetoric not infrequently mention Aristotle at some point in their discussions and imply that they knew his treatise, its direct influence on the tradition was slight. Aristotle did not publish the work. His views on rhetoric were known to those who studied with him and those who read the treatise in the library of the early Peripatetic school. Some of his associates or students, to be discussed in chapter five below, wrote about aspects of rhetoric, and through them some Aristotelian ideas were disseminated to others, who then passed them on to still others or modified them in some way. After the death of Theophrastus (about 285 B.C.) the original text of On Rhetoric, together with other works in the school library, was apparently packed up and sent off to Asia Minor, where the books disappeared from view until early in the first century.[47]

[47] See Kennedy, Aristotle, 305–9.

Though it is possible that some copies of the treatise were in private hands, there is no clear evidence that anyone actually read *On Rhetoric* from the early third century until manuscripts of Aristotle were discovered and brought to Athens and then to Rome in the early first century and were edited and published by Andronicus of Rhodes. Of later writers, Cicero in his dialogue *On the Orator*, Apsines, and the Anonymous Seguerianus make the most use of Aristotle's conceptions; Dionysius of Halicarnassus, Quintilian, and others consulted the work, but it did not inspire them to recast their views of rhetoric significantly and it exercised little further influence on the development of rhetorical teaching. This can perhaps be best explained by imagining a rhetorician of the Roman period looking into *On Rhetoric* for the first time. He would have heard of Aristotle and associated certain ideas about rhetoric with him, especially the division into three species. He probably would have been disappointed by the actual treatise. It discussed in detail propositions of politics and ethics and types of emotion that were not usually included in the teaching of rhetoric and thus seemed irrelevant. Worse, it mentioned only in passing (1.13.10; 3.15.2) the need for a speaker to determine the question at issue in a speech, which, under the name *stasis*, had become the most important part of the teaching of invention. He would have found book 3 disappointing as well. Aristotle's emphasis on clarity would probably have seemed excessive and his discussion of ornamentation lacking in the identification of tropes (except for metaphor) and figures of speech, which had come to be regarded as the heart of the subject. Delivery, though mentioned, was given cursory and patronizing treatment, memory none at all, and what was said about arrangement could be found in fuller form elsewhere. Overall, the Aristotelian treatise would seem too concerned with abstract logical argument and too little interested in the law and in style. *On Rhetoric* survived primarily because, out of date as it seemed, it was by Aristotle, whose other works were seriously studied throughout later antiquity and the Middle Ages. When *On Rhetoric* was translated into Latin in the twelfth century, it was read for its discussion of politics, ethics, or psychology, not for its rhetorical theory.[48] Although interest in the text and references to it increased somewhat in the Renaissance,[49] it was not until modern times that *On Rhetoric* began to be appreciated as a fundamental statement of its subject.

[48] See Murphy, *Middle Ages*, 97–98.
[49] See Brandes, *History of Aristotle's "Rhetoric."*

The Attic Orators

Grammarians working in the Library in Alexandria in the third century B.C. began the process of establishing a *canōn*, or "standard of measure," of the best authors in each of the poetic genres. Canons of prose writers were later added, confined to what were regarded as the three genres of literary prose: oratory, historiography, and philosophy.[1] These canons then determined the texts read in schools and the classic models for literary imitation. According to later tradition the canon of the ten Attic orators, that is, the ten best examples of orators writing in Athens in the late fifth and in the fourth century B.C., included Antiphon, Lysias, Andocides, Isocrates, Isaeus, Demosthenes, Aeschines, Lycurgus, Hyperides, and Dinarchus.[2] Their works were thought to provide the best models of the Attic dialect in Greek as well as a variety of styles appropriate for different subjects. Cicero and Dionysius of Halicarnassus do not seem to have known this canon but regarded certain orators—especially Lysias, Isocrates, Demosthenes, and Hyperides—as more worthy of study and imitation than others. Caecilius of Calacte in the late first century B.C. wrote *On the Character of the Ten Orators*, now lost, which may be the origin of the later canon. The canon first appears clearly in *Lives of the Ten Orators*, preserved among the works of Plutarch but written by an unknown author, perhaps in the second century after Christ. This was the time of the Second Sophistic and the Atticism movement, related to it; the latter sought to return to the linguistic standards of the past in serious writing. We have a few orations by other Greek orators of the classical period, including the sophists Gorgias, Antisthenes, and Alcidamas, as well as some speeches preserved among the works of Demosthenes that are actually by Apollodorus, Hegesippus, and others. The *Apology* of Plato and a similar work by Xenophon are reconstructions of what Socrates said, or might have said, at his trial in 399 B.C.; Plato's *Menexenus* contains a funeral oration; and there are speeches attributed to sophists in Plato's *Protagoras*, *Symposium*, and *Phaedrus*. Finally, there are speeches in the works of historians of the fifth and fourth centuries, including Herodotus, Thu-

---

[1] The best account of the canons is found in Quintilian, the Greek canon in 10.1.46–84 and a parallel Latin canon in 10.1.85–131.

[2] The most convenient English translations are those in the Loeb Classical Library. Antiphon, Andocides, Lycurgus, Dinarchus, and Hyperides are to be found in the two volumes entitled *Minor Attic Orators*, by Burtt and Maidment, the other orators in separate volumes. A selection of speeches by different orators can be found in Connor, *Greek Orations*, and Saunders, *Greek Political Oratory*.

cydides, and Xenophon. Surviving speeches are published versions, often edited after delivery or reconstructions after the fact of what had or might have been said, but taken as a whole they provide a good picture of the practice of rhetoric in classical Athens. It is not really possible to appreciate the rhetorical theory of the fourth century without reading at least some of the speeches of the period. Many are works of great eloquence, admired for their rhetorical and artistic achievement from ancient to modern times.

Judicial oratory is best represented among surviving speeches and was also the central interest of rhetorical theory. Speeches for the law courts are found in the works of Antiphon, Andocides, Lysias, Isocrates, Isaeus, Demosthenes, Aeschines, Hyperides, and Dinarchus, of whom all but Andocides and Aeschines were logographers, or writers of speeches for clients to deliver. The *Olynthiacs* and *Philippics* of Demosthenes are the best examples of deliberative speeches. Epideictic oratory is represented by funeral orations attributed to Lysias, Demosthenes, and Hyperides as well as by Plato's *Menexenus*, and by the *Panegyricus*, the *Panathenaicus*, and other speeches of Isocrates. Discussion here will be limited to consideration of two of the most famous of the orators, Lysias and Demosthenes. Gorgias and Isocrates have been touched on in earlier chapters; other orators are discussed in the original version of *The Art of Persuasion in Greece*.

Lysias

Born about 444 B.C. in Athens, Lysias was a "metic," or resident alien without citizen rights. As a young man he lived for some years in the Athenian colony of Thurii in southern Italy. He then returned to Athens, where he conducted the prosperous family business in manufacturing shields. In 404 his property was confiscated by the oligarchs, who seized control of the Athenian government and are known as the Thirty Tyrants; they put to death Lysias' brother Polemarchus, and Lysias himself barely escaped to Megara, where he aided the cause of the Athenian democrats. When the democracy was restored Lysias was rewarded with a grant of citizenship and prosecuted the individual he regarded as most responsibile for the harm done to himself and his family. This is Oration 12, *Against Eratosthenes*, probably his finest speech and the only one in which he tells us about himself. We do not know the outcome of the trial; Lysias seems to have lost his citizenship on a technicality. According to Cicero (*Brutus* 48), drawing on Aristotle's *Synagōgē*, he then briefly taught rhetoric, but from about 401 he supported himself as a logographer, a writer of speeches for clients to deliver in the law courts. We have, in addition to some fragments, thirty-four speeches attributed to Lysias, of which at least three (nos. 6, 8, and 20) are not by him. He seems to have been active until about 380 and may have lived a few years longer.

Lysias made two great contributions to Greek oratory. The first was a prose style of elegant simplicity, which became the model for the plain style in later centuries. Though unadorned by lofty language and striking figures, it is never bald or dull. Lysias' style conceals its art. The basis of it was, first, word choice that sought the proper term for each object, action, and quality and which was probably encouraged by the philological and lexicographical studies we have noted as current among the sophists. Second, Lysias profited from the experience in composition of Herodotus, Thucydides, Gorgias, and other predecessors; without their mannerisms, he makes use of period, antithesis, rhythm, and assyndeta, woven together harmoniously. Since there had been a Gorgias and was to be an Isocrates, it was well for the history of prose that there was also a Lysias.

Lysias' second great gift to oratory was ethopoeia, his technique of conveying the character of the speaker in the orations he wrote for a client to deliver. This is one part of a recognition, made by Aristotle on the theoretical level, that character is an important means of persuasion. A speech appeared more genuine and less rehearsed if it seemed to be the work of the speaker himself. All speakers need the goodwill of the judges, but the techniques recommended in the handbooks were often trite and stereotyped. Lysias counteracted the bad results of such commonplaces by subtly bringing out unique features of each client's personality. Often, by showing some trivial weakness through a naturalistic touch, he succeeded in establishing a rapport with the audience that could convey the credibility of his client. In the first speech, for example, the defendant is old-fashioned and blunt in his ways; one might not choose him for a friend or even much respect him, but because of Lysias' portrayal it is difficult to believe that he had laid a sly trap for his wife's lover and easy to believe that he killed the lover without premeditation when taken in the act of adultery, which made his action legal. The young man in oration 16 bluffs his way through a tight spot by candid self-confidence. Most famous of all, perhaps, is the so-called "cripple" of speech 24, who is in danger of losing his pension from the state; Lysias wins considerable confidence for a rather suspicious character by a kind of sarcastic humor. In general, character portrayal is effected by what the speaker is made to say, often by the seemingly unconscious revelation of some weakness of character. Lysias does not attempt to vary the diction to suit the speaker; farmers, merchants, and aristocrats all speak the same simple, flawless Attic Greek. Doubtless some of the clients were more successful than others in memorizing and delivering the speeches as Lysias wrote them.[3] We rarely know whether the judicial speeches of the Attic orators were

---

[3] Dover, *Lysias*, 148–96, argues that the speeches of Lysias we have were those preserved by his clients. The more common view is that they derive from Lysias' own files; some may have been published as advertisements of his art.

successful. Clearly there was often much to be said on the other side of the case that the speaker tries to refute or obscure.

Lysias sometimes uses character as a form of persuasion in a more direct way. In several of his speeches a section on the character of the opponent or some person connected with the trial follows after the proof or refutation of the legal charge. Such a section is called an "ethical digression" and can be found in many ancient speeches, especially the most elaborate.[4] In *Against Eratosthenes* (oration 12), for example, after the initial proof of the part of Eratosthenes in the arrest of Polemarchus, Lysias remarks (37) that what he has said is probably suffient indictment, for Eratosthenes cannot follow the common custom of ignoring the specific charges and pointing out his service to the state. He then takes the opportunity to attack Eratosthenes with a list of his disservices to the state, supported by witnesses. This runs for ten sections; it is not strictly relevant to the charge, but it helps to discredit Eratosthenes further by acquainting the audience with his habitual conduct. Later on in the same speech (70ff.) Lysias attacks the character of the well-known politican Theramenes, with whom Eratosthenes had been associated. Another example of ethical digression in Lysias is found in the speech *Against Agoratus*. In section 33 and more specifically in 43, Lysias begins a systematic extension of the charge so that virtually all the misfortunes of Athens are blamed on the villanous, but probably insignificant, figure of the defendant.

It seems possible that the strong party feelings arising out of the troubles at the close of the Peloponnesian War and during the period of the Thirty Tyrants were in part responsible for the appearance of personal invective and for the introduction of emotional passages in speeches. Character assassination becomes a significant feature of Greek and later of Roman oratory, especially as practiced by Aeschines, Demosthenes, and Cicero. Although it would not be acceptable in a modern court and modern readers may have doubts about its fairness, it is a feature of ancient oratory that contributes a great deal to the vitality and readability of the speeches and at the distance of two thousand years can even be enjoyed. The justification for its presence in Greek speeches is connected with the use of argument from probability. If the facts were in doubt, as they often were, the question became one of what such a person as the defendant or the prosecutor was likely to have done. His character was the key. The speaker thus needed to present as favorable an account as possible of his own character and those who support him and as unfavorable an account as possible of the opponent and his friends. Greeks assumed that most individuals had personal enemies who would try to do them harm when possible and that the feeling would be

[4] See May, *Trials of Character*, 28–29.

mutual. They did not find it offensive for these hostilities to be openly expressed, and juries probably discounted the more violent expressions. We should regard it as a feature of the culture.

Some of Lysias' clients were probably guilty of the charges against them or were making unjustified attacks on others. The same is true of clients of other Greek logographers and of clients of Cicero. Like modern lawyers, Greek logographers probably refused some potential clients as politically or personally offensive, but they often took cases in which success required arguments that were inconsistent with values they expressed in other speeches. Their justification in doing so was doubtless that any citizen was entitled to his day in court and the best possible presentation of his case. In addition, Lysias in particular seems to have accepted cases that posed an interesting legal and artistic challenge.

Demosthenes

Demosthenes is an exact contemporary of Aristotle; born in 384, died in 322. His life can be reconstructed in considerable detail from what he says in his speeches, from references to him in the speeches of Aeschines and others, and from the biography by Plutarch, though many questions about his motivation and personal integrity have been raised by scholars.[5] He first became well known from his successes in the law courts and then went on to become a leading speaker in the democratic assembly, where he supported the policies of the conservative leader Eubulus. In midcareer he became greatly alarmed at the growing power of Macedon and tried to arouse his fellow citizens to action against Philip in a series of great speeches, but he was ultimately unsuccessful in preserving Athens' independence. The end of his life is clouded by charges that he received bribes from Alexander's fugitive treasurer, Harpalus. He was convicted and assessed a heavy fine, which he could not pay, but escaped into exile. Recalled to Athens at the death of Alexander in 322, he enjoyed a brief period of favor, but with the defeat of the Greeks by Antipater later in that year he was condemned to death, fled to the island of Calauria, and drank the poison concealed in his pen.

The collected works attributed to Demosthenes contain sixty speeches, an erotic essay, a collection of prooemia, and some letters. Of these, forty-one speeches, the prooemia, and perhaps some of the letters are regarded as genuine. Many speeches were published by Demosthenes himself, no doubt after some editing. He was the first orator so far as we know to publish deliberative speeches, which then could be read and could continue to influence public policy. In the oratorical career of Demosthenes certain

---

[5] Important modern discussions of Demosthenes' life, works, and role in history include Jaeger, *Demosthenes*, and Sealey, *Demosthenes and His Time*.

speeches illustrate critical steps in his development. The following discussion will deal with these in an attempt to outline a critical approach to his rhetoric and achievement.

Demosthenes' earliest speech, his prosecution at the age of twenty-one of his guardian Aphobus for misusing Demosthenes' family inheritance, is a remarkable product, as much a piece of accounting as of rhetoric. The direct evidence is relevant and extensive: statement and substantiation, statement and substantiation, again and again. Argument from probability finds only limited use (e.g., 55). The shamelessness of Aphobus is shown repeatedly, but there is no scurrility. The speech falls into the standard parts: prooemium (1–3, with the usual attack on the intractability of the opponent, expression of inexperience—justified for once—and request for a fair hearing), narrative (4–6), proof (7–48, including a recapitulation at the end), refutation (49–59), and peroration (60–69, with indirect recapitulation and pathos). But the overall impression is one of narrative, as though the orator were telling his story and proving every word.

The second speech against Aphobus, a reply to Aphobus' charge that Demosthenes' father was a public debtor, is very different and less impressive. Direct evidence was apparently not attainable, for the attack had come unexpectedly during the trial. Demosthenes seems to have delivered the first part of the speech extempore; there is no narration, though one is really needed to explain the basis of the charge. Demosthenes filled up the void with a repetition of facts from the first speech and a proportionally longer peroration. The third speech against Aphobus was delivered some time later, after Aphobus had brought a suit of false witness against Phanus, who had testified for Demosthenes. The nature of the attack meant that there was little direct evidence available and required use of argument from probability (e.g., 22ff.). The speech shows considerable versatility both in argument and in style, for example, in the lively imaginary debate between Demosthenes and Aphobus in 40–41. The peroration has been lost.

Cicero, Dionysius of Halicarnassus, Plutarch, the author of *Lives of the Ten Orators*, and others tell a variety of stories about Demosthenes' rhetorical training, some of which may be true. Doubtless he knew some of the handbooks of rhetoric available in his youth, but these pedestrian works were not important contributions to his development. His interest in a career in public speaking is said to have been aroused when, as a boy, he was taken by his pedagogue to hear the orator Callistratus speak in court. Subsequently he studied with the logographer Isaeus and assiduously analyzed and imitated speeches by great orators of the past, taking Pericles as his greatest model. Demosthenes' personal austerity and combination of idealized nationalism and political realism belong in a Periclean tradition. There were no written speeches by Pericles that he could study, but he was certainly familiar with the versions of Pericles' speeches in Thucydides' *His-*

tory and, especially early in his career as a deliberative orator, shows signs of Thucydides' style. He was not a natural orator, initially lacking confidence, adequate control of voice and gesture, and never entirely comfortable with speaking on the spur of the moment. When possible, he preferred to study the issues and write out a speech in advance. According to our sources, elocution lessons with the actor Satyrus are said to have helped him as did private practice in declamation, in an underground cave, or speaking against the roar of waves on the beach, or with pebbles in his mouth (Cicero, *On the Orator* 1.261). Nor was Demosthenes a popular orator; the biographies mention instances of his being shouted down when he tried to speak and of being criticized for a too-studied style. His personality never evoked much warmth in others; he was regarded as lacking in much sense of humor, and his preference for drinking water rather than wine did not encourage conviviality.

Demosthenes' prosecutions of his guardians were successful, though he recovered only a small portion of his inheritance. The speeches he delivered, however, apparently gave him a reputation as an effective orator, which led to a career as a logographer. He seems to have been more selective in his acceptance of clients than was Lysias. He was not the defender of the poor but of the affluent, of the creditor against the debtor; he also wrote speeches for political allies. He emerges as a business-like logographer, who can portray the character of a client with conviction, can narrate with clarity and vigor, and can construct a logical proof without giving the impression of slyness. He did not seek sensationalism, did not deal with adulterers and courtesans, and rarely introduced pathetic effects.

The best-known of Demosthenes' "private" orations (that is, speeches dealing with civil suits) is number 36, for the banker Phormio in a case brought by Apollodorus about 350 B.C. for recovery of a large sum of money. Phormio himself was apparently not capable of speaking on his own behalf; Demosthenes wrote the speech for delivery by a spokesman for him whose name is unknown. It is an example of a common Greek legal procedure called *paragraphē* in which the defendant in a suit turns the tables by prosecuting the prosecutor on the ground that the original prosecution is contrary to law. The grounds alleged in this case are that the question of any money due to Apollodorus had been resolved twenty-five years earlier, that the statute of limitations prevented an attempt to reopen the issue, and that releases had been signed by all parties in the past. This claim is well supported by the evidence of documents and witnesses, but Demosthenes is not content with establishing the facts. Much of the speech is concerned with character, portraying Apollodorus as a greedy spendthrift, distrusted by his own father; as an inveterate litigator of everyone, in search of his own advantage; and as a generally disreputable person, and conversely portraying Phormio as an honorable, generous, and patriotic individual. We know the outcome of the trial, which was a resounding success for Phormio and thus for Demosthenes' speech. Apollodorus failed to get even one-fifth of the jury's votes and by law had to pay a fine for malicious prosecution. But Apollodorus did not give up easily. He subsequently brought a suit for false witness against a minor witness in Phormio's defense named Stephanus. Amazingly, Demosthenes seems to have written the speech *for* Apollodorus in this case, which is oration 45 in our corpus.[6] It not only supports Apollodorus' position but contains a violent attack on Demosthenes' earlier client, and friend, Phormio. In his *Life of Demosthenes* (section 15) Plutarch, writing several hundred years later, severely criticizes this change of sides as an immoral action by one who cynically sold his pen to anyone who would pay. It is possible that Demosthenes had quarreled with the banker over some financial transaction and was getting his revenge; the more commonly accepted explanation, however, is that Demosthenes was paying a political debt. In his *Olynthiac* speeches he had cautiously suggested that the Athenians should take funds used to subsidize theater tickets and convert them to a war chest against Philip. Severe penalties had been written into law to prevent this, and Demosthenes himself did not specifically propose it. Apollodorus apparently took the personal risk of making the formal proposal, as is mentioned in his later speech *Against Neaera* (= Demosthenes 59.4).

As a result of his success in private cases (*dikai*), Demosthenes gained an opportunity to write speeches in suits involving an offense against the state (*graphai*). Greater public interest was of course aroused by these cases, and the speeches are often two or three times as long as speeches in private cases. Since Athens had no public prosecutor, individuals had to bring charges in the public suits, and the actual speeches might be written by logographers, just as in private suits. Demosthenes' function has not changed, therefore, in his speeches *Against Androtion* (355 B.C.), *Against Timocrates* (353), and *Against Aristocrates* (352), but opportunity for imaginative treatment of important subjects and rhetorical development are greater. *Against Leptines* (355) belongs in the same group but marks a further step toward a public career, since Demosthenes is said (Plutarch, *Demosthenes* 15) to have spoken it himself.

In the public orations of Demosthenes it is often necessary to distinguish the objective of a speech from its nominal subject, the real political purpose from the ostensible legal issue. The political objective of *Against Androtion*, for example, was apparently to discredit a political faction that had been hard on the wealthier class of society. Androtion as a tax gatherer had won their ill will, and an excuse for prosecuting him was found when he intro-

---

[6] Aeschines (*On the Embassy* 328) claims that Demosthenes had also shown his original speech for Phormio to Apollodorus before the trial; if so, it did the latter little good.

duced a fairly routine motion to honor members of the outgoing council. As it happened, they had not fulfilled their duty of building new ships, because the treasurer had absconded with the money, and thus the motion was technically illegal. The rhetorical problem Demosthenes faced was to make the action of Androtion seem sufficiently grave to justify condemnation, to convert a legal technicality into a threat to Athens. His technique, and the most striking feature of the speech, is the interweaving of three themes: Androtion is personally vicious, his crimes are a public concern, he is a sophist whose defense should not be trusted. These themes are stated in the prooemium (1–4) but never dropped throughout the speech; the first is the most prominent, but the others continually appear. This technique becomes a characteristic feature of Demosthenes' oratory, known as "psychological planning":[7] though his speeches usually contain systematic treatment of the issues in a logical order, an organic unity of concepts and ideas is achieved by continually playing variations on a small number of themes throughout the speech. These themes often relate to the moral character of the speaker or the lack of moral character of his opponent. In this case, by the end of the speech Androtion seems a monster and the charge a crucial one in the preservation of the state, but there is complete regularity of parts. There is a prooemium dealing with plaintiff, defendant, motive, and significance. A narration is strictly unnecessary, since this is the second speech in the prosecution, but sections 5 to 7 perform the formal function. The proof, extending from section 8 to 68, is divided into a demonstration, with enthymemes and examples, of the illegality of Androtion's action (8–20), of his immorality (21–24), of the legality of the prosecution (25–34), a refutation of the points he has made in his favor (35–46), and an "ethical digression" on his obnoxious character (47–68). The epilogue (69–78) omits a recapitulation and is devoted to awakening the emotions of the jury.

Against Leptines is part of the same political program in the interest of the richer members of society, this time an attempt to repeal a law invalidating grants of immunities to financial burdens imposed on them. It contains (24–25) a spirited defense of private wealth. If Demosthenes did deliver the speech personally, as Plutarch says, we can see in it the image of the character he wished to project: dignified, restrained, somewhat aristocratic.[8] Critics have admired the polished tone and assured elegance of the speech, but its conservatism is equally striking and anticipates Demosthenes' later views as seen in *On the Crown*. The laws and constitution are viewed as a political framework evolved with care through the past, unexcelled in wisdom. Change is most to be distrusted. What has made Athens great once will do

---

[7] See the studies by Delanois, de Raedt, and Rowe listed in the bibliography.
[8] See Jaeger, *Demosthenes*, 65ff.

so again (e.g., 88ff.). On first inspection the speech seems loosely constructed, a series of points strung together and introduced by an almost unvarying connective, *toinun* ("well then"). But this is an illusion contributing to the ethos of the speaker, who seems no slick professional politician but a respectable citizen saying what he has to say. On closer inspection the structure is complex and illustrates another feature of Demosthenes' major orations, a fondness for symmetry. Demosthenes' proposal for a substitute law is set in the very center of the speech (88–104); this is symmetrically framed by two attacks on the law of Leptines; that which precedes is based on positive examples of immunities, and that which follows is the negative side of the case, or refutation. There is a further balance in that the beginning of the speech (2–28) raises general objections to Leptines' law on the basis of topics of justice, expediency, honor, and profit, and Demosthenes returns to these toward the end (134–56).

In 354 Demosthenes delivered his earliest surviving deliberative speech, *On the Symmories*. It is much more compressed than the works just discussed, too compressed, perhaps, for oral presentation; we may well have a revision of what was actually said. This and other early deliberative speeches of Demosthenes seem to reflect both the compression and the style of speeches in Thucydides' history of the Peloponnesian War. The structure, however, is again symmetrical: after a brief prooemium attacking impractical orators, Demosthenes deals first with the proposed Persian war, which he opposes on grounds of expediency (3), honor (6), justice (7), and possibility (9). At the center of the speech is a discussion of ways and means for war: Demosthenes does not oppose preparations, but money should be allowed to remain in the hands of its owners, a course that is possible, honorable, and expedient. The last third of the speech is devoted to a refutation of the need to fight Persia, a peroration emphasizing justice, and a concluding, matter-of-fact recapitulation. Demosthenes regularly concludes deliberative speeches in a calm tone. The topical approach can also be seen in the early speech *On the Liberty of the Rhodians*, given in 351: practicality, expediency, and honor are said all to point to the same conclusion (sections 2, 8, and 28).

About this time two changes take place in Demosthenes' work. After supporting the program of Eubulus, which was based on financial security at home and peace abroad, Demosthenes rather suddenly turns to an aggressive policy in alarm at the continued growth of the power of Philip of Macedon. This can be attributed to Philip's unexpected successes in Thessaly and Thrace. Since such a change must have alienated many of Demosthenes' friends, it seems attributable to a sincere and patriotic belief that determined opposition to Philip was best for Athens. Corresponding to this political change is a rhetorical change. New vigor appears in the *First*

Philippic, unlike anything in Greek oratory since the debates of the Peloponnesian War as described by Thucydides. There is now no question of weighing the relative expediency of courses of action and of attributing them to justice and honor. It is assumed that Philip acts in his own interest, and Athens must act in hers. Territory in the north is the prize of war. The property of the careless belongs to those willing to run a risk. Demosthenes so focuses Athenian interests that the question seems not one of advantage but of necessity, not the choice of a course of action but the pursuit of the only possibility. His major point is that success is possible (2–12). All other rhetorical arguments are only accessory: Athens' failure to act will bring on her the deepest disgrace and will allow Philip to go unpunished (42–43), but no honor is promised for action, and disinterested justice is not invoked. It seems that Demosthenes' patience has been suddenly exhausted: the futility of expecting right to triumph in the course of nature has overwhelmed him. This powerful voice is what later Greco-Roman critics call Demosthenes' *deinotēs*, his "forcefulness" or "awe-full power of urgency."

Succeeding speeches show a similar intensity. The *First Olynthiac*, for example, makes no mention of the honor or justice to be observed in helping Olynthus, only of the fact that it is in Athens' interest to seize the opportunity to fight Philip near his home. In the *Second* and *Third Philippics* Demosthenes takes a further step. To judge from Thucydides and Plato, in the fifth century sophists and orators could brazenly argue that might makes right; this was less acceptable to fourth-century audiences, probably because of the disasters to which it had led and the greater moral sensitivity inculcated by Plato and other philosophers. Beginning with the *Second Philippic* Demosthenes finds a basis for his argumentation in a higher principle than self-interest, one that combines ethical nobility with rhetorical force. This is his concept of national character. Philip, Demosthenes claims, looks only to the immediately expedient, but Athens has the tradition of its past to demand loyalty. Athenian self-interest is thus the maintenance of this tradition. The *Third Philippic*, Demosthenes' most forceful speech, develops this view: older definitions of justice are not discussed, and expedience is coupled with the possibility of preserving Athens. Failure to act will inevitably bring disgrace for all that Athens has been, and the orator's vision of the national character is the point on which he focuses and under which all arguments are subsumed. This is made the centerpiece of the speech (36–40), framed symmetrically by consideration of practical concerns of the moment. A battle for Athens, decadent and fond of flattery, forgetful of its past, is fought out between Demosthenes the unpopular patriot (2) and Philip the violent foreign king, compared successively to a fever (29) and a hailstorm (33).

After the fall of Olynthus Demosthenes apparently became convinced that at least a temporary truce with Macedon was necessary, for Athens was making no progress in the war. Negotiations were conducted in 346 and Demosthenes took part, together with Philocrates, Aeschines, and others. In a speech *On the Embassy* (21ff.) Aeschines describes Demosthenes' conduct during their embassy to Philip: Demosthenes had promised fountains of words and boasted that he would sew up Philip's mouth with an unsoaked reed, but, when the moment came, he collapsed completely. He fumbled his prooemium and finally stopped, helpless. Philip, Aeschines claims, was rather condescending and encouraged Demosthenes to go on, but that just irritated the orator. Finally, the herald imperiously commanded the withdrawal of the ambassadors. As noted earlier, Demosthenes did not have the instinct for replying to a sudden rhetorical challenge; here his collapse may indicate his horror at speaking as an inferior before a barbarian. The incident, assuming Aeschines' account is basically true, may well also be the source of his personal hatred of Aeschines, who claims to have distinguished himself at the time. It was to Aeschines that Philip addressed his reply.

The peace was achieved, though Philip dallied and secured more territory before swearing to it. Contrary to Athenian expectations, which had been encouraged by Aeschines, Philip then advanced into central Greece and reduced the cities of Phocis, which he had prevented from being expressly included in the treaty. Inevitably, those responsible for the peace found themselves attacked. Demosthenes, anxious to show that he had played no active role in negotiations, persuaded a man named Timarchus to bring action against Aeschines for taking bribes from Philip. It was a bad choice; Aeschines immediately charged illegal prosecution on the ground that Timarchus had been a male prostitute and that such a person could not legally initiate suit. *Against Timarchus* is one of the three surviving speeches by Aeschines; long neglected as too unsavory a subject for readers, the speech has recently attracted attention as a major source on Greek attitudes and laws relating to male homosexuality.[9] Demosthenes lost the case; understandably, his speech was not preserved.

Three years later the orator Hyperides successfully prosecuted Philocrates for his part in the embassy to Philip, and Demosthenes followed up with a prosecution of Aeschines in person. Both Demosthenes' prosecution, known as *On the False Embassy*, and Aeschines' successful defense, *On the Embassy*, have been preserved, allowing opportunity for comparison. Demosthenes attempted to achieve on a very large scale the passion of the *Philippics*, the clarity of his earlier judicial speeches, the subtle interweaving of themes, and exposition of his vision of the national character, but the

[9] Neither homosexual acts nor prostitution was illegal, but a man known to have accepted pay for sodomy risked loss of some civic rights; cf. Dover, *Greek Homosexuality*, 19–109, which discusses Aeschines' speech in detail.

speech as a whole was unpersuasive to the ancient jury and is so to modern readers. He had no good evidence that Aeschines had taken bribes and sub-stituted a virulent personal attack on his opponent, his father and mother, his failed career as an actor, and his personal appearance. Aeschines says (section 4) that when Demosthenes charged that he had mistreated a woman of Olynthus the jury shouted him down immediately. Aeschines' reply is his finest speech; it is primarily a narrative account of what was done on the embassy day by day, trying to show that everything was aboveboard and that nobody was bribed. The question of what private understandings may have existed or the personal motivation of the participants is success-fully avoided. Though the truth is not known and some of Aeschines' politi-cal actions have evoked the suspicions of historians, his policy throughout his career can be interpreted as a sincere attempt to find a middle-of-the-road path of independent survival for Athens between Demosthenes' policy of total opposition to Philip, leading to war and defeat (as it did), and an undignified and unpatriotic surrender to Philip's ambitions, which course might be alleged against Isocrates' encomiastic *Philippus* oration.

In 337 B.C., a little over a year after the Battle of Chaeronea at which Philip had decisively defeated the Athenians and their allies, a supporter of Demosthenes named Ctesiphon proposed in the assembly that De-mosthenes be honored with a crown at the festival of Dionysus the following spring because "he continues to speak and do what is best for the people." There was nothing unprecedented in such an award, but the circumstances made this particular motion a question of confidence in the policies of De-mosthenes and a tribute to him in the period of Athens' discouragement and defeat. Aeschines, continuing his personal feud with Demosthenes and opposition to his policies, immediately introduced a charge of illegal motion against Ctesiphon. This suspended the award of the crown until the trial had been held, an event that did not take place until 330. Philip's assassina-tion in the summer of 336 temporary unsettled the political scene. Philip's successor, Alexander, effectively asserted his authority but then left Greece on his great eastern campaign in 334, and the further away he went, the more the illusion grew that Athenians might have some control of their destiny. Thus Ctesiphon apparently pressed his motion and Aeschines his suit. Legally, Ctesiphon was on trial, though the intent was of course to discredit Demosthenes. Ctesiphon probably made a short speech and intro-duced Demosthenes as his advocate, who then delivered the masterful ora-tion known to us as *On the Crown*.[10]

---

[10] Goodwin, ed., *Demosthenes, On the Crown*. In addition to the translation in the Loeb Classical Library, there is a translation by Simpson with rhetorical commentary by Donnelly, in his *Demosthenes on the Crown*; trans. by Keaney, with interpretive essays, in Murphy, *De-mosthenes on the Crown*.

Aeschines' able prosecution has survived. It is most successful in the clarity with which it presents the technical arguments against the legality of Ctesiphon's motion. Broader issues are raised, but they are secondary. Aeschines calls upon Demosthenes to reply in the same order. The first problem of the defense was to avoid this, for it would mean putting weak arguments in a conspicuous position early in the speech. Ctesiphon's motion probably had not been made at the proper time and place. The cleverness with which Demosthenes solves this problem has long been recognized. He denounces Aeschines for making charges foreign to the indictment and insists upon his right to answer these first. What he means are the charges relating to his part in the Peace of Philocrates, foreign to the indictment in the sense that the events were more remote in time from the date of Ctesiphon's motion. Since the basis of awarding the crown was Demosthenes' statesmanship in general, there was no reason why Aeschines should not discuss any period of the orator's activity. Actually, Demosthenes is well satisfied to be able to discuss his services to Athens over a long period. This preliminary issue extends as far as section 52, after which comes the main refutation of Aeschines' charges; but even here the substantive issue of Demosthenes' statesmanship is dealt with first and at great length. Only when he feels that the audience has begun to appreciate his viewpoint does the orator venture to deal, and then briefly, with the technical charges (110–25). An invective against Aeschines is next introduced, and the great torrent of abuse that pours forth effectively removes any attention the audience might have paid to weaknesses in Demosthenes' replies to the technical charges. In other words, what Aeschines wished to be the main issue of the trial became a kind of overlooked valley of detail, lost between the enormous cliffs of Demosthenes' statesmanship and Aeschines' crimes.

A second rhetorical problem that Demosthenes faced was occasioned by the fact that his policies had been unsuccessful. Aeschines made much of Demosthenes' ill fortune and tried to identify Athens' troubles with the person of his opponent. Even without Aeschines' vilification Demosthenes had to plead in the dark shadow of the Battle of Chaeronea and Macedonian domination. This challenge he meets head on and from it achieves great pathos. The most striking passage begins at section 199, which contains the great oath by those who fell at Marathon, much admired by the author of *On the Sublime* (16.2). As in the *Philippics*, Demosthenes insists on loyalty to Athenian traditions; that is the only true expediency. Success or failure are of secondary interest. Athens lost the war but gained a moral victory: "If what was going to be had been clear to all, and if all had known ahead of time, and you, Aeschines, had foretold and prophesied with cries and shouts, though in fact you said not a word, not even in that case should the city have abandoned her traditions" (199). Again and again he hammers out the theme "what else could I have done?" (e.g., 28, 62, 69, 101, 188, 190ff., 301), meaning by "could" within the framework of Athenian traditions. The possibility of shutting his eyes to what seemed inevitable he expressly rejects as impossible (63). This loyalty to national traditions of independence is the foundation on which Demosthenes builds his defense. Neither blunt expediency nor justice to individuals nor honor in the narrow sense play any separate role, but all are synthesized into the single obsession.

Three ways, then, in which *On the Crown* resembles earlier speeches of Demosthenes are its attempt to concentrate attention on wider issues rather than on legal technicalities, its presentation of the need for loyalty to Athenian traditions as the central logical issue and the central rhetorical topic, and its effective use of recurring themes. A fourth way is in the structure of the speech, which shows the tendency to symmetry already noticed in other speeches and an ability to adapt rhetorical conventions to specific occasions. Formally speaking, *On the Crown* has all the traditional parts of a judicial speech: there is a prooemium that performs the usual functions (1–17), including (9–17) preliminary consideration of the procedure that Aeschines had demanded and that Demosthenes knows he cannot successfully follow. Then comes a narration, though it does not deal with the entire circumstances, only with what Demosthenes labels as outside the present case. Yet this gives an excellent background for the body of the speech. When the background is set, he can break off the narrative abruptly and return to it whenever he wishes. Thus he gains several advantages at the same time: he disposes of some of Aeschines' arguments, he gives the impression of logical order and clear narration, he does not tire his audience with a long narrative account, and finally he does not run any danger of repeating himself when he takes up later events further on in the speech. The proof begins in section 53. Demosthenes attempts a brief refutation of the legal charges but soon turns to an extended ethical defense, making up almost one-half the whole speech. This is the substantive account of his motivation and actions in the form of a comparison[11] between the character and policy of Aeschines and that of himself. The midpoint of the speech comes around section 160, and significantly there appears here a turning point in the thought too, for Demosthenes, having made his shattering charges that Aeschines brought on the war and lost Greek freedom (142–

---

[11] The word for comparison in Greek is *synkrisis*. *Synkrisis* is a device of amplification seen in Greek literature as early as the Homeric poems (e.g., the comparison between the city at war and the city at peace in the description of the Shield of Achilles in *Iliad* 19 or the comparison of the tragedies of Aeschylus and Euripides in Aristophanes' *Frogs*). The writing of *synkrisis* later becomes one of the *progymnasmata*, exercises in composition practiced in grammar schools or in the early stages of rhetorical study that in turn influenced its use in literary composition; cf., e.g., the comparison of Demosthenes and Cicero in Quintilian 10.1.105–8 and in Longinus 12.3–4, as well as the "parallel" *Lives* of Demosthenes and Cicero by Plutarch.

59), turns to his own measures to counteract these deeds and to his novel expression of Athenian liberty. A symmetry is thus noticeable in the passage as a whole:

126–40 attack on Aeschines' deeds
> 141 invocation to the gods, echoing that at the beginning of the speech

142–59 attack on Aeschines' deeds

160–98 deeds of Demosthenes
> 199–200 Athenian traditions, beginning with oath by the gods

210–50 deeds of Demosthenes

The contrast between the fortunes of the two orators is then made specific in the following sections. The speech ends with a peroration (297ff.) that is decidedly recapitulatory. Demosthenes again asks the question "what ought the loyal citizen to have done?" (301) and again (315) demands a comparison between himself and Aeschines.

The style of Demosthenes is a unique, powerful instrument, adequately judged only by being read in Greek, where sounds and rhythms can be observed.[12] As Dionysius of Halicarnassus in *On Demosthenes* and Hermogenes in *On Style* stress, he was the master of all styles. One of the greatest passages of *On the Crown* shows well his versatility. It comes at that crucial moment (169) when, after Aeschines has ruined everything, Demosthenes describes himself as coming forward to speak and save what can be saved. The tension of the scene in Athens is conveyed by the narrative in short sentences as the assembly is summoned: evening, the arrival of a messenger, his disastrous news, the meal of the prytanes interrupted. The marketplace is closed, the generals are summoned, and the assembly meets. The herald cries, "Who wishes to address the assembly?" "But no one came forward." The scene is burned into the mind. A tragic pause comes. Demosthenes looks around the assembly: there are the generals, there the orators, there Aeschines. No one speaks. The next touch is typical: the voice of the herald who called for speakers becomes the voice of the fatherland pleading for deliverance. Thunderous parallel contrary-to-fact conditional sentences then roll in to enunciate the gap between desire to act and ability to advise; next, like a red flag, the name of Philip; and finally Demosthenes stands forward in a sentence remarkable for its emphatic word order: "I showed myself, then, this one, on that day, I." In what follows the tone rapidly changes to one of competent comprehension and logical argument.

---

[12] Rhythm in Greek was a matter of long and short syllables, not of word emphasis; cf. Aristotle, *On Rhetoric* 3.8. Demosthenes had a subtle ear for rhythm, avoiding metrical feet and also avoiding a succession of short syllables. The latter feature is known as "Blass's Law," after Friedrich Blass who first noticed it.

The greatness of *On the Crown* consists in part of this command of style, in part of the success with which the contrast of Aeschines and Demosthenes is everywhere developed into black-and-white portraits of evil and good, and in part of the moral tone: intense, noble, sincere, transcendent. Demosthenes' defense is by no means all true—some of the unproven arguments of the embassy speech recur, Aeschines' character is slandered, and the legal issues are weakly dealt with—but the orator is, in his own view, dealing with matters of principle that transcend facts and successfully communicates this to audience and reader. His sophisms are not uttered for the sake of making a good speech, but for the sake of his country. In contrast, Aeschines' speech seems tricky, gaudy, and superficial. Demosthenes was not unaware of the contrast and accused Aeschines (280) of producing a showpiece and of caring nothing about right and wrong. The theme is taken up again in the peroration (308). Demosthenes knew all the techniques of rhetoric, but to him they were means to an important end. As his career developed he made that end the preservation of Athenian democracy and independence and the recovery of the spirit that had made them. He alone of Greek orators shared, perhaps without much realizing it, Plato's belief in absolute values and rejection of rhetorical relativism.

Aeschines lost his case, failed to get even one-fifth of the jury's votes, could not pay the resulting fine, and went into exile on Rhodes, where he taught rhetoric (Plutarch, *Demosthenes* 24). He is also reported to have given readings from his speeches (*Lives of the Ten Orators* 840E). When his audience admired *Against Ctesiphon* and was surprised that it had not succeeded, he replied, "You would not wonder, Rhodians, if you had heard Demosthenes speaking in reply!" It is unfortunate that we cannot experience Demosthenes' delivery. He himself put great weight on it, according to an anecdote in *Lives of the Ten Orators* (845D). When asked what was most important in successful rhetoric, he replied "Delivery." "And second?" "Delivery." "And third?" "Delivery."

Hellenistic Rhetoric

As a result of the conquests of Alexander the Great between 334 and 323 B.C. and the foundation of kingdoms by his successors in Greece, Asia Minor, Syria, and Egypt, Greek culture spread from Greece, southern Italy, and Sicily throughout the eastern Mediterranean. Greek became the international language of government, commerce, and learning. Schools of Greek grammar and rhetoric appeared in every city and town of any importance and provided an entry into the new society for non-Greeks, as well as a traditional education for the sons of Greek families who settled abroad. An ability to conduct business in Greek or speak Greek in a court of law was a necessary skill for a significant segment of the population, and even for those who might never make a formal speech, study of Greek literature and oratory brought with it an understanding of, and acceptance into, the dominant culture. Even the Jews of Palestine, the group with the strongest religious and cultural identity, increasingly attended Greek schools and used the Greek language.[1]

Because the beginnings of the systematic study of rhetoric in Greece were closely related to the needs of democratic government, it might initially seem that study of rhetoric would have declined under the autocratic governments of the Hellenistic period. There were, indeed, few opportunities for deliberative oratory on the scale of the orations of Pericles or Demosthenes addressing an assembly of citizens with the freedom to act on the basis of their collective decisions. A great deal of political debate now took place away from public view, for example in conferences between a ruler and his advisers. An orator might then have the task of announcing policy to the public or of arousing public opinion in favor of the ruler. This opened up the opportunity for epideictic oratory, including encomia and ceremonial addresses flattering a ruler or official at his court or on his visit to some city. Opportunity for deliberative oratory existed when ambassadors were sent, as frequently happened, from one Hellenistic state to another.[2] Among the most important were embassies sent by Greek cities to Rome as the latter became increasingly powerful, or by the Romans to Greek rulers and Greek cities. We have some reports of these speeches, but

---

[1] Summary of the evidence can be found in Kinneavy, *Origins*, 56–100. A crucial step was the translation of the Jewish scriptures into Greek, the Septuagint, made in the Library of Alexandria in the third century B.C. The philosopher Philo of Alexandria and the historian Josephus are the most important Jewish thinkers to write in Greek.

[2] See Wooten, "Ambassador's Speech."

not the original texts. Although international affairs were largely in the hands of the great kings, cities within their rule often retained control of local policy, and these matters were debated in muncipal councils or in the meetings of the leagues of cities that appeared in this period in Greece and Asia Minor. There was thus some continuing opportunity to apply a knowledge of rhetoric in public address. The fact that Hellenistic rhetoric continued to be primarily concerned with judicial oratory suggests that for the average person rhetorical skills were most useful in law courts. In most cases, however, the litigants were now addressing either a single judge or a small panel of judges, not the large juries of the Athenian democracy. A speaker could expect an opportunity to set out his case in a systematic fashion but also to be interrupted and interrogated by the judges.

These centuries were a period in which systematic learning flourished, often under the patronage of powerful rulers. The great Library and Museum at Alexandria was the most famous center of learning and was an institution for advanced research in science and literature: astronomy, geography, mathematics, physics, grammar, philology, and criticism. Athens and Pergamum were the main centers of philosophical studies. The high value put on learning encouraged the further development of theories of rhetoric as an important branch of learning. This took the form of working out in greater detail a system to describe the process of planning, writing, and delivering a speech. Work that was done by one scholar on grammar or dialectic or memory could be adapted by another into a rhetorical treatise. Two of the most conspicuous features of this process were the creation of stasis theory, a systematic method for identifying the question at issue in a speech; and the definition, with examples, of a large number of tropes, figures, and other stylistic devices that could be found in texts or used in composition.[3]

The role assumed by rhetoric in formal education was crucial to its survival and development. The curriculum that evolved continued to be followed through much of the history of the Roman Empire.[4] For a long time schools were private institutions charging fees to support the teacher; a few Hellenistic cities provided public schools, and beginning in the second century of the Christian era the Roman emperors sought to require cities and towns to subsidize teachers. Some girls attended grammar schools, but study of rhetoric was almost exclusively the prerogative of boys.

At the age of six or seven a child might enter a primary school, taught by a *grammatistēs*. The method of instruction was rote memorization of the shapes and names of letters, then the sounds of syllables, and finally the

[3] Murphy, *"Topos* and *Figura,"* has suggested that the development of lists of figures of speech was closely connected with the cataloging of dialectical topics and provides lists that do seem to overlap, though the nomenclature is specific to rhetoric.

[4] Cf. Marrou, *Education in Antiquity.*

pronunciation of words and sentences. Passages of poetry were memorized and recited, and dictations by the schoolmaster were laboriously copied out and corrected. Training of the memory was a pervasive feature of all ancient education.

When a child could read and write it was time to move on to the school of the *grammaticus*, the grammarian, for further study of language and literature. Coincidently a Greek boy had athletic training, perhaps geometry lessons, and often music lessons, but none of these was a concern of the school itself, which was exclusively devoted to literary studies. Our best primary source on Hellenistic grammar schools is a handbook written by Dionysius Thrax about 100 B.C. and used as a textbook for the next fifteen hundred years. Dionysius defines grammar as an acquaintance with what is said in the poets and prose writers, meaning the classical canon as it had emerged in his time. The subject has six parts which were the daily activities of teachers and students in school: reading aloud, including understanding meters used in verse; identification of tropes in the text; explanation of the meaning of rare words and historical references; construction of etymologies; practice in declining nouns and conjugating verbs, and what is called "judgment" of the poets. The latter refers to textual and literary criticism as practiced by professional grammarians, but some teachers probably tried to show their students what they regarded as the special merit of the texts studied.

A distinction was drawn between the teaching of the grammarian and the more advanced instruction of the rhetorician, which boys might begin at the age of twelve to fourteen. Rhetorical schools concentrated on study of prose writers and techniques of argument, amplification, and ornamentation, including figures of speech, but in practice advanced stages of grammar often overlapped with introductory stages of rhetoric, and some teachers taught grammar and rhetoric to different classes. Furthermore, grammarians introduced their students to the first stages of written composition, and this might then be continued in the rhetorical schools. The Greek term for these exercises is *progymnasmata*, exercises "preliminary" to the declamation of speeches. In the rhetorical school the teacher introduced the student to the theory of rhetoric in all its parts of invention, arrangement, style, memory (apparently added in the late second century), and delivery; some teachers may have read from a handbook, which the students then copied down; others lectured on the basis of their own organization of the subject while the students took notes. There is no evidence of written examinations, but teachers probably drilled their students orally about the parts of rhetoric and the definition of terms. Primarily, however, the student was expected to apply his growing understanding of rhetoric in practice speaking in the classroom, *meletē* in Greek, *declamatio* in Latin. The teacher chose a subject, gave a discussion of possible treatments of it, and then declaimed a speech as a model treatment. Students were then assigned subjects for a speech, wrote out a version for correction by the teachers, and when he approved memorized and delivered the speech. The subject matter usually fell into one or the other of two types that in Roman schools were known as *suasoriae* or *controversiae*. The *suasoria* was regarded as the easier and seems to have been common in Greek schools. It provided training in deliberative oratory, for the student was asked to advise some mythological or historical figure what to do in a given situation: for example, "Advise Agamemnon whether or not to sacrifice his daughter Iphigenia"; "Advise Alexander the Great whether to turn back at the Indus river or advance further east." The *controversia* was a declamation in imitation of a speech in a court of law; the student was supplied with applicable laws, real or imaginary, and given a specific case to defend. According to Quintilian (2.4.41), declamation on imaginary deliberative and legal themes was first introduced into the schools in the time of Demetrius of Phaleron, which would mean about 300 B.C. Though there are references to declamation as well as to *progymnasmata* in works on rhetoric from the early first century B.C., most of our evidence, both Greek and Latin, comes from the time of the Roman Empire and will be discussed in later chapters.

At the pinnacle of the Hellenistic educational system was study in one of the philosophical schools. Athens was the main center of philosophy, but there were philosophical schools in Pergamum, Rhodes, and elsewhere. Plato's successors, the Academics, and Aristotle's successors, the Peripatetics, continued their founders' interest in rhetoric, and the Stoic school, founded by Zeno about 300 B.C., studied the subject as well. The fourth leading school, the Epicureans, had little interest in rhetoric until Philodemus took up the subject in the first century B.C. Several philosophers wrote treatises or essays on specific aspects of rhetoric. This is the beginning of monographic treatments, especially of style, which subsequently become common.[5] It was in the philosophical schools rather than in the rhetorical schools that some of the most important advances in rhetorical theory were made.

Theophrastus

Theophrastus (c. 370–c. 285 B.C.), Aristotle's successor as head of the Peripatetic school, probably made the most important contributions to rhetoric of any Hellenistic philosopher. About twenty works on rhetoric are

[5] The earliest antecedent could be said to be works by sophists that collected types of words, e.g., the *Museums of Words* of Polus; Aristotle's lectures on style were probably originally separate from the rest of *On Rhetoric*; Theophrastus' *On Style* may be the model for later monographic treatments, which include the work of Demetrius, Cicero's *Orator*, the treatises of Dionysius of Halicarnassus and Hermogenes, and numerous handbooks of figures of speech in Greek and Latin.

found in the list of his writings given by Diogenes Laertius (5.42–50).[6] In addition to an *Art of Rhetoric* in one book, he wrote separate studies of judicial, deliberative, and epideictic oratory; invention; enthymemes; examples; maxims, nonartistic proof; narration, style; humor; and delivery. What we know about these works, all of which are lost, suggests that Theophrastus closely followed Aristotle's basic views of rhetoric but revised some of his master's teaching and worked out in greater detail subjects that Aristotle had briefly touched on. His attitude toward invention is well brought out in a passage, reminiscent of Aristotle, quoted by Demetrius (*On Style* 226):

> Everything should not be elaborated in detail, but some things should be left for the hearer to know and to reason out by himself; for recognizing what has been left out, he becomes not only your hearer but your "witness," and a very friendly one too. For he thinks himself intelligent since you have furnished him a starting point of understanding, while to tell him everything as though he were ignorant makes you appear to feel contempt for the hearer.

Theophrastus' treatise *On Style* was perhaps the most influential of his writings on rhetoric. Aristotle had said that the virtue of style, the one quality most desirable in prose, is clarity, but also that the language should not be flat nor above the dignity of the subject but appropriate (*On Rhetoric* 3.2.1); subsequently (3.5.1) he added that the first principle (*archē*) of style is to speak correct Greek, and in subsequent chapters he discussed several forms of ornamentation. Theophrastus reorganized this discussion into a theory of four virtues of style, which was adopted by most subsequent writers on the subject. Cicero summarizes the theory in *Orator* 79: "The language will be pure and good [Greek or] Latin, it will be clearly and distinctly stated, attention will be given to what is appropriate; one thing will be lacking[7] which Theophrastus numbers fourth among the virtues of a speech, ornamentation that is pleasant and abundant."

Purity or correctness (Gk. *Hellenismos*, Lat. *Latinitas*) is defined as the first of four virtues, rather than as the first principle of rhetorical style. In *On the Orator* (3.40), drawing on Theophrastus, Cicero says "we shall preserve case and tense and gender and number." Clarity (Gk. *to saphes*, Lat. *perspicuitas*) is achieved by using "common words which clearly indicate what we wish to signify and declare, without any ambiguous word or construction, without too long phrases nor with metaphors too farfetched, without breaking up the thought, without confusing tenses or persons [of verbs], and without disturbing the order" (*On the Orator* 3.49). The virtue of propriety or appropriateness (Gk. *to prepon*, Lat. *proprietas*) had been discussed

[6] All the evidence for Theophrastus' work on rhetoric can now be found, with English translation, in Fortenbaugh et al., *Theophrastus*, vol. 2, 508–59. See also Fortenbaugh and Mirhady, eds., "Peripatetic Rhetoric after Aristotle."

[7] Cicero is here speaking of the plain style, which lacks ornamentation.

by Aristotle (3.7) and was especially important to the Peripatetics in that it was related to their principle, both in ethics and aesthetics, of seeking the mean between extremes. Expression should be appropriate to context and content, neither too elevated nor too colloquial. It may have been in connection with propriety that Theophrastus discussed levels of style, developing the subject beyond the two kinds of style identified by Aristotle (*On Rhetoric* 3.12), where they are identified with the species of rhetoric: the written or epideictic and the agonistic or style of debate, divided into deliberative and judicial. Dionysius of Halicarnassus (*On Demosthenes* 3) found in Theophrastus a discussion of three types of style: plain, grand, and mixed, the latter being a mean between the other two. Dionysius says that Theophrastus cited Thrasymachus as the earliest example of the mixed style; we know that he also discussed the style of Lysias and, from what Dionysius says (*Lysias* 14), criticized it severely as crude and overdone. This judgment is totally at odds with later discussions of Lysias; it certainly suggests that Theophrastus did not cite him as a fine example of the plain style, and it may mean that of the three styles Theophrastus approved only that which was a mean. The theory of three levels of good style (*genera dicendi*) appropriate to the subject was well established by the early first century B.C. when it is found, with examples, in *Rhetoric for Herennius* (4.11–14). Discussion of the three kinds of style there includes their faulty forms, and since Aristotle had included a discussion of faults in diction (3.3), as do several other writers, it is probable that Theophrastus discussed that subject as well.

A division of the subject of style into word choice and composition is implicit in Aristotle (3.2–5 vs. 6–12) and was perhaps specified by Theophrastus as it often is in later writers. According to Dionysius of Halicarnassus (*Isocrates* 3), Theophrastus said that style becomes great, lofty, and unusual through choice of words, harmony (sound and rhythm), and the use of figures. Theophrastus may have divided ornamentation (Gk. *kataskeuē*, Lat. *ornatus*) into sweetness and distinction; the beauty of a word, he said, is inherent in its sound or appearance or in its value in our minds (Demetrius, *On Style* 173). He agreed with Aristotle in disliking overly bold metaphors in prose (Longinus 32.3), and he continued Aristotle's discussion of prose rhythm. We would like to know more about Theophrastus' discussion of figures, since these become such an important aspect of the theory of style. To judge from Dionysius' reference, he used the word *schēmata* for figures;[8] Aristotle did not and indeed had no technical concept of a figure of speech, though he discussed simile, antithesis, verbal techniques used by Gorgias, and various other features of style that come to be known as fig-

---

[8] *Schēma* is common in the fourth century in a general sense of any form or shape; Isocrates describes his *Antidosis* (8) as in the *schēma* of an apology; the earliest known definition of a *schēma* is that attributed by Quintilian (9.1.14) to the fourth-century Cynic philosopher Zoilus, "to pretend one thing and say another," which seems to describe only irony.

ures. Certainly Theophrastus discussed antithesis, probably as a figure; Dionysius says he divided it into three types: when opposites are predicated of the same thing or the same thing of opposites or opposites of opposites.

At the beginning of book 3 Aristotle notes in passing that the subject of delivery as a part of rhetoric had not been much studied. Theophrastus apparently developed the subject in his treatise *On Delivery*, discussing control of voice and gesture, the division of the subject found in later treatments. His discussion, however, seems not to have been restricted to delivery in oratory, probably ranging widely over music, acting, and recitation of poetry.[9] Theophrastus himself is said to have lectured to as many as two thousand at once and to have given practical attention to his presentation (Diogenes Laertius 5.37), anointing and dressing himself with care and using gestures (Athenaeus 1.21a–b). We do not know whether he specifically divided rhetoric as a whole into the four parts of invention, arrangement, style, and delivery, though he did discuss all of these subjects separately.

Later Peripatetics

Although Cicero, Quintilian, and others refer to Peripatetic rhetoric on a number of occasions, they sometimes mean Aristotle and Theophrastus, rather than later Peripatetics, and it does not seem possible to identify a specifically Peripatetic tradition in Hellenistic rhetoric. According to Strabo (13.1.54), writing about three hundred years later but with good sources of information, Theophrastus' successors did not have the unpublished writings of Aristotle or Theophrastus until these were rediscovered and published in the first century B.C.; as a result they did not continue their founders' philosophical thought and engaged primarily in dialectical debate on general issues, of which Strabo had a low opinion. Quintilian gives a somewhat more positive version, saying (12.2.25) that the Peripatetics "boast" that they are engaged in rhetorical study, "for they are more or less the ones who instituted debate of theses for the sake of practice." The Peripatetics had, of course, Aristotle's published works, including the *Gryllus*, which discussed whether or not rhetoric was an art. Individuals who had studied personally with Aristotle or Theophrastus would have been familiar with their theories and used them in their lectures or writings.

One such person was Demetrius of Phaleron. He was a statesman, orator, man of letters, and teacher with some following, and he wrote some books on rhetoric of which we know very little. He is more often mentioned for his style. According to Cicero (*Brutus* 37–38), it was more suited for the wrestling school than for combat: "He delighted the Athenians rather than

---

[9] See Fortenbaugh, "Delivery."

inflamed them, for he came out into the sun and dust (of the public arena) not as one emerging from an army tent but from the shady retreat of Theophrastus, a most learned man. He was the first to modulate oratory and make it soft and delicate and he preferred to seem delightful, as he was, rather than serious."

Some insight into Hellenistic debates about the nature of rhetoric, continuing the discussions in Plato's *Gorgias* and Aristotle's *Gryllus*, can be found in Quintilian's survey of definitions of rhetoric (2.15) and whether it should be regarded as an art (2.17). The head of the Peripatetic school in the middle of the second century was Critolaus. Quintilian says (2.15.23) that he denied that rhetoric was a faculty (Aristotle's *dynamis*), a science (*epistēmē*), or an art (*technē*), and called it a *tribē*, a "knack," as does Socrates in Plato's *Gorgias*. Yet on the previous page (2.15.19) Quintilian attributes to Ariston, a pupil of Critolaus, a definition of the end of rhetoric in the following terms: "a science of seeing and pleading in civil questions by means of speech of popular persuasion," and he adds that Ariston, as a Peripatetic, regarded rhetoric as a science, not as a virtue as the Stoics did. This is very confusing; the definition is partly Aristotelian, partly not. Quintilian was probably relying on secondary sources, and given the Peripatetic practice of debating issues, perhaps what we have are bits of such debate. But in the second century B.C., as noted in chapter 1, all the philosophical schools show a reaction against rhetoric, and Critolaus, lacking direct knowledge of Aristotle and Theophrastus' views, may have gone back to more negative sources in the *Gorgias* and *Gryllus*. With the publication of Aristotle's works in the first century, the Peripatetics resumed an interest in his theories. One of them, name unknown, went so far as to argue that Demosthenes had learned his art of rhetoric from Aristotle's treatise on the subject, a view Dionysius of Halicarnassus seeks to refute on chronological grounds in his first *Letter to Ammaeus*.

Demetrius, *On Style*

A Greek textbook that shows direct knowledge of writings of Aristotle and Theophrastus on rhetoric, perhaps the earliest to do so, is the treatise *On Style* attributed to an otherwise unknown Demetrius.[10] The date of composition has been much debated; a possible conclusion is that it was written in the early first century B.C., after Aristotle's treatise *On Rhetoric* had been rediscovered but before the debate over Atticism, of which it shows no

---

[10] He was long thought to have been Demetrius of Phaleron; this seems impossible, even though Philodemus, writing about 70 B.C., may have attributed the work to him; see Grube, *Demetrius*, 54–56. There are English translations of the treatise by Roberts, *Demetrius* (reprinted in the Loeb Classical Library volume of Aristotle's *Poetics*); by Grube, *Demetrius*; and by Innes in Russell and Winterbottom, eds., *Ancient Literary Criticism*, 171–215.

awareness. If this is right, Demetrius' work is the earliest surviving monographic treatment of style. It begins abruptly—perhaps the introduction is
lost—with a discussion of periodicity that resembles Aristotle's account but
introduces a novel distinction of three kinds: historical, conversational, and
rhetorical. The historical period is a mean beween the other two.

The rest of the treatise consists of a discussion of four styles—the plain,
the grand, the elegant, and the forceful—in terms of diction, composition,
and subject matter, each with a corresponding faulty style and each illustrated with examples from classical Greek poetry and prose. This section
begins (36–37) with criticism of earlier writers who recognized only two
distinct styles, plain and grand, and regarded the others as intermediate,
possibly a restatement of Theophrastus' view. Theophrastus is not mentioned here but is quoted on four other occasions (41, 114, 173, 222). A
theory of four rather than two or three styles is unusual; the only other
reference to four styles is found in Philodemus' *On Rhetoric* (vol. 1, p. 165,
Sudhaus), written about 70 B.C., which, however, speaks of the "middle"
rather than Demetrius' "forceful" style. Demetrius' work is a sensitive piece
of literary criticism, based on an implicit concept of taste (e.g., 67, 137,
287).[11] It is the earliest extant Greek work that makes a distinction between
figures of thought and figures of speech and the earliest to show knowledge
of technical names for figures, names that they often retain in later writers:
examples include *aposiōpēsis, prosōpopoeia, anadiplōsis,* and *klimax.* It is,
however, difficult to compose a complete list of what the author regards as
a figure. Is there any difference between *epanaphora* (61) and *anaphora*
(141)? Figures of speech are described (59) as a "species of composition"
involving repetition, changes of word order, or variation of grammatical
forms. No definition of a figure of thought is offered, but examples of forceful figures of thought are given in 263–66 (pretending to pass over some
subject, suppressing a word or statement when it is about to be made, and
personification). After the discussion of figures in the forceful style there
follows a discussion of diction, which includes the simile (273), also treated
as something other than a figure in section 146. There is thus considerable
confusion, in part because the author is not drawing up a list of figures but
trying to describe the effect of different kinds of style. He is apparently
unfamiliar with the concept of a trope but does treat metaphor as something distinct from a figure; the discussion of metaphor in 78–89 much
resembles that in Aristotle and even quotes *On Rhetoric* on the subject (81).

An unusual feature of Demetrius' work is his discussion of letter writing,
citing letters of Aristotle and others (223–35). Letters, we are told, should
be written in a mixture of the plain and elegant styles and are like one side
of a dialogue. This discussion presumably reflects the increasing role of the

---

[11] See Kennedy, *Cambridge History,* vol. 1, 196–98.

epistle, public and private, literary and nonliterary, in the Hellenistic period. What is puzzling is not that Demetrius should discuss the subject but why other rhetoricians do not, considering the fact that the epistle was a widely used literary genre, beginning at least with Isocrates, and that the subject had practical value for students of rhetoric. Nor, so far as we know, was letter writing taught by grammarians. Cicero has much to say about letter writing in his own letters, and what he says seems to suggest classifications of different kinds and perhaps the existence of some manuals of letter writing, of which we have examples from later antiquity.[12]

The Stoics

The Stoic school of philosophy was founded by Zeno of Citium in Athens about 300 B.C. and was the most dogmatic of the Hellenistic philosophical movements, claiming that a wise man could have absolute knowledge of truth and should rise above all emotion, and insisting on an extremely austere concept of virtue. Many Stoics were notorious for their crabbed style of speaking and writing. Cicero says (*De Finibus* 4.7) that the Stoics Cleanthes (third century) and Chrysippus (second century) each wrote an *Art of Rhetoric,* "but of such a sort that it is the one book to read if anyone should wish to keep quiet. . . . They point the argument with their puny little syllogisms, like thorns. People may assent, but they are not convinced in their hearts and go away much as they came." Yet Stoicism became the most popular of the philosophical schools, especially with Romans who found in it something resembling their own tradition of personal austerity. Diogenes Laertius (7.42–43) gives a brief account of Stoic rhetorical theory, which is probably chiefly derived from writings of Diogenes of Babylon, head of the Stoic school in the first half of the second century. The theory is of a standard sort:

> They regard rhetoric as the science (*epistēmē*) of speaking well in exposition and dialectic as the science of correct discussion in question and answer. . . . Rhetoric itself they say to be threefold: one part is deliberative, one judicial, one encomiastic. Its divisions are invention, expression (*phrasis*), arrangement, and delivery.[13] A rhetorical speech is divided into prooemium, narration, the parts against the opponents, and epilogue.

Discussing Stoic grammar a little later, Diogenes says (7.59),

> The virtues of speech are five: Hellenism, clarity, brevity, propriety, ornamentation (*kataskeuē*). "Hellenism" is expression without mistake in grammar and with no careless usage. "Clarity" is style expounding the

---

[12] The evidence has been collected by Malherbe, "Ancient Epistolary Theorists."

[13] Memory was not yet recognized as a separate part of rhetoric.

thought intelligibly. "Brevity" is style employing only what is strictly necessary for making the matter clear. "Propriety" is style suitable to the subject. "Ornamentation" is style avoiding vulgarity. Of the faults of style "barbarism" is style contrary to the usage of well-bred Greeks and "solecism" is a statement in which the grammatical categories are not in proper agreement.

The Stoics were especially interested in grammatical correctness. They taught that everything should be called by its proper name and carried this to the extreme of denying that any word is in itself obscene (Cicero, *To His Friends* 9.22.1). They preferred a simple, straightforward style, and their definition of ornamentation is a narrow one. According to Plutarch (*On the Contradictions of the Stoics* 28.1047a–b), in the first book of his work on rhetoric Chrysippus required "a liberal and simple adornment of the words," while rejecting such niceties of style as avoidance of hiatus.

Stoic contributions to rhetoric came in part from their study of grammar. The student of classical Greek is required to learn a formidable number of irregular verbs and nouns, but in the spoken language, as in colloquial English, there was a tendency to simplify the inflectional system into a smaller number of patterns of conjugation and declension. Chrysippus wrote four books on "anomaly," the doctrine that traditional usage, not regularity of forms, should determine what is grammatically correct. In this he was followed by Crates, the leading figure in the Stoic school at Pergamum in the second century. Grammarians at Alexandria took the opposite view and supported the doctrine of "analogy," that insofar as possible consistency ought to be imposed on grammatical forms.[14]

Stoic grammatical studies probably created the theory of tropes. A trope is a single word used in a novel way, either because the idea to be expressed has no name of its own (no "proper" word) or for the sake of imagery or embellishment. The earliest study of tropes by a grammarian that is mentioned in our sources was the work of Crates' pupil Tauriscus in the second century (Sextus Empricus, *Against the Professors* 1.249). Subsequently, Dionysius Thrax, as noted earlier, included exegesis of poetical tropes as a part of grammar. The difference between a trope and a figure is parallel to the difference between barbarism and solecism as defined above: a trope (in classical grammatical theory but not necessarily in modern literary theory), like a barbarism, involves only a single word; a figure, like a solecism, involves at least two words. So viewed, a metaphor is a trope, a simile is a figure. But, as Quintilian notes (9.1.1), many teachers did not clearly distinguish tropes from figures, and there is often much confusion in the discus-

---

[14] In English, "I go, I went" is an example of anomaly; the colloquial barbarism "I go, I goed" results from analogy. Our main source on the anomaly/analogy controversy is Varro, *On the Latin Language* 9; Julius Caesar wrote a work entitled *On Analogy*, now lost.

sions. It is possible that the distinction between figures of thought and figures of speech is also a Stoic innovation, for Fronto (*On Eloquence* 1.15) quotes a list of figures of thought from Chrysippus.

The most important Stoic philosopher of the second half of the second century was Panaetius of Rhodes, who visited Rome and became a close associate of the Roman statesman Scipio Aemilianus. His philosophy was more eclectic than that of earlier Stoics, for he was an admirer of the writings of Plato and Aristotle, and he sought to adapt Stoic ethics to the needs of upper-class Romans. One of his most important works was *On Duties*; this is now lost, but it was a major source for Cicero's treatise of the same name. The passage on the power of speech in Cicero's *On Duties* (1.132–37) is probably derived from Panaetius. It is part of a discussion of the virtue or duty of propriety. The power of speech is here said to be of two sorts, seen equally in formal debate and in conversation. The rhetoricians supply rules for the former; the latter subject has so far been neglected. The voice is the organ of speech; it should be clear and pleasant. Clarity can be improved by practice; a harmonious tone can be achieved by imitating those who speak in a restrained and smooth way. Some suggestions for conversation are offered. It should be easy, not too assertive, and show wit, with the tone adapted to the subject, whether serious or humorous. It should also keep to the subject and, consistent with Panaetius' Stoic values, should generally avoid emotion. It is acceptable to reprove someone sternly, in which case the speaker may seem angry, but he should not allow himself actually to feel anger. Even with bitter enemies, even when treated outrageously, we should maintain dignity and repress anger.

Later in the work (2.48–51), as a part of a discussion of how to win true glory, the importance of eloquence is considered. Cicero says that although there are opportunities in assemblies and senates, the law courts are the primary source of fame for an orator. One should not prosecute a capital charge against a person who may be innocent, but to defend one who may be guilty is sanctioned by popular opinion, custom, and humane feeling; this, Cicero says (2.51), was the view of Panaetius. There is finally (2.66–69) a section on the duty of the patron to his client in legal cases. He will win gratitude but will offend others, to whom he needs to explain why he has done what he has done, offering future service to them.

Some Stoics sought to popularize their views by a kind of informal preaching, attacking the vices of society. Something similar, even more outrageous in tone, was practiced by Diogenes the Cynic in the fourth century, by Bion the Borysthenite in the third, and by other individuals who lived in poverty and wandered from city to city inveighing against the stupidity of social conventions. This kind of preaching is often referred to in modern times as the Stoic-Cynic diatribe.[15] Some of its style and themes of invective

---

[15] See Kustas, *Diatribe in Ancient Rhetorical Theory*.

can be found in the literary satires of the Roman poets Lucilius, Horace, and Juvenal. Aristotle (*On Rhetoric* 3.17.10) uses *diatribē* of a passage in a speech that dwells on a subject, such as the vices of an opponent or the virtues of a speaker, in an emotional way. In philosophical schools the word was used to refer to informal remarks of a teacher in which he addressed and rebuked students or refuted logical objections to his teaching.[16] Versions of this are found in essays by Seneca, in speeches by Dio Chrysostom, in the *Discourses* of the Stoic Epictetus, and in Christian writing.

The Academics

Plato's Academy developed into the Academic school of the Hellenistic period, but in the third and second centuries Platonic dogmatism was abandoned by Arcesilaus and Carneades in favor of skepticism. Cicero regarded himself as an Academic, and we know their teachings best from his works, especially his *Academics*, which stresses their technique of disputation on two sides of an issue (*in utramque partem disputare*). In the late second century B.C. Academic philosophers, in common with Peripatetics and Stoics, became hostile to rhetorical study. Cicero says (*On the Orator* 1.46–47) that they all rejected the orator's claims to greatness and restricted rhetoric to what was useful in law courts and assemblies; Plato's *Gorgias* was studied in the school at this time and gave authority to such a view, while Aristotle's *On Rhetoric* was still unknown. It is possible that the Academics were responsible for making memory a part of rhetoric; Cicero (*On the Orator* 2.360), after telling a traditional story of the use of a mnemonic system by Simonides of Ceos in early Greek times, jumps down to its practice by the Academics Charmadas and Metrodorus in the late second century, and Pliny the Elder (*Natural History* 7.89) says Metrodorus brought the system to perfection. Metrodorus subsequently abandoned Academic philosophy and became a teacher of rhetoric (Strabo 13.609).

At the end of his treatise *Classifications of Oratory* (*Partitiones Oratoriae* 139), a rhetorical catechism he wrote for his son, Cicero says the contents are derived from the teachings of "our Academy," meaning the Academic school of the late second and early first century, but as the passage goes on to indicate, what he has in mind is Academic dialectic and ethics rather than a distinctive Academic rhetorical theory.

The Epicureans

In 306 B.C. Epicurus founded a new philosophical school in Athens that differed sharply from the others of the period both in its physics—its doctrinaire materialism based on a theory of atoms and void—and its ethics,

[16] See Stowers, *The Diatribe*.

which sought imperturbability in retirement from the turmoil of life. Participation in public affairs was not encouraged, and study of political rhetoric was discouraged; Quintilian (12.2.24) says that Epicurus banished orators from his presence, ordering his followers "to flee all systematic study on the swiftest ship possible."[17] Epicureanism did, however, provide an opening for poetry and rhetoric that taught Epicurean doctrines or contributed to aesthetic pleasure and were nonpolitical. The Latin epic of Lucretius, *On the Nature of Things*, expounds Epicureanism in verse to free human beings from superstition and fear of death, using poetry to sweeten the bitter medicine of philosophy (1.935–50).

The only Epicurean whose writings on rhetoric are at all known to us is Philodemus. He came to Italy from Palestine early in the first century. Portions of his numerous Epicurean works have been discovered on charred papyri from a library excavated at Herculaneum, where they had been buried in the eruption of Mount Vesuvius about a century after his death. The papyri are exceedingly difficult to decipher, since the brittle rolls have to be opened with great care and the writing is essentially now black on black. Even when the text can be read, Philodemus' Greek prose style is difficult, often ironic and idiosyncratic. Yet over the course of the last century scholars have had considerable success in reconstructing Philodemus' writings; research continues today and in the course of time they will be better understood and additional portions may be discovered.

We have a considerable part of Philodemus' *Hypomnēmatikon*, a handbook that seems to set out the views on rhetoric of Philodemus' Epicurean teacher Zeno of Sidon, and a longer, perhaps more original work, *On Rhetoric*.[18] The most characteristic doctrine of Philodemus, and apparently of some Epicurean predecessors, is that of the three Aristotelian species of rhetoric only epideictic is artistic; success in judicial and deliberative rhetoric is solely the result of practice. Epideictic rhetoric, which Philodemus usually calls "sophistic" and of which the works of Isocrates are taken as the main model, is useless but gives pleasure from its beauty. These views are set out in both the *Hypomnēmatikon* and in fragments of books 1 and 2 of *On Rhetoric*. Book 3, largely lost, apparently argued that sophists do not produce statesmen and are often harmful. Book 4 contained an original discussion of rhetorical invention, in which Philodemus seems to have argued that neither discovery nor judgment of arguments rightly belongs to

---

[17] Some Romans, active in public life, were attracted by Epicureanism. The best example is L. Calpurnius Piso, whose Epicurean views are attacked by Cicero in his oration *Against Piso*.

[18] References to Philodemus' rhetorical works are usually given by volume and page number in the old edition by Sudhaus; there is now a better edition by Longo-Auricchio. Hubbell, "The *Rhetorica* of Philodemus," provides an English paraphrase based on Sudhaus' text; a collaborative project to produce complete translations of Philodemus' writings is currently under way, though none has yet been published.

the art of rhetoric; they are functions of other intellectual disciplines concerned with the specific subject matter of the arguments. What remains for rhetoric is the function of focusing and applying these arguments for rhetorical effect. This is reminiscent of Aristotle's distinction between "specific" and "common" topics; knowledge is extrarhetorical, but there are rhetorical techniques in its utilization.[19] Book 4 also discussed style, with some modification of Theophrastus' theory of four virtues or the Stoic list of five, mentioned above. Philodemus seems to have identified six qualities to be sought in good prose style: correctness, clarity, forcefulness, brevity, propriety, and ornamentation.[20] Forcefulness (*emphasis*) is an addition to the Stoic list and anticipates the interest in that quality, usually called *deinotēs*, in Dionysius of Halicarnassus, Hermogenes, and other writers of the imperial period, though there is no evidence that they knew Philodemus' work. Book 5 contrasted the unfortunate rhetor and the fortunate philosopher; book 6 attacked those philosophical schools that taught rhetoric, and this may have been continued in a seventh book.[21] Although there are thus some positive views on rhetoric in Philodemus' writings, his characteristic method is to set out and criticize views of earlier writers. His work *On Poems*, in at least five books, is especially important in this respect since it is a major source for otherwise lost Hellenistic poetic theory.

Asianism

A change toward greater artificiality in style is characteristic of the Hellenistic period. Demetrius of Phaleron, as mentioned above, spoke more like a student of philosophy than a practical politician. Other forms of artificiality were especially noticeable away from Athens.[22] Cicero describes the development in a colorful passage (*Brutus* 51):

> But outside of Greece there was great enthusiasm for speaking and the greatest honors accorded in praise of it made the name of orator illustrious. For when eloquence once sailed from the Piraeus [the port of Athens], it passed through all the islands and visited all parts of Asia, with the result that it was infected with foreign diseases and lost all that healthiness and what might be called saneness of Attic diction and almost unlearned how to speak. From this came the Asiatic orators, not to be despised for their rapidity and abundance of speech, but too little restrained and too redundant.

[19] See Gaines, "Philodemus on the Three Activities of Rhetorical Invention."

[20] See Gaines, "Rhetorical Expression in Philodemus."

[21] See Innes, "Philodemus," 218.

[22] The discussion of Asianism here is based on the account of Wooten, "Style asiatique." His article largely replaces earlier accounts.

This is the phenomenon known as Asianism, which Cicero elsewhere (*Orator* 25) describes as "fat and greasy." He distinguished two forms (*Brutus* 325): one is described as epigrammatic and pointed; the other swift and impetuous, with ornate words. Cicero was writing *Brutus* and *Orator* in 46 B.C. and was trying to combat the more extreme forms of the new Atticism movement of that time. "Asiatic" as a pejorative description of style seems to have originated then; when in Cicero's earlier writings an orator is called "Asiatic" it only means he came from Asia Minor.

The earliest orator described as Asiatic is Hegesias of Magnesia, who lived in the third century; we have only short quotations from his speeches. These sound as though they come from declamations, and they seem to fall into the class Cicero described as "epigrammatic." Hegesias favored short, rhythmical phrases and avoided long periodic sentences. The effect is somewhat reminiscent of the style of Gorgias. Hegesias' style is, in fact, a continuation of developments of the fourth century that turned to greater artificiality, seen in fragments of speeches of Charisius and Cleochares, for example. Charisius, however, regarded himself as imitating Lysias (*Brutus* 286), and most orators would have claimed to be Attic. No critic ever promoted a theory of Asianism as the best style. What was out of fashion for a time was the style of Demosthenes, not fully appreciated until the writings of Cicero and Dionysius of Halicarnassus.

The best examples of the impetuous and ornate style in the third and second centuries come from elaborate inscriptions preserving letters of Hellenistic kings, such as that of Ptolemy II at Miletus around 260 B.C.[23] This had apparently become the standard style for formal correspondence and official proclamation. It can also be found in formal writing on papyri in the Hellenistic period. In the late second and early first centuries a number of famous orators and teachers of rhetoric were active in Asia Minor. They included the brothers Menecles and Hierocles of Alabanda, who represent the epigrammatic style, and Aeschines of Miletus and Aeschylus of Cnidus in the ornate style. Theirs was the oratory Romans heard when they visited and studied in the East, and it had some effect on Latin oratory of the early first century. Cicero's rival Hortenius was thought of as showing Asian characteristics, and they are not lacking in Cicero himself, especially in his earlier orations, including the *Verrines*. A rhetorical school on the island of Rhodes was started by Apollonius of Alabanda (also called Apollonius Molon) in the early first century, more restrained in style than the schools of Asia Minor. Cicero (*Brutus* 317) credits Apollonius with showing him how to control his own youthful impetuosity, reduce his tendency to redundancy, and generally discipline himself to become the great orator he was destined to be.

[23] See Norden, *Antike Kunstprosa*, 140–55.

Hermagoras and Stasis Theory

The most famous professional teacher of rhetoric in the Hellenistic period was Hermagoras of Temnos, who lived about the middle of the second century B.C. and who first worked out in detail a theory of the stasis or determination of the question at issue in a speech. His work is lost but can be reconstructed in some detail from use of his theory in Cicero's *On Invention, Rhetoric for Herennius,* and later rhetorical writings.[24]

Hermagoras' original book was a comprehensive rhetoric handbook for students in rhetorical schools, preparing them for declamation of judicial themes, though the nominal goal was ability at public speaking. Invention was given the most extensive treatment; arrangement and style were grouped under the heading "economy," which was subdivided into judgment, division, order, and style (cf. Quintilian 3.3.9); discussion of memory and delivery perhaps followed.[25] Hermagoras defined the duty of the orator as "to treat the proposed political question as persuasively as possible" (Sextus Empiricus, *Against the Professors* 2.62). He seems to have concerned himself only with logical proof, not with ethos or pathos. "Political questions" were divided into two classes: theses and hypotheses. A thesis is a disputation that does not involve specific individuals or situations. Cicero (*On Invention* 1.8) attributes to Hermagoras such philosophical theses as "Whether there is any good except the honorable? Whether the senses are reliable? What is the size of the sun?" Hermagoras perhaps introduced debating of philosophical theses into his rhetorical school, for the Stoic philosopher Posidonius attacked his discussion of theses, perhaps as inappropriate for a rhetorician (Plutarch, *Pompey* 42.5). Hypotheses are specific cases involving persons and occasions. Seven attributes of the rhetorical situation (*peristasis*) were identified: actor, action, time, place, cause, manner, and starting point.

Aristotle (*On Rhetoric* 1.3.9) had distinguished between cases in which the question at issue (*amphisbētēsis*) was one of fact (had someone done something?) and those in which it was one of law (was the action illegal?) and also (3.17.1) noted four possible questions in dispute: fact, injury, importance, and justice. Although he recognized the need to define the question at issue in a trial, Aristotle did not develop a theory to cover the various possibilities, nor did he use the term stasis. According to Quintilian

---

[24] A fuller account, primarily drawn from Matthes, "Hermagoras," is given in my *Art of Persuasion in Greece,* 303–21.

[25] See Matthes, "Hermagoras," 107ff. If so, this would be the first discussion of memory in a rhetoric handbook. *Rhetoric for Herennius,* often indebted to Hermagoras in other respects, gives an excellent account of memory but says (3.38) that there were many Greek discussions of the subject. One may have been that of Metrodorus, mentioned among the Academics above.

(3.6.3), it was first employed either by Naucrates, a pupil of Isocrates, or by Zopyrus of Clazomene, and he points to the use of the word in Aeschines' speech *Against Ctesiphon* (206) where the orator demands that Demosthenes be forced to speak about the real "stasis" of the case. The word literally means "stand, standing, stance," describes the "stance" of a boxer toward an opponent, and perhaps was transferred from that context to the stand taken by a speaker toward an opponent. Quintilian (3.6.23) saw the influence of Aristotle's dialectical categories of substance, quantity, relation, and quality on concepts of stasis, which in Latin is called *constitutio* or *status*. Hermagoras was certainly familiar with logic and dialectic as taught in the Peripatetic and Stoic schools of philosophy and probably drew on this knowledge.

In determining the question at issue in a judicial speech, Hermagoras began with the *kataphasis*, or charge of the prosecutor, which defined the *aition*, or cause of action. This was answered by the *apophasis*, denial by the defendant, which provided the *sunechon*, containment of the issue, and focused the basic conflict. Out of this process emerged the *zētēma*, question, or *krinomenon*, the matter under judgment, which was then classified as either "rational" (subdivided into four types of stasis) or "legal" (also subdivided into four types, though these were not called staseis). Although a negotiation of the central issue goes on in the assertations and replies of speakers on the two sides of a case, the issue is really determined at the point where the defendant takes a final stand. Thus the process can be viewed as one of elimination of each type successively; for example, in the case of a rational question the defendant's *apophasis* will, if possible, define the issue as stasis of fact ("you did"; "I didn't"); if such a claim is not possible, recourse is had to stasis of definition ("you did"; "yes, but it wasn't theft"), and only failing that to one of quality ("you did"; "but I had to," or "I didn't mean to"). Some cases were regarded as *asystata*, lacking stasis; these should not come to trial because the evidence is insufficient, is equally balanced on both sides, or is too one-sided, or because the subject presents some contradiction or difficulty that makes decision impossible.

Hermagoras' four types of stasis in rational questions were the following:[26]

1. *Stochasmos*, Latin *coniectura*, "conjecturing" about the fact at issue, whether or not something had been done at a particular time by a particular person: e.g., Did X actually kill Y?

2. *Horos*, Latin *definitiva*, whether an admitted action falls under the legal "definition" of a crime: e.g., Was the admitted killing of Y by X murder or homicide?

---

[26] The chief sources for the terms are Cicero, *On Invention* 1.10; Quintilian 3.1.56, 3.5.14, 3.6.56; and Augustine, *On Rhetoric*, in Halm, *Rhetores Latini Minores*, 142–43.

3. *Kata symbēbēkos* or *poiotēs*, Latin *generalis* or *qualitas*, the issue of the "quality" of the action, including its motivation and possible justification: e.g., Was the murder of Y by X in some way justified by the circumstances?

4. *Metalēpsis*, Latin *translatio*, objection to the legal process or "transference" of jurisdiction to a different tribunal: e.g., Can this court try X for a crime when X has been given immunity from prosecution or claims the crime was committed in another city?

Each of the four staseis was discussed in detail by Hermagoras, and subdivisions were made. In stasis of fact it is necessary to prove or disprove motive, ability, and desire. Further, the defendant's person and character furnish evidence to indicate the probability or improbability of the alleged action. Cicero, following Hermagoras' system (*On Invention* 2.28ff.), lists as topics name, nature, way of life, fortune, habits (subdivided into six headings), zeal, and purpose. The act itself furnishes evidence also, for the orator should consider its attributes, performance (place, time, and occasion), adjuncts, and result.

If the stasis is one of definition (*On Invention* 2.53ff.), the speaker should define the crime, prove the definition, compare it with the act of the person accused, introduce commonplaces on the enormity and wickedness of the crime, or, in the case of the defendant, on the utility and honorable nature of the act, attack the definition the opponent offers, compare similar cases, and finally attack the opponent personally. Though the speaker might make use of a law in establishing a definition of a crime, the applicability or justice of the laws was not at issue in stasis of definition; that fell under the rubric of legal questions, to be discussed later.

The most complicated type of stasis was that of quality. It was to be employed when the speakers agreed about what had been done and about the legal term to describe the action, but disagreed about such matters as whether the action was important, just, or useful. Here the defendant could claim mitigating circumstances. Hermagoras divided stasis of quality into four parts (throughout the system he seems to have favored division in four headings): deliberative, demonstrative, judicial, and pragmatic (*On Invention* 1.12; Quintilian 3.6.56ff.). Cicero protests the use of the species of rhetoric as names for types of stasis of quality, but they were probably intended by Hermagoras to refer to topics characteristic of the species, which could be used to justify an action. The topic of the "advantageous," for example, is characteristic of deliberative rhetoric but useful in judicial speeches in explaining the quality of an action in terms of the speaker's view of what a person should or would have sought or avoided; similarly, what is praiseworthy or blameworthy (epideictic), what is just or unjust (judicial).

"Pragmatic" probably referred to what was or was not useful or practicable (cf. *On Invention* 1.12). Clearly the most important quality would be the justice or injustice of an action, and this Hermagoras further divided. The defendant might claim that an action was appropriate, in accordance with custom, and just in itself (*kat' antilēpsin*). If that could not be substantiated, he would have to look for some other mitigating circumstances (*kat' antithesin*), "assumptive" stasis of quality. Hermagoras divided the latter into four types: *antengklēma*, when the defendant brings a countercharge (e.g., "He was killed, but he was a robber"); *antistasis*, when the defendant claims some advantage resulted for somebody or that the act prevented something worse from happening; *metastasis*, when the blame is shifted to someone else, for example by a soldier to his commander who ordered an action; and *syngnōmē*, when a plea is made for forgiveness on the basis of having acted in ignorance or by accident.

Metalēpsis, or stasis of transference, is used when the defendant argues that the prosecutor has no right to prosecute or the court has no jurisdiction over the case.

Parallel to these four types of stasis are four legal questions (*nomika zētēmata*). The first of these, "by word and by intent," involves whether a law should be interpreted literally or in accordance with the intention of the original framers of the law. An example in *Rhetoric for Herennius* (1.19) concerns a law that anyone remaining on board an otherwise abandoned ship can gain possession of it and its cargo. Yet, if one person is too ill to abandon a ship in a storm but unexpectedly survives, can that person claim possession? Did the lawgiver intend to reward only one who braved a storm? The letter of the law seems to include anyone remaining aboard, for whatever reason. The second involves contrary laws, when two laws seem in conflict. The third occurs when the law is ambiguous, and the fourth when there is no law covering a specific situation and the speaker has to reason from existing laws about analogous situations.

The discussion of stasis and legal questions seems to have made up Hermagoras' account of invention. There followed an account of rhetorical "economy," divided into the four parts of judgment, division, order, and style (Quintilian 3.3.9). Grouping these matters under economy was unusual and was not adopted by later rhetoricians, even when they follow Hermagoras in other ways. Hermagoras may have been responsible for expanding the number of parts of an oration from four, as commonly seen earlier, to six. Both Cicero's *On Invention* and *Rhetoric for Herennius*, often dependent on Hermagoras in other ways, list six parts: introduction, narration, *partition*, confirmation, *refutation*, and conclusion. Hermagoras perhaps formalized the logical basis of the prooemium by distinguishing four kinds of cases: the honorable, the paradoxical, the doubtful, and the disreputable. These appear in *Rhetoric for Herennius* (1.5) as *honestum, turpe, dubium*, and *humile*. We know nothing about Hermagoras' discussion of style; Cicero (*Brutus* 263, cf. also 271) says "the teaching of Hermagoras was meager in ornamentation, detailed in invention."

Hermagoras' system was a scholastic and even pedantic discipline. The constant use of four headings probably facilitated its memorization by a student. Later rhetoricians continued to debate how best to determine the question at issue in a speech, reduced or increased the number of categories and subcategories, and varied the terminology, but once introduced, stasis theory became a major part of classical inventional theory, most applicable to judicial rhetoric but often extended to include deliberative and even epideictic forms. Hermagoras seems to have envisioned the judicial process as it had existed in classical Greek courts of law, imitated in declamation, where the principals in a case spoke on their own behalf. The system could, however, with minor changes be adapted to the situation in Roman courts of law, where the speakers were more often advocates speaking for clients.

By the time of Hermagoras Romans had begun to study rhetoric with Greek teachers. Cicero describes the awakening in the following words (*On the Orator* 1.14):

> When our empire over all the waves had been established and enduring peace made leisure possible, there was hardly an ambitious young man who did not think he should strive with all zeal for the ability to speak. At first, ignorant of the whole study, since they did not realize the existence of any course or exercises or rules of art, they did what they could with their own native ability and reflection. Afterward, when they had heard Greek orators and become acquainted with Greek literature and had studied with learned Greeks, our countrymen took fire with an incredible zeal for speaking.

We thus turn now to the beginnings of rhetoric in Rome.

Early Roman Rhetoric

The early history of the Roman republic was filled with dissensions, especially strife between the "orders," the patrician aristocracy and the plebeian citizenry, and this must have involved public debate. Much of what we know about it, however, comes from later writers, especially the historian Titus Livy. These writers were trained in rhetoric and adopted the forms of Greek historiography, including the composition of speeches for the leading figures in events, based on oral tradition or imaginative reconstruction of what might have been said. A famous example is the speech attributed by Dionysius of Halicarnassus (*Roman Antiquities* 6.83–86) and more briefly by Livy (2.32.8–12) to Menenius Agrippa in 494 B.C., in which he uses the fable of war between the belly and the other parts of the body as a parable for class strife. The ideal early Roman male was, however, austere and laconic, a man of action rather than of words, relying heavily on personal authority. This traditional role was assumed by speakers even in the second century, when Greek rhetoric had begun to be studied by some Romans. An example is a speech attributed to Scipio Africanus, who had been charged with having accepted money from King Antiochus of Asia. According to Aulus Gellius (4.18.3), his defense before the assembly was as follows: "I recall that this is the anniversary of the day on which I defeated Hannibal the Carthaginian, a man most hostile to your rule, in a great battle in the land of Africa and secured for you peace and glorious victory. Therefore, let us not be ungrateful to the gods, and, I suggest, let us leave this scoundrel [his prosecutor] and go from here straight to give thanks to Jupiter the Best and Greatest."[1]

Cicero's *Brutus* is a history of Roman oratory from the beginnings to his own time. The only Latin speech from before the end of the third century of which Cicero claims direct knowledge (*Brutus* 61) is that of Appius Claudius Caecus ("the Blind") to the senate in opposition to the proposed peace with King Pyrrhus of Epirus about 280. The beginning of the speech was best remembered. Plutarch (*Pyrrhus* 19) gives the following version: "In the past I was distressed at the misfortune to my eyes, Romans, but now I regret not being deaf as well as blind when I hear your shameful plans and recommendations for overturning Roman glory." What we know of the speech suggests that Appius, like Scipio, relied heavily on personal authority and bitterly attacked any compromise with Rome's enemies. Although

---

[1] The standard collection of evidence for Roman republican oratory is Malcovati, *Oratorum Romanorum Fragmenta*.

Plutarch's version introduces logical arguments, we can probably conclude that the most characteristic feature of native, early Roman rhetoric was heavy reliance on ethos and pathos, the latter often taking the form of moral outrage.

An important difference between Greek and Roman courts was that in Greece litigants had ordinarily been expected to speak on their own behalf and the teaching of judicial rhetoric assumed this situation. At Rome, by the time of the later republic, most members of the upper classes may have been able to speak in court, but they regularly got their more eloquent friends to help them. The purchase of a speech to be memorized by a litigant was very rare in Rome. In practice, major cases were pleaded by professional orators, called "patrons."[2] The procedure was an extension of the patron / client relationship of the early republic. Originally a patron was a patrician who had certain responsibilities toward a number of "clients," who might be citizens or freedmen in Rome or in allied states. The clients looked to the patron primarily for legal help. Much of the law was not published or well known, with the result that clients were ignorant of procedure in cases in which they might be involved, and they also lacked the social prestige to defend their own rights in a society heavily dependent on personal authority. The original patron/client relationship was permanent and inherited; though a client might acquire more than one patron, he could only free himself from the relationship by being himself elected to one of the higher offices of state. By the later republic "patron" is also used of anyone who pleaded a case for another. Though this relationship often involved some kind of social or political tie, it was not permanent. On the other hand, it was not supposed to be a source of income for the patron, though gifts were often made in place of fees. The *Lex Cincia* of 204 B.C. prohibited the payment of pleaders in court.

In the second century a patron was still expected to have technical legal knowledge useful in the case, but this gradually changed so that by the first century a patron or client usually sought legal advice from a jurisconsult, an authority on the law. The patron, like a barrister in a British court, then determined the tactics and rhetorical presentation of the case. In important cases several patrons appeared on both sides, each making a full, formal address to the jury. Throughout the late republic many of the chief men of the state, even when holding public office, appeared frequently in court to act as patrons. The effect on the rhetorical situation was to make the prestige and authority of the patron a factor in the case. Not only the ethos of the two principals, but the ethos of the patrons was an issue, and a skilled

[2] The original meaning of the Latin word *orator* was "ambassador," but by the second century it was applied to any spokesman for others and then to any public speaker. Cicero's dialogue *On the Orator* is largely responsible for the term's taking on the connotation of special powers of eloquence.

patron like Cicero took advantage of this, often speaking about himself and his opponents as well as about his client and his opponents, and sometimes exploiting differences between himself and his client as a way to strengthen his case.

The normal sequence of events at an extortion trial may be taken as an example of Roman court procedure in the late republic in its fullest development. At a preliminary hearing the defendant was summoned before a praetor by a patron chosen by those aggrieved, and the charge was made. If the praetor accepted the charge as possibly actionable, he then adjourned the proceedings for a specified length of time so that evidence could be gathered and a defense prepared. By the appointed day a jury (fifty to seventy-three citizens) had been chosen from a pool of those eligible. The praetor presided at the trial, which took place out-of-doors in the Roman forum. The prosecution opened its case with a set speech (*oratio perpetua*), in which a patron often had a great deal to say in general about the wrongs committed by, and the wickedness of, the defendant, but in which he might well not reveal the evidence to substantiate the charges. He would be followed by other patrons for the prosecution, who might develop aspects of the charge in greater detail. The defense then had a chance to make a series of opening replies, trying to anticipate the evidence that would be introduced. Several patrons might deliver extensive speeches for the defense. The result was a situation that greatly encouraged flights of eloquence, ethical digressions, and emotional appeals, drawing on all the rhetorical skills of a speaker, with little limitation by what was relevant or provable. This procedure probably more than anything else contributed to the development of judicial rhetoric in the grand style, which was brought to its fullest form by Cicero. Only after the speeches on each side had been delivered was any evidence introduced, followed by an opportunity for cross-examination, and an *altercatio*, or debate, between the patrons on the main points in dispute. The trial might take several days, in contrast to Greek trials, which were settled in one day. Extortion cases were then adjourned for a second action, which repeated the process, though with better knowledge of the evidence. In other cases the jury voted at this point, but if a majority was not convinced of guilt or innocence, a second hearing was held. This procedure was altered in 52 B.C. by a law of Pompey that required the evidence in cases of violence or bribery to be introduced before the speeches and limited the length of speeches and the number of patrons. Writing a hundred and fifty years later, Tacitus makes a character in his *Dialogue On Orators* (38) claim the change was the beginning of the end for great Latin oratory.

A common form of deliberative oratory in the Roman republic was the *contio*; the word means "meeting," but was transferred to a speech at any public meeting except sessions of the senate. The Roman citizens were regularly convened in assemblies that performed different functions and bore

different names depending on the voting procedure used. Consuls or tribunes could convoke formal meetings of one or another of the assemblies to
consider legislation, in which case the proposed bill usually had had prior
senatorial approval and was posted publicly. The two consuls, elected by the
assembly for a term of one year, were the official heads of state; the original
function of the ten tribunes, also elected for a term of one year, was to
protect ordinary citizens from unjust arrest at the instigation of patricians,
but their right to veto (literally "I forbid") gave them wide authority to
block any action they regarded as against the interest of the public or themselves. At legislative assemblies ordinary citizens had an opportunity to
come forward and speak from the rostrum in the forum, but much of the
speaking was done by public officials or well-known persons. The Roman
republic was an oligarchy, not a democracy; most power most of the time lay
in the hands of a small number of members of noble families, often rich,
working through their clients, but popular leaders, or demagogues, often
using the office of tribune, arose to demand change and at times completely
disrupted the government. This breakdown of constitutional government,
accompanied by economic problems, led to the dictatorship of Caesar and
the establishment of the Roman Empire by Augustus in the second half of
the first century B.C.

Although Roman officials were popularly elected and campaigned for office, public address does not seem to have been a major factor at elections.
Campaigning took the form of personal visits by the candidate or his clients
to talk informally with others or of negotiations for support behind the public view, and in some periods bribery was common.

The popular assemblies met frequently in some periods, but the major
scene of regular debate in the Roman republic was the senate, which consisted of several hundred men who had been elected to some public office
in the past and who served for life unless removed by the censors, usually on
the ground they lacked property qualification, sometimes for moral or political reasons. The greatest period of the senate's authority came in the second century B.C., but it continued to debate public policy even under the
empire. The senate was a highly oligarchic body whose decisions, though
influenced by speeches, were also very much the result of family ties, financial interests, or political alliances and the prior decision of an inner group
of senators. The senate did not pass laws; that, and declaring war, was the
prerogative of the assemblies. Instead, it passed decrees, which were nominally only advice to the consuls or other officials, but which had the effect
of law in empowering them to take specific actions, including a "final decree," which was the equivalent of a declaration of martial law. The senate
played a major role in advising the consuls, generals, and governors about
foreign policy, and it received ambassadors from abroad. Before the first
century all speeches in the senate had to be in Latin, delivered through

interpreters if necessary,[3] and the translations of the speeches of Greek ambassadors, even if rather roughly done, provided Romans with rhetorical models of invention and arrangement. They saw there the workings of enthymemes and examples; of argument from probability; of topics of expediency, justice, and honor, and they began to imitate. It is surely no coincidence that Roman oratory began to achieve artistic form in the years when Romans first heard in their own city and partly in their own language highly skilled and persuasive Greek orators.

Epideictic oratory of the Greek sort was largely nonexistent in Rome. The only native epideictic form was the funeral eulogy (*laudatio funebris*) for members of noble families. The traditional form seems to have been little more than a list of the accomplishments and virtues of the deceased and the deceased's ancestors. Cicero (*On the Orator* 2.341) speaks scornfully of the literary qualities of these speeches, and what little has been preserved of them seems to confirm his judgment. Texts of speeches were apparently preserved among family records, where they could be used in composing the next such speech when needed, and they were sometimes inscribed on funeral monuments. Women had a more influential role in Roman society than in Greece, though they could not vote, hold office, or plead in law courts. Noblewomen were thus accorded funeral orations equally with men, and their personal virtues as set out in such speeches doubtless contributed to the concept of proper womanhood as understood in the culture. The *Laudatio Turiae* is a funerary inscription recording the virtues of a noblewoman named Turia and probably a version of what was said at her funeral. One funeral oration that perhaps included more rhetorical amplification than usual was Julius Caesar's speech for his aunt, mentioned by both Plutarch (*Caesar* 5) and Suetonius (*Julius* 6).

Cato the Elder

Although Cicero in *Brutus* cites examples of earlier Romans who achieved some fame as orators, the first of whom we can form a distinct impression is M. Porcius Cato, consul in 195 and censor in 184 B.C. We know Cato's speeches only from quotations of them by later writers, but these provide an understanding of his style, and in some cases it is possible to grasp the organization or argument. Though it is difficult to be exact because of the varying titles under which his speeches are cited, we seem to have bits of about eighty different speeches, the majority of them either *contiones* or speeches in the senate; there are, however, also a number of judicial

---

[3] Valerius Maximus (2.2.3) says Apollonius Molon was the first person to address the senate in Greek, probably in 81 B.C. Gellius (6.14.9) reports that C. Acilius translated for Carneades and the other ambassadors from Athens in 156–155 B.C.

speeches.[4] Cato early acquired a reputation as a patron and throughout his career was respected for his legal knowledge as well as for his oratorical ability. He was the quintessential old Roman, hard-headed, austere, and uncompromising on matters of morality or national interest, and his help was available to anyone who wanted to undertake prosecution of corruption, decadence, or vice. He himself repeatedly undertook prosecutions of anyone and for anything when he thought traditional values were being undermined. This was a time of great change, when Romans acquired wealth from exploitation of new provinces abroad, when the allurement of Greek culture captivated some of his contemporaries, and when traditional Roman morals and mores were thus being challenged.[5] Cato played his part in the extension of Roman rule into Greek-speaking countries, and he seems to have learned a good deal from Greeks (cf. Plutarch, *Cato* 2.4), but he was the most outspoken opponent of Hellenization and thought Romans could only be corrupted by it. "I shall tell in its proper place," he wrote his son Marcus, "what I found out about those Greeks, and I shall prove that it is a good thing to glance at their literature, not to study it thoroughly. Their race is quite worthless and unteachable, and I speak as a prophet in saying that when it gives us its literature it will ruin everything." (Pliny, *Natural History* 29.14).

The best-known of Cato's judicial speeches, *On His Own Expenses*, seems to be a reply to charges made against him that he was privately living in greater luxury than the law allowed, the hope being that he could be made to seem a hypocrite. This speech shows how the charge hurt his feelings and is noteworthy for its use of an emotional *praeteritio*, the figure by which a speaker itemizes the topics he will not discuss. Whether learned from Greeks or invented by Cato's own genius, it shows a control of dramatic technique requiring careful changes in the tone of voice and delivery, and producing stringent irony. In the portion quoted by Fronto (vol. 2, pp. 44–46, Haines), Cato describes himself as seated in his study planning his speech and dictating to his slave:

> I ordered to be brought out the book in which my speeech had been written on the matter of the legal wager I had made with M. Cornelius. The tablets were brought; the merits of my ancestors were read through; then the things I had done for the state are read. In the passage which immediately follows these there was written in the speech "I never lavished money, neither my own nor that of my associates, in canvassing for office." Alas, don't, don't write that, I said, they don't want to hear. Then he read "I never imposed commandants on the towns of your allies who

---

[4] For the texts and evidence, see Malcovati, *Oratorum Romanorum Fragmenta*, 12–97. The major source for Cato's life is the biography in Plutarch's *Lives*.

[5] See MacMullen, "Hellenizing the Romans."

ravaged their goods or their children." That too delete, they don't want to hear. Read on: "I never divided up the booty which had been captured from the enemy nor the proceeds from its sale among a few of my friends in order to keep it from those who had earned it." That too erase; they certainly do not want this to be said; there is no need of its recital. "I never gave free passage by the public post so that my friends might by their passes earn vast sums." Go on and delete that entirely. "I never distributed silver so that my servants and friends could drink my health, nor made them rich at the public cost." You must scrape that out of the tablets right down to the wood. See I beg you where the state stands, in that the deeds which I meritoriously performed for the state, and for which I used to receive thanks, now I do not dare mention, lest I incur ill will. Thus it has been brought about that it is possible to do harm with impunity, but not to do good with impunity.

Note that Cato has written copies of earlier speeches to which he turns for topics in composing a new speech, that he does not pretend that his defense is extemporaneous, and that he expects his audience to have some interest in the process of composition.

For centuries students have been told that Cato ended every speech in the senate with the words *censeo Carthaginem esse delendam*, "I think Carthage ought to be destroyed." He did not live quite long enough to see its fulfillment at the end of the third Punic War in 146 B.C. It cannot be shown that he actually used these words, though he may sometimes have said something like them.

The best-known of all Cato's speeches is that delivered in the senate in 167 B.C. on behalf of the Rhodians, who had sympathized but not actively aided Perseus of Macedon, just defeated by the Romans. The Rhodians had sent ambassadors to dissuade the Roman senate from taking punitive action against their city, but they were much cowed and did not speak very well when they appeared. Cato was the principal supporter of Rhodes on this occasion and included his speech in his historical work *Origines* (Livy 45.25.2). We know it from portions quoted by Aulus Gellius (6.3.1–50):

> I know that it is customary when circumstances are favorable and expansive and prospering for the spirits of most men to exult and for their pride and boldness to grow and enlarge. As a result, my great concern at present, since this matter has turned out so favorably, is that there be no mistake in deliberation which might check our good fortune and that this happiness may not turn out too unchecked. Adversity disciplines and teaches what needs to be done, prosperity is apt to turn men aside from right deliberation and understanding. Thus all the more earnestly I say and advise that this matter should be put off for some days until we return from our excessive joy to control of ourselves.

For my part, I do not think that the Rhodians wanted us to win the war as we won it, nor for King Perseus to be defeated. But the Rhodians were not the only ones who did not want us to win, for I believe many peoples and many nations had the same hope, and probably among them there were some who were not motivated by a desire for our disgrace, but were afraid that we would do whatever we wished if there was no one whom we feared and that they might be under our sole rule in servitude to us. It was for the sake of their own liberty, I think, that they adhered to this hope. Yet the Rhodians never publicly helped Perseus.

Consider how much more suspicious we are in private affairs among ourselves. For each and every one of us, if he thinks something is being done against his own interest strives with all his strength to prevent that adverse thing from happening; but the Rhodians endured what they saw happening.

. . . These great advantages on both sides, this great friendship, shall we suddenly abandon? Shall we be the first to do what we charge them with wanting to have done?

. . . He who speaks against them most strongly says, "They wished to become our enemies." Is there any one of you, I want to know, who, in a matter in which he himself is involved, thinks it right to be punished because of having *wished* to do wrong? No one, I think; for I would not in a matter related to me. . . . What more? Is there, I want to know, any law so severe which says "If anyone *wishes* to do such and such a thing, let the fine be a thousand sesterces provided that is less than half his estate; if anyone *wishes* to have more than five hundred acres, let the penalty be so much; if anyone *wishes* to have a greater number of sheep, let him be fined so much?" Yet we all wish to have more of all of these, and we go unpunished for it. . . . But if it is not right for honor to be given because someone says that he *wanted* to do right but did not do it, will it be prejudicial to the Rhodians because they did not do harm, but because they say that they wanted to do harm?

. . . They say that the Rhodians are insolent, charging what I would not at all want said of me and my children. Let them be insolent. What business of ours is it? Are you angry if someone is more insolent than we are?

Cato's motive in defending the Rhodians may have been the fear that their wealth would be plundered and confiscated by Romans, whom he regarded as already too given to luxury, but there is rather little of his usual moral indignation and character projection in the speech. Livy (45.25.2) noted its mildness. The essay of Gellius in which the excerpts given above are quoted is an interesting piece of rhetorical criticism. Gellius, writing in the second century after Christ, had a special interest in early Latin literature. He says that Cicero's secretary Tiro wrote a letter in which he criticized

Cato's rhetorical methods in this speech in a rather pedantic way: the opening was insolent, for Cato should have tried to win over the good will of his audience; the argument of the second excerpt is a confession of guilt, not an acceptable defense; the third excerpt is an invalid argument; the fourth, fifth, and sixth are invidious sophistries, built on deceptive examples. Gellius answers each objection. He shows that Cato was not addressing those whose good will he needed but was a senator speaking on public policy to others already much concerned with the issue. He tries to show that the arguments are more valid than Tiro recognized and sums up the effect of the speech in these words (6.3.52–53):

> It is to be noticed that throughout that speech of Cato all the arms and assistance of the rhetorical discipline are brought into play. But we do not see it done as we do in mock maneuvers or in battles simulated for entertainment. For, I repeat, the matter is not handled with excessive care and elegance and smoothness, but as in a contest where the outcome is in doubt, when the battle line has been scattered, and the fighting goes on in many places with varying success, so in this speech when that very well known arrogance of the Rhodians was stirred by the hatred and ill will of many, Cato employed every means at once of defense and offense, and one minute commends them as innocent, another charges that their possessions and riches should not be sought, another intercedes as though they had erred, another shows their friendship to the state, another appeals to mercy or to traditional Roman clemency or to the public interest. All of these things could perhaps be said in a more polished way or with greater rhythmical smoothness, but it does not seem possible for them to be said more strongly or vigorously.

The analogy between war and oratory seen in this passage is a commonplace in Latin;[6] indeed, the Latin word *ornatus*, "ornamentation," is derived from a verb that means "to prepare," used especially of preparing and polishing arms for battle. Gellius' statement that Cato employed the arms of the rhetorical discipline raises the question of Cato's familiarity with the teaching of Greek rhetoricians. Cicero says that all oratorical virtues are to be found in Cato's speeches (*Brutus* 65–69), including examples of tropes and figures of speech, though he felt also a roughness in Cato's composition, particularly because words, phrases, and sentences were not smoothly joined together, and he missed the rhythmical cadences of his own day. Although there was a tradition that Cato learned Greek only in old age (Cicero, *On Old Age* 26; Plutarch, *Cato* 2.4), he probably did so much earlier. He had spent many years in Greek-speaking provinces and employed a Greek grammarian named Chilo to tutor his son. In the same passage Plu-

---

[6] Contrast this with the analogy between oratory and athletics in Greek, as at the beginning of Isocrates' *Panegyricus*.

tarch says that Cato's writings were ornamented with Greek thoughts. It was part of his public persona to play down his indebtedness to Greeks.

In fact, Cato even wrote a survey of rhetorical theory, which probably utilized Greek sources. For use by his son he wrote and then published the first Roman encyclopedia, with sections on agriculture, medicine, rhetoric, and other subjects. Quintilian (3.1.19) calls him the first Roman rhetorician. We know very little about the contents of the discussion of rhetoric. Three quotations are perhaps taken from it: "An orator, son Marcus, is a good man skilled at speaking" (Seneca, *Controversiae* 1.pr.9); "seize the subject, the words will follow" (Julius Victor, p. 374 in Halm, *Rhetores Latini Minores*); and the term *vires causae*, "the strong points of a case" (p. 308, Halm).

According to Suetonius (*On Grammarians and Rhetoricians* 25), in 161 B.C. the praetor Pomponius consulted the senate on the subject of the presence of Greek philosophers and rhetoricians in Rome, and it was decided that he should have authority to expel them from the city. Two Epicurean philosophers had probably already been expelled in 173 (Athenaeus 12.547a). About 156 the heads of the three major philosophical schools in Athens—Carneades the Academic, Critolaus the Peripatetic, and Diogenes the Stoic—were sent to Rome on an embassy and attracted audiences to the philosophical lectures they gave there. Carneades in particular incensed the conservatives by lecturing one day in favor of justice and the next, in a manner typical of an Academic, against justice, "not out of serious philosophical belief, but in a kind of oratorical exercise of speaking *in utramque partem* (on both sides of an issue)."[7] Cato urged that he be sent packing (Plutarch, *Cato* 22), but no official action seems to have been taken. Nor were steps again taken against Greek rhetoricians or grammarians, who were teaching in Rome by the mid–second century. All such Greek teachers would necessarily have had Roman patrons, in whose homes they lived and taught.

Roman Orators of the Late Second and Early First Centuries B.C.

Cicero's *Brutus* is a history of Roman oratory, tracing its artistic development up to his own time. He singles out (section 82) S. Sulpicius Galba (consul in 144) as the first Roman to aim at ornamentation, to try to charm his audience, and to amplify his subject with pathos and commonplaces. C. Papirius Carbo (consul in 120) was the first Roman to practice oratorical exercises (*Brutus* 105), which he did even in his tent on military campaign (Quintilian 10.7.27). C. Scribonius Curio (praetor in 121) was famous for

---

[7] Lactantius, *Divine Institutes* 5.14.3–4; see also Cicero, *On the Orator* 2.155, and Aulus Gellius 6.14.8–10.

his speech defending Servius Fulvius on a charge of incest, amplified with commonplaces on love, torture, and rumor, which by Cicero's time seemed rather childish (*Brutus* 124).

The most important orators of the late second century were the two brothers Tiberius and Gaius Sempronius Gracchus, both of whom used the office of tribune and meetings of the popular assembly to try to secure economic and political reforms. With them begins the century of strife, reform, reaction, and war that brought the Roman republic to a close, certainly one of the awesome spectacles of history. We have no true fragments of speeches of Tiberius Gracchus, the older of the two. He was tribune in 133, and his major achievement was a bill to distribute public land among the urban proletariat. His mother, Cornelia, had seen to it that he was given a Greek education, and he had studied rhetoric with Diophanes of Mytilene (*Brutus* 104). His speeches were apparently more distinguished for their thought than their style.

Gaius Gracchus, who followed his brother's path as liberal reformer to the tribunate (in 123 and 122) and death by assassination, was perhaps the greater, and certainly the more impassioned, orator. His style of delivery included striding up and down and tearing his robe from his shoulder; his anger and voice would rise to fever pitch as he addressed the assembly. To maintain some control over himself, he is said to have stationed a servant near him with a pitch pipe to sound if he went beyond predetermined limits and thus to bring him back to a reasonable tone and order without interrupting his speech.[8] The most famous words of Gaius, spoken on the last day of his life, were, according to Cicero (*On the Orator* 3.214), so effective that even his enemies burst into tears: "Where can I flee in my misery? Where turn? To the capital? It reeks with the blood of my brother, To home? That I may see my mother wretchedly crying and prostrate?" This dilemma has antecedents in Greek poetry (e.g., Euripides, *Medea* 798–99) and oratory (e.g., Andocides, *On the Mysteries* 148).

Marcus Antonius, consul in 99 and grandfather of the triumvir Mark Antony, is praised by Cicero for his invention, arrangement, memory, and delivery (*Brutus* 139 and 141), in other words, for his ability in all the parts of rhetoric except style. His greatest strength was in establishing belief in a fact in the minds of the audience or in arousing or allaying suspicion (144). Consequently, Cicero thought him more effective in judicial than in deliberative oratory (165), and with Crassus he became the most popular advocate of his day (207). He was capable, if sincerely moved, of powerful emotional appeals, as in the peroration of his speech for Manlius Aquilius, on trial for extortion, when, so we are told (*On the Orator* 2.194–96), he ripped

---

[8] See Cicero, *On the Orator* 3.225, and Dio Cassius 25.85.2, where the servant has become a flute player, who provides a steady accompaniment.

the toga from the scarred body of the old soldier to exhibit his wounds and evoked the jury's sympathy by calling upon the name "of every god and man, citizen and ally." He had little knowledge of the law, and in Cicero's dialogue *On the Orator* (1.172 and 248), in which he is a character, he claims he never felt the need for it. He refused to publish his speeches, so that if taxed with having taken a different position in a previous speech he could flatly deny it (Cicero, *For Cluentius* 140). "On behalf of the life of those in danger," Valerius Maximus says (7.3.5), "he was prepared not only to use his eloquence, but to abuse his self-respect."

Cicero gives an account of Antonius' defense of Norbanus on a charge of treason in 95 B.C. (*On the Orator* 2.197–201). What we know about the speech shows how stasis theory and ethos could be applied by a patron in a Roman trial. Antonius admitted that the facts seemed to be against his client and that he himself had been criticized for taking on the case, especially since he had recently been censor. His justification was that Norbanus had been quaestor under him in Cilicia; Romans liked to think of a governor and quaestor as tied by permanent loyalty. Antonius began with that personal tie and made no concealment of his fears and doubts of success, but once he had acquired the sympathy of the jury for himself, if not for his client, he went on to his principal argument that the mob scene, in which Norbanus had admittedly acted with some violence, could not be blamed on Norbanus and was in fact justified in the circumstances. This he supported by historical examples of civil progress at the expense of disturbances between the nobles and the people. The legal question of what constituted treason (*maiestas*) Antonius glossed over as briefly as possible, and he sought to shift responsibility for the incident (Hermagoras' *metastasis*) to Caepio on the ground that the public disturbances in which Norbanus took part had been set off by the prosecution of Caepio, who was blamed for a disastrous Roman defeat. This gave Antonius an opportunity to expatiate on the sins of Caepio. The tactic diverted anger from Norbanus and was also effective with the jury, all from the equestrian class, who as a group hated Caepio for an earlier proposal to take control of the juries away from them. The crimes of Caepio also made a good contrast with the modesty of Antonius himself and his loyal friendship for Norbanus, to which the orator reverted at the end of the speech. It was, all in all, very successful, as even Norbanus' accuser had to admit, and it secured Norbanus' acquittal.

Like Cato, Antonius wrote a handbook on rhetoric. Cicero (*Brutus* 163) calls it "meager enough" and makes Antonius claim (*On the Orator* 1.94, 208) that it was published against his will and dealt not with the art of rhetoric as taught in Greek schools but with what he himself had learned in practice. A quotation from it by Quintilian (3.6.44) indicates that it discussed stasis theory, but without technical vocabulary: "The matters are few in number from which all speeches are born: a thing done or not done, a legal right or legal injury, a good thing or a bad one." That is to say, it can be argued in defense of a client that an act was not committed, or that it was done legally, or if it were done and in violation of law, that it was morally justified or necessary in some way. This indeed seems to have been what Antonius argued on behalf of Norbanus. In *On the Orator* (1.94) Cicero makes Antonius quote a famous statement from his "little book," in which he claims that he had known some speakers who were *diserti* ("accomplished, skilled") but none "yet" who was *eloquens*. He then explains this to mean that he had not found anyone who could "marvelously and magnificently amplify and ornament whatever he wished and who held within his own mind and memory every source of all those things which pertain to speaking." The discussion contributes to Cicero's view of the ideal orator as set out in the dialogue and not too subtly suggests his own subsequent achievements.

L. Licinius Crassus, consul in 95, is Cicero's chief spokesman in *On the Orator* for an orator with a wide and deep knowledge of all subjects. Although when speaking in court he pretended to look down on Greek learning (2.4), he was thoroughly familiar with it, had studied Greek rhetoric (1.137–47), and had given a good deal of time to practice exercises (1.154–57). Cicero (*Brutus* 165) attributes two qualities to Crassus that Antonius lacked, a knowledge of the law and an accurate and elegant but unaffected style. He aimed at brevity, and his delivery was restrained (*Brutus* 158). His published speeches, to Cicero's regret (*On the Orator* 2.8), were few, but some quotations from his flashes of wit were famous (2.240–42).

The most interesting of Crassus' speeches was that delivered in the centumviral court about 93 B.C. in the celebrated *causa Curiana*, the case of Manius Curius. An unnamed Roman had drawn a will leaving his estate in the first place to an as yet unborn child, or, if that child should die before coming of age, to Manius Curius, whose connection with the family is unknown. The testator then died almost immediately. No child was born, and after ten months Curius claimed the estate. M. Coponius, a relative of some sort, objected and engaged the services of Mucius Scaevola, distinguished for his knowledge of the law. Curius obtained Crassus as his patron. Because of the fame of the advocates, the tribunal was surrounded by an expectant crowd (*On the Orator* 1.180), and the proceedings took on something of the appearance of a test case. Scaevola naturally took the line that the literal requirements of the will had not been fulfilled: no orphan being born, there could be no heir under the will. This he supported with extensive remarks on testamentary law and ancient formulas, with warnings about the dangers of trying to interpret the intent of a testator and subverting straightforward statements by clever interpretations. His speech was learned, succinct, and polished (*Brutus* 195–97). Crassus began his reply with a flash of his famous wit, saying that Scaevola reminded him of a boy who saw a thole pin and immediately wanted to build a whole boat; he had figured out that people were born before they died, but since here nobody was born, nobody died, and he thought by that tiny point to capture the court (*On the Orator* 1.243; *Brutus* 197). Crassus' argument naturally hinged on the intent of the testator, and he had much to say *pro aequo et bono*, "for what was equitable and good." He overwhelmed the opposition with an exhaustive series of arguments and examples (*Brutus* 144–45). At the same time, he insisted that he was not attacking the system of civil law, but that Scaevola did not understand it. In his refutation of his opponent, he proceeded to an ironic reductio ad absurdum and ad hominem argument, from which comes the one literal quotation of the speech that we have: "For, Scaevola, if no will is rightly made unless you write it, all of us citizens will come to you tablets in hand; you alone will write everybody's will. What will happen then? When will you have time for public business? Or your legal practice? Or your own affairs? When will you even find time to do nothing? A man does not seem to me to be free who does not sometimes do nothing!" (*On the Orator* 2.24). Crassus won the case.

The question of the word versus the intent of a testator, or for that matter of a law, had surely come to the attention of a Roman court before, but of this case it was remarked that the most learned in law of the orators had met and triumphed over the most eloquent of those learned in the law (*Brutus* 145). Roman law was heavily dependent on precedent and thus what an orator successfully argued in a particular case could influence the development of the law.

Latin Rhetoricians

In 92 B.C. Crassus was censor with Domitius Ahenobarbus and the two of them, in rare agreement, issued an edict as follows (Suetonius, *On Grammarians and Rhetoricians* 25.2; Aulus Gellius 15.11.2):

> It has been reported to us that there are men who have instituted a new kind of study, that youths are going to school to them, that they have taken for themselves the name Latin rhetoricians, and that young men are wasting whole days there. Our ancestors arranged what they wished their children to learn and to what schools they wished them to go. These new ways, which are a departure from custom and from the principles of our ancestors, neither please nor seem right. Wherefore both to them who hold these schools and to them who are accustomed to go there, it seems necessary to show our opinion: *We do not approve.*

Censorial disapproval carried a threat to the civil status of anyone who infringed the decree. Suetonius goes on to say that rhetoric gradually became more acceptable, citing evidence that Cicero and others declaimed in

Latin. From the context it seems likely that he thought objections were against schools that taught rhetorical exercises in Latin. He mentions analysis of rhetorical texts and exercises in narration, translation, praise and blame, and the evaluation of customs and myths. Cicero (*Brutus* 309–10) says that in his youth he let no day pass without oratorical exercises: "I planned and delivered declamations, as they are now called, often with Marcus Piso and Quintus Pompeius or with someone else every day, doing it much in Latin but more often in Greek, both because the Greek language, with its abundance of stylistic ornaments, gave me the habit of speaking similarly in Latin, and because unless I spoke Greek I could not be corrected or taught by Greeks, who were the best teachers." Antonius refers contemptuously to school exercises in Cicero's *On the Orator* (2.100) and indicates that what are later called *controversiae* were already common: "A law forbids a foreigner to ascend the wall; he ascends; he drives off the enemy; he is accused. There is nothing difficult in studying such a case. They rightly therefore give no directions for mastering it. This is more or less the form of cases in a school." Although Carbo and Crassus had practiced exercises, they had done so privately, not in schools, and perhaps in Greek rather than in Latin. The first person to conduct a school of declamation in Latin, and presumably one of the teachers to whom the censors of 92 objected, was L. Plotius Gallus. Suetonius (26) quotes a letter written by Cicero in 92, when he was fourteen years old, saying that he wanted to join the crowds of young men who studied with Plotius Gallus, but was restrained by the authority of very learned men (he must mean Crassus and his friends), who thought that ability could better be nurtured by Greek exercises.

The dramatic date of *On the Orator* is 91 B.C., and Cicero makes Crassus discuss his edict of the previous year (3.93–94). His motive, he claims, was not (what had been alleged) that he did not want the abilities of the young to be sharpened; rather, he was afraid their abilities would be blunted and their *impudentia*, "shameless self-confidence," be confirmed. "For among the Greeks, of whatever sort, I saw in addition to this exercise of the tongue some kind of learning and knowledge worthy of mankind, but these new teachers, I knew, could teach their students nothing but to be bold." Crassus' rejection of the notion that he opposed sharpening the wits of the young is probably intended to answer the charge that political motivations on the part of conservative aristocrats were the real basis of the censorial edict. Plotius Gallus was a friend and supporter of the popular leader Marius, and he might be viewed as runing a school for future demagogues. *Impudentia* certainly has a political implication, and the demand that rhetoric be studied in Greek implies the need for extensive prior study of that language and of its literature and philosophy, which could take years and be costly— beyond the means of many Romans. Crassus probably wanted to restrict access to public life to an elite group, not necessarily conservative but likely to be so. Like those who argued for Greek and Latin rather than an immediately practical education in nineteenth century American universities, he cast his arguments in terms of real understanding versus superficiality, and he reinforced this with his obligation as censor to defend Roman tradition.

Crassus died in 91 B.C., Antonius in 87. Cicero did not speak in public until the late 80s and was not an acknowledged orator of the first rank until his victory over Verres in 70. In the intervening years the greatest Roman orator was Q. Hortensius Hortalus. To the ambitious young Cicero, Hortensius was the rival to be overcome, all the more because of a certain affinity of personality between them (*Brutus* 317). We know Hortensius' oratory almost solely from Cicero's descriptions of it and the references to him in speeches in which they spoke on opposite sides, or occasionally on the same side. Cicero calls Hortensius' style Asianist (*Brutus* 325) and says that the manner seemed appropriate in a young man, but not later in life.

Cicero's *On Invention*

Cicero was born at Arpinum, about seventy-five miles east-southeast of Rome, on January 3, 106 B.C. Though his paternal ancestors had not held public office, and when he came to stand for office himself he was thus what the Romans called a *novus homo*, "new man," his family had important connections by marriage. When Cicero was between twelve and fifteen, he, his brother Quintus, and some other members of his family went to live in Rome with no less a person than the orator Crassus. "We learned," Cicero wrote later in *On the Orator* (2.2), "what Crassus approved and were taught by the teachers he employed. In as much as we were at his home we observed often what was clear even to us boys, that he spoke Greek as though it were his native language, and we saw him propound topics for discussion to our teachers and treat other topics himself in his conversations so well that nothing seemed new or unheard of to him." Cicero goes on to say that he met at this time the other great orator of the age, Antonius, and had many talks with him. About 92, the Athenian rhetorician Menedemus visited Antonius (*On the Orator* 1.85); Cicero is likely to have heard him lecture and declaim. He also frequented the home of Aelius Stilo, who was a Stoic philosopher and taught grammar, maybe rhetoric as well (*Brutus* 206–7). Crassus died suddenly in 91, and the Social War of 91–88 partly disrupted conditions in Rome, but Cicero continued his rhetorical studies. In 89 he turned to study of the law and attended the legal consultations of Q. Mucius Scaevola; in 88 the Academic philosopher Philo arrived from Athens, and Cicero claims that he gave himself up wholly to philosophy (*Brutus* 306).

Sometime between 92 and 88 Cicero began an ambitious Latin rhetorical treatise but never completed more than the first two books dealing with

117

invention. He later (*On the Orator* 1.5) refers to the work as "inchoate and crude," based on the notebooks of his boyhood or adolescence, which in Roman terms means around the age of fifteen or sixteen. There is nothing in *On Invention* that Cicero could not have known around 90 B.C., and no historical reference to any event later than the nineties. It is the work of a teenager, though a precocious teenager in a period in which young men grew up rapidly and even sometimes pleaded cases in court while still in their teens.[9] When, later in his life, Cicero wrote accounts of Greek philosophy in Latin, he often stressed his desire to provide Romans with an access to Greek learning. Possibly this was his motive in writing *On Invention*, though he does not say so. The work could be viewed as an attempt to meet the objections of Crassus and others to the teaching of rhetoric in Latin, which they criticized as superficial and which was apparently largely practice in declamation, by providing a theoretical account of the subject. There were, of course, the precedents of Cato and Antonius, both of whom had written accounts of rhetoric without meeting the need for a comprehensive treatment of the subject, and a few years later an unknown author was to write *Rhetoric for Herennius*. Cicero does not identify an audience for *On Invention*. He may have written primarily to improve his own understanding of the subject and did not expect the work to be read by others than friends and members of his family. The author of *Rhetoric for Herennius*, writing about ten years later, clearly did not know of Cicero's treatment of invention.[10] After Cicero's death it became very well known indeed. Quintilian refers to it repeatedly; Victorinus and Grillius wrote commentaries on it in late antiquity; it was the commonest Latin rhetorical textbook of the Middle Ages—many manuscripts and many commentaries still survive—and it continued to be studied in the Renaissance. In contrast, Cicero's mature works on rhetoric—*On the Orator*, *Brutus*, and *Orator*—were little known after the classical period until rediscovered by Italian humanists in the fifteenth century. The appeal of *On Invention*, or Cicero's *Rhetorici Libri* as it was more often called, was surely that it was, unlike his major rhetorical works, a genuine textbook that offered a full, systematic, easily comprehended account of its subject and at the same time carried the authority of Cicero's name. Even the pretentious self-assurance of its youthful author, who seems to think he knows all there is to know not only about rhetoric but about philosophy, literature, history, and law, was a recommendation to later teachers and students.[11]

Book 1 begins with a celebrated preface, frequently quoted from medi-

[9] For further evidence of the date of *On Invention*, see my *Art of Rhetoric in the Roman World*, 106–10.

[10] At least he claims (1.16) to have been the first to "think out" the use of *insinuatio*, which Cicero discussed in a very similar way in *On Invention* 1.23.

[11] The only available English translation is that of Hubbell in the Loeb Classical Library.

eval to modern times, in which with all the self-assurance of his sixteen or seventeen years Cicero reflects on the relationship between wisdom and eloquence, or philosophy and rhetoric. The position he takes anticipates his efforts in *On the Orator* to argue for a new synthesis of philosophy and rhetoric:

> Often and long have I contemplated in my mind whether abundant resources for speaking and great zeal for eloquence have brought more good or evil to human beings and communities. For when I consider the troubles of our republic and compile a list in my mind of the disasters that befell the greatest states of the past, I see that no little part of their misfortunes was brought about by those who were most skilled in speaking; when, however, I undertake to recover from written records a knowledge of events lost from our memory because of their antiquity, I recognize that many cities were founded, numerous wars extinguished, the strongest alliances, the most sacred friendships were brought about more easily by eloquence than by the reasoning power of the mind. And after long reflection, reason herself brings me to this opinion above all: I hold the belief that wisdom without eloquence has been of little benefit to states, but eloquence without wisdom has for the most part been a great hindrance and never an advantage. (*On Invention* 1.1)

The preface continues for some pages with a disquisition on the origin of culture, the original brutish condition of mankind, the appearance at some time in the remote past of a great man with the wisdom to see how order and prosperity could be brought to human life, and the eloquence such a person must necessarily have had to persuade others to follow him.

For all his claims to original research and reflection, Cicero is amplifying a thesis that was a common topic of rhetorical teaching in his youth. Some of what he says goes back to celebrations of eloquence by Greek sophists and Isocrates; he is, however, probably directly indebted to some unknown recent work or to lectures by one or more of his teachers of rhetoric, or to the views of his mentor Crassus. As we have seen, Cicero did not study with a Latin rhetorician, only with Greeks. Although not expressly stated, his justification for claims of originality in *On Invention* is that he is writing a discussion of rhetoric in Latin. The immediate source of the rhetorical theory that makes up the bulk of *On Invention* may also be largely derived from some one of his Greek teachers, though in the preface to book 2 (2.4) he claims to have collected "all" the works on rhetoric and to have excerpted the best precepts. When he cites the views of Gorgias and Aristotle, as he does in section 7 of the first book, we should not necessarily conclude that he has actually read their works—indeed, Aristotle's *On Rhetoric* was almost certainly not available in Rome at this time; he is simply setting out what he has been taught or found in some secondary source. There are, he says, different "families" derived ultimately from two sources, Aristotle and Isocrates. He does not claim to have read either; he has heard of a treatise on rhetoric by Isocrates but has not seen it; what he knows of the Isocratean tradition are "precepts" of Isocrates' students. The two traditions—the more philosophical, Aristotelian, and the more purely rhetorical, Isocratean—were then fused, he says, by later teachers who took whatever they thought was best from both. "Their works," he says, referring to these later teachers, "and those of earlier writers, in so far as opportunity offered, we have before us, and we have added some things of our own to the common tradition."(2.8). He perhaps did consult Hermagoras' rhetorical treatise; a major part of *On Invention* is devoted to discussing stasis theory, and Hermagoras is named four times. In 1.16 he says that Hermagoras is regarded as the inventor of stasis of transference (thus not of stasis theory as a whole). "After he invented it, however, many have objected to it; we think they were not so much misled by ignorance (for the matter is clear) as blocked by envy and a desire to disparage (a rival)." But Cicero, or more likely his teacher, did not hesitate to disagree with Hermagoras. The first reference to him (1.8) objects to his division of the subject matter of rhetoric into theses and hypotheses, and in 1.97 he criticizes Hermagoras' identification of the digression as a formal part of a speech.

In 1.9 Cicero says that "according to most authorities the parts of rhetoric are invention, arrangement, style, memory, and delivery." The five parts, and in this order, were therefore already canonical, even though this is the earliest context in which they are so listed. At the end of the second book (2.178) he notes that he has completed discussion of the first part (i.e., invention) and will discuss the others in the remaining books, but these were never written.

The discussion of invention, after the philosophical preface, consists of a section on definitions (1.6–9)—rhetoric is a part of politics; the art and faculty of the orator is concerned with the materials of epideictic, deliberative, and judicial speeches; there are five parts of rhetoric—followed by a discussion of the four *constitutiones* or basic issues of a speech (1.10–19): questions of fact, definition, quality, and jurisdiction. *Constitutio*, which is also found in *Rhetoric for Herennius*, was the original Latin translation of Greek *stasis*, but later writers usually adopt the more literal translation *status*. The rest of book 1 (20–109) is taken up with discussion of the parts of a judicial oration—*exordium, narratio, partitio, confirmatio, refutatio, digressio* (not, however, accepted as necessary), and *peroratio*. The discussion of each part takes the form of a list of topics (*loci*) that can be used, sometimes with examples from literature. In discussing the exordium Cicero spells out for the first time (1.23–25) the technique of *insinuatio*, the "subtle approach" to be adopted when a case is perceived to be difficult or an audience hostile. The discussion of the *confirmatio* includes an account of argumentation, divided into induction (1.51–56) and deduction (57–77). In the section on deduction (*ratiocinatio*) we meet for the first time the theory of the five-part argument. Cicero claims (1.61) that this is a teaching of the followers of Aristotle and Theophrastus; it is in fact a kind of amplification of the Aristotelian syllogism and enthymeme in which a proposition (part 1) is supported by a variety of reasons (part 2), then a second proposition (what would be the minor premise in a syllogism) is stated (part 3), and that is followed by a variety of reasons for believing it (part 4). The fifth part then states the conclusion. Such an argument in Greek is sometimes called an *epicheirēma*, literally "a handful."[12]

The second book of *On Invention*, after a preface on the eclectic sources Cicero claims to have followed and the history of the discipline, is divided into three parts, devoted to the three kinds of oratory: judicial is given by far the longest discussion (2.14–154) and is subdivided into accounts of the arguments to be used in each kind of stasis and discussion of cases involving interpretation of written evidence. A shorter discussion of arguments in deliberative speeches follows (2.155–76). The last part of the work (2.176–78) is apparently intended to dispose of epideictic oratory. The most striking omission throughout, especially considering that Cicero claims to draw in part on an Aristotelian tradition, is that there is no discussion of ethos and pathos as means of persuasion, and little is done—nothing in the case of epideictic—to adapt rhetoric to specifically Roman needs.

The *Rhetoric for Herennius*

Rhetoric for Herennius,[13] the earliest surviving treatise to discuss all five parts of rhetoric, was studied through the Middle Ages as a work by Cicero, known as the *Rhetorica Secunda*. Renaissance Latinists realized that it was not by Cicero, and the claims of Cornificius were put forward on the basis of some reference to him in Quintilian's discussion of figures. The author may or may not have been named Cornificius, but even if he was, we know nothing more about him except that he was clearly an upper-class Roman, writing an account of rhetoric from his notes, and addressing one of his peers. He speaks of "our teacher" (1.18), of his busy private affairs and interest in philosophy (1.1), and of his hopes of studying other subjects (3.3, 3.28, 4.17). Maybe he was thinking of putting together an encyclopedia as Cato had done or as Celsus was to do. He claims to write at Herennius'

---

[12] See *Rhetoric for Herennius* 2.2; on different meanings given by different authors to the terms "enthymeme" and "epicheireme," see Quintilian 5.10.1–7 and the discussion of Hermogenes' *On Invention* in chapter 10 below.

[13] The standard English version is that of Caplan in the Loeb Classical Library, with valuable introduction and notes. Since publication of my *Art of Rhetoric in the Roman World*, two new editions of the treatise have appeared, one edited by Calboli and the other by Achard.

request, and in so doing he is the first of a series of authors, including Cicero, Seneca the Elder, Quintilian, and Tacitus, who fulfill, or pretend to fulfill, the urgent requests of their friends, relations, or publishers, but in this case he may have been providing an overview of rhetorical theory to a friend who had not had the opportunity to study Greek rhetoric. We cannot identify the addressee, C. Herennius, with much greater certainty than the author. There was a tribune of that name who opposed Sulla in 80 B.C., a C. Herennius was convicted of extortion in the early 70s, and a general of that name fought for Sertorius and was killed in Spain in 75. Possibly they were all the same person. On the basis of political interests shown in the treatise, the date of composition is probably between 85 and 80 B.C.; the latest historical references are to the death of Sulpicius (88 B.C.) and Marius' seventh consulship (86 B.C.). *Rhetoric for Herennius* has a more Roman quality than Cicero's *On Invention*. As as been recently observed, "the Auctor endeavors to teach his reader the technique of appealing to the social code of the ruling elite of Rome, for it is the knowledge of the maxims of that class and the rhythm of its discourse that will empower the reader politically."[14]

The first two and a half books of *Rhetoric for Herennius* cover the same ground as Cicero's *On Invention*, sometimes showing close verbal similarities, but they differ somewhat in organization and detail. There follows a brief discussion of arrangement (3.16–18), then an account of delivery (3.19–27), then memory (3.28–40). In 3.1 the author postpones discussion of style to the fourth book, which is almost a separate monograph on the subject. In 1.3 he gives the parts of rhetoric in the canonical order, with memory before delivery, but in book 3 reverses the order of treatment. The only explanation offered (3.19) is that delivery is very important and that no one has written "carefully" on the subject before.[15] Probably we should understand this to mean that no one had written carefully on it in Latin. The author's sources are similar to Cicero's, and verbal similarities between the two works may be explained by their using the same sources or having studied with the same Greek teacher, though at different times. The author of *Rhetoric for Herennius* (1.18) says that his teacher thought two of Hermagoras' categories of stasis could be combined into one, whereas Cicero does not note this. The teacher may have changed his views over time, as Quintilian did about stasis theory.

[14] Sinclair, "Sociology of Rhetoric," ad fin. Sinclair gives special emphasis to the author's treatment of *sententiae* as revealing his belief in what is appropriate for an upper-class Roman to say and how he should say it.

[15] Quintilian (11.3.143) knew of a work on gesture by Plotius Gallus, the "Latin rhetorician," which contained remarks on arranging the toga. It may not have treated use of the voice or have been "carefully" written, e.g., not have been based on what the author regarded as good Greek theory.

The author's discussions of delivery, memory, and style are of the greatest interest, since we have no earlier sources on these three parts of rhetoric as they had developed during the Hellenistic period. Delivery is divided into control of the voice and motion of the body, or gesture. Voice is treated in terms of magnitude or volume, stability or rhythm, and flexibility or tone, adaptations of Aristotle's suggestions in *On Rhetoric* 3.1. Tone consists of three styles of speaking: *sermo*, "conversational tone"; *contentio*, "argumentative debate"; and *amplificatio*, the "grand manner of harangue." The three categories correspond to the three kinds of style—plain, middle, and grand—which are discussed by the author in the fourth book. Of movement of the body the author says it must make what is said more probable. Facial expression is apparently the most important, and here a great deal of variety of sentiment is to be sought. Ordinarily the speaker should stand in one place, hold his body straight, and use only his right hand to gesture, but in *sermo* it is possible to incline the shoulders forward as though to bring the face closer to the hearer, in debate to walk up and down and even stamp the foot, and in pathetic amplification to strike the brow or, what was apparently terribly exciting to a Roman audience (see Quintilian 11.3.123), to slap the thigh. In *Brutus* Cicero mentions the delivery of some orators: for example, the lively manner of Antonius (141), whose hands, shoulders, side, foot, stance, and pacing all suited the words and thoughts. Asianist orators are said to have had a marked singsong tone (*Orator* 57). Theophrastus' *On Delivery*, from which some of the teachings in *Rhetoric for Herennius* may ultimately derive, had apparently included discussion of acting, and professional actors or teachers of singing certainly influenced rhetorical teachings about delivery. The author recommends consulting them (3.20).

Memory systems had clearly developed during the Hellenistic period. The author of *Rhetoric for Herennius* mentions Greek writings on the subject (3.38), but his own account is the earliest that survives. As in the case of other parts of rhetoric, including stasis theory, memory as described in the treatise was taught in Greek schools as a discipline that, once learned, could function as a structure or tool to be utilized as needed in actual speaking. The author recommends (3.39) verbatim memorization of what a student has written as an exercise to strengthen the more important memorization of subject matter. His main interest, however, is in the artificial memory system that is built on the use of *loci*, "backgrounds," and *imagines*, "images." A *locus* is a real place with which the student is familiar. In modern life a street or a campus is often a good background, though the author warns against choosing one with too much traffic that might confuse the mind. The background should be mentally divided into separate scenes, about thirty feet apart, each somewhat different from the other; a row of shops would do, but not the intercolumnar space along a perfectly regular portico. It is, however, important that the background form a continuous series in the mind, since this is what provides the linkage and insures memory of the material in the right sequence. Every fifth scene can be identified by imagining in it something involving a number, for example a golden hand with five fingers for number five.

This series of backgrounds, once thoroughly learned, can be used again and again just as a wax tablet, we would say a blackboard, can be erased and reused. When something is to be memorized, its subject matter is divided up into scenes and each salient point represented by a physical object. The author gives (3.33–34) as a specific example a scene that a speaker might want to remember while prosecuting someone on a charge of poisoning motivated by a desire for an inheritance. Against one of his familiar backgrounds the speaker imagines the testator in bed, the defendant at his side, a cup in his hand, the will in the other, and a purse hanging from his finger. This scene can come to the speaker's mind at the point in his speech where he is to deliver a refutation and should be put against the background sequence that he would have reached in his mind at that point.

It is possible, but more difficult, to use the system to memorize words. Here the images should not be the meaning of the words so much as their sounds. The former has the danger of suggesting synonyms, but the latter gets the tongue started. Thus, for an English speaker, the opening words of Virgil's *Aeneid*—*Arma virumque cano*, "Arms and the man I sing"—should not be memorized by envisioning a pile of weapons and a man singing, but perhaps as an arm cut off at the shoulder, lying on a weir, out of which projects a cannon. A speaker or an actor can use the verbal system occasionally to remember a particular phrase or sentence, especially one he has trouble getting right, or the text of a crucial law. The whole system was doubtless used much more in schools or in public address by a young man making one of his first appearances than by practiced orators. For the latter, thorough knowledge of the subject, careful observation of the effect on the judges, and self-confidence were more important than rote memory. Many great orators did not plan ahead the words they would use throughout a speech, though they did plan their opening words, the arrangement of the material, and arguments to be used, and they may have used a memory system to keep to the order of what they had planned. In the schools, speeches were usually written out, memorized, and delivered; in public life a published speech was usually not the text an orator had delivered from memory but one he wrote out after delivery, often with embellishments and improvements on what he had actually said. Cicero's secretary Tiro developed a system of shorthand ("Tironian Notes"), and in later antiquity speeches were sometimes taken down in shorthand by scribes, then edited and published.

The fourth book of *Rhetoric for Herennius*, making up nearly half the work, shows how rhetoricians' interest in style had grown into a highly developed system since the fourth century. It begins (1.1–10) with an extended preface, in which the author argues against those who illustrate features of style with quotations from earlier writers or speakers rather than create their own. An example, he thinks, should not be borrowed testimony, but proof of the skill of the author of the discussion. The whole passage is a good example of arguing a "thesis," as practiced in some schools, first seeking to refute the opposing view, then offering evidence for the proposition of the speaker. This thesis is peculiar to the author, who is perhaps using it to assert his originality. Most writers on rhetoric, from Aristotle to modern times, have quoted examples of style, only occasionally coining their own, and have not seen any problem in the practice. The significance of the author's position in the history of rhetoric is that he clearly does not believe that excellence in style is best cultivated by imitation of great speakers and writers of the past. That view was gaining ground in his time, and by the second half of the first century, in Cicero's *Brutus* and *Orator*, in the rhetorical works of Dionysius of Halicarnassus, and ever afterward, imitation is a fundamental doctrine of rhetoric. The author's practice is not quite so rigid as his theory: some of his examples seem to be unacknowledged paraphrases of what could be found in earlier Latin examples or Latin versions of Greek examples, and he does not object to quoting examples of faults in style from famous writers (e.g., 4.18).

The author divides the subject of style into two headings (4.10 ad fin.): *genera*, the three kinds of style, and *res*, the materials or qualities of style. He often uses *res* ("things") where a Greek or later Roman author would use a more technical term. The discussion, with examples, of the three kinds of style is the earliest surviving account of the subject, but it is certainly not original and may go back to Theophrastus, as noted in an earlier chapter. The author says that style "always" takes one of the three forms, but his contemporaries did not always agree (e.g., Demetrius and Philodemus, as noted in chapter 5). The *genera* consist of three "figures": *gravis*, or "grand," based on smooth and elaborate composition with imposing words; *mediocris*, or "middle," based on more ordinary though not vulgar language; and *adtenuata*, or "plain," which uses everyday language but possesses purity of Latin diction.

Res are also three in number (4.17): *elegantia*, elegance or taste; *compositio*, composition; and *dignitas*, dignity. These are apparently an echo of Theophrastus' four virtues of style as developed by unknown rhetoricians of the Hellenistic period: "elegance" includes Theophrastus' purity and clarity; the three qualities together make the style *adcommodata*, or "appropriate." "Composition" is only briefly discussed: the author only cites (4.18) a list of faults to avoid: frequent hiatus, excessive alliteration or repetition of the same word or homoeoteleuton, and hyperbaton. The composition of periods, which Aristotle had treated, is discussed later (4.16–27) among figures, and rhythm is mentioned only once in passing (4.44).

The discussion of *dignitas* takes up most of the book (4.19–68). The choice of the term "dignity" to describe ornamentation is unique and one of the ways the author seems to accommodate Greek rhetorical teaching to Roman traditions, but, like Cicero, he fails to discuss ethos as an aspect of rhetoric. Since as noted at the beginning of this chapter, ethos was a marked feature of Roman oratory, this omission probably means that ethos was not directly discussed in the author's Greek sources. It reemerges in rhetorical theory only after the publication of Aristotle's *On Rhetoric* later in the century. *Dignitas* as described here is a list of sixty-four tropes and figures, with definitions and examples, showing the results of the study of the subject by grammarians and rhetoricians in the centuries since Aristotle and Theophrastus. The word *figura* as a translation of Greek *schēma* had not yet come into use in Latin, and the author's term is *exornatio*, but figures are, as in Demetrius' *On Style*, divided into ornamentations "of words" and "of thoughts" (4.18 and 46). A figure of words, or figure of speech, consists in the polish of the diction. The first example given is *repetitio*, or anaphora, when the same word is used at the beginning of successive phrases. Among the figures of words are ten (4.42–45)—including metaphor (*translatio*) and, for the first time, metonymy (*denominatio*)—that are set apart and correspond to "tropes," though no special term is used of them. Figures of thought derive their *dignitas* from what they say rather than how they say it. The discussion begins (4.47) with *distributio*; for example, "The duty of an accuser is to bring charges; of the defense to explain and refute them; of a witness to say what he knows or hears, ..." The author replaces the Greek names for figures with Latin translations; later Latin rhetoricians often transliterate the Greek or use somewhat different Latin terms.[16] The author makes an effort to identify when a particular figure is useful and what its effect is, and he warns against overindulgence in figures (e.g., 4.32), but he cannot be said to have a general theory of the psychology of figures.

Taken together, *On Invention* and *Rhetoric for Herennius* show the contents of Greek rhetorical teaching as it existed in the early first century B.C.

---

[16] *Rhetoric for Herennius* is in many ways the best brief introduction to rhetoric in Latin, but in using it for rhetorical analysis, the student should be aware that its terminology is in many respects unique. The author supplied descriptive words that his contemporaries might understand and did not create a technical rhetorical vocabulary for Latin. In general, it is probably better for modern scholars to use the Greek names for figures, though even in Greek the terminology was not entirely consistent. But since *Rhetoric for Herennius* contained a discussion of figures well known in the Middle Ages, its terminology will sometimes recur in medieval texts. For the names and definitions of Greek and Latin figures and for other technical rhetorical terms, consult Lausberg's *Handbuch der literarischen Rhetorik*.

and of the attempts to translate this into Latin. Both authors express an interest in philosophy, and Cicero in his prefaces anticipates his later interest in the relationship between philosophy and rhetoric, but both works are practical manuals, closer in spirit to *Rhetoric for Alexander* than to Aristotle's *On Rhetoric*. Neither gives much attention to logical proof and neither discusses ethos and pathos as means of persuasion. Although the anonymous author, more than Cicero, reveals the values of the ruling Roman elite, neither do much to adapt Greek rhetorical theory to the special conditions of Roman legal procedure. Without directly acknowledging it, they seem to address primarily the conventions of judicial declamation as it was practiced in schools of rhetoric. For that they provide a theory, especially stasis theory, that was apparently not previously set out in Latin, and thus they may be said to attempt to answer some of the objections of Crassus and others to the superficiality of the teachings of the Latin rhetoricians of the time.

Cicero

Cicero's political challenge throughout his career, and thus the focus of much of his rhetoric, was how to preserve the Roman republic and the society in which he grew up from revolutionary threats fostered by the ambitions of demagogues, administrative corruption, foreign and civil war, and economic chaos. He was a political moderate, ambitious for personal honor and influence within the traditions of the Roman republic, but well aware of the many economic, social, and administrative problems of his time. There were no organized political parties in Rome; as in Athens, there was instead a fluid pattern of personal relationships among the leaders, influenced by class, ideology, and wealth. Cicero became the leading spokesman for the *optimates*, the conservatives who claimed to uphold what was "best" for the state,[1] and for what he called a *concordia ordinum*, responsible cooperation in the national interests by the aristocracy, the prosperous upper-middle class (the "knights"), and the urban and rural citizens of less social and economic standing. As a practical politician he often made compromises and temporary alliances with others with whom he differed, but overall his career shows a commitment to humane principles of justice, fairness, and tolerance of diversity. In the effort to save republican government he ultimately failed but gained the admiration of posterity. We know him better than any other person who lived in classical times, primarily because of the survival of hundreds of personal letters, which he wrote to friends and members of his family and which reveal his thoughts, reactions to contemporary events, discouragement, and hopes, sometimes on a daily basis. Although he had a high opinion of himself and could at times be pompous, he also had a splendid sense of humor, and above all he had a gift for eloquent spoken and written expression that has rarely been approached since. Among ancient statesmen, Cicero is most often compared to Demosthenes, and indeed he came to take Demosthenes as his chief model in his later work.[2] He excelled Demosthenes in the many facets of his knowledge and interests, in his urbanity and sense of humor, perhaps in his humanity. Speaking of their oratory, Quintilian has this to say about the two (10.1.106): "Demosthenes is more concentrated, Cicero more copious; the former draws his sentences together more briefly, the latter at greater length; Demosthenes always fights with the dagger, Cicero often also with the bludgeon; from De-

---

[1] He often refers to his political associates as the *boni*, "the good guys."
[2] See Wooten, *Cicero's Philippics*.

mosthenes' speeches nothing can be taken away, to Cicero's nothing can be added; in Demosthenes there is more careful attention to detail, in Cicero more natural ability."[3]

Cicero wrote about rhetoric, and philosophy as well, chiefly in those periods of his life when he was prevented from taking full part in public affairs in Rome, for his public career as statesman and speaker in the law courts took priority in his own mind over other activities. It is thus appropriate to begin with his speeches and introduce his theoretical writings in the context in which they were written. Fifty-eight speeches survive in whole or in part.[4] He himself usually published his speeches after delivery, often with some revision.[5] There is space here to discuss only a few of the most significant of them.

Cicero's Orations in the Years from 81 to 56 B.C.

Cicero's earliest surviving speech is *For Quinctius*, delivered in 81 B.C. in a case involving a business partnership. He was twenty-five years old at the time. Although the speech illustrates many of the precepts of rhetoric that Cicero had learned from his teachers and had discussed in *On Invention*, he adapted the rules to the situation in a flexible way. For example, issues of fact, law, quality, and jurisdiction are all brought in to some extent, even though stasis theory as set out in *On Invention* does not provide for their combination into a single case. The speech also relies heavily on ethos, anticipating some of the techniques Cicero will later use to great effect.[6] The style shows some of the characteristics of Asianism, to which the young Cicero was attracted: sentences are often long because of amplification of both ideas and language, including listings and doublings of words. In this early work the result at times seems cumbersome; he gradually developed more smoothness and suppleness, even in highly complex sentences.

The speech that first made Cicero famous in the law courts was his brilliant and exciting defense of Sextus Roscius of Ameria on the chilling charge of parricide, probably delivered in 80 B.C.[7] The case occurred during the rule of the dictator Sulla, soon after the proscriptions that had legalized murder and confiscation of the property of many opponents. According to Cicero, the accusation that Roscius had murdered his father was a plot to dispose of Roscius, concocted by the actual murderer and two others who

---

[3] See also the comparison of the two in Longinus, *On Sublimity* 12.3–5.

[4] For English versions, see Grant, *Murder Trials* and *Selected Political Speeches* in the Penguin series, and the volumes by a variety of translators in the Loeb Classical Library series.

[5] For a fuller account of many of the speeches, see my *Art of Rhetoric in the Roman World*, 138–48, 149–204, and 259–282.

[6] See May, *Trials of Character*, 14–21.

[7] See Craig, *Form as Argument*, 27–45

shared in the loot. After the murder they put the name of Roscius' father on the list of those proscribed by Sulla, though in fact he was a supporter of Sulla, and in this way made possible the sale of his property. This was arranged through the connivance of Sulla's freedman Chrysogonus, who bought the property at a fraction of its value and ejected Roscius from it. No one was apt to run the risk of bidding against Chrysogonus, and it was perhaps hoped by the confederates that Roscius would not be able to find a defender when indicted for the murder. None of the better-known *patroni* would accept the defence. Cicero undertook it out of personal friendship for his client, with the hope that as a young man who had the nerve to cross swords with the corrupt, wicked tool of the dictator, he could make a popular name for himself, and perhaps with the knowledge that some of Sulla's more powerful supporters would not be sorry to see Chrysogonus discredited. Chrysogonus was, however, unscrupulous and nasty and could be counted on to put up a good fight. The key to success was to take him by surprise. In this Cicero was entirely successful. His intention to defend Roscius and attack Chrysogonus was apparently kept secret until he rose and spoke.

Cicero's defense of Roscius has three parts, combining stasis of fact with that form of stasis of quality that shifts responsibility for the action to another person and ultimate responsibility for guilt to still another: he argues that Roscius did not murder his father, that the murder was in fact the work of Magnus, one of the accusers, and that the whole proceeding was conducted with the help, and to the advantage, of Chrysogonus. In fixing the guilt (84) Cicero states a famous phrase, which he attributes to Cassius Longinus, *cui bono*, "Who stood to gain?" The unexpected personal attack on Chrysogonus opens with one of Cicero's celebrated puns: "I come now to that golden name of Chrysogonus [in Greek: "the golden born"], under which name the whole gang hides"(124). He is exceedingly careful to make no criticism of Sulla: Sulla, he asserts, knew nothing about it at all, made no money by it, is so taken up with great affairs of state that he cannot possibly know what all his followers do, any more than Jupiter can know the wickedness of individual men (131).

A striking feature of the speech, and a prevailing characteristic of Cicero's rhetoric, is its employment and extension of ethos.[8] The emphasis on character is evident from the very beginning, where Cicero's references to his own youth and lack of authority help to awaken the sympathy of the jury. Throughout the speech his own character and that of his client are developed in contrast to that of his opponents and other actors in the drama in ways not provided for in rhetorical handbooks, and toward the end of the speech (143) he takes a further step in the development of ethos by distin-

---

[8] See May, *Trials of Character*, 21–31.

guishing between his client's feelings and his own, something which was not ordinarily possible in classical Greek procedure where the principals spoke on their own behalf and thus not envisioned by Greek rhetoricians. Cicero here claims that Roscius has no personal ill will against Chrysogonus and company; he is not even trying to recover his property; all he wants is acquittal on the charge of killing his father. What has been said against Chrysogonus comes from the heart of Cicero himself, who is unafraid, who cannot keep silent. The speech ends with an attempt to convert the case from that of Q. Roscius to the universal grounds of law and order at Rome. This technique can be found in Greek oratory but is much used by Cicero and was especially suited to Roman procedure, since Roman law was based on precedent to a much greater extent than was Greek law; here the generalization of the issue and the stress on the case as establishing a precedent was especially effective, since it came at a time when many Romans were anxious to reestablish order in society.

Cicero won his case and seems not to have suffered for his attack on Chrysogonus. Plutarch (*Cicero* 3) says fear of Sulla was the reason Cicero chose to go to Greece in 79 B.C., but Cicero himself claims (*Brutus* 314) that his habit of speaking at the top of his voice and with tension in his whole body was ruining his health and that he wanted to study with Greek teachers. It was, after all, not unusual for a young Roman to spend some time studying in Greece, and what Cicero learned there made an important contribution to his later writings, including his dialogue *On the Orators*. He spent six months in Athens studying philosophy with Antiochus the Academic and practicing declamation under the direction of Demetrius the Syrian. Then he continued to Asia Minor, where he worked with the famous rhetoricians there. Finally, in the spring of 78, he arrived in Rhodes, where he joined the new Rhodian school of Apollonius of Alabanda. Here he learned how to control his voice and repress the excesses of his style (*Brutus* 315–16). Sulla had now died, and Cicero returned from the East to reenter political life in Rome. He was elected quaestor for the year 75 B.C. and assigned to duties as an assistant to the governor of Sicily, after which he returned to Rome, took the seat in the senate to which his quaestorship entitled him, and resumed his activities in the courts. The governor of Sicily from 73 to 71 B.C. was Gaius Verres. Even allowing for some exaggertion in Cicero's description of him, it seems impossible to refute his reputation as the most notorious example of a rapacious Roman governor. Cicero's prosecution of him in 70 was overwhelmingly successful and confirmed his position as the leading orator in Rome. He was forced, however, to adopt a strategy of introducing the evidence immediately at the beginning of the trial, thus losing the opportunity for an elaborate opening address. To make up for this, he then published what is known as the Second Action against Verres, a series of five undelivered speeches, rhetorically elaborated beyond any of his actual speeches. For one with a taste for flamboyance, they make excellent reading and show Cicero's powers of dramatic narrative and lurid invective.[9]

Cicero's cleverness in a very complex case is evident in his defense of Cluentius, delivered in 66 B.C.[10] He later chose it as an example of speech employing all varieties of style (*Orator* 103). It is his longest, and Pliny (*Epistles* 1.20.4) regarded it as his finest speech. The complexities result from the cast of characters, from the circumstances of previous trials that bear on the case, and from the legal procedure, since Cluentius was apparently being tried under two different provisions of the law on assassins and poisoners. The more straightforward charge was that Cluentius had tried to poison Oppianicus; the more complicated charge was that he had earlier tried to bring about Oppianicus' judicial murder by bribing a jury to convict him on false charges of murder and attempted murder. This was the source of great prejudice against Cluentius, both in Rome generally and in the court, and Cicero's primary rhetorical challenge was how to counteract the prejudice. This he does at such length that not until section 143 does he come to the immediate charges. The charge of judicial murder he wants to dismiss on the ground that it did not apply to knights, but quite cleverly he introduces a dispute between himself and his client in planning the defense, Cicero seeking to stress the legal technicality, Cluentius insisting on having his reputation cleared and not trying to escape by a technicality (144). This is one of Cicero's many effective uses of contrast and comparison between patron and client. In the same part of the speech he employs another of his favorite topics, the generalization of the immediate issue into a threat to all law in the state. The discussion of the poisoning charge comes at the end of the speech (169–94) and seems to show that no good evidence had been offered against Cluentius. Cicero's arguments that the allegations are improbable look perfectly adequate, and by this point one is willing to believe that Cluentius' enemies would stoop to anything. The defense is in large part a matter of constructing a satisfactory ethos for the major characters: Cicero even manages to make it seem to Cluentius' credit that his most persistent opponent has been his own mother! Cicero won the case and later boasted that he had pulled shades of darkness over the eyes of the jury (Quintilian 2.17.21). He perhaps meant specifically in connection with the bribery accusation, where his argument is a dilemma: either Oppianicus or Cluentius bribed the jury, and since Oppianicus can be shown to have made an attempt, Cluentius must be innocent. The near certainty that both parties had tried bribery is not considered,[11] but Cicero's argument (62) that Cluentius' case was too good to make bribery necessary is hardly convincing,

---

[9] For discussion, see my *Art of Rhetoric in the Roman World*, 156–65.

[10] See Kirby, *Rhetoric of Cicero's Pro Cluentio*.

[11] In *For Caecina* 29 Cicero indicates that Cluentius had used bribes.

considering the state of the Roman courts at the time. To meet Oppianicus' bribery with bribery may have seemed the only prudent course. The case as a whole is a fine example of what ancient critics admired in an orator: not legal knowledge (though Cicero displays a good deal) or logical clarity, but the ability to charm the jury and sweep it off its feet by colorful narrative, vivid characterization, radiant confidence, skillful emphasis and deemphasis, and in general the creation of a work of art.

Cicero was elected praetor in 66 and for the first time addressed a deliberative speech to the Roman people at an assembly.[12] He says he purposely waited to speak until he was sure of his authority with the people and of his oratorical ability (*Manilian Law* 2). The subject he chose to support was a law proposed by the tribune Manilius, under which Pompey, successful beyond all expectation in a special command against pirates who had been a plague in the Mediterranean, would now be given command in the long-drawn-out war against Mithridates of Pontus. Julius Caesar also spoke in favor of the law (Dio 36.43.2). Both orators were eager to show themselves friends of the great Pompey, and the law was apparently certain of success with equestrian and proletarian voters, who idolized Pompey and were weary of the conduct of the war in the East. Cicero thus spoke as a popular public official before a friendly audience. The rhetorical problem he faced was not so much how to convince his audience as how to avoid antagonizing those in the senatorial party who opposed Pompey, and especially to avoid criticism of Lucullus, the previous commander against Mithradates. But this was not impossible; Lucullus, though unpopular with his troops, was a man of great ability and had had successes in the past that could be openly saluted. Cicero's argument is essentially that Lucullus had been frustrated in his recent efforts and it was time to give a new man a chance, especially since such a man as Pompey was already in the East.

Though the expediency of Pompey's appointment is brought out, as it should be in such a case, the speech has strong epideictic elements in its expression of political affiliations and ideals, in its attempt to unify opposing groups, and in its praise of Pompey. In dealing with the latter subject (27–28) Cicero proceeds through a list of topics as found in Greek epideictic oratory and discussed in Greek ethical philosophy but perhaps not previously applied by a Roman orator. Pompey is recommended on the basis of his knowledge, courage, authority, and luck. The practical virtues discussed include fortitude, industry, promptness, and wise policy; the ethical virtues are morality, temperance, trustworthiness, affability, intelligence, and humanity. Cicero idealizes Pompey beyond historical recognition into a picture of what every great Roman commander ought to be, much as Pericles' *Funeral Oration* is a picture of what Athens ought to be rather than what it was. The speech has the complete regularity of form associated with a judi-

---

[12] The primary function of praetors at this time was administration of the judicial system.

cial rather than a deliberative speech; there is exordium, narration, partition, proof, refutation, and peroration. Cicero himself regarded the speech as the best example among his works of the "middle style" (*Orator* 102).

The high point of Cicero's career was his consulship in 63 B.C. With it, he acquired a new rhetorical weapon, which he never failed to wield: consular prestige. We have nine speeches dating from that year: three speeches against the grain law of Rullus delivered early in the year; the defense of Rabirius on a charge of treason (a consul did not necessarily cease from activity as a patron in the courts); four speeches against Catiline, two in the senate and two before the assembly of the people; and the speech for Murena, charged with bribery in connection with the elections for the following year. The fragmentary speech for Rabirius is remarkable as the only extant judicial speech delivered before the assembly, since the case was brought by an antiquated procedure to the centuriate assembly. In the *Orator* (102) Cicero takes it as the best example of the "grand style" in contrast with the "plain style" of *For Caecina* and the "middle style" of his speech on the Manilian law. "In it," he says, "I blazed forth with every kind of amplification." No speech by Cicero has a more sober tone, adopted in part as Cicero's protest at the almost comic-opera proceedings by which Rabirius was being made a victim.

The *Catilinarians* are doubtless the best known of all Latin speeches. They make good school texts, because they present stirring events of considerable historical significance,[13] because they are rather short, and because they are not written in especially difficult Latin. The rhetorical anaysis of the *Catilinarians* is, however, complex. They do not conform well to the ordinary requirements of deliberative oratory, though the first and fourth were delivered in the senate and the other two before an assembly of the people. Only the fourth can be said to deliberate about a course of action, and actually that action is judicial, not political. Furthermore, the parts of the speeches do not necessarily perform their usual functions or relate very clearly to each other. This complicates any attempt to define the rhetorical problem that Cicero had posed for himself and to describe the techniques by which he has chosen to answer it.

One reason that the *Catilinarians* seem to aim at more than one objective is that Cicero did not publish them until 60 B.C., three years after delivery,

[13] The conspiracy of Catiline was one of a series of attempts in Cicero's lifetime to overthrow the republican constitution and wrest control of public policy from the senate, replacing it with a dictator or small oligarchy. Catiline himself was a dissolute aristocrat, motivated chiefly by a personal desire for money and power, but he attracted support from others like himself and from lower classes of society suffering from economic difficulties. Unlike other popular leaders who preceded or followed him—the Gracchi, Marius, Julius Caesar, and Octavian—he lacked personal integrity and offered no real program of administrative, social, and economic reform.

when he issued them in an edition with eight other speeches dating from his consulship and compared them to Demosthenes' *Philippics* (*To Atticus* 2.1.3). Cicero's career was in serious difficulties during these years, stemming from his actions as consul. As early as the last day of 63 he had been prevented from delivering the customary speech of one going out of office, on the ground that he had put to death Roman citizens—the Catilinarian conspirators, though not Catiline himself, who was killed in battle—without a trial. Though some disliked Cicero personally, the real issue was senatorial direction of affairs, and the chief legal point in question was the *senatus consultum ultimum,* or general decree of emergency by which the senate authorized the consuls to see "that the state suffer no harm." What a consul could do under this decree was largely a matter of his own prestige and the support he could get from the senate and public opinion. The senate had passed the decree in late October 63 and it was the basis of Cicero's actions in putting down the conspiracy, though not apparently of his order to strangle the conspirators, since that had separately and specifically been authorized by the senate. In any event, Cicero was criticized for years and eventually driven into exile, on the ground that he had exceeded his authority. He naturally replied by trying to make clear his view of the situation in 63 and to glorify his rescue of the constitution. In the first *Catilinarian* some passages relating to Cicero's fears and justifications (e.g., 6, 9, 11, and 22) may be additions or revisions for later readers, and the fourth *Catilinarian* may be a conflation of two different speeches at the same session of the senate.

The first speech, delivered in the senate on November 8, has several different addressees. First, it is addressed to Catiline and aimed at getting him to leave Rome, without forcing official action against him. Breaking with all conventions of senatorial procedure and rhetorical rules for an exordium, Cicero opens with the famous words "How long, O Catiline, will you abuse our patience?" But the speech is also more properly addressed to the senate, aimed at arousing it to the danger and explaining why Cicero has taken the course he took, specifically why he did not take more stringent measures. Third, it is addressed to readers in 60 B.C. and tries to show them why he was justified in taking as stringent measures as he did.

It is likely that Cicero went into the senate not expecting to see Catiline, but intending to report some preparations he had made. Catiline's effrontery in coming made him alter the form of his speech. Cicero not only breaks with precedent in addressing him directly but violates the injunction given in *On the Orator* (2.213–14) against an emotional beginning. The topics of the exordium are the present danger, the historical precedents, Cicero's anxiety, and his plan. These are of interest to a varied audience. The present danger is for the senators, though expressed in indignation to Catiline. The historical precedents and legal weapon were well known to the senate, but were a warning to Catiline and of interest to future readers. Cicero's anxiety is a negative factor in dealing with Catiline but important for his justification in the eyes of posterity. His plan interests the senate and Catiline.

There follows (7–10) a narration of Cicero's knowledge of the conspiracy. Great suspense is created: Catiline presumably did not know how much Cicero knew, and he is not immediately told. The allusion is vague in section 1, warmer in section 6, but in section 8 breaks out in all clarity. The heart of the speech (11–27) is an argument aimed at persuading Catiline to leave Rome. Rhetorically, the high point of the section is a *prosōpopoeia*, the address of the Laws to Catiline, reminiscent of a similar personification in Plato's *Crito*. This is followed by a short refutation of Catiline's logical demand that the senate vote: possibly some debate had intervened, possibly Cicero was anticipating a demand, or possibly the section was put into the published speech to answer a demand made after the real speech. Cicero here seems on rather weak ground, and he may have received less support from the senate than he hoped for. The fourth part of the speech (27–32) is a refutation, addressed to the senate, of complaints that Cicero had not gone far enough in putting down the conspiracy. The complaint is put in the mouth of the Fatherland, which thus makes a contrast with the earlier address of the Laws to Catiline. Finally comes a brief peroration.

The second *Catilinarian*, delivered the next day to the people, does not have so clear a structure but is similarly composed of explanations of caution and justifications of action, while the third, also to the people, describes the capture of the conspirators in Rome and pleads with the people not to allow Cicero's actions to injure him. The fourth speech purports to come from the debate in the senate on the punishment appropriate to the prisoners after the conspiracy was put down and reads like a speech in a trial before the senate. According to the historian Sallust (*Catiline* 50.3), the senate first judged the conspirators guilty of treason, then debated the appropriate punishment. Although Sallust in his account of the conspiracy praises the first *Catilinarian* (31.6), he passes over the other three and, in reporting the senatorial trial, composed his own version of speeches of Julius Caesar, arguing against the death penalty, and of Cato the Younger, arguing for it. These speeches well represent the alternatives and offer a striking political and personal contrast of the two speakers. Cicero himself later admitted (*To Atticus* 12.21.1) that Cato had summed up the matter in the clearest and fullest way. The senate's decision was to execute the prisoners.

Cicero's speech *For Murena* is closely connected with these same events. In the election in the summer of 63 the candidates for the consulship of 62 were Catiline, Servius Sulpicius, Decimus Silanus, and Lucius Murena. Catiline was already engaged in the plot to overthrow the senatorial government, which came to be known as the Catilinarian conspiracy. His defeat

was essential in the eyes of the senatorial party, and bribery was used extensively to secure the election. This aroused the indignation of Cato the
Younger, great-grandson of old Cato and an imitator of him as guardian of
public morality. Though as anxious as anyone for Catiline's defeat, he
threatened prosecution for bribery of anyone who was elected. The winners
turned out to be Silanus and Murena. Silanus was Cato's brother-in-law and
was left alone, but Murena was prosecuted for bribery by Cato, the defeated
Sulpicius, and two others. The charge of bribery was not unwarranted nor
unusual in Roman politics but was extremely inconvenient for orderly government: Murena's conviction would mean that only one consul would be
in office at the beginning of 62, when the plots of Catiline might well still
hang over Rome, and he or one of his followers might hope for success at a
special election. Cicero had campaigned for Sulpicius but found it possible
to support Murena and decided that it was vital to defend him against the
charges. The case was heard in November, sometime between the second
and third *Catilinarian*, after Catiline had withdrawn to Etruria, but before
he had been defeated. In Murena's defense there appeared the most presti-
gious patrons to be found: Cicero's old opponent, the silver-tongued
Hortensius, now cooperating with him; the rich and influential Crassus; and
the incumbent consul, Cicero. Cicero says (*Brutus* 190; *Orator* 130) that
when speaking in collaboration with others he customarily spoke last, delivering as it were a peroration for which his abilities were well suited. *For
Murena* appears to be an instance: he says (48) that he must sum up the
case, repeating some of the arguments of Hortensius and Crassus, and (54)
that Murena had particularly asked him to deal with the third and most
specific part of the prosecution, though the others had already answered it.
Cicero's particular function, however, was to destroy the great moral authority of his friends Sulpicius and Cato as prosecutors in this particular
case. Though he persists in denying the charge of bribery, it was apparently
well founded and could not be effectively refuted. Nor could he very well
directly attack the character of the prosecutors, who were in fact his own
personal friends and highly respected in Rome. The answer he so effectively
constructed was to admit their virtue but to present them as well-meaning,
unrealistic dabblers in affairs whose significance they did not understand.
Let them ride their hobbies of the legal scholarship in one case or Stoic
virtue in the other, good enough in their way, but not of much value in the
real world, especially when it was a question of saving the republic. As a tour
de force in the construction of rhetorical ethos, *For Murena* is rivaled only
by Cicero's later speech *For Caelius*.[14]

The exordium (1–10) begins in a solemn and religious tone, not unlike
Demosthenes' *On the Crown*. Cicero explains why he has taken the case,

[14] See May, *Trials of Character*, 58–69.

though consul, though himself author of a bribery law, though a friend of Sulpicius and supporter of his candidacy. All of this lends weight to the defense of Murena, for there must be an overriding necessity to bring Cicero to Murena's side. Then comes the partition into the three topics of the prosecution (11): the *reprehensio vitae*, or criticism of Murena's life—this ought to be the most important, Cicero says, but the opposition had not found much to criticize—the relative claims of Murena and Sulpicius to the consulship (*contentio dignitatis*), and the charge of bribery (*crimen ambitus*). Under Roman procedure all were relevant issues. The account of Murena's life and merits (11–53) is chronological and functions like a narration. Inserted in the middle of it is the attack on Sulpicius. Murena, whose military exploits were perhaps rather modest, is made into a symbol of the contribution to Roman life of the soldier; Sulpicius, into that of the jurisconsult, and the game is on in a charming *synkrisis*, or comparison. The law is represented at its hairsplitting, literalist worst and the archaic ritualism of legal formulas irreverently ridiculed. A lawyer is nothing in comparison to an orator (24), Cicero says, and he claims he could easily learn all civil law in three days (28). The answer to Cato comes in refutation of the bribery charge (54–85). Cato is described as a man with "a doctrine not moderated or gentle, but, it seems to me, a little too harsh and more austere than the truth or nature allows" (60). He believes all sins are equal: equally wrong, without cause, to wring the neck of a fowl or a father (61). Then comes a spirited imaginary dialogue.

The ridicule, thorough as it is, produced no bitterness. Cato went away from the trial remarking "What a witty consul we have," a contradiction in Roman terms, but he became a friend and close adviser of Murena all the next year. More important, he came to modify his views slightly and, in what he regarded as the public interest, condoned bribery against the election of Julius Caesar in 60. To alter the view of a Cato may be fairly labeled a great triumph. Critics who do not understand the rhetorical problem of the case have sometimes found Cicero's humor in November 63 puzzling. How could he be so flippant with Catiline in Etruria? The answer of course is that only by flippancy did he think he could keep Catiline from Rome. It was doubtless widely appreciated that Cicero had elsewhere eulogized the civil law in glowing terms and was personally quite interested in Stoicism; he was not, however, regarded as slippery or insincere, but as clever and quick-witted. The rational argument that moved the jury was the quite real necessity for having two consuls when the year opened. What the jury needed was some excuse, some pretext, to reject the complaints of such important accusers and to overlook the immediate issue of bribery. Cicero furnished them with such an excuse.

The years following Cicero's consulship were among the most difficult in his life, as he saw his achievements and even personal security more and more seriously threatened until finally he was driven into exile in 58 B.C. His actions as consul had made him a symbol of senatorial government. Pompey, Caesar, and Crassus, who joined together in the informal cabal called "the first triumvirate" to control the government in 59, solicited his support unsuccessfully and then turned against him. There are a number of speeches from the period before and after his exile that show different rhetorical approaches and different sides of his character. Among them is the short and charming speech for the poet Archias in 62, which contains a famous passage on the role of poetry in society (12–20),[15] and the speech *For Sestius* of 57, which includes an important discussion of Cicero's political philosophy and the goals of the *optimates* (96–143). But the speech of this period most popular with modern readers is the defense of Caelius Rufus on a charge of violence and poisoning, delivered in 56.

For Caelius is another example of Cicero's success in defending a client by cleverness, wit, and style rather than by evidence or proof.[16] He even boasts of relying on arguments rather than witnesses (22)! As a parade of characters in a titillating drama, the speech is splendid:[17] there is the young pleader for the prosecution, Atratinus, treated with humiliating condescension in the opening of the speech; there is Clodia, sister and alleged mistress of Cicero's enemy Clodius, "the Medea of the Palentine" as he calls her, not less interesting to posterity as the former lover of the poet Catullus; and there is Caelius himself, whose exploits are dismissed by the sophisticated orator as youthful wild oats. Indeed, Cicero makes considerable effort to present Caelius as potentially a young Cicero who may be expected to develop into a statesman like himself.

The primary rhetorical problem was doubtless the weakness of Cicero's case, and the answer to it is the brilliant color, the entertaining irrelevancies, the vigor and self-assurance of the presentation, and the consular authority shed on Caelius by Cicero himself. The charge that Caelius took gold from Clodia to buy the assassination of the philosopher Dio, who had come on an embassy from Alexandria, is met by a sophistic dilemma reminiscent of that in *For Cluentius*: if Caelius was intimate with Clodia, he surely would have told her why he wanted the gold and she would have refused it; if he was not intimate with her, she would not have given it to him (53). The charge of poisoning is met by the claim that Cicero can see no motive (56), and the orator elaborates into a most improbable comic farce a scene in the baths, when the poison is supposed to have been delivered. There are two admirable *prosōpopoeiae*, first of old Appius Claudius rising from the grave to rebuke his profligate descendant, Clodia, then of her brother Clodius,

---

[15] See Gotoff, *Cicero's Elegant Style*, which contains discussion and commentary on the speech, with special attention to style.

[16] See Craig, *Form as Argument*, 105–21.

[17] See Geffcken, *Comedy in the Pro Caelio*.

Cicero's most inveterate enemy, addressing his sister (33–36). Cicero's embarrassment is most evident when he tries to play down Caelius' association with Catiline. Caelius had originally been a protégé of Cicero, then became estranged. Cicero probably undertook the case because Caelius had been attacked by their common enemy rather than for great sympathy with his recent actions.

Soon after the victory for Caelius, Cicero's career reached a turning point. He thought that the triumvirs—Pompey, Caesar, and Crassus—were drifting apart, and he attempted to get the senate to undo some of the actions of Caesar's consulship (59 B.C.). Cicero's efforts, however, contributed to the renewal of the triumvirate for another five years and to a tightening of control of the government by the triumvirs. The alternatives open to Cicero narrowed to cooperation or retirement, and he chose to cooperate. He had already discovered the horrors of exile. Cooperation took the form of supporting in the senate policies of the triumvirs and, worse, undertaking on request the defense of their friends in the law courts. In a long letter to Lentulus written in 54 (*To His Friends* 1.9), Cicero discusses his motives, the changed condition of the state, the limited opportunities for public service now open, and the way some of the senatorial party had failed to support him. His basic justification was that he did sincerely respect Pompey, to whom he owed a debt of gratitude for past actions, and that Caesar had been his friend in the past and had preserved the appearances of friendship in recent times. Personal friendship was always important to Cicero, and personal relationships in Rome often played a stronger role than ideology. Although at the request of the triumvirs he defended in court some men he did not like and had fought in the past, Vatinius and Gabinius for example, consistent with his usual policy, he did not undertake prosecutions. The virulent invective *Against Piso* is not a prosecution; it was given in the senate in 55 and is primarily an expression of his frustrations and pent-up emotion. An interesting feature is the attempt to use Piso's interest in Epicureanism to discredit him, just as Cato's Stoicism had been used in *For Murena*. In public life Cicero could play on Roman suspicion of Greek philosophy as a rhetorical tool, though he himself was deeply interested in it and later published a series of works to make it available to Roman readers.

On the Orator

Cicero found another outlet for his rhetorical energy during the course of the year 55. While contemplating his own checked career and the limitations imposed on an orator under the triumvirate, he composed a dialogue discussing what a perfect speaker could and should be, the three books that comprise *On the Orator*. It is one of his most admired works and stands only slightly behind Aristotle's *On Rhetoric* and Quintilian's *Education of the Orator* as a rhetorical classic.[18]

Each of the three books has a prologue with comments by Cicero and a brief description of the scene of the ensuing dialogue, which is represented as having taken place at various spots on the estate of Crassus at Tusculum in September 91 B.C. As noted in the previous chapter, Crassus was Cicero's mentor in those years. The characters are the great orators of the time, all of whom Cicero had known: Crassus, Antonius, Scaevola, Sulpicius, Cotta, Catulus, and Julius Caesar Strabo. Cicero claims to have heard about the discussion from Cotta; probably it never actually took place, but he has assigned each of the characters a role in the discussion consistent with what he knew of their views of rhetoric and their personalities (cf. 3.16). Crassus died a few days after the dramatic date of the dialogue; the others all subsequently found their freedom of speech checked by enemies, and Antonius, Sulpicius, Catulus, and Strabo lost even their lives. In the prologue to the third book Cicero draws a comparison to his own experience.

In a letter to Lentulus (*To His Friends* 1.9.23) Cicero tells something about the form and contents of the work: "Since I am dissociating myself from orations and turning to gentler muses which appeal to me now very greatly, as they have since youth, I have written in the manner of Aristotle, in so far as I wanted to conform to that, three books of discussion and dialogue *On the Orator*, which I think may be helpful to your son Lentulus. They avoid the trite rules and embrace the oratorical theory of all the ancients, both the Aristotelian and Isocratean." "In the manner of Aristotle" refers not to *On Rhetoric*, but to Aristotle's now-lost dialogues, such as *Gryllus*. These seem to have differed from Platonic dialogues in that the author claimed to have been present at the discussion and allowed the characters to expound their views at length rather than to search for truth by question and answer in the Socratic manner. In another letter (*To Atticus* 13.19.4) Cicero speaks of the work as resembling the dialogues of Heraclides Ponticus, in which the characters are people of a previous generation and the writer plays no part in the discussion. The last sentence quoted above from the letter to Lentulus is borne out in that *On the Orator* is not a technical treatise: it avoids technical terminology and focuses on major issues that go back to Plato's *Gorgias* and *Phaedrus* and Aristotle's *Gryllus*: whether rhetoric is an "art"; the relative importance of natural ability, theory, and training in fostering eloquence; and the kinds of knowledge required for successful

---

[18] The most imporant additions to the bibliography since publication of my *Art of Rhetoric in the Roman World* are the volumes (five are planned) of an extensive commentary in German, edited by Leeman, Pinkster, et al. See also Wisse, *Ethos and Pathos*. A new English version with notes, drawing on this commentary, is in preparation by May, Wisse, and Leff. Until the latter is published readers need to rely on the Loeb Classical Library edition of Sutton and Rackham, whose translation is at times faulty and whose paragraphing and marginal notes can be misleading. The best version of the Latin text is that of Kumaniecki in the *Bibliotheca Teubneriana*.

public speaking. Cicero has tried to bring the Isocratean tradition (that of professional teachers of rhetoric in Greece) and the Aristotelian (the philosophical approach) as well as the functions of the traditional Roman orator together in a new synthesis of the ideal statesman and leader under constitutional government, the role he himself had sought to fulfill.

The structure of *On the Orator* shows careful planning, but there is also considerable repetition, especially of the speakers' views on the major issue of the knowledge required by the orator. This is probably a deliberate tactic on Cicero's part, for it gives greater emphasis to the ideas he wanted to stress while at the same time preserving the style of an informal conversation, in which repetition could be expected. The discussion of the first book takes place in a garden under a plane tree, reminiscent of Plato's *Phaedrus*, and sets out differing views of the knowledge required of a successful orator and the relative roles of natural ability, rhetorical theory, and practical exercises. Crassus, who is clearly Cicero's major spokeman, is made to argue for broad knowledge of philosophy, politics, history, and law, and to emphasize the importance of natural ability. Scaevola thinks this ideal unattainable in practice and stresses the need for a technical knowledge of law. Antonius rejects Crassus' claim that an orator is one who can speak on any subject; to him an orator is one who can use language and argument effectively in the law courts and in public meetings. This requires some specific knowledge of the subject, but in practice not much knowledge of philosophy or law is needed.[19]

The long second book is largely given over to Antonius, who is made to have moderated his views over the intervening night. He no longer pushes his restricted view of the orator, but as the company strolls about a portico, reminiscent of Aristotle's "Peripatetic" school, he discusses the orator on the basis of his own experience. His remarks include speculation on the possibility of rhetorical historiography and in the case of oratory range over invention, arrangement, and memory, described in nontechnical terms. Most important is the discussion of the three functions of the orator, later known as the *officia oratoris*: to win over the audience's sympathy; to prove what is true; and to stir the emotions to the desired action (2.115). This is Cicero's version of the three Aristotelian modes of persuasion: ethos, logos, and pathos. In dealing with the emotions the use of humor is mentioned, and an extensive account of that subject is given by Caesar (2.217–90).

The third book takes place in the afternoon of the same day, when the company meets in a shady spot, again reminiscent of the *Phaedrus*. Crassus is the chief speaker and primarily concerns himself with style and delivery, but he is twice led into an excursus on the orator's need for a liberal educa-

[19] Cf. Aristotle's distinction in *On Rhetoric* 1.1.21 between the "specifics" of a case and the "topics" of dialectic and rhetoric.

tion and especially knowledge of philosophy. He reviews ancient intellectual history and blames Socrates for separating rhetoric and philosophy (3.60–61). He considers the view of rhetoric of the various Hellenistic philosophical schools (3.62–68) and finds that of the Academy most satisfactory. A second excursus (3.104–43) is suggested by the importance of amplification in great oratory. To be able to amplify, the orator must have knowledge of a variety of subjects. The discussion of style is structured around the four virtues, derived from Theophrastus, of Latinity, clarity, ornamentation, and propriety. The extended account of ornamentation treats diction (3.148–70) and composition (3.171–208) and includes the first discussion in Latin of prose rhythm, which the speaker regards as a part of the emotional element in oratory. The book ends with a tribute to Hortensius, in 91 a rising young orator, which is an imitation of the reference to Isocrates at the end of Plato's *Phaedrus*.

On the Orator is dedicated to Cicero's brother Quintus as a result of discussions between them about rhetoric and oratory (1.5). Cicero gives a brief account of his own position in the prologue to the first book (1.16–33). It is this that he presumably expected to be confirmed by the dialogue as a whole. Rhetoric, he says, is a vast subject. Without knowledge of many things it is empty verbiage. Style should be developed by practice and the emotions studied, "because all the force and theory of speaking must be applied in calming or exciting the minds of those who constitute the audience" (1.17). There is need for humor, knowledge of history, and knowledge of law, all of which are fully exemplified in Cicero's own speeches. Delivery must be understood and memory must be sound. Neither rules nor teachers nor exercises can make a person an orator, but only knowledge of all great subjects and all arts. In practice, however, knowledge of everything is too much to demand, and like others Cicero concerns himself with the knowledge required for judicial and deliberative oratory.

Crassus and Antonius are made to speak of their studies of rhetoric and philosophy in Athens in the late second century.[20] Although they may have told Cicero in his youth something of the views of teachers they met, writing in 55 he was probably largely dependent on what he learned himself during his visit to Athens in 79 and on written sources for the debates between rhetoricians and philosophers.[21] One such work was a handbook of rhetoric by Charmadas the Academic, mentioned in 1.93–94, which seems to have anticipated some of Cicero's views (see 1.88). *On the Orator* is, however, the first datable discussion of rhetoric since the time of Theophrastus that shows a direct knowledge of Aristotle's *On Rhetoric*. As ex-

[20] Crassus in 1.45–48 and Antonius in 1.84–89.
[21] Hendrickson, in "Literary Sources," argued that it is a regular technique of Ciceronian dialogue to attribute to an oral source doctrines and information that were in fact derived from written works.

plained in chapter 5, some works of Aristotle, probably including *On Rhetoric*, were not accessible to scholars after the death of Theophrastus. Early in the first century the books were recovered, brought to Athens, and then around 83 seized by Sulla and brought to Rome. In a letter written about the time he composed *On the Orator* (*To Atticus* 4.10), Cicero says that he has been studying in the library of Sulla's son and mentions Aristotle. This may well be the direct source for the Aristotelian elements that reappear in *On the Orator* and are not found in Hellenistic discussions of rhetoric. Specifically, the discussion of invention in 2.114–306 is Aristotelian in that it does not deal with the parts of the oration, as did Cicero's *On Invention* or *Rhetoric for Herennius*; these are left to be mentioned under arrangement (2.307–332). As in Aristotle, Cicero's account of invention identifies three means of persuasion: logical proof that what we claim is true, the effective presentation of moral character (ethos), and appeal to the emotions (pathos) (2.115, cf. 121 and 128). The first kind of persuasion is based either on presentation of evidence or on rational argument, and each of these is discussed, as in Aristotle. The account of rational argument consists primarily of a list of topics usable in many cases (2.162–73), the sort of thing Aristotle had discussed in the *Topics* and adapted for *On Rhetoric*. Antonius acknowledges (2.152–53) that the material is Aristotelian and claims to have read both *On Rhetoric* and the *Synagōgē* (2.160), but this may be Cicero's way of indicating his own indebtedness to Aristotle. That indebtedness is not, however, complete. He has not included discussion of the enthymeme and the example. His account of ethos does not follow Aristotle; it is more influenced by Roman conditions and considers both the character of the patron and that of the client (2.182). Cicero regards ethos as consisting in presentation of the gentler emotions (2.183): it conciliates and charms the audience and is essentially good natured, a lower level of dramatic intensity than the raging fire of pathos, which is the real triumph of the speaker's art. The discussion of pathos (2.185–215) seems to have been based on observation of the actual practice of Antonius and Crassus. Like Aristotle, however, Cicero does discuss how to arouse or allay some specific passions: jealousy, for example (2.209–10).

The use of humor for rhetorical purposes is a tactic that Cicero frequently employed in his speeches and to a much greater extent than is found in other extant Greek and Latin oratory.[22] He mentions a number of ways in which humor is important to an orator (2.236):

> because it secures good will for him by whom it is aroused, or because all admire the sharpness inherent often in a single word, especially in replying to criticism and sometimes in attacking, or because it breaks the

---

[22] Quintilian (6.3.4) mentions a collection of Cicero's witticisms in three books, probably published by Cicero's secretary Tiro after the orator's death.

adversary or hinders or makes light of or discourages or refutes him, or ~~because it shows the orator himself is a man of culture, learned, sophisti-~~ cated; and most of all because it softens and relaxes seriousness and tension and by laughter often dissolves troublesome matters which could not easily be disposed of by arguments.

Cicero belittles Greek treatises on humor (2.217) but proceeds to divide up the subject along lines that resemble Greek theory as known from other sources.[23] In general, two kinds of humor were recognized by ancient theorists, one good natured and pervasive, the other caustic and intermittent. Cicero calls them *cavillatio* and *dicacitas* respectively (2.218). Humor was thought to be based on the unseemly or deformed, but within limits. Great wickedness or great misery were not appropriate subjects (2.236–37). The key to the use of humor was "propriety," which suggests a Peripatetic source. A more formal division was that into humor based on words and humor based on a fact, an action, or a thought. This distinction was easy for rhetoricians, since it paralleled their commonly made distinction between *verba* ("words, style") and *res* ("things, subject matter") and between figures of diction and figures of thought. Among later rhetoricians, only Quintilian (6.3) gives much attention to humor in rhetoric; his account is indebted to what Cicero says in *On the Orator*.

On the Orator is an important account of the ideal of the citizen-orator that dominated the culture of the Greco-Roman period, in contrast to the theological and scientific ideals of medieval and modern culture in the West, and was also an important statement of the need for a liberal education.[24] In the introduction to *On Invention* Cicero had made great claims for the orator, but the precepts of rhetoric that follow in that work largely obscured any grand concept. In *On the Orator* the inadequacy of rules is constantly stressed, almost too much so, perhaps, considering the debt of many portions of the work to rhetorical theory. Cicero was convinced from personal experience of the power and richness of oratory. It was to him a true art form, not in the sense of a science reducible to rule with predictable results, but in the sense of a product of the creative imagination, working with defined forms and materials. Cicero had a certain kind of imagination in a very strong form; he was never highly original in thought, always heavily

---

[23] In addition to the bibliography cited in my *Art of Rhetoric in the Roman World* 223, see Janko, *Aristotle on Comedy*. Janko provides (19–41) text and translation of the *Tractatus Coislinianus*, which outlines a theory of comedy and humor and may derive from the lost second book of Aristotle's *Poetics*. Theophrastus had also written a treatise on "the ludicrous"; see Fortenbaugh et al., *Theophrastus*, vol. 2, 557.

[24] See Bird, *Cultures in Conflict*, 11–24, and Kimball, *Orators and Philosophers* 12–42. *On the Orator* directly influenced Roman views until late antiquity but was not well known in the Middle Ages; the full text was rediscovered in the fifteenth century, it was the first book printed in Italy (1465), and its subsequent influence was considerable.

indebted to his predecessors, but he had an ability to see a larger picture and to maximize materials and opportunities. But *On the Orator* is not entirely satisfying. The dialogue form has some charm but covers up imprecision, for despite the extended speeches it resembles a real conversation in which people forget what they have said or change their views for the sake of argument or politeness and in which general agreement does not represent conviction so much as weariness or good manners. Moreover, the dramatic situation and the characterization are not really good enough to make the work stand as a purely literary achievement. One of the best speeches is that of Antonius in book 1, arguing that the orator needs only a rather superficial knowledge of philosophy or law. This is never adequately answered. In fact, Antonius only somewhat overstates what Crassus and most other Romans believed. Philosophy, Crassus says (3.79), does not take much knowledge; it is not like geometry or music but can be understood by any intelligent person, and he then makes the rather outrageous claim (3.79) that unless a person can learn a subject quickly he can never learn it at all. We see here that characteristic view of many Romans that it is good to know something about philosophy, and many other subjects, but not to become too deeply involved in its study or, like Cato the Younger, to become too extreme in applying its doctrines. Roman society encouraged a kind of deliberate, gentlemanly, superficiality of learning, or at least its affectation. *On the Orator* begins as a work intended, at least in part, to counteract superficiality and pedantry in rhetoric, but it ends by accepting such a view. Cicero also fails to consider the active and contemplative life as two aspects of the same person; it is, after all, the total man that needs liberal education. Another subject largely untouched in *On the Orator* is that of the moral responsibilities of a speaker, whether to himself or society. We know from his letters that Cicero agonized over these issues, and his later work *On Duties* takes them up, but he does not introduce them into the discussion in *On the Orator*.

Subsequently, perhaps between 54 and 52 B.C., Cicero wrote a very different, much shorter work on rhetoric, *Partitiones Oratoriae*, or *Classifications of Oratory*.[25] It is a rhetorical catechism, unrelieved by characterization, digression, or adornment, intended to provide his son with a Latin statement of the rhetorical theories of invention and arrangement he had been studying in Greek. Modern students have sometimes found it a convenient short introduction to the parts of the oration and stasis theory as understood in the first century B.C. In section 139 Cicero says that the oratorical "partitions" he has described derive from the teaching of the Academic philosophical school, to which he himself adhered. What he appears to mean is

[25] English translation by Rackham in the second volume of the Loeb Classical Library edition of *On the Orator*.

that an understanding of the process of logical definition and division as taught in Academic dialectic is fundamental to the method he has followed. There is little or nothing in the work that classifies it as a unique Academic view of rhetoric.

For Milo and Cicero's Later Speeches

Because of the prevailing political conditions and his opposition to those in power, Cicero only occasionally spoke in the law courts during the last ten years of his life. The triumvirate of Pompey, Caesar, and Crassus had been renewed in 54 B.C.; this was then followed from 49 to 45 by civil war between Caesar and Pompey, who unsuccessfully took up the cause of the senate; Caesar became dictator during the war and ruled until his assassination in March 44; Caesar's political heir, Mark Antony, and his personal heir, Octavian, who later became the emperor Augustus, then defeated the republican leaders Brutus and Cassius in a second civil war and together with Lepidus formed a second triumvirate, which proscribed Cicero and authorized his murder in December 43.

The most famous defense Cicero undertook during these years was that of Milo in 52. The dramatic and complex circumstances are described in a commentary on Cicero's speech For Milo written by Asconius a hundred years later.[26] Almost complete chaos reigned in Rome in the fall and winter of 53–52, and elections were repeatedly put off, so that the year 52 opened with no consuls in office. One candidate was T. Annius Milo, who had helped to bring Cicero back from exile in 57 and had become the leader of an armed band of thugs opposed to the triumvirs. Cicero's enemy Clodius was a candidate for praetor and the leader of another gang. Early in 52 Milo and company met Clodius and company more or less by accident on the Appian Way about ten miles southeast of Rome, a fight took place, and Clodius was killed. His followers treated him as a fallen martyr and cremated him in and with the senate house. The senate passed a *consultum ultimum* and called upon Pompey to restore order. Pompey had supported Clodius in the past and was now standing on the sidelines watching the collapse of constitutional authority with some satisfaction. He quickly accepted the position of sole consul offered him by the senate, an unprecedented position almost analogous to that of the later emperors, secured passage of new laws on violence and bribery, and set up a special court with streamlined procedures to deal with the recent lawlessness, including the action of Milo.

Cicero had to defend Milo under very limiting conditions. Instead of the usual opening speeches with their opportunity for generalization and ampli-

---

[26] Translation by Squires, *Orationium Ciceronis Quinque Enarratio*.

fication, the trial began with three days of evidence from witnesses, carefully recorded in the presence of a jury. Then on the fourth day a new jury of eighty-one members was summoned; they had not necessarily heard the evidence but presumably had access to it in written form. On the fifth day came the trial with speeches on each side, completed in one day.[27] The prosecution was allotted two hours, the defense three. Just before the vote, each side had the right to challenge fifteen jurors, leaving a total of fifty-one. In order to use the time to the best advantage, Cicero was the only speaker for Milo. Not only did he have only a short time to counteract specific sworn testimony, but he had to speak in the forum surrounded by armed men and with Pompey anxiously looking down from the steps of the temple of Saturn. Cicero was brought to the trial in a covered litter, was very nervous, and was repeatedly interrupted while speaking. Milo was convicted by a vote of thirty-eight to thirteen and sent into exile.

The speech Cicero delivered was never published. Instead, Cicero published a revised version—what he might have said under different conditions—which rhetoricians and modern critics have regarded as an almost perfect judicial speech.[28] According to Dio Cassius (40.54.3), when Milo received a copy he remarked with irony that it was just as well Cicero had not delivered it or he would never have had a chance to enjoy the seafood of Marseilles. The basic argument of the two speeches was probably much the same, but the arrangement and style were improved in the published version. Cicero's major challenge was to avoid offending Pompey and to persuade the jury, weary of civil unrest, that there was some possible justification for Milo's actions.

The speech begins with an exordium (1–6) dealing with the unprecedented conditions under which Cicero had to plead. The virtues of Pompey, as well as those of Milo and the madness of Clodius, are stressed. Then comes a refutation of three charges made by the opposition, which had aimed to show that Milo was so clearly guilty that a trial was hardly necessary (7–23). One charge was that Milo was an admitted murderer and thus deserved to die. Milo had not denied that Clodius was killed by his slave acting under his authority; Cicero seeks to establish the stasis as one of law rather than one of fact, claiming that Milo acted in self-defense. The other two charges were that the senate had judged Milo to have acted against the interests of the state and that Pompey had already judged the case by his law and procedures. Neither of these was legally valid, since the senate and Pompey were investigating a situation, not making judicial judgments. Next comes a brief narration (24–30), in which Cicero tries to show that Milo had not premeditated the encounter with Clodius: up to the point of their

[27] Tacitus (*Dialogus* 38) regarded Pompey's law as permanently changing the conditions of pleading, but only the imposition of a time limit seems to have been retained; under the empire evidence of witnesses followed the speeches of the patrons, as earlier (see Quintilian 5.7.25).

[28] See Donnelly, *Cicero's Milo*, and May, *Trials of Character*, 128–40.

meeting each other, it was an ordinary, relaxed day in Milo's life. Most famous is the picture of Milo going home from the senate, changing his clothes, and sitting waiting for his wife, "as happens to us all" (28). Then comes Cicero's statement of the crucial question "Which laid a plot for which?" (30–31) and the "proof" (32–91) that it was not in Milo's interests to do so and that the circumstances of time and place made it improbable that he had actually done so. All of this is admirably worked out along the lines taught in the rhetorical schools. The emotional element in the speech becomes increasingly strong, culminating in the peroration (92–105).

Quintilian (6.5.10) did not know what to praise most about Cicero's speech *For Milo*. He mentions specifically the placement of refutation before narration, the way Clodius is shown to have been the aggressor, the combination of the plea that Milo did not intend murder with Cicero's approval of Clodius' death, and the use of an emotional plea by Cicero in place of any demonstration of pathos by Milo himself. The stasis of the speech always interested rhetoricians. Cicero could not deny the fact that Clodius was killed by Milo's slave, for which Milo was responsible. He had, however, the choice of two arguments: the legal one that the action was justifiable homicide in self-defense, or the qualitative one that the action, even if deliberate, was in the national interest. Brutus, always attracted by grand gestures, favored using the latter and wrote a speech to show how it should have been done (Quintilian 3.6.93). The argument would not have been legally valid; it would have had hope of success only in circumstances in which Cicero could have dominated the court with emotional power, and this he could not do. He makes it clear that he regards Clodius' death as a good thing, but he does not try to save Milo with that argument. Cicero was selective in his choice of material for the speech. He says as little as possible about Pompey's new law against violence; it was occasioned by Milo's actions and could only prejudice his case. There was, apparently, no specific provision for killing in self-defense in Roman law, and Cicero has to deduce it from the right to bear arms in self-defense. There is also a good deal of selecting and coloring in the picture of Milo, whose patriotism and other virtues have not been so evident to historians.

Cicero was initially ambivalent during the early stages of the civil war between Caesar and Pompey. He felt that Caesar's actions were clearly unconstitutional but had less than complete confidence in Pompey as a defender of the constitution and the senate. In March 49 he wrote his friend Atticus a letter (9.4) that gives a glimpse of one role declamation could play in Roman life:

> In order not to give in entirely to depression, I have taken up certain so-called "theses," which are both of a political nature and appropriate to the times, that I may keep my mind from complaints and practice myself in the subject proposed. They are of this sort [he gives the list in Greek]:

whether you should remain in your country when it is ruled by a tyrant; whether you should by every means bring down a tyranny, even if the state will be generally endangered; whether you should be on guard against letting one [e.g., Pompey] who abolishes tyranny rise too high himself; whether you should try to help the state under a tyrant by the right word at the right time rather than by war; whether retiring somewhere and keeping quiet is politically justifiable under a tyranny or whether you should go through every danger for the sake of liberty; whether war should be waged against a place and siege laid when a tyranny rules it; whether, even if you do not approve of overthowing tyranny by war, you ought yet to enroll yourself among the constitutionalists; whether in politics you should share the danger of benefactors and friends even if their overall policy does not seem right; whether a man who has served his country greatly [e.g., Cicero himself], but because of this has suffered irremediably and been envied, should face danger willingly for his country or should at some point think of himself and his family and abandon political action against those in power.

Practicing myself on these propositions and speaking on both sides of the question, now in Greek, now in Latin, I both divert my mind for a bit from my troubles and deliberate about a relevant problem.

Cicero eventually decided to join Pompey. After the latter's defeat at Pharsalus in 48 B.C., Cicero returned to Italy; he eventually received pardon from Caesar and returned to Rome. He did not take much part in public affairs, but we do have three speeches he addressed to Caesar.[29] They had been friends in the past and were never personal enemies; Cicero consistently opposed Caesar's politics and policies, but consistently admired his intelligence, shared many of his personal interests, and came to respect his humanity and clemency toward opponents. *For Marcellus* was delivered in the senate to thank Caesar for pardoning a stubborn old aristocrat. It is not a defense of Marcellus but a panegyric of Caesar, and thus of all Cicero's speeches the closest to epideictic oratory. Like many good panegyrics it tries to influence the future by selected praise of the past. Caesar, Cicero says, must give the state stability, which requires a constitutional basis. Among the most striking passages is one (29) in which Cicero calls on Caesar to consider the verdict of history. A much cleverer speech is *For Ligarius*; Ligarius was another member of the senatorial party still in exile whose case was brought before Caesar as sole judge. In Plutarch's life of Cicero (39) there is a memorable description of the trial, in which Caesar asks his friends, "What harm in hearing Cicero speak after so long a time, since the accused has long ago been judged a wicked man and an enemy?" But Caesar was in for a surprise and was thoroughly moved by the speech, turning pale,

[29] See Gotoff, *Cicero's Caesarian Speeches.*

shaking at mention of Pharsalus, dropping his papers while Cicero spoke. At the end, "He was forced to acquit the man of the charge." The speech thus came to be viewed as a signal triumph of pure eloquence. It is exceedingly clever, a delight to read, though there remain questions about the extent to which the occasion may have been staged with Caesar's cooperation.[30] A third speech to Caesar is *For King Deiotarus*. The case was tried in Caesar's own house, a custom many of the emperors later followed, to the disadvantage of orators. Apparently Caesar never got around to making a decision before his death. After Caesar's death and before Antony, Octavian, and Lepidus had firmly secured power came the series of deliberative orations known as the *Philippics*, consciously modeled on Demosthenes' speeches against Philip of Macedon. The *Second Philippic*, with its violent invective against Antony, is the most famous.[31]

Brutus and *Orator*

It is ironic but not entirely surprising that the first major treatises on Roman rhetoric, *On the Orator*, *Brutus*, and *Orator*, were written at a time when Roman public address was being checked. In the 50s and 40s B.C. there was enforced leisure among orators in Rome and with it a concern about the potential role of the orator.

Cicero's vision of the statesman-orator in *On the Orator* is presented as controversial, and reaction to it might be expected. The kind of oratory Cicero approved and practiced—amplified in content, rich in style, open to ethical and pathetical appeals—belonged to a tradition to which Galba, Crassus, and Hortensius may earlier be assigned. There was, however, also a continuing tradition of preference for a simple or plain style, seen in what we know of speeches by Cato the Elder, Rutilius Rufus, Brutus, Calvus, and Julius Caesar. Roman awareness of the study of language by Greek grammarians and Stoic philosophers gradually converted this older tradition from a blunt straightforwardness in treatment of the subject to a search for purity of diction (*Latinitas*). The orator of the plain style was not necessarily unemotional, but he expressed his emotion by choice of forceful words and vigorous delivery, not by the number of words, the piling up of clauses, or other kinds of amplification. The orator of the plain style regarded verbosity as diluting rather than intensifying communication; the orator of the grand style thought emotion should be fed a rich diet to develop its strength to the full.

Connected with the interest in pure Latinity was the grammatical move-

[30] See my *Art of Rhetoric in the Roman World*, 260–64; May, *Trials of Character*, 140–48; Montague, "Paradox of Cicero's *Pro Ligario*."

[31] See my *Art of Rhetoric in the Roman World*, 268–82, and Wooten, *Cicero's Philippics*.

ment called "analogy," mentioned in chapter 5. This is the preference for regularity in grammatical forms, taught by the Stoic school at Pergamum and brought to Rome in the mid–first century. Its opposite was "anomaly," the acceptance of irregularity as developed in common use, the doctrine taught in Alexandria. Julius Caesar wrote a treatise entitled *On Analogy*, applying Greek doctrine to Latin. It seems likely that the work was at least in part a reaction to the rather slighting treatment of purity and clarity in Cicero's *On the Orator* (3.48–49). We do not know the exact time of composition, but Caesar wrote it during one of his passages over the Alps on return to Gaul from Italy (Suetonius, *Julius* 56.5). It was dedicated to Cicero and dealt broadly with the principles of speaking Latin accurately. In the introduction Caesar addressed Cicero in the following words: "If some men have labored with study and practice to be able to express their thoughts with distinction—and here we must recognize your contribution to the fame and dignity of the Roman people as a kind of leader and inventor of richness—should we as a result regard knowledge of simple and familiar language as something to be left aside?" (*Brutus* 253). The pure, clear style Caesar favored is seen in his commentaries on the Gallic and Civil Wars and appeared also in his oratory (*Brutus* 252).

Another movement with which Latinity and anology became involved was "Atticism," the pursuit of allegedly Attic Greek standards of purity and grace. Among the Greeks of the first century this was a reaction against stylistic developments of the Hellenistic period, Asianism at one extreme and the simplified Koine, or vernacular, at the other. We hear about Greek Atticism first from Dionysius of Halicarnassus,[32] whose rhetorical works were written in the generation after Cicero's death, but Dionysius, in the introduction to his study *On the Ancient Orators*, claims that the reform in style, especially in diction, had begun somewhat earlier and was by his time almost victorious. He attributes this reform to Roman influence. Modern attempts to identify a Greek source in the second or early first century have proved unsuccessful. Cicero had not heard of Atticism when he wrote *On the Orator* in 55 and never alludes to any Greek source for the movement. Thus it seems possible to regard Atticism as something developed first in Rome in the period around 50 B.C. with increased study of classical Greek models of prose in rhetorical schools. If so, it is one of the relatively few instances of Roman influence on Greek rhetoric and literature.

The most interesting aspect of Atticism is its tendency toward classicism. As adopted in Greek, Atticism rejected two hundred years of language and

---

[32] Demetrius' treatise *On Style*, perhaps a work of the early first century, shows the potential for Atticism among Greek teachers but uses the term "Attic" (e.g., sections 175 and 177) to refer to the Attic dialect rather than to a new movement in style, and it is not as strictly classicizing as is Dionysius.

literature and saw the standard of language, composition, and rhetoric in the achievements of the fourth century B.C., especially in the speeches of the Attic orators.[33] "Imitation" became the road to literary excellence. The result was often rather sterile; there is, in fact, little first-rate literature in Greek for several centuries, though there are works of learning important for their contents. The imitation of Greek models in Latin was for some time a more creative process, since it brought into the literature new ideas and a new standard of excellence. Virgil, Horace, Propertius, Ovid, and others imitate Greek originals, but in doing so experiment with the possibilities of Latin and incorporate Roman themes in a new synthesis and with new perspectives. Latin writers, of course, could not utilize Attic Greek; they sought to create a counterpart to classical styles in their own language. A few, however, the historian Sallust among them, took the Latin of the second century as a linguistic counterpart to Attic Greek and thus introduced an archaic flavor into their writing.

Cicero's principal literary antagonists, in addition to Caesar, were Calvus and Brutus. He carried on a correspondence, now lost, with Calvus and Brutus on the subject of style. Tacitus (*Dialogus* 18) later sums it up as showing that to Cicero, Calvus seemed "bloodless and dry," Brutus "tedious and disjointed," while Calvus called Cicero's style "formless and flabby" and Brutus found it "pulpy and out of joint." Note the use of physiological metaphors in describing style, a characteristic of ancient criticism.

Cicero's dialogue *Brutus*, written in 48 B.C. when he was largely withdrawn from public life, is a discussion of the history of Greek and Roman oratory in a dialogue among Cicero, Brutus, and Cicero's friend Atticus, culminating in a consideration of contemporary conditions and the Atticism movement. The style of Calvus, Cicero says (*Brutus* 283–84), was carefully worked; he spoke with elegance, but was excessively self-critical, and the result was a loss of vitality. Brutus responds that Calvus liked to be called "Attic," and that was why he purposely aimed at this thin or meager style. The remark suggests that Brutus would not call himself an Atticist, but elsewhere (*To Atticus* 15.1a.2) Cicero treats Brutus as an Atticist. Here he goes on to represent Calvus as misled by his own theories and as not appreciating the variety of the Attic orators. Cicero's response to Roman Atticism was to redefine the term: "Attic" should not be taken to mean imitation only of the plain style of Lysias; it equally includes the smooth style of Isocrates, the varied style of Hyperides, and the forceful style of De-

[33] Classicism can be said to have begun with the work of the Alexandrian grammarians of the third century who edited and commented on archaic and classical Greek poetry and produced "canons" of classical texts to be studied as literary models. Their interests, however, were largely limited to poetry, and classicism in Greek prose does not appear before the first century.

mosthenes (289), which by this time had become Cicero's favored model among the Greeks.[34] "All who speak well speak in the Attic style" (291). A result of Cicero's tactics is that "Attic" was often used by later writers in a rather general sense to describe any admired, disciplined prose style, while "Asian" often means any style perceived as inflated and faulty.[35]

Brutus[36] opens with a a prologue in memory of Hortensius, whose style had been closer to what Cicero admired than was that of the Atticists. It is not, however, his eloquence that is stressed here so much as his good fortune in dying in 50 B.C., before opportunities for great oratory were checked under the rule of Caesar. He is repeatedly referred to throughout the dialogue, and his oratory is discussed in some detail at the end, where he is called an Asianist (325) and where Cicero explains the meaning of that term, as quoted in chapter 5. Hortensius thus becomes a unifying rhetorical and political symbol throughout the work.

After the introduction comes (10–24) a description of the circumstances of the dialogue, which represents a conversation among Cicero, Brutus, and Atticus while waiting for news about Caesar's war in Africa early in 46 B.C. Cicero dedicates the work to Brutus in return for Brutus' literary epistle *On Virtue*, which had been dedicated to Cicero. Dedication of another work to Atticus is promised in return for his treatise on Roman chronology, inspired in turn by Cicero's work *On the Republic*. Atticus' treatise suggested and facilitated Cicero's study of the history of Roman oratory.

There follows a brief review of the history of Greek oratory (25–52), rather like a narration in a speech. Eloquence is said to have reached full development in Greece later than the other arts. Its history is marked by stages of development: Pericles was the first really great orator and the earliest to have been influenced by theory, for which relative peace was necessary. The high point of Greek oratory came in the fourth century with Isocrates, who was the first to pay attention to rhythm, and especially with Demosthenes (35). In the Hellenistic period, eloquence sailed to Asia, where its style was corrupted, and then to Rhodes. The main body of the work, discussing Roman orators, proceeds by generations, discussing consular orators first in each section, then lesser figures. The first Roman definitely known to have been eloquent, Cicero says (57), was M. Cornelius

---

[34] Cicero's special admiration of Demosthenes is a feature only of his later writing and speaking, including his *Philippic* orations; see Wooten, *Cicero's Philippics*, 46–57.

[35] In the sixteenth and seventeenth centuries "Attic" is used by Justus Lipsius and others of the reaction against Ciceronianism in style, for which Seneca and Tacitus are taken as Latin models. See Kennedy, *Classical Rhetoric*, 213–15.

[36] Latin text and English commentary by Douglas, *Ciceronis Brutus*; English translation by Hendrickson in the Loeb Classical Library series. On *Brutus* and *Orator* as works of literary criticism, see Fantham, "Growth of Literature and Criticism at Rome," 235–41.

Cethegus, consul in 204 B.C. The first orator whose speeches are worth reading is Cato the Elder, but his style is not sufficiently polished (69). A richer style begins with Sulpicius Gallus, but the first Roman to wield the legitimate tools of the orator, to digress, to delight, to move, to amplify, to employ pathos and commonplaces, was Galba (82). A new high point came with Gaius Gracchus, outstanding for native ability, dedication, and learning (125). At last, in Antonius and Crassus, Latin oratory attained something approaching the level of Demosthenes and Hyperides (138). There are, Cicero admits (201), two kinds of good orators, "those speaking simply and succinctly, and those grandly and amply," but "that is better which is more splendid and magnificent." Purity of diction is a negative virtue: "it is not such a wonderful thing to know good Latin as it is shameful not to know it" (213–14). In section 279 Cicero turns to consideration of Hortensius as the leading orator of the period after Crassus and Antonius, and this allows him to work in the account of his own rhetorical studies and development (304–19), on which the summary at the beginning of this chapter is largely based. Cicero himself thus emerges by implication as the highest point yet reached in the history of oratory at Rome. Though his ambition is clear from the beginning, what he says about himself recognizes that he could not have done what he did if others had not gone before him, acknowledges his early faults and problems, and stops with the trial of Verres, in which he defeated Hortensius.

The chronological sequence of *Brutus* is varied by carefully placed digressions that relate to the Atticism controversy. One digression (183–200) is placed at the midpoint of the book and deals with how oratory should be judged, whether by esoteric literary standards, as the Atticists were doing, or by popular effectiveness, as Cicero reasonably demands. The three functions of the orator, identified earlier in *On the Orator* (2.115), are here (185) taken up in the form "that the hearer be taught, be delighted, and be strongly moved." Two other digressions are closely connected and balanced. The first (70–76) comes early in the account of Roman oratory and after reference to its first great practitioner, the elder Cato. Cicero here compares the historical development of oratory to that of sculpture and painting, with reference also to the history of poetry. The objective of the digression is to suggest that Cato should be viewed as a Roman counterpart to Lysias, though the Atticists ignore him. Balancing this is a third digression (292–300), in which Atticus is allowed to ridicule Cicero's glorification of early Roman orators, including the assertion that Cato was a Roman Lysias. Cicero sticks to his guns, but the digression adds liveliness to the dialogue and shows that he did not mean his claim to be taken too literally. *Brutus* is one of Cicero's more carefully written works; he seems to have sought a prose style that would be approved by his opponents.

A second work dedicated to Brutus is the treatise known as the *Orator*,[37] written soon after *Brutus*. Cicero here abandons the dialogue form to give an account of the style of oratory he most admires. Although there is considerable repetition in the work, an overall plan is easily recognized. An introductory section (1–36) deals with the purpose of the work: to describe an ideal orator beyond any who has ever lived. Cicero uses the Platonic forms to help explain what he has in mind. He goes on to expound the doctrine, met earlier in *Rhetoric for Herennius*, that there are three good styles, not one. The perfect orator should master all (20); no Roman has done so, and among the Greeks only Demosthenes comes close (23). Then the errors of the Atticists are revealed (28–32). Their definition of Attic is too narrow, and those who adopt Thucydides or Xenophon as models do not even imitate orators.[38]

The second part of the work (37–139) is a rather uneven survey of rhetorical theory, not unlike that given by Antonius and Crassus in the second and third books of *On the Orator*. The usual categories and topics are there: the kinds of oratory and the parts of rhetoric with some discussion of each, but Cicero elaborates only what is relevant for the picture of the orator he wishes to construct, defined (69) as "one who can speak in the forum [i.e., in courts of law] or on public questions in such a way that he proves, delights, and stirs his audience." We meet here again the three functions of the orator. In the picture of this man it is style that is most fully discussed, using the Theophrastan categores of the virtues of style (79). Propriety will determine what style to use: the plain style (75–90) avoids rhythm and periodicity and has no objection to hiatus. Its ornamentation should not be noticeable. A distinctive feature should be use of wit. The middle style as described (91–96) is really that of Isocrates, though he is not named and Demetrius of Phaleron is made the example. It has little vigor but much smoothness and ornamentation. The grand style (97–99) is full, rich, stately, elaborate and powerful, but it needs to be varied with the other styles, and unless skillfully managed it can fall flat. Though Cicero insists on the necessity of combining styles in a single speech (74), he confusingly persists in speaking of the middle or grand orator (e.g., 98–99). He cites examples of each style and of varied styles from his own speeches (102–8). Then, as in *On the Orator*, the knowledge needed by the speaker is discussed (113–20), including logic and other parts of philosophy, law, and history. Here is inserted (121–39) a dry summary of rhetorical rules for invention, partition, and style, which goes over some of the ground already covered.

The first two parts of the *Orator* are preparatory for what follows. Cicero

---

[37] English commentary by Sandys, *Ad Brutum Orator*; translation by Hubbell in the Loeb Classical Library volume with Hendrickson's translation of *Brutus*.

[38] The Roman writers known to us of whom this might be said are the historians Sallust and Asinius Pollio, both writing somewhat later. See Leeman, *Orationis Ratio*, 136–67.

repeatedly indicates that what is most important and most difficult is still to come (e.g., 51, 61, 75, 100, 134). The third part (140-238) is a very full discussion of the aspect of style most neglected by the Atticists, composition. This is introduced by an apology aimed at counteracting contempt for teaching rhetoric: "Why is it shameful to learn what it is honorable to understand, or why is it not glorious to teach what is most becoming to know?" (142). The basis of what Cicero says is derived from Isocrates, Aristotle, and Theophrastus, but he has applied Greek theories to Latin and has much more to say about prose rhythm than any earlier author (174). Into the discussion of the collocation of words is inserted an attack on the analogists (155–62). The account of the periodic sentence recognizes two forms, that in which the grammatical structure gives the balanced rounding or completeness, for example an antithesis, and that in which, quite appart from the meaning, the rhythm of the words achieves a form that is complete because satisfying to the ear. The discussion of rhythm (168–216) is the most detailed part of the work. It begins with an introduction (168–73), followed by a division of the subject (174). The origin, cause, nature, and use of rhythm are successively handled, and examples of the effect of rearranging words and thus breaking up the rhythm are given (232–33). There should not be complete lines of verse nor usually a succession of similar feet, but combinations of different feet are needed. Cicero praises combinations of cretic, paeon, and spondee with iamb, tribrach, and dactyl, but some of these are not common features of his own style. A discussion of the utility of rhythm is then added (227–36). At the end of the work Cicero does not seem particularly optimistic about his success in convincing Brutus of the superiority of his conception of styles, and we know from a letter to Atticus (14.20.3) that he did not succeed. Cicero failed to convince Brutus because of Brutus' personal tastes, not because he failed to make a good case. Surely Lysias, Thucydides, and Xenophon were not the best models for imitation at the Roman bar. Surely the best orator should be a master of all styles and know how to employ each. In stating his case Cicero has neatly, and apparently with originality, combined the three functions of the orator with the three kinds of style: the plain style is best for proof, the middle style for delighting, the vehement style for moving the passions (69).

In addition to the works already discussed there are other minor works by Cicero relating to aspects of rhetoric. *On the Best Kind of Orators* is an introduction to a projected, but apparently never completed, translation of Aeschines' and Demosthenes' speeches in the case of Ctesiphon. *Topics*, written in the summer of 44 B.C., is an exposition of the topics of argument (genus, species, similarity, and so forth) as taught in Peripatetic dialectic, to which are added notes on stasis theory and other aspects of rhetorical invention.

In the years 45 and 44 B.C. Cicero wrote a series of works, chiefly in dialogue form, that provided introductions to Hellenistic Greek philosophy for Roman readers. On abstruse subjects he tends to follow the Academic custom of letting others expound different sides of a question and avoiding much expression of his own views. Cicero is no less a rhetorician when he is a philosopher, and behind his pose of suspending judgment there lies a desire to persuade, and perhaps especially to persuade himself of the truth and consolation to be found in philosophy. Of all the philosophical works the one most closely related to rhetoric is the last, *On Duties*, which is a systematic exposition of ethics, not a dialogue, and largely based on a work by the Greek Stoic philosopher Panaetius.[39]

Cicero's career was spread over about forty years, and some changes and development in his theory and practice of rhetoric were to be expected. *On Invention* is purely a work of school learning. It was supplanted by *On the Orator*, the thoughtful outgrowth of his own experience and wider study. Changes from that work to *Brutus* and *Orator* are not fundamental ones. Indeed, Cicero never changed his basic view of the orator. His interest in styles, however, seems to have increased as his opportunities for persuasion were curtailed and as new issues were raised by the Atticists. Cicero put a distinctive personal stamp on classical rhetoric, and his orations and writings on rhetoric have remained classics ever since; it is not an overstatement to say that the history of rhetoric in western Europe from his time to at least the seventeenth century is the history of Ciceronianism.

[39] See discussion in chapter 5 above and in my *Art of Rhetoric in the Roman World*, 264–68.

Rhetoric in Augustan Rome

The victory of Caesar's heir, Octavian, over Antony at the Battle of Actium in September 31 B.C. marked the end of the Roman republic and the beginning of the empire. In 27 Octavian took the title "Augustus," under which he reigned until his death in A.D. 14. Although not a distinguished public speaker, he had a profound understanding of the rhetoric of empire. A variety of republican titles and religious forms were used to mask the reality of his power; art, architecture, inscriptions, and urban planning conveyed the aura of a new golden age; and support was given to writers, who in turn were expected to celebrate the achievements of the emperor and the legitimacy of his rule. Yet criticism of the age, within limits, was tolerated and is often present in the writings of its greatest poets, Virgil and Horace. Virgil's *Georgics* and *Aeneid* and many of the *Odes* of Horace, for example, celebrate the greatness of Rome, but with regret for the violence that has accompanied it and with implicit warnings of dangers to come. The greatest prose work of the period, Livy's *History of Rome*, celebrates the republic's origins and military achievements but views its recent history as a moral decline.

Throughout the Greco-Roman period there is no clear differentiation between literary criticism and rhetorical theory.[1] In formal education the teaching and criticism of poetry was the province of grammarians, but they also taught prose composition and introduced students to rhetorical techniques. The whole subject of style, and in particular the use of tropes and figures, was of interest to both grammarians and rhetoricians, and rhetoricians often cited examples of rhetorical techniques from poets. In Rome, the teaching of declamation became the obsession of the rhetorical schools in the early empire, often to the exclusion of literary interests; Greek rhetoricians put more emphasis on the study and imitation of classical literary texts, both poetry and prose, and some—Demetrius earlier, Dionysius of Halicarnassus in the Augustan period, and Longinus later—wrote treatises that deserve to be called literary criticism. The only real examples of literary criticism in Latin from the Augustan period are the *Epistles* of Horace, including the *Art of Poetry*. His discussions of word choice, composition, characterization, and some other subjects show an indebtedness to contemporary rhetorical teaching. Stoic philosophers continued their interest in

---

[1] On the relation between literary criticism and rhetoric in the Augustan period, see my *Art of Rhetoric in the Roman World*, 384–419, and Innes, "Augustan Critics."

applying allegorical criticism to uncover meanings congenial to their doctrines in poetic texts. The most important surviving example from the early empire is the work known as the *Homeric Allegories* of Heraclitus.[2]

Greek Rhetoricians of the Second Half of the First Century B.C.

We know the names of several Greek teachers of rhetoric from this period, especially those who were attracted to Rome, in a few cases we have glimpses of their teaching, and we have extensive writings by one, Dionysius of Halicarnassus. Rhetorical schools continued to flourish in Greek cities, but relatively little is known about them. Cicero's son studied rhetoric in Athens with a certain Gorgias, who wrote a work on figures of speech that survives in a Latin translation by Rutilius Lupus and shows rather Asian taste in style.[3] Apollodorus of Pergamum was selected by Julius Caesar to teach rhetoric to Octavian in 45 B.C. There are references by Quintilian and other later writers to the continued existence of an "Apollodorean" school, characterized by inflexible rules for the structure of a judicial oration. His younger contemporary, Theodorus of Gadara, was the teacher of the future emperor Tiberius and founder of a competing school of "Theodoreans," more flexible on some matters, equally pedantic on others.[4] A third teacher of importance was Caecilius of Calacte; his numerous works on style were influential and are a major loss in reconstructing the history of rhetoric. Titles known from the Byzantine encyclopedia *Souda* clearly show his interest in Atticism: for example, *How the Attic Style Differs from the Asian* and a lexicon called *Against the Phrygians* (i.e., Asianists). His Atticism was apparently radical, for he argued that Lysias was a superior writer to Plato (Longinus 32). *On the Character of the Ten Orators* may have been the first work to establish the canon of the "ten Attic orators." He was also author of a work on sublimity, criticized by the author we know as Longinus in his extant work on the subject as taking a narrow view of the topic. It did not discuss pathos and probably was largely devoted to dicussion of word choice and figures of speech. Another treatise in which he classified, named, and illustrated figures of speech was apparently a standard work. According to Quintilian (9.1.10–13), there was an ongoing debate among rhetoricians as to whether all language was in some sense "figured." Apollodorus, Dionysius, and the unknown author of chapter 9 in a rhetorical handbook falsely attributed to Dionysius seem to have thought all language was figured, as do many modern critics. Caecilius' position, perhaps influenced by

---

[2] Edited with French translation by Buffière, *Héraclite*; see Russell, "Greek Criticism of the Empire," 320–22.

[3] Text in Halm, *Rhetores Latini Minores*, 3–21.

[4] See Granatelli, *Apollodori Pergameni ac Theodori Gadarei Testimonia et Fragmenta*, and Grube, "Theodorus of Gadara."

Stoic language theory, apparently was that plain, unfigured language could and did exist and that a figure (*schēma*) was "a turning to a form of thought and diction which is not in accordance with nature."[5]

Dionysius of Halicarnassus

In the introduction to his *Roman Antiquities*, a history of early Rome, Dionysius says that he came to the city about 30 B.C., had lived there for twenty-two years, learned Latin, and knew many of the learned men of the time. It is likely that he had taught rhetoric earlier in Halicarnassus or Athens and that he became the private tutor of rhetoric to sons of various Roman aristocrats. *On Literary Composition* is dedicated to a young man named Metilius Rufus as a birthday tribute and refers to their daily exercises together. His historical work he calls "the monument of my soul" (1.1.2) and should probably be viewed as the occupation of leisure hours, intended to be a literary masterpiece. Although it preserves some valuable information derived from earlier sources, it is chiefly remarkable as an example of rhetorical amplification in historiography. There are numerous vivid descriptions and long, elaborate speeches attributed to early Romans, written in the style of prosopopoeiae practiced in grammar and rhetoric schools.

The surviving rhetorical treatises of Dionysius were written in Rome between 29 and 10 B.C. The essays on Lysias, Isocrates, and Isaeus are probably the earliest; an introduction was then added to them to create the beginning of a work entitled *On the Attic Orators*. The first *Letter to Ammaeus* probably dates from about the same time. Dionysius later began a fourth essay, *On Demosthenes*, but before completing it wrote the treatise *On Literary Composition*. The first two books of the treatise *On Imitation* and the *Letter to Pompeius* were probably also written in this period. The essay *On Thucydides*, the second *Letter to Ammaeus*, and *On Dinarchus* were written later.[6] The *Art of Rhetoric* that carries Dionysius' name is wrongly ascribed to him and was probably written in the second century after Christ; it will be discussed in chapter 10. Dionysius' overall objective as a writer on rhetoric was to reestablish Attic standards of style in diction and composition by imitating classical Greek writers in oratory and historiography. Like Cicero,[7] he saw an historical development in artistic prose from the fifth to the

---

[5] See the quotation by Phoebammon in Spengel, *Rhetores Graeci*, vol. 3, 44.

[6] There is now a translation, by Usher, of all these works except the fragmentary treatise *On Imitation* in the Loeb Classical Library series. *The Three Literary Letters* and *On Literary Composition* were translated earlier, with commentary, by Roberts. There is a translation of *On Thucydides*, with commentary, by Pritchett. The order of composition listed above is that proposed by Usher, vol. 1, xxiii–xxvi.

[7] Living in Rome, Dionysius may well have had some knowledge of Cicero's rhetorical works; he does not refer to them, but such reference would not be expected when writing for a Greek audience.

fourth century, culminating in the work of Demosthenes, and recognized a variety of styles all equally "Attic." He shows no knowledge of an established canon of ten orators; instead, he seems to establish his own canon of the models that will most repay study. In the course of his research he faced the necessity of judging what works were genuine, what spurious, and the influence of one writer on another. Dionysius' interests are predominantly in style, the various kinds—for which his usual word is *charactēres*—and virtues to be imitated in composition, but he also discusses the orators' treatment of subject matter, the topics they employ in different parts of a speech, and their use of ethos and pathos; he does not discuss stasis theory or declamation.

The introduction to *On the Ancient Orators* provides the best information about Dionysius' attitude to the issue of Atticism. He says that after the death of Alexander (323 B.C.) "ancient and philosophical rhetoric" was "scorned and subjected to insult." It was replaced by something theatrical and ignorant, which he develops in a metaphor of the rejection of an Attic wife for an Asian mistress. He claims, however, that in his own age a reaction has set in; possibly this is an act of God or the operation of a natural cycle, or possibly it comes from an intelligent human impulse. Orators and writers are again "conscious of philosophy," and only in Asia does the tasteless style linger on. He attributes much of the responsibility for improvement to the influence of the virtuous and responsible rulers of Rome, men of education and judgment, whose "commendation has encouraged the intellectual element in every city and has forced the ignorant to learn sense." He himself wishes to strengthen this new eloquence with an evaluation of the ancient orators and historians and their characteristics, which should be useful to "persons practicising political philosophy." Thus he plans a comparative account of three older orators, Lysias, Isocrates, and Isaeus (already written) and then orators of the next generation, Demosthenes, Hyperides, and Aeschines. In the beginning of the later essay *On Dinarchus* he labels Lysias, Isocrates, and Isaeus the "inventors" and Demosthenes, Hyperides, and Aeschines the "perfectors" of style, but so far as we know he never wrote the essays on Hyperides and Aeschines. He seems to use "philosophy" and "philosophical" somewhat in the sense in which Isocrates used it: a serious, disciplined responsibility to express the traditional society and culture of Greece. The word does not refer to the teachings of any particular philosophical school.

The essay on Lysias is divided into four parts: Lysias' life (chapter 1); the "virtues" of his style (2–14); his treatment of the subject matter in each part of an oration (15–19); and examples of his writing, with some analysis. The essay on Isocrates was apparently intended to follow a similar scheme, but less attention is given to style and more to subject matter in terms of moral and philosophical issues, and a section is inserted on criticisms of Isocrates.

The essay on Isaeus follows the same basic plan, though much comparison of Isaeus with Lysias is inserted. In these essays Dionysius follows the concept of virtues set out originally by Theophrastus and somewhat modified by Hellenistic writers: the style of Lysias and Isocrates has purity, propriety, and clarity, and that of Lysias has brevity as well.

In considering Lysias' treatment of the subject matter, Dionysius cites the requirements set forth in rhetorical handbooks and shows how Lysias conforms to these. Study of Isocrates, however, can instill philosophical eloquence, and those who give attention to it can become not only good speakers but noble in character and useful to family, city, and all of Greece. Study of particular passages in Isocrates will help to develop patriotism, nobility, justice, reverence, eloquence, and persuasive power. The short essay on Isaeus is of interest for its critical method. Dionysius wants to distinguish the style of Isaeus from the rather similar style of Lysias. He does this by taking up specific qualities common to both, illustrating and distinguishing them by quoting from similar contexts. The essential difference that emerges is the greater artificiality of Isaeus' style and thought. Usually Dionysius assumes that his feeling for particular passages will be shared immediately by readers, but twice (7 and 11) he takes the additional step of rewriting sentences to illustrate the effect of the composition. This procedure, sometimes called *metathesis*, is followed also occasionally in his other works. *On Isaeus* ends with a note on why discussion of other orators has been omitted from Dionysius' plan. He has taken Isocrates, he says, as the best example of poetic adornment and what is elevated and impressive and has thus omitted both his predecessors, Gorgias, Alcidamas, and Theodorus, and his contemporaries or successors, Anaximenes, Theodectes, Theopompus, Naucrates, Ephorus, Philiscus, and Cephisodorus. Similarly, Lysias is superior to Antiphon, Thrasymachus, Polycrates, Critias, and Zoilus among those who aim at exactness of word and practical oratory.

The first *Letter to Ammaeus* is a refutation of the claim of an unnamed Peripatetic that Demosthenes owed his knowledge of rhetoric to Aristotle.[8] Dionysius assumes that what is meant is that Demosthenes had read *On Rhetoric*, not that Demosthenes had attended lectures by Aristotle; thus he relies on the argument that historical references in *On Rhetoric* show it to have been written after most of Demosthenes' speeches had been delivered.

Only a portion of the treatise *On Imitation* has been preserved.[9] One fragment offers a definition of rhetoric as "an artistic faculty of persuasive speech on a political matter, having the goal of speaking well." Aristotle's definition is here expanded to specify civic discourse, and Quintilian's defi-

---

[8] Possibly the Peripatetic in question was Andronicus of Rhodes, who first published *On Rhetoric* earlier in the first century.

[9] The Greek text is in Usener and Radermacher, *Dionysii*, vol. 6, pt. 2, 197–217.

nition of rhetoric as "the science of speaking well" is anticipated. Another fragment defines "imitation" (*mimēsis*) as "an activity receiving an impression of a model through inspection of it," while "emulation" (*zēlos*) is "an activity of the soul moved toward admiration of what seems fine." The remaining parts of book 1 and the epitome of book 2 make clear, what Quintilian also teaches (10.2), that imitation as understood by rhetoricians was not a matter of copying the mannerisms of a classical writer but of understanding the special qualities of writers and producing a counterpart to them on different subjects; also that exclusive imitation of a single model, however great, was not adequate to produce excellence in style. Dionysius then gives a survey of Greek literature, both poetry and prose, which should be studied to attain full control of style. Quintilian probably drew on this in his similar survey.

Chapter 3 of *On Imitation* offers a somewhat different account of the virtues of style from what is found in the essays on Lysias, Isocrates, and Isaeus, and the system is further clarified in the essay *On Thucydides* (23). Correctness, clarity, and brevity (or conciseness) are thought of as "necessary" virtues. To these should probably be added propriety, which is subsequently stressed. The place of ornamentation is taken by a series of possible or "supplementary" virtues, achieved through word choice and composition of sentences. *On Imitation* mentions ethos (or characterization), pathos (or emotion), beauty, magnificence, strength, force, intensity, abundance, a multitude of figures, sweetness, persuasion, grace, and naturalness; *On Thucydides* gives a somewhat different list, including sublimity (*hypsos*), elegance, solemnity, magnificence, intensity, gravity, pathos, and combativeness. The importance of these lists is that they represent the first step toward the "ideas" of style later formulated by Hermogenes and fundamental to subsequent Greek concepts of style. The inclusion of *hypsos* is of interest, since we know it was the subject of a treatise by Caecilius and it is of course also the subject of the celebrated work attributed to Longinus, *On Sublimity*.

The beginning of the essay *On Demosthenes* is lost. Our text starts in the middle of a quotation from Thucydides, after which Dionysius says that Thucydides is the "standard and canon" of a style that is elaborate, extravagant, ornate, and replete with all additional ornament. Over against the Thucydidean "character" of style is set the plain style of Lysias. The various writers exhibit a "harmony" of styles, with Thucydides (and Gorgias) at one extreme and Lysias at the other. What lies between the two extremes should, he thinks, be viewed as a "mixture" of features of each. Isocrates among the orators and Plato among the philosophers are his preferred examples. This all leads up to Demosthenes, who combines the best features of the styles of all previous orators and writers (8). He is compared first with Thucydides (9–10), then with Lysias (11), and later with Isocrates (18–22) and Plato (23–32). Dionysius' view of Plato's style was not laudatory enough for Platonists of the time; in *Letter to Pompeius* he seeks to defend himself against criticism and also explains his judgment of the style of Herodotus, Thucydides, Xenophon, and Theopompus.

While writing *On Demosthenes* Dionysius seems to have turned aside to compose the treatise known as *On Literary Composition* (*Peri syntheōs ono-matōn*, literally "On the Putting Together of Words"), to which he refers in section 49. This work outlines a somewhat different theory of three styles or harmonies (chapters 21–24): the "austere," the "polished," and the "well blended." Isocrates is to be regarded as a writer of the mixed style, of polished harmony, and of the epideictic genre; Thucydides is grand style, austere harmony, and also epideictic genre; Demosthenes is mixed style, blended harmony, and all genres. When Dionysius resumed writing *On Demosthenes*, at chapter 34 he adopted this terminology. He gives a short but interesting discussion (36) of why different authors use different harmonies. The reasons given are, first, natural predisposition (reminiscent of remarks of Aristotle in chapter 4 of the *Poetics*); second, acquired principles of taste; third, contemporary fashion; and fourth, imitation of a model. Not only orators and historians but also poets can be classified by this system (38–41): Aeschylus and Pindar are "austere"; Hesiod, Sappho, and Anacreon are "polished"; Homer is "blended." After outlining his theory Dionysius considers the style of Demosthenes, including his rhythm (47–48) and delivery (53), how to recognize his genuine speeches (50), and Aeschines' criticisms of Demosthenes' style (55–57). Comparative criticism is repeatedly evident, and there is some reworking of passages to illustrate discussion of qualities (e.g., 20).

On Literary Composition is the most detailed account we have of how educated Greeks reacted to the beauties of their native language. After a short introduction, Dionysius considers first (6–9) the grouping, shaping, and tailoring of clauses, then (10–20) the sources of *hēdonē* or "charm" and *to kalon* or "beauty." There are four sources: melody, rhythm, variety, and propriety. Next (21–24) comes discussion of the three kinds of harmony resembling that in *On Demosthenes*: the austere, of which Pindar and Thucydides are examples; the polished, illustrated by Sappho and Isocrates; and the well blended, of which Homer and Demosthenes are the best examples. Dionysius makes it clear that he is developing ideas of his own and that no technical terms were in use for the concepts he is identifying. Indeed, in the introduction he had stressed that the whole matter of composition had been neglected by his predecessors. He had investigated Stoic writings on language but found nothing useful in them (4). Greek prose since the fourth century was, in his judgment, an artistic wasteland; he never praises the style of any writer of the third, second, or first century, and he lists quite a number, including the great Polybius, as writers whom no one has the patience to read. We are also told in the introduction that study of composition is necessary for all who would practice political speech. Study of ideas and subject matter is too difficult for the young; it requires understanding and experience. What fascinates the young, what they can be led to understand, what they should be trained in are the beauties of language. Not a word in what follows relates composition to persuasion. This might suggest that Dionysius is writing primarily for teachers and students of grammar rather than of rhetoric, but it also reveals a point of view current in the schools of declamation in Rome, where emphasis on style often eclipsed argumentation.

At the request of Q. Aelius Tubero, a prominent Roman jurisconsult and historian, Dionysius wrote his essay *On Thucydides*. Cicero had criticized those Atticists who took Thucydides as a model for oratory but admitted he might be used as a model in historiography and ended with the observation that if Thucydides had lived later in the development of artistic prose his style would have been mellower and softer (*Brutus* 287–88). Dionysius had earlier associated Thucydides with an early stage in the development of artistic prose and had also made him the example of one pole in the stylistic spectrum. Here he tries to be fair and admits some virtues in Thucydides' treatment of his subject (5–20), but his judgment of Thucydides' archaic, disjointed, and sometimes obscure style is severe. He should not be proposed even as a canon for historical writing, let alone for public speaking (see chapters 2, 35, and 55). The second *Letter to Ammaeus* amplifies some of what is said in *On Thucydides*.

The final essay by Dionysius discusses the orator Dinarchus. It is primarily of interest as a source of information about him and his works, including which ones were genuine and which spurious. Dionysius thought that Callimachus as librarian in Alexandria and the Stoic scholars in Pergamum had been misled in a number of cases.

Declamation and Seneca the Elder

There are passing references to rhetorical exercises in *Rhetoric for Herennius* and in the writings of Cicero. Suetonius' work *On Grammarians and Rhetoricians* provides a little more information.[10] Cicero continued some practice of rhetorical exercises throughout his life, as well as occasional disputations on philosophical theses, as mentioned in chapter 7. Other prominent individuals who are said to have practiced some form of declamation in private include Pompey, in preparation for a speech against Curio (Sue-

[10] There is a translation by Rolfe in the Loeb Classical Library *Suetonius*, vol. 2, 396–49, but the English words or phrases adopted by Rolfe to describe grammar and rhetoric exercises are often misleading.

tonius, *On Grammarians and Rhetoricians* 25.3), and Antony and Octavian, in intervals during the war at Mutina (Suetonius, *Augustus* 89). These individuals gave respectability to declamation as a mental exercise or for recreation in a society that had relatively few forms of entertainment.

Our major source of information on declamation in the early Roman Empire is the work of Seneca the Elder entitled *Sententiae, Divisions, and Colors of Orators and Rhetors*.[11] It consists largely of quotations from speakers he had heard in his youth, to which are added prefaces discussing the practice of declamation and the chief declaimers he had known. Seneca gives the following account of the development of declamation in Rome:

> Cicero did not declaim what we now call *controversiae* nor the kind of exercises which were spoken of before Cicero's time, called *theses*. This particular kind of exercise which we practice is so new that its name also is new. We speak of *controversiae*, Cicero called them *causae*, or legal cases. The term *scholastica*, originally Greek but so completely taken over into Latin that it is used as though it were Latin, is even more recent than *controversiae*. Similarly, *declamatio* is not found in any author earlier than Cicero and Calvus, who distinguished declamation from *dictio*, or "speaking." Calvus said that by then he declaimed not too badly and that he spoke well. To declaim he thinks to be a form of practice at home, *dictio* is a matter of real speaking. The name has only recently come to be applied, for the enthusiasm itself is recent. There is no difficulty in my having known from the cradle a thing born since I was. (*Controversiae* 1.pr.12)

There is some confusion here, or perhaps Seneca does not express himself very well. Hermagoras had made the distinction between *theses* and *hypotheses*, or general issues and particular cases (including imaginary particular cases). The philosophical schools, especially the Peripatetics, had certainly practiced disputations of theses, and Cicero had done so as well. Suetonius reports that *controversiae* were originally drawn either from history or from some recent real happening and that older published collections included reference to specific details (*Rhetoricians* 25.6). Although a few *controversiae* in Seneca's collection contain specific names and historical references, more are imaginary cases designed to test the speaker's ingenuity. Seneca is doubtless correct in suggesting that through the time of Cicero declamation was occasionally practiced by adults at home; he fails to make it clear that it had long been a major activity in Greek rhetorical schools and had been imitated in Latin schools at least by the early first century, when

---

[11] Translation by Winterbottom in the Loeb Classical Library; discussions by Bonner, *Roman Declamation*; by Sussman, *The Elder Seneca*; and by Fairweather, *Seneca the Elder*. Seneca is sometimes referred to as Seneca Rhetor, but this is misleading in that it wrongly implies that he was a teacher of rhetoric.

it provoked the censorial edict of Crassus. In the Augustan period declamation continued as a major activity in the schools, but it also became a public activity on the part of teachers of rhetoric and educated adults of the upper classes. Seneca was born about 55 B.C., and it is public declamation of the last third of the Augustan period that he views as having grown up with himself.

The usual setting of declamation was a rhetorical school that was open, at least on certain days, to visitors. The teacher gave an exhibition of his own skill, often with some introductory explanation of the treatment of the case he was going to adopt, and others were welcome to join in. Students kept notebooks in which they collected passages from declamations praised by their teacher (Quintilian 2.11.7). Professional rhetoricians published some of their better declamations, which could then be studied by others. Seneca, however, claims to have relied on his memory of speeches, or at least parts of speeches, given many years before; this is not incredible. Ancient schools put great emphasis on training the memory, and there are numerous examples of Greeks and Romans with a remarkable verbal memory for poetry, prose, names, and lists of all kinds. Students were usually expected to write out a declamation on a theme proposed by the teacher; he then criticized it and after revision the student memorized it and spoke it to the school, thus getting practice in memory and delivery. Adults probably usually spoke extemporaneously.

Declamation was not a form of debate as known in modern times or in the dialectical exercises of Greek philosophical schools: participants were not paired against each other, and no side won the argument. Each speaker was assigned or chose one side of a case, and sometimes only one side would be represented by several speakers. Insofar as a winner emerged, this was an informal judgment by the teacher or others present that one speaker had best handled the challenge he set for himself.

Declamation provided exercise in both deliberative and judicial oratory. The deliberative exercise was regarded as the easier and by the Augustan Age was undertaken by students when they finished the program in composition in the grammar schools. Adults in Rome only occasionally tried their skill at this, though professional rhetoricians often did so in Greek schools. In deliberative declamation a speaker composed a *suasoria*, a speech dealing with a dilemma confronting some mythological figure or some famous historical person in the past. Contemporary subjects were avoided as potentially dangerous. The speech could be a *prosōpopoeia*, for which grammatical exercises had provided some training and in which the speaker impersonated a specific individual giving advice to another or debating with himself what action to take in a given situation, or it could be addressed to someone in the second person. In the first *suasoria* cited by Seneca, the speaker gives advice to Alexander the Great on the question of whether or not to cross the ocean after having conquered the known world; in the third, Agamemnon deliberates with himself whether to sacrifice Iphigenia. Historicity was not important; in Seneca's seventh *suasoria* Cicero is imagined deliberating whether to burn his writings when he is told he can thereby save his life. There is no reason to believe he was given this choice.

The more difficult, but much more popular, judicial declamation was the *controversia* in which one or more laws, Greek, Roman, or often imaginary, was stated. Seneca's first example is "Children should support their parents or be imprisoned." Then some unusual circumstances are imagined: "Two brothers are on bad terms; one has a son, the other falls into poverty. Despite the orders of his father the young man provides support for his uncle. As a result he is disowned. The uncle adopts him and subsequently becomes rich through an inheritance. At the same time the young man's natural father begins to be in want. Against the order of his adoptive father he aids his natural father. He is again disowned, this time by the adoptive father" (*Controversiae* 1.1). The orator may speak in the person of any of the individuals involved or as an advocate for any of them. He may imagine any mitigation, complication, or motivation he wishes; he is not bound by any law other than that specified or by any rule of legal procedure or evidence. For example, a young man who has been thrice disinherited and thrice reinstated by his father is found preparing a drug under suspicious circumstances (*Controversiae* 7.3). Is it a poison destined for the father or for the young man himself? Is it perhaps only a sleeping potion? The declaimer may choose whatever suits him for prosecution or defense or may invent any other explanation.

As a school exercise, declamation was intended to give students practice in public speaking. Teachers gave lectures on rhetorical theory and illustrated possible techniques; students also studied rhetorical handbooks and applied what they learned there to their own compositions. Special emphasis was put on the three features of a speech identified in the title of Seneca's work: *sententiae*, divisions, and colors. *Sententiae* are what Aristotle (2.21) had called *gnōmai*. These are maxims or epigrammatic generalizations about life and human beings, couched in a novel form to give them "point." Typical is one by Porcius Latro, Seneca's friend and favorite declaimer: "I have no fear that judges may bind hands which pirates have loosed" (1.7.1). Some declamations were little more than a string of *sententiae*. "Division" refers to the division of the subject into its principal issues. This involves the application of stasis theory. Determination of the question at issue in a declamation was largely left to the speaker. Different approaches were taken by different speakers, and there was much controversy about the best choice in traditional cases. The divisions used by Porcius

Latro almost always involved the questions "Is it permitted?" and "Is it right?" which fall respectively under legal stasis and stasis of quality (e.g. 1.1.3; 7.1.16–17). Declaimers, however, often neglected argumentation and relied on ethos, pathos, and general hyperbole for proof. They were much given to arguing along a fortiori lines from an unwarranted assumption to a foregone conclusion; for example, (1.6.1), "I deny my house to one who should be denied the earth." A "color" is an interpretation given by a speaker to events or to the motivation of those involved, and also relates to stasis. A defense against a murder charge might, for example, be the "color" of insanity. The first *controversia* in Seneca's seventh book is a complicated case involving a father, a stepmother, two sons, a charge of parricide, and adventures with pirates. Should a declaimer speaking for one of the sons employ the "color" of attacking the stepmother, a traditional virago, and to what extent? Seneca praises Latro (7.1.20) for the subtle and incidental way he brings a disparaging reference to the stepmother into a narrative where the principal color is the son's plea that he could never have brought himself to kill his father, an argument based on the ethos of the speaker.

There were traditional themes for *controversiae*, for which a speaker needed to find a new twist, and new themes were constantly invented. Most were lurid, often involving sex and violence. Rape, capture by pirates, mutilation in war, and disinheritance or other problems with parents constantly appear. The original reason for this choice was probably an effort to keep adolescent boys interested in their studies, or later to entertain audiences of visitors. The effect was to create a bizarre, unreal world of declamation, remote from most actual cases in the law courts. Some adults who participated in public declamation were patrons regularly practicing at the bar, and some teachers of declamation had a legal practice on the side, as Quintilian did later, but many who were regarded as brilliant declaimers were unsuccessful if they tried to appear in court, and others—the so-called *scholastici* or "declamation buffs"—never even tried. Habits learned in schools could be disastrous in the forum, as Albucius discovered when he tried a high-flown figure of thought while pleading a case:

> "Swear," he called out to his opponent, "but I shall dictate the oath: swear by the ashes of your father which are unburied; swear by the memory of your father; swear. . . ." and all the rest of the commonplace. When he had finished Lucius Arruntius [patron for the opponent] arose and said, "We accept the condition; my client will swear." "I wasn't offering a condition," protested Albucius, "I was employing a figure." Arruntius persevered. The board of judges was eager to put the finishing touches on a case all but concuded. Albucius shrieked, "If you get away with this it is the end of figures of speech!" Arruntius replied, "Let it be the end; we can live without them." Arruntius won, and Albucius never accepted another

brief. He told his friends, "Why should I speak in the forum when more people hear me at home than hear anyone in the forum? I speak when I want to; I speak as long as I like; I speak for whichever side I wish." (7.pr.7–8)

Feelings among declaimers were often intense and discussions at public declamations sometimes acrimonious. Cassius Severus, an effective speaker in the courts, especially distrusted the affectations of the schools. Seneca quotes his description of a dispute with Cestius Pius:

"I remember going to his school when he was about to recite his version of a speech against Milo. As was his wont, Cestius spoke admiringly of himself: 'If I were a Thracian gladiator I would be the great Eusius; if I were an actor I would be the great Bathyllus; if a horse Milissio.' I couldn't contain my anger and cried out, 'If you were a sewer, you'd be the Cloaca Maxima [the great sewer of Rome].' Everybody laughed loudly and the students all turned around to see who had such thick-necked insolence. Although Cestius had been going to improve on Cicero, he couldn't think of anything to say to me and refused to continue unless I left the house. I said that I wouldn't leave a public bath unless I had been washed. [Thus, he wouldn't leave before hearing the declamation.] Subsequently I decided to get satisfaction for Cicero from Cestius in the forum. As soon as I met him I summoned him to court before the praetor, and after I had poured forth as much as I wanted of our jokes and insults, I demanded that the praetor indict him under the law against 'undefined offense.' Cestius was so upset he hired a lawyer. I then brought him before another praetor and demanded an indictment for 'ingratitude.' Next, before the urban praetor I demanded that a guardian be appointed for him [on the ground that he was insane]. When his friends came running to this scene and making complaints, I said that I would cease to be troublesome if he would swear that Cicero was more eloquent than he, but neither in jest nor in earnest was it possible to get him to do this." (3.pr.16–17)

Seneca emerges from his book as an amiable old man, pleased to relive what he regarded as the good old days by putting down what he remembers in order to inform his three sons. He believed in the imitation of writers and speakers of an earlier, more classic age as the basis of excellence. As a hard-headed man of property, conservative and disdainful of philosophy, he might be expected to view with suspicion the ornaments of style or wit that he in fact loves. Yet to his son Mela, whose avoidance of a public career he rather approved, he says: "Devote yourself to eloquence. The passage from it to all the other arts is an easy one; it provides a useful tool even to those whom it does not train to be professional speakers" (2.pr.3). In the preface to his tenth book of *controversiae*, however, Seneca confesses weariness with his work: "Studies of the *scholastici* have this quality: touched upon lightly they delight, dwelt upon and brought under closer scrutiny they become tiresome." The criticisms of declamation that he quotes from others chiefly involve the remoteness of the conditions of declamation from actual speaking in the forum. Most Latin writers of the empire had been educated in the schools of rhetoric, and its influence, especially its emphasis on *sententiae*, is easily seen in their works, in the poetry of Ovid, Lucan, and Juvenal, for example, but also in the more disciplined prose of Seneca the Younger and of the historian Tacitus.

If we ask why declamation gained such popularity with adults, the answer is probably to be sought in the social conditions of the time. Formal education almost exclusively stressed verbal skills. Originally these had been preparatory to some participation in public life. Instilled with a love of speech, adults sought opportunities to practice it in competition with others. Opportunities to do so in public assemblies declined under the empire. Constraints on freedom of thought and expression appeared. Procedures in the law courts became more professonalized; knowledge of the law became more important; busy judges became less tolerant of rhetorical amplification irrelevant to the issues. For many educated adults, declamation thus became an outlet for personal, creative expression. Literary composition, in which dangerous subjects could be touched on implicitly, subtly, or in an apparently imaginary context, was another outlet, indulged by many in their leisure time, and friends were then invited to hear recitations of their writings. As noted earlier, other forms of group activity were limited in Rome. The public attended equestrian and gladiatorial shows in large numbers, and theatrical performances continued intermittently, but in both cases members of the public were only spectators. For most, there were no organized games to play in competition with others, either sports or games of skill. Nor were there coffeehouses or private clubs where individuals could while away the time, though conversation and exercise could be had at the baths. The greatest attraction of declamation was probably that it gave people something to do that engaged their minds and satisfied their needs for competition.

Latin Rhetoric in the Silver Age

The period from the death of the emperor Augustus in A.D. 14 until the reign of Marcus Aurelius in the second half of the second century is known as the "Silver Age" of Latin literature in contrast to the "Golden Age" of the Ciceronian and Augustan periods. The rhetorical schools dominated formal education, declamation continued a popular activity for adults, and an extensive body of elegant, though not highly original, literature showing the influence of rhetorical teaching was produced in traditional genres: epic by Lucan, Silius Italicus, Valerius Flaccus, and Statius; tragedy and philosophy by the younger Seneca; satire by Persius and Juvenal; lyric and epigram by Martial; historiography by Tacitus. There are also a number of scholarly works on scientific and technological subjects showing the learning of the period. "Imitation" reigns as the principle of literary composition; a Latin canon including Catullus, Virgil, Horace, and Ovid in poetry, and Cicero, Sallust, and Livy in prose gradually emerges; and writing is richly allusive to earlier texts. Some strong literary voices, however, are heard—Lucan, the younger Seneca, and Tacitus, in particular—and one work, the bawdy, cynical, and imaginative novel-like *Satyricon* of Petronius, is unprecedented in form in extant classical literature. Although oratory retained great prestige as a literary genre, and orators published their best efforts, few examples survive except for the versions of speeches given by historians in their accounts of the period.[1]

Latin prose style goes through a series of reactions in the Silver Age that are paralleled by rhetorical doctrines taught in the schools. Augustan prose—Livy's *History of Rome*, for example—continues to resemble writings of Cicero in its inclination to amplification, its use of connective words, and its preference for rhythmical periodic constructions. Reaction was under way, however, and the declamatory style gained popularity, resulting in increasing use of short sentences, abrupt transitions, strained metaphors and figures, and above all fondness for *sententiae*. In the last third of the first century there is a reaction against the declamatory style and a return to something like the standards of Cicero. Among rhetoricians, Quintilian is the great spokesman for this movement. Its application can be seen in the

---

[1] A portion of a speech by the emperor Claudius on the adlection of Gallic senators is preserved on a bronze tablet at Lyons (translation by Hardy, "The Speech of Claudius") and can be compared with the version in Tacitus' *Annals* 11.24. Other than that, the only surviving speeches are the *Panegyricus* by Pliny the Elder and the *Apology* by Apuleius, both discussed later in this chapter.

writing of Quintilian's student, the younger Pliny, and in the *Dialogus* of Tacitus, though Tacitus' historical works continue to show the influence of the declamatory style. In the mid–second century a new mannerism appears in the writings of Aulus Gellius, Apuleius, and Fronto, characterized especially by a fondness for archaism; Fronto also taught rhetoric and set out some of his principles in writings about eloquence.

We know the names of a number of teachers of rhetoric and writers of rhetorical handbooks in first-century Rome, chiefly from references in Quintilian. The person he most admired (10.1.86; 12.11.3) was, however, primarily an orator, Domitius Afer, who was practicing in the courts from about A.D. 25 to his death in 59 (Tacitus, *Annals* 14.19) . As a young man, Quintilian was closely associated with Afer and quotes from or refers to a number of his speeches in important cases and records personal anecdotes about him. Afer was especially famous for his wit, of which the most famous examples were collected and published (Quintilian 6.3.42). He wrote at least one work on rhetoric, a treatise on proof and evidence (5.57). It is probably from Afer that Quintilian initially derived his strong feeling that the study of rhetoric and rhetorical exercises in the schools should aim at a practical skill and should avoid the excesses of the declaimers.

Afer also had a political career, culminating in a consulship in A.D. 39. This necessarily involved him in flattery of the emperor, especially during the oppressive regime of the erratic emperor Caligula (see Dio Cassius 59.19). Quintilian is silent about any moral failures on the part of his mentor, but Afer appears in the pages of Tacitus as "a man of humble background and ready to shine by any means" (*Annals* 4.52). What Tacitus implies is that Afer was an "informer" (*delator*), an unscrupulous orator who advanced his own career by prosecuting well-known persons, including relatives of the emperors when he had reason to believe that he would please the court by so doing and would gain influence and money as a result. (An informer received a portion of the estate of a person he convicted.) The rise to power of a series of successful informers, especially under the autocratic rule of Tiberius, Caligula, Nero, and Domitian, was an unsavory aspect of rhetoric in the time of the Roman Empire. It is, however, only fair to add that most of our information about the history of the period comes from writers of the senatorial class, especially from Tacitus, who was bitterly opposed to the court and its policies. Tacitus' speeches are lost, but his rhetorical power can be judged from his historical works, which, more than anything else, have persuaded posterity to view the early empire as a time of loss of liberty, moral decline, official corruption, and ostentatious wealth.

In reviewing the history of rhetoric at Rome, Quintilian provides (3.1.21) a short list of major writers on rhetoric of the first century: Cornelius Celsus, Popilius Laenas, Verginius Flavus, Pliny the Elder, and Tutilius. None of their writings survives, though something is known about the works of

Celsus, Verginius, and Pliny. Celsus was the author of an encyclopedia, probably written in the reign of Tiberius. Quintilian says that it included rhetoric, military science, agriculture, and medicine; perhaps there were other sections as well. The writing of encyclopedias, including sections on rhetoric, seems to have begun with Cato the Elder, was continued by Cicero's contemporary Varro and others, and in late antiquity produced the extant works by Martianus Capella, Cassiodorus, and Isidore of Seville, which were important sources on the liberal arts throughout the Middle Ages and include dry compendiums of rhetorical theory. The only portion of Celsus' encyclopedia to survive is that on medicine, a straightforward statement of Greek medical knowledge written in clear Latin. Celsus was not a physician and perhaps not a teacher of rhetoric either. He simply collected information from other sources. Quintilian refers to Celsus' discussion of rhetoric twenty-five times, usually to disagree with it; he seems to be trying to counteract the influence of a popular work that he regarded as misleading. Celsus' definition of rhetoric reminded Quintilian (2.15.22) of that of Theodorus: "to speak persuasively on doubtful matters of interest to a citizen." The orator's prize, Celsus said, is not a good conscience, but victory, to Quintilian an unacceptable position (2.15.32). Other references indicate that Celsus discussed stasis theory and the arrangement of arguments, that he demanded strict relevance in the exordium; suggested that a narration should be omitted if the fact of a crime was denied; opposed word coinage; and discouraged rhythmical effects in the exordium of a speech. Like others of the period, Celsus was apparently much interested in figures of speech; Quintilian thought he distinguished too many kinds (9.1.19) and later (9.2.104–5) lists nineteen devices that Celsus had unnecessarily labeled figures.

Verginius Flavus was teaching rhetoric in Rome around A.D. 49, when the poet Persius studied with him, and continued until exiled by Nero "because of the fame of his name" in 65 (Tacitus, *Annals* 15.71). Quintilian refers to him with respect half a dozen times and may have studied with him as a young man (11.3.126). He says (7.4.40) that Verginius wrote a textbook for declamation in which he severely limited stasis of quality. Verginius also discussed Theodorus' rule that the exordium should mention the points to be made later in the speech; Quintilian says (4.1.23) that he misinterpreted Theodorus' requirement, which was only that the judge should be prepared for the chief questions.

Pliny the Elder was a man of independent wealth who devoted his life to scholarship until killed helping others to escape in the eruption of Mount Vesuvius in A.D. 79. Of his many writings, only his enormous *Natural History* survives, but his nephew, the younger Pliny, in *Epistle* 3.5, lists other works including histories and a treatise entitled *The Student*, which he says educated and perfected the orator beginning from the cradle. This furnished the only known precedent for Quintilian's decision to begin his great work on *The Education of the Orator* with the earliest training of a child. Quintilian, however, describes Pliny's work as "pedantic" (11.3.143). According to Aulus Gellius (9.16), *The Student* included a discussion of declamation with examples of argument.

Seneca the Younger, son of the author of the work on declamation discussed in the previous chapter, combined uneasily the roles of a man of great private wealth, a Stoic philosopher who preached the simple life, and a powerful minister of state at the court of Nero, who ordered Seneca's suicide in A.D. 65. In addition to numerous works on philosophy he composed a series of tragedies, the only Latin examples of the genre to survive, which are highly declamatory. What Seneca has to say about rhetoric reflects traditional Stoic views of the subject and is mostly found in his *Moral Epistles*.[2] These are really a series of short philosophical essays, addressed to an unknown Lucilius. Rhetoric, he says (20.2), is one of the rational parts of philosophy along with dialectic. It deals with words, meanings, and arrangement (89.17). Students should engage in continuous reading and writing (84.1–2), but it is best to study a small number of works thoroughly (2). Just because a subject for composition has been used by an earlier writer does not necessarily mean that it is exhausted; the latest writer actually has an advantage in that the words are ready before him (79.6)—a form of the doctrine of imitation.

Much of what Seneca has to say relates to style. "Speech which addresses itself to the truth should be simple and unadorned" (40.4). "If a man is sound, self-controlled, serious, temperate, his artistic ability is also dry and sober; if the former is vitiated, the latter is also affected" (114.3). Speech has no fixed rules, Seneca claims (114.13); it varies with the taste and vices of the times. Excessive use of archaism should be avoided, as should a too-pedestrian or an overwritten style. Those who write unrhythmically or too rhythmically are equally at fault. His views are perhaps best summed up in remarks to Lucilius in *Epistle* 59.4–5: "You have the words under control. The language does not carry you off nor draw you further than you intended. There are many who are summoned by the charm of some pleasing word to write something which they had not planned, but this does not happen to you. Everything is compact and suited to the subject. You say as much as you wish and mean more than you say. This is an indication of a rather great subject. It is clear that your mind as well has nothing empty, nothing vainly puffed out." Judgments differ somewhat as to whether Seneca's own prose style accords with his precepts. It is jerky and brittle and to some has seemed mannered and artificial. At the same time, it is appropriate for expression of his own complex personality. The word choice in his prose works is simple,

---

[2] Translation by Gummere in the Loeb Classical Library.

sometimes even colloquial; his many metaphors are usually drawn from daily life. His sentence structure is equally simple but is constantly given "point" by an epigrammatic or ironic twist. The only feature of declamation that is markedly present in his writing is his constant creation of *sententiae*, which is characteristic of all writing of the Silver Age. His poetry is a different matter; he favored mythological themes that are psychological studies of violence and insanity, for which his tense, emotional poetic style is an appropriate medium. Although he was regarded as a fine orator, none of his speeches survives.

Quintilian

Marcus Fabius Quintilianus, the greatest teacher of rhetoric at Rome, was born in Calagurris in Spain (modern Calahorra) sometime in the late 30s, perhaps as late as A.D. 40.[3] His early education was probably in Spain, but he was in Rome at least by 57, probably a little earlier, and there came to know Domitius Afer. He may have studied declamation for a time with Verginius Flavus (11.3.126), but his choice of the practicing orator Afer as his mentor suggests that he hoped for a career in the law courts rather than in the rhetorical schools as declaimer and teacher. Possibly he began his career as an assistant to Afer in court. Apparently he had some early success, for he published one speech "led by a youthful desire for fame" (7.2.24). Sometime around A.D. 60 or soon after he returned to Spain, where he probably pursued a career in the provincial courts. When the governor of Spain, Galba, was saluted emperor and marched to Rome to overthrow Nero in 68, Quintilian went with him (Jerome, *Chronicles* s.v. 68, probably derived from Suetonius). This might have proved disastrous for him during the appalling year of the four emperors that followed, but somehow he survived. Apparently he turned to teaching rhetoric at this time, perhaps to support himself when there were few opportunities in the courts.

Vespasian emerged as the victor in the contest for the throne. In the spring of 71 the new emperor began a program for reform of government and society, in reaction to the decadence and corruption of Nero. One feature of it was the appointment of Quintilian to a chair in rhetoric supported by the state treasury, the first such appointment ever made.[4] It is significant that Vespasian chose a person whose inclinations were toward the practical application of rhetorical skills rather than a famous declaimer, a person who

---

[3] The summary of Quintilian's life given here reflects a reexamination of the sources and differs in some details from those found in earlier books. Quintilian's references in 5.7.7, 10.1.23, and 86 are the most important for the chronology of his early life.

[4] On this fact, see Jerome, *Chronicles* s.v. 88; Jerome's date, however, is clearly wrong, since Quintilian retired in the early 90s, after twenty years of teaching (1.pr.1), and can be corrected from Zonaras 11.17 (Epitome of Dio Cassius 65.12).

took Cicero as his model in oratory, who disliked the style of oratory that had flourished under Nero, represented by the speeches of Seneca (10.1.26), and who also distanced himself from the activity of informers,[5] but to get the appointment Quintilian must have had some influence at the court. Throughout his career he remained a loyal supporter of Vespasian and his successors, Titus and Domitian. During his tenure as a professor he occasionally undertook to plead legal cases (4.1.19; 4.2.86).

Quintilian gives some information about his teaching methods: he offered a preliminary course of lectures for boys who may have been fourteen or fifteen years old (1.pr.7; 8.pr.1–7). He complains that they were coming to him at an older age than was necessary (2.1). This preliminary course apparently gave an outline of the system of rhetoric in simple terms and suggested that there was only one right way to do things; the boy would learn later that what he thought was the only way was usually the best (8.pr.4). At one time he experimented with reading and analysis of historical and oratorical texts with this younger group, but the study got in the way of the work of the more advanced students, whose parents had sent them to study declamation, and was abandoned (2.5.1–2). Quintilian does not question that the teaching of declamation was his major duty (2.10.2), but he wished it to be a practical preparation for public life. He repeatedly criticizes the choice of unrealistic themes, swollen style, and impractical conventions. To bring declamation back into line as training for the law courts, he suggests some modest reforms (2.10.9): use of proper names, more complicated cases, more normal diction, some sense of humor. Some of the examples of declamation scattered through his work show what he had in mind but also suggest that he did not or could not push reform very far.[6] As a teacher, Quintilian regarded himself as in loco parentis (2.2.4), with a strong moral responsibility toward developing the values and discipline of students, but also with an obligation to make learning seem natural and even fun. Almost alone of ancient educators, he was strongly opposed to corporal punishment of the young (1.3.13–14). In return, he expected students to develop a sense of duty to the teacher: the student should both obey and love him (2.9). He is also unusual in stressing the need for the education of women (1.1.6–7), though by this he did not mean that young women should attend rhetorical schools.

In the preface to the sixth book of his great rhetorical treatise, *Institutio Oratoria*, Quintilian tells us something about his private life. The events he mentions can be reconstructed roughly as follows. Around A.D. 83, when he was in his forties, he married a woman young enough to be his daughter. It is at least possible that she was the sister of Marcellus Vitorius, to whom the

---

[5] See Winterbottom, "Quintilian and the *Vir Bonus*."
[6] See, e.g., 3.6.96–97; 5.10.111–12; 7.3.30–34.

Institutio is dedicated and who had probably been Quintilian's student a little earlier.[7] They had two sons, of whom the younger died at the age of five. His wife died a few months later, probably in 89 or early 90. At that time he had begun to write a treatise entitled *On the Causes of the Corrupted Eloquence*, which has not been preserved. The older son, in whom his father placed great hopes, died while Quintilian was writing the *Institutio*.

After twenty years of teaching, probably in the summer of A.D. 91 or 92, Quintilian retired from teaching.[8] As he describes in the preface to the first book, he was then persuaded to begin writing a treatise on rhetoric. There were of course many such works, but his friends pointed out that their theories were inconsistent and urged Quintilian to give his own judgment of the views of his predecessors. Another reason for writing was the unauthorized publication of lecture notes taken by his students, which he regarded as an unsatisfactory account of his views. He says he found the subject more extensive than he expected and devoted two years to research. This seems to suggest that he was not very familiar with earlier writings on rhetoric, except presumably those of Cicero. The resulting treatise is valuable for the history of rhetoric because of the views of earlier writers Quintilian offers and evaluates in connection with each aspect of rhetoric, but it has to be said that his methods were somewhat casual. Though he certainly had some knowledge of Greek, he shows a preference for Latin sources whenever possible, including Latin translations of Greek works (e.g., 2.15.21) or Latin sources for Greek theories. He is thus not always precise in his quotations or paraphrases of what Greek writers had said. He cites Aristotle and Theophrastus from time to time, but does not seem to have appreciated the special qualities of Aristotle's *On Rhetoric*, and despite his extensive discussion of the virtues of style running from book 8 through the first chapter of book 11, he never attributes this theory to Theophrastus, which he could have learned from Cicero even if he did not read Theophrastus' own work. Throughout, he picks and chooses, sometimes out of context, what is most useful for him in arguing for his view of rhetoric as the "science of speaking well" (2.15.34: *bene dicendi scientia*) and the development of his view that only a good man can be a perfect orator (first stated in 1.pr.9 but often repeated).

After about two years of preliminary research, thus perhaps in A.D. 93, Quintilian began writing the *Institutio*. The books were written in the order in which they now stand, except that the preface to book 1 was written last. In the preface to the fourth book he describes how, after completing three books, he was asked to take charge of the education of the two heirs to the throne. The likely date is sometime in 94. These boys were the sons of

---

[7] In 6.pr.13 Quintilian speaks of his son's uncle as praetor. Marcellus was praetor about the time Quintilian was writing; see Statius, *Silvae* 4.4.59–60.

[8] Presumably a successor was appointed, but we do not know who that was; possibly Julius Tiro, whose name appears after Quintilian's in the list at the end of Suetonius, *On Rhetoricians*.

Domitian's neice, Domitilla, who was married to Flavius Clemens. According to Ausonius (20.7), perhaps relying on Suetonius, Clemens secured for Quintilian the *ornamenta consularia*, an honorary distinction that gave him the rank of a former consul without any duties. Clemens himself was suffect consul early in the year 95;[9] the appointment had probably been agreed to by the emperor the previous year. In 6.pr.13 Quintilian mentions that his own son had been adopted by a man of consular rank. Such adoptions were not unusual in Rome. We do not know who the consular was, but it is at least possible that it was Clemens. If so, Quintilian's son could appropriately be included with the two young princes in the small group of boys he was expected to teach. Quintilian's patron, Marcellus Vitorius, is likely to have had some part in the arrangements, and his son Geta, mentioned in 1.pr.6, may have been included in the small group. Quintilian's son was at least nine years old at the time, possibly a little older, and the other boys may have been around the same age. That would make them younger than the students Quintilian had taught as a professor of rhetoric, but the study of early education he had completed for the first book of his treatise had made him something of an authority on the subject, which was doubtless known to his close associates and influenced them in arranging his appointment.

Flavius Clemens is never mentioned by name in Quintilian's treatise, which might seem odd if the circumstances just described are true. But there was an excellent reason for omitting his name: before the year 95 was over Clemens had been discredited and executed on the unusual charge of atheism (Dio Cassius 67.14.1–2). We do not know what happened to his sons; probably they were sent into exile, and in any event they disappear from history. Quintilian's own son had died. He himself, in grief and loneliness, managed to complete and publish his treatise, probably before the end of 95, certainly before the murder of Domitian in 96. A letter to his publisher Trypho, prefixed to the first book, indicates that pressure was put on him to get the work out. Marcellus Vitorius survived and was one of the consuls of the year 105 under Trajan. His son Geta did not have a political career as Quintilian had hoped; he did, however, survive and was appointed to the college of Arval priests by Hadrian in A.D. 118. We do not know when Quintilian died; 96 is a reasonable estimate. His former student, the younger Pliny, seems to refer to him as already dead in a letter written late in 97 (*Epistles* 2.14.9).[10]

---

[9] Under the empire the consulship was usually held only for periods of two months or less. The first to serve were the official consuls of the year, sometimes including the emperor himself; subsequent holders were known as "suffect consuls." They presided over meetings of the senate and had ceremonial functions but little real power.

[10] The Quintilian addressed in *Epistle* 6.32 is another person of the same name.

Quintilian emerges from his work as a humane, likeable, and in many ways admirable man. He was a professional educator with high standards, patience, and respect for his students; he had a sense of humor and combined the authority of his position with personal modesty; his lofty cultural vision of the ideal orator, something he thought still possible in Rome, is tempered with a realistic sense of what individuals could achieve and the times demanded. When the complete *Institutio* was rediscovered in the fifteenth century, it became the major classical authority on education for the Renaissance. His rhetorical theories are rarely original, but his judgment is usually sound, and he significantly contributed to the return to Ciceronian standards of style from the excesses of the declaimers. His own voice can frequently be heard through his Latin style, speaking informally to his reader; when he seeks to rise to the grand style, as at the beginning of book 12, the result can be rather labored, but he can also write eloquently and movingly, as in the preface to the sixth book and in the last chapter of the twelfth. The criticisms that can be made of him are chiefly of two sorts: as noted earlier, he is not as precise as we would wish in his discussions of earlier views of rhetoric, for he was more a teacher than a scholar. The second, and more serious, criticism is that he flattered the emperor, shut his eyes to abuses of power, and tolerated the activities of informers. The passage (10.1.92) in which he celebrates the achievements of the emperor Domitian in epic poetry seems to most modern readers a tasteless piece of fawning, but it is typical of other references to that touchy emperor at the time. Domitian's father Vespasian, who was responsible for Quintilian's rise to fame, was one of the best of the emperors of the century, and Domitian himself, especially during the early years of his reign, was a competent administrator. Quintilian was a loyal supporter of the regime. As such, he doubtless had to overlook some actions with which he may not have been personally comfortable. In understanding the Roman Empire it is in fact extremely valuable to know that a man like Quintilian could support it enthusiastically, and his view helps to counterbalance the lurid picture of the time given by Tacitus, Suetonius, and Juvenal. Quintilian's political views were probably close to, and perhaps influential on, those of his student Pliny. Pliny cooperated as best he could with Domitian and as a result advanced his own career; after Domitian's death, under the greater freedom of Nerva and Trajan, he candidly recognized the faults of the earlier regime, though without regret at his personal role at the time. Unlike Pliny, Quintilian did not survive to enjoy what Tacitus (*Histories* 1.1) calls "the rare felicity of times when it is permitted to feel what you wish and to speak what you feel."

The title Quintilian chose for his treatise, *Institutio Oratoria*, means "oratorical education," or as it is usually translated "The Education of the Orator."[11] The title reflects his desire to give an account of the education and study from childhood to adulthood required to produce a "perfect orator," who will be not only an eloquent speaker but a political leader and moral spokesman for Roman society. Quintilian's ideal resembles that of Cicero in *On the Orator* and is modeled on what Cicero says there and elsewhere and on Cicero's conception of his own role, but Quintilian puts less emphasis on knowledge of philosophy than did Cicero. He speaks with respect of great philosophers of the past (e.g., 12.2.22), but he scorned contemporary philosophers: the philosophical ideal, he thinks, lacks civic virtues; philosophy can be feigned, eloquence cannot (12.3.12). This is consistent with the attitude of Vespasian and Domitian; the latter emperor even banished philosophers from Italy in 89 and again in 95. They were regarded as social and political troublemakers. The moral standards Quintilian requires of his perfect orator are, however, reminiscent of Stoicism, and his definition of rhetoric as "the science of speaking well" is expressly identified with the definitions of the Stoics Cleanthes and Chrysippus, "the science of speaking rightly" (2.15.35). At the end of his work (12.11.25) Quintilian raises the question of whether anyone can ever achieve the stature of his ideal orator. His answer is that because it has not yet been reached it does not follow that it cannot be, that all great and admirable things require time, and that even second or third rank is worth striving for. Although he stops short of speaking of an orator-emperor analogous to Plato's philosopher-king, this may have been his private goal in teaching the ill-fated heirs of Domitian. That Quintilian's ideal was not totally impossible can be seen in the person of the five emperors who succeeded Domitian: Nerva, Trajan, Hadrian, Antoninus Pius, and Marcus Aurelius. In this period succession was determined by adoption by each emperor of the most respected candidate rather than by inheritance, and the last three had something like the training for the throne, the cultural values, and the eloquence that Quintilian desired.

Quintilian describes his vision of the perfect orator in the preface to the first book of the *Institutio* (1.pr.9–20) and follows this with an outline of the treatise, which had already been completed:

> The first book will contain those things which are prior to the work of the rhetorician. [He means the account of the earliest training at home and study in a grammar school, which is our only full account of the

---

[11] The only commonly available translation of the *Institutio* is that of Butler in the Loeb Classical Library. It needs, however, to be revised on the basis of the much improved Latin text of Winterbottom, *Quintiliani Institutio*. There are commentaries in English on book 1 by Colson, on book 10 by Peterson, and on book 12 by Austin; there is a commentary on book 3 in German by Adamietz. Cousin's Budé edition (*Institution oratoire*) contains a less reliable text, a French translation of the whole and extensive notes to be used with caution, based in part on his earlier *Etudes sur Quintilien*. See also Little, *Quintilian the School Master*, which contains a paraphrase of the whole work, and Kennedy, *Quintilian*.

subject]. In the second book we shall consider the first lessons with the rhetorician and problems involving the nature of rhetoric. Five books will then be devoted to invention (for arrangement is a subdivision of it), four to style, in which part will also come memory and delivery. There will be one final book in which we shall say in so far as our poor powers allow what ought to be the orator's way of life, what his policy in undertaking, studying, and pleading cases, what his kind of style, what limit to his pleading, what his studies after retirement. (1.pr.22)

This is, of course, the order of nature as the child grows and develops into a man. In the earlier books Quintilian tends to address parents or teachers; in the later books he speaks directly to the would-be orator. The concept of nature is important throughout: Quintilian wants to produce a natural style, he wants a speech to grow naturally and organically, and he wants to bring each speaker to full, natural development.

Later (2.14.5) Quintilian introduces a different structural principle: this is the idea of *ars* (theory), *artifex* (speaker), and *opus* (the work of art). These concepts are reminiscent of the poetic theory of Neoptolemus, reflected in Horace's *Art of Poetry*, which concerned itself with poetry, poet, and poem.[12] The concepts are, however, very unevenly dealt with: all the *Institutio* from book 3 to book 11 deals with *ars*, and all of book 12 except chapter 10 on the kinds of style deals with *artifex*. The heart of the *Institutio* (books 3 to 11) is a discussion of rhetoric. It deals with all traditional parts of the subject and in greater detail than does any other classical treatise— 11.3, for example, is the only really good account of delivery and of the experience of both hearing and seeing a Roman orator—and it contains discussion of some subjects not found elsewhere in Latin. The most famous of the latter is book 10. At the end of book 9 Quintilian has completed discussion of ornamentation as a virtue of style; he does not discuss the final virtue, propriety, until 11.1. In between comes a book devoted to how an orator can obtain *copia*, or "abundance" of ideas and words by reading and writing, and how he can develop facility in public speaking. The first chapter of book 10 discusses what the student should read in Greek and Latin.[13] Quintilian's account of the canon of Greek poetry and prose resembles that in Dionysius of Halicaranssus' work *On Imitation* and may be directly indebted to it; his parallel account of Latin authors represents his own judgment and is famous for its brief characterizations, often quoted by historians of Latin literature. The prevailing metaphor is one of a contest between Greek and Latin achievements in each genre: in epic, the Roman Virgil is surpassed only by the Greek Homer (10.1.85–86); in satire the victory be-

[12] See Innes, "Augustan Critics", 259–67.

[13] Quintilian divided his work into books; the chapter divisions were made by later scribes and editors.

longs solely to Romans (93),[14] but in comedy they "limp" badly (99); in history Latin writers hold their own (101); their greatest success is in oratory, where Demothenes' one advantage over Cicero is that he came first and to a great extent made Cicero what he was (108). The second chapter of the book is the best surviving account of the theory of "imitation" of literary models as the source of excellence in writing. The student is recommended to imitate the style of a variety of writers and especially to imitate strong examples of qualities in which he is weak.

There are a number of passages where Quintilian claims some originality in rhetoric and some additional places where his theories differ to some extent from what is found in earlier discussions of rhetoric. In book 2, chapter 20, he discusses whether or not rhetoric is a "virtue," a view he attributes to (Stoic) philosophers. Their arguments are subtle, but Quintilian prefers an argument he says is not found elsewhere, "from the actual work of the orator" (2.20.8): "What can the orator accomplish in praising unless experienced in the honorable and shameful? Or in persuading a course of action unless what is useful is perceived? Or in the lawcourts if he is ignorant of justice?"[15] At times the orator needs bravery, as Cicero did pleading for Milo (not perhaps the best possible example, considering that Cicero lost his nerve). Thus the orator needs to know, and to have virtues and rhetoric is a "virtue."

A characteristic feature of Quintilian's teaching is the desire to give practical advice. For example, the first chapter of book 4 deals with the exordium, and Quintilian remarks "Since it is not enough to demonstrate to learners what is contained in the theory of the prooemium [sic] but one must say how it is most easily accomplished, I add that a speaker should look at what is to be said, before whom, for whom, against whom, etc." (4.1.52) His contemporaries think one can start anywhere, but the best test of a topic is whether it would lose effect by being placed elsewhere. He repeatedly warns against a literal acceptance of rules and pleads for naturalness and simplicity. In the chapter on memory (11.2) he outlines the traditional system but expresses some doubt about its practical utility and gives his own less technical advice at length. His own experience as an orator is occasionally reflected in what he says. For example, he refers to one of his cases that could only be handled in a "figured" way (92.73), and after explaining how *visiones* can be used to produce a real and necessary emotion in the speaker he adds, "I could not keep quiet about these matters by which I believe I attained whatever reputation for ability I have or had; I have frequently been so stirred that not only have tears overwhelmed me, but pallor and symptoms of real grief" (6.2.36). Two of the most interesting and unusual

---

[14] Quintilian does not say what he is often taken to mean, that only Romans wrote satire.

[15] The theory here is Aristotelian, but Quintilian shows no awareness of that.

chapters are 5.7, on the examination of witnesses, and 6.4, on debate in the presentation of a case. Both passages provide instruction in the pleading of real cases and have no application to declamation.

While writing the *Institutio* and reconsidering the subjects discussed, Quintilian occasionally changed some of the theories he had taught in the past. An example is the revised version of stasis—his word is *status*—theory set out in 3.6.63–82. This subject was of course applicable to declamation as well as to actual pleading. He warns the reader that he has come to regard his lectures as containing a logical fallacy in treating legal stasis as part of stasis of reasoning and in identifying a separate stasis of jurisdiction. He now thinks that the question at issue in a case is either one of reasoning or one of law. Questions of reasoning can be divided into three kinds: fact, definition, or justice. Questions of law are divisible into various species, but these can similarly be classified as matters of fact, definition, or justice. Jurisdiction is not a separate kind of stasis, since it involves either reasoning or law and can be rephrased as one of the three kinds of stasis. This account is then followed by "an easier and more open road" (3.6.83), a practical way by which a student may approach the case at hand and in which the various categories are less rigorously stated: in legal questions, for example, three *simulacra*, or mirror images of stasis are accepted.

As in most other treatises except that of Aristotle, judicial rhetoric is the overwhelming concern. There is a chapter on epideictic rhetoric (3.7), but even there some of Quintilian's interest is the use of praise or blame in judicial speeches. He mentions funeral oratory and the Capitoline competition, instituted by Domitian in honor of Jupiter Capitolinus, but does not discuss the various epideictic forms of address to emperors and other officials that were developing in Greece and may have had some Latin counterparts even before Pliny expanded the speech of thanks by a consul to the emperor into his *Panegyricus* and established a new genre. At the end, a brief attempt is made to apply stasis theory to epideictic rhetoric. The following chapter on deliberative oratory is longer and also refers to stasis (3.8.4). At the outset Quintilian expresses surprise at the view of some authorities—Aristotle would be one but is not mentioned here—that the goal of deliberative oratory is *utilitas*, which might be translated "expediency." This is morally repugnant to Quintilian, who prefers to say that the goal is "the honorable" (*dignitas, honestum*), or an action that combines the two. Much of the chapter is devoted to *suasoriae* in rhetorical schools, with mention also of deliberative oratory in historical writing (3.8.67). In 2.16.19 and 12.1.28 there is passing mention of addresses by an officer to his troups, something often found in historical works. At the end of 3.8 he discusses practical uses for deliberative rhetoric and sees them in counseling friends, in speaking in the senate, and in advising the emperor when asked. He conspicuously avoids discussion of the decline of the importance of public deliberative oratory under the empire. There was clearly much deliberation among advisers to the emperor and other officials, of which we get occasional glimpses; a good example is Tacitus' reconstruction of the advice of his freedmen to Claudius on choice of a new wife, which opens the twelfth book of the *Annals*.

Two collections of declamations carry Quintilian's name in the manuscripts. The *Minor Declamations* consist of 385 themes for declamation with *sermones*, or short lectures, by a teacher of rhetoric advising how the theme can best be treated, and short quotations from declamations on the theme. Some of the themes, possibly also some of the instructions, may go back to Quintilian's school and are not inconsistent with his teaching, but the collection as a whole is probably a compilation made in late antiquity from many sources. The nineteen *Major Declamations* are less likely to have originated with Quintilian, but they are our only complete examples of Latin *controversiae* and are highly readable examples of the genre.[16]

Discussions of the "Decline of Eloquence"

The cultural optimism of the regime of Augustus was a rather artificial construction, and as time passed Romans reverted to their more normal pessimism about the state of the world. This includes speculation on what was perceived as a decline of eloquence in public address and of literature as well. Cicero had noted it in a passage in *On Duties* (2.67), perhaps derived from the Greek philosopher Panaetius. We have a series of discussions of the causes of decline as perceived in the first two centuries of the empire. Though there are two important Greek discussions, the topic is more frequent in Latin texts, where differences between the age of Cicero or Virgil and the next century were more evident; in Greek texts, decline was viewed by Dionysius of Halicarnassus and others as occurring much earlier in Hellenistic Asianism, which was now being replaced by a renascent Atticism.

A Greek writer of the generation after Dionysius who took a more gloomy view of the state of culture was the Jewish philosopher Philo of Alexandria.[17] In his essay *On the Work of Noah as a Planter*, he says that people of his time were inferior to the wise men of the past in both language and deeds. Language, he claims, has become diseased and inflated. Men are effeminate;

---

[16] There is no English translation of *Minor Declamations*; there is a good English version of *Major Declamations* with introduction and notes by Sussman.

[17] The only firm date in his life is that of his embassy as an old man to Caligula to ask exemption for Jews from worship of the emperor in A.D. 39–40. He gives an account of this in *Legatio ad Gaium*. His other works were written earlier. They include a pamphlet in oratorical form attacking Flaccus, the governor of Egypt, and extensive writings on the Old Testament, interpreted allegorically with concepts from Platonic and Stoic philosophy. There is a translation of Philo's writings by Colson and Whitaker in the Loeb Classical Library.

few care for ancient ambition. In ancient days, "poets and prose writers and those interested in other liberal arts flourished; they did not sweeten and enervate the ears with rhythmical language, but they roused any part of the mind which was weak and broken down, and as much of it that was in tune they harmonized with the instruments of nature and virtue"(159). There is a similar passage in his essay *Every Good Man Is Free* 62–74. Philo's view is that there has been a general moral decline in society; a symptom is evident in writing and speech. Philo and other writers use a common set of metaphors to describe the decline; some are physiological: bone and muscle have degenerated to flabbiness; others are sexual: virility has become effeminacy; still others are drawn from fondness for fancy dress and bodily ornament or from rich food.

The elder Seneca, writing in Latin about the same time, regards the decline of eloquence in his lifetime as obvious and suggests three causes for it: "Whatever Roman eloquence achieved to rival or excel Greek insolence reached its peak in the time of Cicero. . . . Since then, day by day, things have become worse, whether because of the luxury of the times (for nothing is so deadly to natural abilities as luxury), or because when the prizes to be won in this very honorable task became less, all ambition took itself to other areas more promising in fame and profit, or by some Fate whose malign and eternal law it is in all things that whatever has been brought to the highest point falls again to the lowest more swiftly than it rose" (*Controversiae* 1.6.6–7). He continues with observations on the prevalence of laziness (including poor memory), lust, effeminacy, braiding the hair, and wearing disgusting finery, leading to quotation of the elder Cato's definition of an orator, "a good man skilled in speaking," now a thing of the past. As noted in the last chapter, Seneca does report criticisms of declamation elsewhere in his work, but here he does not attribute decline to the artificiality of declamation. Presumably he thought that more a symptom than a cause. Of the causes he mentions, the decadent luxury of the times clearly impresses him most, and for this he sees no cure. By the fading of ambition, the second cause, he seems to mean loss of interest in public life and in seeking public office in contrast to ambition for private wealth. He thus suggests, but does not elaborate, the possibility that political changes from republic to empire may be at the root of the decline. Elsewhere (10.pr.5) he speaks of Labienus as "one who in this time of overwhelming peace had not yet laid down the energies characteristic of the Pompeian party." "Peace" was consistently claimed by the emperors as the greatest achievement of their rule, but when mentioned by others it can carry the implication of the disappearance of vigorous debate and the loss of freedom. The writings of Labienus and Cassius Severus were burned at the order of the senate, as Seneca mentions in the same preface, and Labienus committed suicide. This was under the ostensibly mild Augustus. By the time Seneca was writing, treason trials had

187

become an ugly feature of the reign of Tiberius. Cremutius Cordus was accused of praising Caesar's assassins, Brutus and Cassius, in an historical work, calling Cassius "the last of the Romans"; Tacitus puts into his mouth a splendid oration on freedom of speech (*Annals* 4.34–35), but the younger Seneca says (*Consolation to Marcia* 22.7) that Cremutius Cordus committed suicide before his trial.

That there was some law of fate or at least a natural cycle in human activity that made literary decline inevitable was the view of Velleius Paterculus, writing about the same time as Philo and the elder Seneca. Velleius was an enthusiastic admirer of the empire and especially of Tiberius, in whose army he had served, but he also believed that there had been a moral decline among the Romans. After retirement he wrote a short history of Rome, unusual in that it contains some chapters on literary history. At the end of the first book (1.16–18) he ventures some thoughts on what might be called the "progression of the genres." That he originated the idea seems unlikely; something like it is implicit in Aristotle's *Poetics* in regard to the history of tragedy, in the view of Callimachus and other Hellenistic poets that traditional epic and tragedy were not suited to their own age, and in the observation of Dionysius of Halicarnassus in the preface to *On the Ancient Orators* that there are natural cycles in the history of style. The basic idea is that great writers in each literary genre are approximate contemporaries: tragedy flourishes at one time, oratory at another, and so on. "What distinction was there," Velleius asks, "among orators before Isocrates or after his pupils and their followers?" The same phenomenon could be observed in Latin texts, where, despite the work of Cato and a few others, the greatest achievement came in the time of Cicero. Few before him and his contemporaries can delight a reader and none can arouse admiration. The explanation given for this phenomenon, rather hesitatingly, is that emulation and rivalry produce a series of good works in a particular form for a period of time, but the effect of a great genius in any genre is inhibiting on others. They become discouraged at the possibility of surpassing an Isocrates or a Cicero and turn to something else. "This frequent and fickle jumping from one genre to another is the greatest obstacle to a perfected work of art." At the end, Velleius remarks on, but does not try to explain, the fact that excellence is not shared by all cities: Athens had more eloquence than all the rest of Greece put together. Velleius' theory applies best to the history of poetry, and a version of it has been advanced in modern times by the Russian formalist critics; it applies less well to oratory that is intimately connected with the challenges and opportunities of political and legal conditions.

The opening scene of the surviving text of Petronius' *Satyricon*, written in the time of Nero, is a conversation between Encolpius, the young hero—or perhaps better antihero—of the novel, and Agamemnon, a rather pompous teacher of rhetoric. Encolpius has visited a rhetorical school and is in the middle of an attack on the artificiality of declamation, which he claims is the cause of the decline of eloquence (1–2). Declaimers are insane, and their art, a world of pirates, tyrants, and immolated virgins, is entirely foreign to the forum, for which it pretends to train. The declaimers' "honied globules of words and all the sayings and doings sprinkled with pepper or sesame" have corrupted style so that eloquence has lost its force. Things were better in classical Greek times, when there was no need of declamation, but "Asianism" has ruined everything. Agamemnon replies with a defense of the teachers (3–5). They have to teach the way they do or they would not have students. The real blame lies with parents, who are in a great hurry to rush their sons through school and out into the forum unprepared. Eloquence is a difficult study, needing a long period of training. The system is all right in theory, but the professors are not given a chance.

This is the earliest passage that specifically blames the decline of eloquence on the unrealistic practice of declamation. It occurs, however, in a brilliantly satiric work in which virtually every seemingly serious statement is undercut by the morally dubious character of the speakers. Encolpius is trying to impress Agamemnon as being a serious and thoughtful young man, in hopes of being invited to a free dinner; Agamemnon, for his part, defends his profession but is cultivating Encolpius in hopes of enjoying his sexual favors. What each says, therefore, should probably be thought of as a satire on commonplaces of the time, not as Petronius' serious views. Petronius doubtless had his own views, but little in the *Satyricon* can be trusted as a source for them, except its cynical view of life.[18]

Another writer of the Neronian period is the satirist Persius; according to the short biography preserved with his poems, he had studied with Verginius Flavus, but he clearly did not enjoy declamation (3.44–47). His first satire deals with literature, including some references to oratory (83–87), which help to confirm that the remarks of Encolpius are a commonplace of the time. Even in a serious trial, he says, an orator thinks first of being complimented for his speech. Answering a charge is less important than figures of speech. Writers would not produce the rot they do if they had any manhood (103–4).

Quintilian's lost work *On the Causes of Corrupted Eloquence* probably took up these themes. Given his positive attitude toward the regime he is not likely to have acknowledged any political causes for decline: great orators, he says (10.1.122), still speak in the forum. He was, however, anxious to counteract the influence of the excesses of declamation. What he regarded as the corrupted style can be seen from a passage late in his work (12.10.73): "They are much deceived who think that the vitiated or corrupted style of speaking is popular or persuasive. It exults in license in the

---

[18] See Kennedy, "Encolpius and Agamemnon."

use of words or runs riot with childish epigrams or swells with unrestrained pomposity or leaps about with empty commonplaces or glitters with adornment which will collapse if lightly touched or substitutes extravagance for sublimity or goes mad in a semblance of free speech." In 8.3.58 he says that the ways in which speech is corrupted are similar to the ways in which it is adorned.

The most extensive discussion of the decline of eloquence is *Dialogue on the Orators* in Ciceronian style by Tacitus, probably written in A.D. 97.[19] It may be at least in part a negative reaction to Quintilian's views, but since it is set dramatically in 75, long before publication of either of Quintilian's works, there is no opportunity to refer to him specifically. That Tacitus chose to write a Ciceronian dialogue rather than an essay in the abrupt, pointed style of his historical works is, however, some indication that Quintilian's program for return to Ciceronian standards was having results in the late first century. But Tacitus' Ciceronianism is ironic, for the question posed is "Why is oratory dead?" In the course of the dialogue there is examination of the assumption of decline, and one character, Aper, denies it vigorously, but his views are not accepted by any of the others, and the flourishing oratory Aper describes turns out to be that of the informers. Tacitus claims to have been present at the discussion as a young man but to have taken no part in it. His spokesman is Curiatus Maternus, at whose home the conversation takes place and who, at the end, gives what is apparently to be regarded as Tacitus' final answer. Maternus is also a figure for Tacitus in that he has abandoned public oratory for literary composition, in Maturnus' case tragic poetry on historical themes, while Tacitus in 97 was in the process of abandoning oratory for historical writing.

Most of the *Dialogue* consists of five extensive speeches. First, Aper attacks Maternus' abandonment of oratory and attempts to demonstrate the overwhelming greatness of eloquence (5–10). He does not hesitate to allude to contemporary orators, including the informer Eprius Marcellus. Maternus replies briefly (11–13): he is weary of the labors of speaking, finds a better defense in personal integrity than in eloquence, and longs for the quiet life of a poet. Clearly he is anxious to avoid any identification with the informers. There is then an interlude, marked by the arrival of Vipstanus Messala and a general discussion of the relative merits of the ancients and the moderns (14–16). Tacitus touches lightly on the fact that Messala is half brother to the informer Regulus, whom he had even defended in a famous case a few years before (*Histories* 4.42).

Aper then delivers a second speech (16–23), which is a defense of contemporary oratory. He argues that the term "ancient" is ambiguous: Cicero

---

[19] The date has been much debated but seems to have been settled by Murgia, "Pliny's Letters and the *Dialogus*." Translation of *Dialogus* by Peterson in the Loeb Classical Library and by Benario in the Library of Liberal Arts.

is in a sense a modern orator. But Aper severely criticizes speakers of the early empire and praises his contemporaries as briefer, clearer, more brilliant, and more graceful. Messala replies to Aper (25–35) by praising the eloquence of the past and criticizing that of the present as more the art of an actor than of an orator. Maternus urges Messala to get to the causes of decline (27), and the latter promptly attributes it to "the laziness of youth, the neglectfulness of parents, the ignorance of teachers, and forgetfulness of ancient discipline" (28.2). This echoes what we have met in Seneca the Elder and in Petronius. Maternus again interrupts to ask for more detail about training, and we are given a picture of the contrast between old Roman education and the schools of declamation, with their subjects remote from reality (34.4–5). At this point, some of the text is lost. Messala apparently had something more to say, and Julius Secundus may have entered the conversation.

When the text resumes Maternus is speaking. Apparently he regarded the explanation advanced by Messala as a description of symptoms rather than of the cause of decline. His own speech puts the blame primarily on the lack of subjects for great oratory. The disorders and dissensions of the republic had naturally fanned the flames of political eloquence, but now this is no longer necessary under the orderly and peaceful government of the empire. We have seen a reference to "peace" as the possible cause earlier in the remarks of Seneca the Elder, but here this is given greater stress. An additional factor mentioned is that the law courts are now more practical and just but allow less scope to an orator. Maternus repeatedly says that in most ways the change is an improvement and should not be regretted, but there is a note of nostalgia, and toward the end (41.4) there is a distinct ironic note in the description of the senate as the best men, unanimous in policy, of the emperor as the wisest individual, and of the general absence of wrongdoing, so that criminal prosecution is not needed. Throughout the dialogue, loss of freedom of speech is only lightly touched on, for example, in section three when Maternus is asked if he is not worried that his tragedy *Cato the Younger* may be "misunderstood," that is, taken as an attack on tyranny and thus "cause trouble," to which he responds that he will do his duty and if his *Cato* left anything unsaid, his *Thyestes* will say it.

The one remaining important discussion of the decline of eloquence is in Greek and comes at the end of the essay *On Sublimity*, attributed to an unknown author whose name may have been Longinus. This is one of the most perceptive works of ancient literary criticism, which for a long time was little known but was popularized by Boileau in the late seventeenth century and became the inspiration for the cult of "the sublime" that flourished throughout the eighteenth century and anticipated some aspects of the romantic movement. The best manuscript attributes the work to Dionysius (of Halicarnassus?) or Longinus (presumably Cassius Longinus, a rhetorician of the third century), or elsewhere to Dionysius Longinus. Since it claims to be a reaction to Caecilius of Calacte's work on sublimity, it has been dated as early as the Augustan period, or to some time in the next century; more commonly it is now dated in the early or mid–second century.[20] It certainly belongs to the classicizing, Atticizing movement of this whole period. The author is interested in helping a young student understand elevation in style by study and imitation of great models; in the process he relies heavily on rhetorical concepts. The five sources of sublimity he identifies (chapter 8) are the power to conceive great thoughts and the use of strong and inspired emotion (*pathos*), which are aspects of rhetorical invention, and three features of rhetorical style: figures, word choice, and composition or word arrangement. He gives special emphasis to Plato and Demosthenes as stylistic models and compares the latter with Cicero (12.4) in somewhat the same terms used by Quintilian in 10.1.105–7.

In chapter 44 Longinus, as he may as well be called, describes a recent conversation he has had with a "philosopher." The latter remarks that there are many people with natural ability alive but there are no great minds, and the result is a "cosmic dearth of discourse (*logoi*)." Longinus replies that "the explanation generally mentioned" is the loss of political freedom and loss of political rewards. "We are educated from boyhood for a just servitude" and end up as "flatterers on a grand scale." This explanation is not advanced so frankly in the other discussions we have seen but may indeed have been often expressed in private conversations. Longinus, however, does not think it is "the peace of the world" that is the cause. The fundamental cause, he says, is avarice: greed, pride, love of luxury, to which he adds idleness. He thus returns to more general cultural causes resembling those proposed by the elder Seneca.

Pliny the Younger

The younger Pliny was the nephew of Pliny the Elder, a student of Quintilian, a distinguished orator, and author of the *Panegyricus*, the first extant Latin oration since those of Cicero. His public career was rapid and successful: probably quaestor in A.D. 90 and praetor in 93, both under Domitian, and suffect consul in the fall of 100 under Trajan. His career ended as special legate of Trajan to govern the province of Bithynia in the years around 112. It was in that office that he was called upon to deal with complaints against Christians, the earliest reference to them in Latin literature. He describes the problem in a letter to Trajan (10.96) and was advised by the emperor to exercise restraint (10.97).

[20] See the discussion by Russell, "Greek Criticism of the Empire," 306–11. The best translation is also that of Russell, *'Longinus' On Sublimity*; translation by Hamilton in the Loeb Classical Library volume with Aristotle's *Poetics*; commentary by Russell, *'Longinus' On the Sublime*.

Pliny is principally known from ten books of *Epistles*;[21] unlike Cicero's letters these represent his own selection, carefully revised for publication. Several of the letters touch on questions of prose style. The principles that emerge are largely consistent with Quintilian's teaching: style should be suited to subject and will vary within a speech; it can best be learned by imitating writers like Demosthenes and Cicero (1.2). Writing to a young friend, Pliny lists useful exercises in imitation and composition (7.9). "Corrupted eloquence" once flourished, but taste has now been reformed to more austere standards without debarring the florid where it is appropriate (3.18.8–10). One of the most interesting letters is a long communication urging upon the deaf ears of Tacitus the superiority of copiousness over brevity (1.20). Pliny's letters are written in an elegant, simple style showing the influence of Quintilian's teaching. Although he enjoyed hearing the Greek sophist Isaeus (2.3), he shows little interest in declamation and may not have practiced it as an adult.

There are numerous references to Pliny's own speeches and those of others and to trials in the law courts. As an advocate in the courts he claims to have restricted his cases to four categories (6.29): those of his friends, those of people left helpless, those important as legal precedents, and those that were particularly significant in some other way. He took pains to avoid any activity smelling of the informer and, since he was a wealthy man, did not accept payment for his services to clients (5.13.8). The emperor Claudius had legalized fees for patrons, which was standard procedure thereafter.

In the Augustan period the orator and historian Asinius Pollio had introduced the custom of "recitation" of new compositions to invited guests and the public at large (Seneca, *Controversiae* 4.pr.2). This remained a permanent feature of the literary life of Rome. For both poets and prose writers it was a way of trying out a work and receiving criticism from a sympathetic group, thus allowing for further revision in advance of formal publication. Pliny adapted this process in the case of important speeches that he wished to leave as monuments of his rhetorical art. The earliest speech Pliny decided to publish was apparently one he gave at the dedication of the new library he presented to his native city of Comum in A.D. 96. As he describes it in *Epistle* 1.8, he first wrote and revised the speech as carefully as he could. Apparently it was a success, though he says nothing about the actual delivery. He then invited a group of friends to hear him recite the speech and to give criticisms of a general sort. Subsequently he sent a copy of the speech to a friend to be corrected and criticized in detail. Finally he published the revised version, which has not survived. Careful preparation, delivery, recitation, circulation of a written draft to friends for criticism, and careful revision before publication was his standard procedure (7.17.7). Although his letters are written in a simple style, his speeches ranged over the full register

---

[21] Translation by Radice in the Penguin series and in the Loeb Classical Library.

of styles as appropriate to the subject. For example, he says (7.30.5) that he took Demosthenes' passionate attack on Midias as a model for imitation in a speech he gave in the senate early in the reign of Nerva to try to bring Publicius Certus to justice for activities under Domitian. Publication of course performed the practical function of keeping the issues of a speech alive and affecting public opinion beyond that of the original audience. A few days after publication of Pliny's speech, Certus was taken ill and died. Pliny heard reports that he had imagined himself hunted down by Pliny, sword in hand. *Epistle* 1.2 is a request for revisions and corrections of another speech, which Pliny says was modeled on Demosthenes, Calvus (the Atticist acquaintance of Cicero), and Cicero himself. This indicates that the speech ranged over a variety of styles.

Epistle 2.11 is a long letter describing Pliny's prosecution of Marius Priscus for extortion, conducted in the senate with the emperor Trajan presiding. Under the empire the senate acted as a court of law when charges were made against any of its members. The case was a difficult one, since some senators thought Priscus had already been punished enough by previous convictions on lesser charges and regarded the trial as a threat to their privileges. The presence of the emperor was inhibiting also, though Trajan could be counted on to be fair. Pliny was allowed to speak for twelve larger (twenty-minute) and four smaller (fifteen-minute) measures by the water clock, or a total of about five hours. He says that the emperor was very kind and repeatedly had a freedman whisper in Pliny's ear that he should be sparing of his voice and strength. Possibly Trajan found five hours of Pliny's eloquence rather too much of a good thing. The principal issue in the case was a legal one: Pliny had to show that the law against extortion covered the actions of Priscus, which he did by analogy with the interpretation of other laws. The second day of the hearing was taken up by a speech by the defendant, a second speech for the prosecution by Tacitus, spoken "very eloquently" Pliny says, and an emotional peroration for the defense by Catius Fronto. On the third day the documentary and other evidence was produced, and the members of the senate debated what decision to reach, as in Cicero's fourth *Oration against Catiline*. Two main views were expressed: restitution to the state of the money extorted in bribes, together with perpetual banishment from Italy; or restitution of the money without banishment. The emperor's influence seems to have persuaded the majority to the heavier sentence. Both Pliny and Tacitus received the thanks of the senate. It is not clear whether Pliny published this speech; he did recite it once to a group of friends, though hesitantly, saying that judicial speeches are really effective only in the actual circumstances of a court (2.19).

Pliny describes a number of other cases in which he appeared, whether for the prosecution or the defense. *Epistle* 4.9 gives an account of his defense of Julius Bassus for extortion as governor of Bithynia. His personal conclusion was that Bassus was a good man who had acted incautiously in some respects but deserved to be acquitted. In terms of stasis Pliny ruled out denial of the facts, which were well known. He had to admit also that the actions were prohibited by law. To admit everything and throw his client on the mercy of the senate seemed imprudent. He was thus left with stasis of quality, but here too he felt he could not insist that what had been done had been done "rightly." In this dilemma, he says, he "thought it best to hold a middle course." Apparently he thus claimed that his client's intentions had not been evil, that he had acted unwittingly, and that his real friendship with those from whom he received presents mitigated the wrong done; the prejudices against Bassus from previous incidents were probably brought out and the motives of his accusers questioned, with the object of showing that the case was not clear-cut. Pliny's defense of Bassus was successful, in large part because of the pity he was able to awaken for the misfortunes into which Bassus had fallen under Domitian.

Pliny often practiced before the centumviral court, which handled inheritance cases. He was especially proud of his defense of Attia Variola, whose father had acquired a new wife at the age of eighty and changed his will in favor of her and her son by a previous marriage, to the exclusion of his own daughter. The jury consisted of four separate panels, who were probably charged with separate decisions involving several claimants to the estate but who sat together, making a total jury of 180. The basilica was crowded and victory only barely achieved. Pliny describes the speech as follows (6.3.7–11):

> Long as it is, I do not fail to hope that it will gain the favor of a very short speech, for there is refreshing variety in the abundance of matter, the adroit arrangement, the numerous short narrative passages, and the variation of the style. There are many elevated passages . . . , much determined argument, and much that is elegant. It often happened that the need for facts and figures and for all but calling for a counting table obtruded upon those ardent and noble parts so that the dignity of the centumviral court was suddenly transformed into the scene of a private case. We gave sails to indignation, to anger, to grief, and in the swell of this splendid case we were borne on as though on the high sea with many winds. In a word, some of my associates like to think that this speech (I shall say it again) is as it were the "Ctesiphon" among my orations [i.e., the equal of Demosthenes' speech *On the Crown*].

When he entered on his term as consul in A.D. 100, Pliny delivered in the senate a speech of thanks to Trajan for his appointment. Such a speech is known as a *gratiarum actio*. Previous consuls had expressed their appreciation of the honor, but Pliny seems to have been the first to seize the occasion as an opportunity for a major address dealing with the role of the emperor and his relationship to the senate and his other subjects.[22] Both in the text of the speech as we have it (e.g., 45.6; 73.6; 75.3–5) and in a letter discussing it, Pliny states his fundamental goal: "that the virtues of our emperor be reinforced by sincere praise of them and secondly that future emperors be admonished, not as by a teacher, but in the form of example, by what road they best might attain the same glory" (3.18.1–2). Pliny spoke of course as a member of the senate and of the senatorial elite that had often formed the major opposition to previous emperors; he is holding out an offer of their loyal cooperation with Trajan in return for the emperor's acceptance of principles of liberty and constitutional government. His confidence in Trajan was not misplaced, and his speech may have contributed to the justice of Trajan's reign, which was honored throughout the empire.[23]

Pliny's objectives required that the speech be published and read by his contemporaries and successors. After delivering it he amplified it and circulated it to friends for suggestions (3.13). He also delivered some or all of it before a large audience in three sessions of recitation (3.18.4). Finally he published it under the title *Panegyricus*, reminiscent of Isocrates. The text as we have it runs to nearly a hundred pages of Latin. It is impossible to be certain what parts come from the original speech and what is later, though the passages prophesying a future triumph may be additions after the fact. The speech falls into six main parts, which accord with the advice for the composition of epideictic oratory as given by classical rhetoricians (e.g., Quintilian 3.7.10–18): there is a short introduction (1–3), a narrative of Trajan's earlier career (4–24), an account of Trajan's services to Rome as emperor in the immediately preceeding period (25–55), a description of his activities in A.D. 100 (56–80), an account of the virtues of his private life (81–89), and finally Pliny's personal gratitude to him (90–95). As a political and social document of the time the *Panegyricus* has great importance; as a piece of oratory it is extremely tiresome. The main problem is the homogeneity of tone. There are no emotional high points, no changes of speech or style, no flashes of passion or wit. Throughout, Pliny maintains the same highly worked flow of noble *sententiae*. Even the exclamations and the rhetorical questions do not ruffle the surface of his praise. It is a fitting tone for the oratory of a glorious, but static, empire.

Fronto and Gellius

A leading figure in the literary life of Rome in the middle of the second century was M. Cornelius Fronto. He was born in North Africa about A.D. 100; came to Rome, where he practiced in the courts and held public office,

---

[22] See Morford, "Pliny's *Panegyricus*." Translation by Radice in the Loeb Classical Library.

[23] The speeches of Dio Chrysostom entitled *On Kingship*, addressed to Trajan somewhat later, have a similar objective. They will be discussed in the next chapter.

culminating in a suffect consulship in 143; and was regarded as the greatest Latin orator of the age (Dio Cassius 69.18). As such, he was appointed by Antoninus Pius as teacher of rhetoric to the two heirs to the throne, Marcus Aurelius and Lucius Verus. He continued a close friendship with them both when they jointly succeeded to the throne in 161, even though Marcus turned away from rhetoric to Stoic philosophy as a more meaningful private study.

Fronto is best known from a collection of letters, including many of his own and some replies from Antoninus, Marcus Aurelius, and Verus. The text survives only in a palimpsest manuscript; some time in later antiquity an attempt was made to erase the writing as much as possible and to reuse the pages in two codices of Christian works. The original text can only be read with difficulty; the pages are out of order, and some are not preserved at all.[24] The letters are largely devoted to personal and literary matters. Some of the earlier letters give a glimpse of Fronto's methods in teaching his royal pupils: on one occasion he sent Marcus a piece from the early Roman historian Coelius Antipater to study with an assignment in composition (vol. 1, p. 18); he also assigned the composition of maxims, similes, and commonplaces (vol. 1, pp. 12, 34, and 54), and suggested themes for declamation (vol. 1, pp. 210 and 214).

The amount of historical information in the letters is disappointing, but there is an interesting exchange between Fronto, Verus, and Marcus on the encomiastic history of Verus' Parthian War that Fronto composed (vol. 2, pp.194–98 in Haines). Verus supplied the information; Fronto then elaborated it into a propaganda document. Nobody involved seems to have thought that historical veracity was significant. Only the preface survives (vol. 2, pp. 198–218), largely based on rhetorical commonplaces and literary imitations. A number of the letters refer to Fronto's activities in the law courts, with short quotations of what he said, or to speeches in the senate. Like Pliny, he gave a speech of thanks on assuming the consulship. In a few comments on it (vol. 2, p. 118) he says that the greatest virtue of an orator is to find a path between what he wants to say and what his hearers want to hear.[25]

Included among the letters are some short examples of sophistic epideictic: an *Eroticus*, inspired by Plato's *Phaedrus* (vol. 1, pp. 20–30), and parts of *Praise of Smoke and Dust* (vol 1, pp. 38–44) and *Praise of Negligence* (1.44–49). Fronto says (vol. 1, p. 40) that no composition of this kind previously existed in Latin; the requirements are abundance of *sententiae* and finish of

[24] The best edition of the Latin text is by Van den Hout, *Frontonis Epistulae*. The only available translation is that of Haines in the Loeb Classical Library, made from an earlier version of the Latin text. Passages in the letters are here referred to by volume and page in Haines' translation.

[25] For discussion of Fronto's speeches, see my *Art of Rhetoric in the Roman World* 595–97.

style, and the objective is "sweetness." Another sophistic work is *Arion*, a rhetorical narrative about the Greek lyre player saved by a dolphin (vol. 1, pp. 54–58). In his historical and epideictic writings and in his overall view of rhetoric, Fronto is the best Latin counterpart of the Greek "Second Sophistic," which flourished in this period and will be discussed in chapter 11. He also knew several of the Greek sophists personally, including Herodes Atticus. The Second Sophistic was an Atticizing movement imitating the style, and often taking up themes, of classical Greek writers of the fourth century. Fronto and several of his contemporaries seem to want an analogous movement in Latin, imitating Greek subjects but turning back to early Latin models of diction. The result is archaizing. A letter that summarizes Fronto's views was regarded by Haines as the earliest extant and thus put first in his collection. It takes the search for unusual or unexpected words as the most important feature of stylistic study. Cato, Sallust, Plautus, Ennius, and a few other authors are praised for their skill at finding the right word; Cicero's neglect of it is criticized. Fronto is doubtless wrong if he thought early Latin writers chose their words with greater care than did later writers. The Augustan poets, of whom Fronto is not very fond, deserve more praise in that respect, but by Fronto's time their language seemed trite. Although Fronto bases his theory of style on search for the "right" word, it seems clear that he was attracted by the flavor and novelty of archaism; genuine, old Latin words no longer in use had for him a special charm. But this predilection is applied with some restraint in Fronto's own writing.

Fronto tried to rescue Marcus Aurelius for rhetoric, partly by the influence of his friendship, partly by flattering his oratorical abilities, partly by argument. The first of four letters collectively entitled *On Eloquence* addressed to Marcus exhorts him to pursue the subject as something useful and necessary to a ruler. Fronto tries to answer Marcus' complaint that when he has said something brilliant he feels pleased and that this feeling is wrong (vol. 2, p. 62). Chastize yourself for self-satisfaction if you must, he says, but why chastize eloquence any more than you would good judgment, which might also give satisfaction. The third letter praises Marcus' ability at oratory and his continuing need of rhetoric to express his thought. The fourth letter is a critique of a recent speech by Marcus, which Fronto says was not entirely characterized by *elocutio novella*. Although that phrase, translated as "the new style," has sometimes been taken as the name for a movement led by Fronto, it occurs only here and perhaps only means "novelty of expression." In a letter to Marcus entitled *On Speeches*, Fronto castigates the hectic, trivial style of the younger Seneca and the empty repetitions of Lucan (vol. 2, p. 102 and 104), and he rebukes the choice of words in a recent edict of Marcus as inappropriate: "Keep to the old mintage. . . . Seek some word, not one coined by you, for that would be absurd, but employed more neatly, more suitably, more appropriately" (vol. 2, p. 114).

Fronto's literary tastes were shared by his friend Aulus Gellius and can be found in a miscellany of antiquarian studies that Gellius compiled over many years, entitled *Attic Nights*.[26] Gellius often discusses the style and rhetorical skill of early Latin writers, with quotations from their works. It is to Gellius (6.3) that we are indebted for preservation of the better part of Cato's speech *For the Rhodians* and Tyro's criticism of it, discussed in chapter 6 above.

Apuleius

The greatest Latin writer of the mid–second century is another North African, Apuleius, author of the prose-romance *Metamorphoses*. This is the story of the transformation of a certain Lucius into an ass and his resulting adventures until converted to the worship of Isis. It is written in difficult, highly artificial Latin, reminiscent of Greek sophists, Roman declamation, and the teachings of Fronto. Archaism and a search for novelty of expression abound.

Apuleius also wrote the only judicial oration preserved from the time of the Roman Empire, his *Apology* in defense of the charge that he used magic to gain the hand and estate of an African woman in Oea near modern Tripoli.[27] We should probably assume that the speech was revised for publication and does not in all respects preserve what Apuleius actually said in court, but given the nature of the charge, the fictional world of declamation or of Apuleius' novel here merges with the real world of the law courts. He adapts rhetorical precepts for invention and arrangement to the needs of the occasion. There is first an exordium (1–3) drawn from the opponent, the judge, and the case. The charge is generalized, for Apuleius argues that it is not only himself but "philosophy" that is on trial. Taken together with the title and a number of references to Plato, this suggests that Apuleius is trying to present himself as a kind of Socrates, on trial for his beliefs in a mystical, Platonic religious creed and for his way of life. Most of the speech, however, deals with details of the charge and their refutation. His opponent has tried to arouse prejudice against him by referring to his beauty, his eloquence and poetry, his personal vanity, the poverty that led him to his action, and his place of birth; these slanders Apuleius shows to be mutually contradictory (25). He then gives a preliminary refutation of the charge of magic (25–27). Section 28 is a *partitio* in which he promises first to refute the fact of his use of magic, second to show that even if he were a magician he has not engaged in evil practices, third to discuss the real motivation and circumstances of his marriage (thus postponing the narration until late in

[26] Translation by Rolfe in the Loeb Classical Library. See discussion by Fantham, "Latin Criticism of the Early Empire," 294–96.

[27] Translation by Butler, *The Apologia and Florida of Apuleius*.

the speech), and finally to show how his stepson has been turned against him. This division of the subject, however, is not systematically carried through. He largely relies on stasis of fact rather than of quality. The narrative of his relationship with his wife (66–96) is well handled. The most convincing part of the argument is the discussion of a letter by his wife (81–83), which the opposition quoted out of context to try to show that she regarded her husband as a magician. The fourth topic, relating to his stepson, is treated briefly (98–101), and the speech ends with a short peroration. Apuleius rather plays with his adversaries in the first two-thirds of the speech, before springing the trap of the evidence he has to support his defense. We do not know if he won the case; he seems to have moved to Carthage soon after.

Other works by Apuleius include *On the God of Socrates* and *Florida*. The former is a piece of sophistic oratory resembling speeches of Greek sophists of the time—for example, Aelius Aristides or Maximus of Tyre—on Platonic subjects. *Florida* is a collection of twenty-six short rhetorical pieces of considerable variety. We do not know whether they are rhetorical exercises or selections from his writings made by himself or by someone else. Two could be regarded as short speeches: number 9, in which he compares himself to the sophist Hippias and praises the governor Severianus, and number 16, which thanks Aemilianus Strabo and the senate of Carthage for a statue that has been ordered in his honor as a priest. Others resemble school exercises: comparisons, descriptions, and fables. The style varies with the subject. Overall, they show the interest of a Latin writer in experimenting with epideictic rhetoric of the sort practiced by Greek sophists of the time.

After the mid–second century there are no important secular works of Latin literature until the fourth century. Christian Latin, however, developed rapidly. Its relation to rhetoric will be discussed in a later chapter.

Greek Rhetoric under the Roman Empire

During the first two centuries of the Roman Empire, from the time of Augustus to that of Marcus Aurelius, there was extensive communication between Greek- and Latin-speaking areas, and a common culture evolved, in which the traditional understanding and teaching of rhetoric remained an important feature. Beginning in the last third of the second century of the Christian era, however, East and West begin to draw apart, leading by the fourth century to the existence of two empires with two different languages, Greek and Latin; two different Christian churches, Orthodox and Catholic; and two different understandings of rhetoric, the Hermogenic tradition in the East and the Ciceronian in the West. Some signs of what was to come, however, can be detected as early as the Augustan period. Dionysius of Halicarnassus came to Rome, taught rhetoric there, learned Latin, and wrote a history of early Rome; but he also began the development of new ways of looking at the "characters" of style, as described in chapter 8. In the East these led to the influential formulation of the "ideas" of style by Hermogenes, but Latin rhetoricians generally preferred the older system of the three *genera dicendi*. Quintilian shows little awareness of new Greek approaches to rhetoric in his own age and transmits Cicero's understanding of the subject with only minor revisions. Latin rhetoric always retained primary focus on judicial oratory and thus on an interest in Roman law; Greek rhetoric put greater emphasis on epideictic oratory and thus on an interest in philosophy.

Most formal education in antiquity was in private schools in the homes of teachers or in rented space in a city; parents paid fees directly to teachers. Some Hellenistic cities had public schools, endowed by benefactors.[1] Vespasian was perhaps imitating this model when he appointed Quintilian to teach rhetoric in Rome. In the mid–second century Antoninus Pius appointed Lollianus to a chair of rhetoric in Athens (Philostratus, *Sophists* 23). In a letter addressed to the cities of Asia, but applicable to the whole empire, he took a further step toward providing for public education in ordering that sophists—the standard term for teachers of Greek rhetoric under the empire—teachers of grammar, and physicians be given relief from taxes, the number being limited to five each in provincial capitals, four in cities where law courts met, and three in other towns.[2] These teachers were apparently paid a stipend from municipal funds. There were

[1] See Marrou, *Education in Antiquity*, 160–62.
[2] See Justinian's *Digest of Roman Law* 27.1.6.

of course numerous other teachers who supported themselves from students' fees and did not enjoy immunity from taxes. In the fourth century the national system of education was further standardized. The price edict of Diocletian, published in 301, set salaries of sophists at 250 denarii per student per month, that of grammarians at 200. In the later Theodosian Code (13.3), officially designated sophists were exempted from public obligations and court summonses, and their salaries were paid by the local municipalities.

Progymnasmata

Grammar schools and some rhetorical schools taught exercises in composition that were "progymnastic," that is, they were "preparatory" to the writing and delivery of declamations. Until the fifth century B.C. Greek schools emphasized understanding and memorization of poetic texts. Students were not expected to write original compositions. The early sophists introduced exercises in composition and for the first time encouraged some originality on the part of their students. Speech writing by students was a major activity in the school of Isocrates. The first reference to *progymnasmata* as "preparatory exercises" is found in *Rhetoric for Alexander* (chapter 28). Probably they became common in the Hellenistic period, various types were developed, and some of these were taken over by Roman teachers. The author of *Rhetoric for Herennius* is familiar with "narrative" as an exercise in composition (1.12); paraphrase is a feature of later exercises and was practiced by Crassus, according to Cicero (*On the Orator* 1.154). In discussing training in grammar Quintilian (2.4) mentions twelve exercises in composition, which he calls *primae exercitationes*. Some, including narrative of a myth or the plot of a play, he regarded as properly taught by grammarians, whereas he thinks that historical narrative is best taught by a rhetorician. He says that a teacher sometimes dictated fair copies of exercises as models for students to imitate; otherwise teachers presumably assigned a problem, such as to write a comparison of two historical figures. Latin literature, beginning in the Augustan age, shows the influence of exercises in composition, which even became literary genres. The *Heroides* of Ovid are versified *prosōpopoeiae*, or "personifications," a common exercise in schools. Often literary versions of exercises are combined as structural units in larger works: Ovid's *Metamorphoses* uses myth, personification, narrative, comparison, and *ekphrasis* (vivid description of a place or work of art).[3] The comparisons of Greeks and Romans that Plutarch included in his *Lives* are literary versions of *synkrisis*, another exercise common in schools. Although progymnasmata were clearly practiced in Roman schools of grammar and rhetoric,

[3] On the importance of exercises in composition for Greek and Latin literature, see Cairns, *Generic Composition.*

there is no extant Latin handbook of them until the sixth century, when the grammarian Priscian made a Latin paraphrase of the Greek survey attributed to Hermogenes.[4]

There are four surviving handbooks of progymnasmata in Greek, by or attributed to Theon, Hermogenes, Aphthonius, and Nicolaus. In addition, there are fair copies of progymnasmata, including ninety-six examples representing all the common forms by the fourth-century sophist Libanius. The handbook by Theon is apparently the earliest.[5] Quintilian (3.6.48; 9.3.76) mentions a rhetorician of that name who is usually identified with the sophist Aelius Theon, listed in the Byzantine encyclopedia *Suda* as the author of progymnasmata and other works on grammar and rhetoric.

Theon's treatise begins with a preface in which he criticizes students who undertake declamation without preliminary training and even without a liberal education; the exercises he will describe are useful for all kinds of composition: rhetorical, historical, and poetic. Progymnasmata, Theon claims, are the foundation of every "idea" of speech; if properly introduced into the souls of the young, that is, if students are trained to work with these compositional units, good results will follow. The preface ends by advising that all the exercises should involve reading examples aloud, listening to others read, and paraphrasing models. Original composition and the argument of opposing views should come only after the student has attained facility in copying.

A second work on progymnasmata is that attributed to Hermogenes, the most important rhetorician of the second century. Its authenticity, however, is doubtful. The Hermogenic treatise lacks a preface and gives a very brief account of thirteen exercises with little illustration. The third, and most important, treatise is by Aphthonius of Antioch, a student of Libanius in the second half of the fourth century.[6] The clarity of his discussion and divisions and his inclusion of examples won for Aphthonius' work an authoritative place in Byzantine education. An extensive body of commentary was built up over the next millenium, and the treatise was translated into Latin by Rudolph Agricola in the late fifteenth century, making it available for use in the schools of western Europe.

Aphthonius describes the following fourteen exercises:

1. *Mythos*, or fable. The exercise took the form of assigning the student to write a simple fable in imitation of those attributed to Aesop. Aphthonius distinguishes three forms: rational, involving a human being;

---

[4] English translation of the Hermogenic treatise by Baldwin, *Medieval Rhetoric*, 23–38, and of Priscian's version by Miller et al., *Readings in Medieval Rhetoric*, 52–68.

[5] Text and translation by Butts, "The Progymnasmata of Theon"; translation of the first two chapters by Matson et al., in *Readings*, 254–62.

[6] Translation by Nadeau, "Aphthonius"; revised translation by Matson et al., in *Readings*, 267–88.

ethical, involving an animal; mixed, involving both. The moral can be stated either at the beginning or the end.

2. *Diēgēma*, or narrative. The "narration" of a judicial speech is usually called *diēgēsis*; it ordinarily sets forth a series of actions; the exercise in narrative is simpler, describing only one action. Its divisions are fictitious (mythological), historical, and political. The topics to consider are agent, time, place, manner, and cause. These are derived ultimately from Aristotle's theory of categories. The "virtues" of narrative are four: clarity, brevity, persuasiveness, and purity of language. These may derive from Isocrates (see Quintilian 4.2.31).

3. *Chreia*, or anecdote, defined as "a brief reminiscence referring to some person in a pithy form." It is called *chreia* because it is *chreiodes*, "(morally) useful." The anecdote may report a saying, an action, or a combination of the two. Students were given a saying or a description of an action by a famous person and assigned to work it out (*ergasia*) by writing a paragraph expanding and developing the meaning with the following headings: praise of the chria; paraphrase; statement of the cause; example of the meaning; contrast and comparison; testimony of others; epilogue. The chria selected as an example by Aphthonius is "Isocrates said that the root of education is bitter, but its fruit is sweet." In modern times students of biblical studies have shown special interest in the chria as a compositional unit in the Scriptures.[7] The Christian mass originates in the chria of Mark 14 and Matthew 26, which describes the action and words of Jesus in offering the bread and wine to his disciples at the Last Supper.

4. *Gnōmē*, or maxim. As a rhetorical form this was first described by Aristotle in *On Rhetoric* 2.21; it became the *sententia* beloved by the Roman declaimers. Aphthonius divides it into protreptic, apotreptic, declarative, simple, and compound. The student was given a moral generalization from a classical writer and expected to work it out in the same way as a chria.

5. *Anaskeuē*, or refutation. Up to this point, the exercises only required a student to describe, paraphrase, or amplify the material assigned by the teacher. "Refutation" is the first exercise to require logical reasoning on the student's part. It was studied before "confirmation," because it is generally easier to find objections to someone else's thesis than to offer an independent proof. Aphthonius divides the exercise into attack on those who hold the view, followed by exposition using the following headings: impossible, illogical, unsuitable, and inexpedient. What was to be refuted was drawn from myth, narrative, or chria. Aphthonius' example is refutation of the story of Apollo and Daphne as improbable.

[7] Cf., e.g., O'Neil, "The Chreia in Greco-Roman Literature"; Robbins and Mack, *Patterns of Persuasion*, 1–106; Williams, "Parable and Chreia."

6. *Kataskeuē*, or confirmation. What is confirmed should be neither self-evident nor impossible, and the treatment is the reverse of refutation. Aphthonius' example is an argument that the story of Daphne is probable.

7. *Koinos topos*, or commonplace. In Theon's handbook and in the Hermogenic treatise this is defined as amplification of either vice or virtue, but in Aphthonius and in general it means attacking vice. It is called "common" because it envisions criticism of stereotypes—tyrants, for example—rather than specific individuals. The headings to be used in "working out" the commonplace are contradiction, comparison, maxim attacking the motivation of the type of person described, digression on earlier deeds, rejection of pity, and what are called *telika kephalaia*, "final headings." These are used in some other progymnasmata and are important topics in public address: legality, justice, expediency, practicability, honor, and result. As in the case of refutation and confirmation, the negative skill was taught first as easier and was followed by the positive skill in the next exercise.

8. *Enkōmion*, or praise. The progymnasmatic encomium provided the basic training in epideictic rhetoric practiced by the sophists, although it could have some application in passages of praise in deliberative and judicial oratory as well. Subjects on which a student practiced were praise of persons, things (like justice), times (like spring), places, animals, and growing things (like olive trees). A whole people—for example, the Athenians—can be praised or an individual singled out. Aphthonius' examples are encomia of wisdom and of the historian Thucydides, favorably compared with Herodotus. Headings to be used are prooemium, *genos* (divided into nation, city, ancestors, and parents), upbringing (divided into habits, skills, and laws), deeds (divided into those of body, soul, and fortune), comparison with another person, and epilogue, which may be a prayer. These topics are regularly found in epideictic rhetoric beginning with Athenian funeral orations and continuing through the encomia of emperors and other officials of the Roman Empire.

9. *Psogos*, or invective. Aphthonius says it differs from commonplace in that it does not seek punishment, but it differs more significantly in that it attacks a specific, named individual. The example he gives is an invective against Philip of Macedon, which would presumably draw heavily on Demosthenes.

10. *Synkrisis*, or comparison. This can be viewed as a double encomium or the combination of encomium of one person or thing and invective against another. The subjects compared should not be dealt with seperately but compared heading by heading, using topics listed under encomium. Aphthonius' example is a comparison of Achilles and Hector.

11. *Ēthopoeia*, or personification. Aphthonius thinks of ethos in Aris-

totelian terms as the presentation of moral character by a speaker through words and arguments. There are three species: *eidolopoeia* is a speech attributed to the ghost of a known person (an example would be Cicero's personification of Appius Claudius Caecus in his speech *For Caelius*); *prosōpopoeia*, the term used by Theon and some other writers for the exercise in general but by Aphthonius to mean personification of an imaginary or mythological character; and *ēthopoeia* in the narrow sense of personification of a historical character. The divisions of ethopoeia are pathetical, ethical, and mixed. The "characters" of style to be sought in the exercise are clarity, conciseness, floridity, lack of polish, and absence of figures. Instead of headings, there are to be divisions into past, present, and future time.

12. *Ekphrasis*, or description. The subjects, like those of encomium, may be persons, actions, times, places, animals, and growing things. The description should be complete: of a person, for example, from head to foot; of actions, from start to result. The "character" of style should be *aneimenos*, "relaxed," but ornamented with figures. Aphthonius' example is an ekphrasis of the acropolis of Alexandria. Ekphrasis is an important feature of classical literature, beginning with the description of the Shield of Achilles in the eighteenth book of the *Iliad*. Ekphrasis is often found in historical writing, but in oratory is confined to works given literary amplification, Cicero's published speeches against Verres, for example. The Homeric model produced a series of descriptions of works of art in which the narrator expresses the emotions awakened on seeing a statue or painting. The best examples from the time of the Roman Empire are the *Eikones* by Philostratus and his grandson of the same name.

13. *Thesis*, or argument. This comes late in the sequence, since it is an introduction to argument in the philosophical schools. The forms are political and social—Should a city be walled? Should one marry?—or theoretical—Is the heaven spherical? "Hypotheses" add particular names and circumstances, real or imaginary. Aphthonius seems to regard thesis as a progymnasma, hypothesis as a fully developed declamation (the *controversiae* of Roman schools). The divisions of thesis are *ephodos* or approach, which takes the place of a prooemium, followed by the "final headings" noted under commonplace (number 7).

14. *Nomou eisphora*, or introduction of a law. This exercise Aphthonius calls a gynnasma rather than a progymnasma, and it has many characteristics of a deliberative hypothesis, though persons are not necessarily named. It takes two forms, *synēgoria*, or advocacy of a proposed law, and *katēgoria*, or opposition. The headings are constitutionality, justice, expediency, and practicability. The argument for or against the law is to be stated, then the counterargument is to be given, then the headings are to be discussed. The example given is a speech opposing a law requiring

that an adulterer, taken in the act, be killed. This has some application not only to deliberative rhetoric but to declamations involving husbands, wives, and adultery, frequently cited in the Hermogenic corpus and found also in Roman *controversiae*.

The fourth treatise on progymnasmata is by Nicolaus, who had studied with the Neoplatonists Plutarch and Proclus in Athens and taught rhetoric in Constantinople in the reign of the emperor Leo (A.D. 457–74).[8] This is the most thoughtful of the discussions of the subject and, like the treatise of Aphthonius, was used as a textbook in the Byzantine period. By Nicolaus' time the study of rhetoric had been reorganized in Greek schools to incorporate new approaches to invention and style introduced by Hermogenes and to make it more useful as an introduction to the study of philosophy, in accordance with Neoplatonist teaching. These changes will be discussed in greater detail later in this chapter. One feature of the new program was the writing and study of prolegomena, or introductions to the study of rhetoric from a philosophical point of view. Nicolaus provides such an introduction, though he does not use the structure of four or ten questions commonly found elsewhere. At the end of the introduction he defines rhetoric in somewhat Aristotelian terms as "an ability in invention and orderly expression of the available means of persuasion in every discourse." The duty of the orator is to consider what should be said on every subject, to arrange the material, and to express it in the best way. The goal of rhetoric is not to persuade, but to speak persuasively.

Another feature of the new program was greater emphasis on logical organization of a subject and its parts. In Nicolaus' work this takes the form of identifying the species of rhetoric for which each exercise offers preliminary training—whether judicial, deliberative, or epideictic—the part of an oration to which it applies, and the appropriate style to be used. Also consistent with the interests of the time is the emphasis given to encomium and the division of that subject into a variety of genres similar to those found in the somewhat earlier treatises on epideictic rhetoric by Menander.

One might have expected that the schools would have provided some instruction in letter writing, an important skill for students and adults throughout the Hellenistic and Roman periods. Many examples of private, public, and literary letters survive, either separately or in large collections of the letters of individuals. Theon mentions letters once and Nicolaus refers to letter writing briefly, but epistolography was never a progymnasmatic exercise, and it is not entirely clear how the average student gained command of the conventions of form. The only Greek rhetorical treatise to give any attention to letter writing is Demetrius' *On Style* (223–25); references in Cicero, however, imply that a theory of letter writing existed and that

[8] Translation of the preface by Matson et al., in *Readings*, 264–65.

various types of letters were recognized. Collections of model letters were made, of which fragments are preserved in papyrus; the techniques could thus be learned by imitation, but we do not know in what context this was practiced. It is possible that by later antiquity, when the civil service had developed into a vast bureaucracy, courses in letter writing and shorthand—a skill also much developed during the Roman Empire—were offered those training to become public scribes. Some short handbooks of Greek epistology survive that give basic patterns of composition. The earliest of these, perhaps from the Hellenistic period, identifies fourteen types of letters: friendly, commendatory, blaming, and so on. Another, from late antiquity, has a list of forty-one types, with brief examples.[9]

Hermogenes and the Formation of the Hermogenic Corpus

The most important Greek rhetorician of the Roman Empire was Hermogenes. He has generally been assumed to be identical with Hermogenes of Tarsus, described by Philostratus (2.577) as a young prodigy in declamation who, at the age of fifteen, was honored by a visit from Marcus Aurelius in A.D. 176. After an early flowering, his oratorical powers waned. Philostratus makes no mention of Hermogenes' technical writings; according to later commentators they were also written in his youth, but they are not student notebooks like Cicero's *On Invention*, and it seems more likely that after losing facility at oratory he turned to teaching rhetoric and writing technical manuals.

Five works survive under Hermogenes' name.[10] The short handbook of progymnasmata has already been mentioned and is probably not a genuine work of Hermogenes. The extended treatise *On Invention*, to be discussed later in this section, is probably not genuine either, though it may be indebted to a lost work by Hermogenes on the subject. *On Staseis* and *On Ideas of Style* can be regarded as genuine. *On Method* is probably not by Hermogenes but may date from his time.

As explained in chapter 5 above, Aristotle recognized the need to define the question at issue in a judicial speech; in the second century B.C. Hermagoras developed the subject into a detailed account of stasis theory, versions of which are found in Cicero's *On Invention* and in *Rhetoric for Herennius*. Subsequently, teachers of rhetoric exercised their ingenuity in criticizing

---

[9] Two late Latin treatises have short sections on letter writing: Julius Victor (pp. 447–48 Halm) and Anon. *Excerpta Rhetorica* (p. 589 Halm). For translation of passages in Greek and Latin on letter writing, see Malherbe, "Ancient Epistolary Theorists." See also my *Greek Rhetoric under Christian Emperors*, 70–73.

[10] The standard Greek text is Rabe, *Hermogenis Opera*. For translation of the Progymnasmata, see n.4 above; translations of other works include Nadeau, "Hermogenes *On Stases*," and Wooten, *Hermogenes' On Types of Style*.

and revising Hermagoras' system. Quintilian surveys the results up to his own time and offers his own system in *Institutio* 3.6. Lollianus, mentioned early in this chapter as holding a chair of rhetoric in second-century Athens, and his contemporary Minucianus seem to have introduced new approaches in works now lost.[11] Minucianus' treatise was in fact better known than that of Hermogenes for the next two centuries, but thereafter Hermogenes' work gained acceptance as the authority on the subject. Numerous commentaries were written throughout the Byzantine period. Hermogenes' treatise consists of an introduction, a chapter on method (a favorite term with him), and an extended account of the *diaeresis* or division of stasis into fourteen *kephalaia*, or "headings." It is this systematic treatment of the subject that greatly appealed to later Greeks, including Neoplatonists who saw in it training in logical method.

Hermogenes begins with the claim that the most important part of rhetoric is *diaeresis* and *apodeixis*, or division and demonstration, of political questions. A "political question" is a logical disputation dealing with particular instances arising under the laws or customs of a state on the matter of what is just, honorable, or advantageous or all of these together. It is, however, the function of philosophy, not rhetoric, to investigate these topics in general terms. Most of Hermogenes' account of stasis deals with judicial situations, some with deliberative; passing reference is made to epideictic. The laws and customs he cites are not those of the Roman Empire; the Greek student did not learn law by studying rhetoric. A few are derived from classical Greek city-states, but most are imaginary laws devised by rhetoricians as themes for declamation. Deliberative themes were often inspired by incidents in Greek history or speeches of the Attic orators, but no attempt was made to preserve historicity. Not only did declamation not teach law, it did not teach history either.[12]

Subjects for declamation, according to Hermogenes, are divided into persons and deeds. Persons fall into seven divisions (the process of diaeresis begins in earnest here): specific and proper, like Pericles; related, like a father; discreditable, like a profligate; ethical, like a farmer; combined, like a rich youth; combining quality and act, like an effeminate youth accused of prostitution; and descriptive, like a soldier. Deeds are those of the accused, those of others that connect an accused with a crime (e.g., a man is charged with treason when the enemy erect a statue of him), and intermediate, when the evidence is circumstantial. Questions are capable of stasis if there are persons and acts to be judged (or at least one of these), if plausible arguments are available, and if the decision is uncertain. Otherwise the case is *asystaton*, not capable of stasis. Of this, Hermogenes lists eight headings.

[11] See my *Greek Rhetoric under Christian Emperors*, 75–77.

[12] For a good introduction to the world of the Greek rhetorical schools, see Russell, *Greek Declamation*.

The introduction ends with the statement that different kinds of speeches should have different styles, but stasis should be studied before style. This is the opposite of what Dionysius of Halicarnassus had argued and indicative of the view of rhetoric as a logical discipline, which recommended it to the Greek Neoplatonists.

The discussion of method is a brief statement of Hermogenes' system of headings of stasis, followed in the body of the work by consideration of each heading and examples of it taken from themes of declamation current at the time. The unusual feature of the system is that it links the various headings in a progression of alternatives rather than separating them into parallel categories, as others had done.[13] A subject for decision, according to Hermogenes, falls under the heading "unclear" if it is not agreed by the disputants whether an action was performed at all. If the defense denies doing the action, the issue becomes *stochasmos*, stasis of fact. If the action is "clear," that is, admitted by the defense, the case is either "incomplete" or "complete"; incomplete if there are questions about the meaning of terms in the law, which leads directly to stasis of definition (*horos*), complete if applicability of the law is admitted, in which case the issue turns on the "quality" (*poiotēs*) of the act or its doer. The latter is again divided into two headings, legal (*nomikē*) and rational (*logikē*). In the detailed discussion of the headings that follows the chapter on method, the four legal headings are postponed to treatment at the end: word versus intent, inference, conflict of law, and ambiguity.

Rational stasis is either *pragmatikē*, relating to action in the future and thus the field of deliberative rhetoric, or *dikaiologia*, relating to the past and thus judicial. The latter is what most interests Hermogenes, and he proceeds with his binary distinctions. First, a deed is either unintentional, providing *antilēpsis* or "defense" as the stasis, or it is intentional, called *antithesis* ("opposition"). The latter is either *antistasis*, meaning defense on the ground that the action was "beneficial," or not beneficial. If not beneficial, it can be defended by *antengklēma*, the claim that the action was caused by the opponent; if that claim cannot be supported, the alternatives are *metastasis*, transferring the blame to someone else, or admission of blame with *syngnōmē*, a plea for forgiveness. Finally, there are two forms of stasis outside the systematic structure of the others. One is *paragraphē*, the claim that the case is outside the jurisdiction of the court, or *metalēpsis*, the claim that there is no prima facie evidence.[14]

[13] For a diagram of the headings, showing the constant division to the right, see my *Greek Rhetoric under Christian Emperors*, 83.

[14] Hermogenes uses *metalēpsis* as a general heading for transference and in the special sense of denial of evidence. Most of the later Greek commentators say there are fourteen headings of stasis in his system, but Marcellinus in his *Prolegomenon* counts thirteen because of the double meaning of *metalēpsis*.

The discussion of *stochasmos* is the longest and is subdivided into ten headings, several of which are similar to headings of *poiotēs*. Some of these subheadings are actually topics that can be used in a variety of kinds of stasis. What Hermogenes calls *ap' archēs achri telous*, or "from beginning to end," is an example. It consists of the particulars of Who? What? How? When? Why?—adaptations of Aristotelian categories—and is used to lay out a narrative account from the point of view of prosecution or defense. As applied to *stochasmos* it brings out the performance or nonperformance of a deed, but it can also be used to show motivation or the gravity or triviality of an admitted offense.

The division between *pragmatikē* and *dikaiologia* is the basis of inclusion of deliberative and judicial oratory respectively in the system. *Pragmatikē* is subdivided into the lawful, the just, the expedient, the possible, the honorable, and the anticipated result. Each of these headings draws on subdivisions of other kinds of stasis for its arguments, on *nomikē*, for example, to demonstrate legality. A declaimer usually relied on a single heading of stasis, and Hermogenes does not consider their combination, but in a court of law defense was usually offered on more than one ground and the prosecution was forced to answer each. Later Greek rhetoricians sometimes lectured on speeches of the Attic orators and discussed the combinations of stasis found there. These lectures are the ultimate source of the surviving scholia to Aeschines and Demosthenes, where such points are repeatedly made.[15]

In the preface to *On Staseis* Hermogenes remarks that invention and stasis theory overlap, but that some features of invention are not included under stasis. Later (p. 53 Rabe) he refers the reader to a work in which he has discussed features of a rhetorical prooemium and in *On Ideas* (p. 378 Rabe) mentions his treatise on invention, of which it was probably a part. A work entitled *On Invention* survives, attributed in the manuscripts to Hermogenes. The contents are generally consistent with Hermogenes' teaching about stasis and "ideas" of style, but the style is somewhat different, and there are other problems of attribution.[16] The treatise we have is probably the work of an unknown teacher of declamation from the third or fourth century who perhaps made some use of Hermogenes' original work on invention and improved on it. This work then came to be accepted as a standard textbook in place of Hermogenes' treatise. The first two books of the treatise we have are brief, not very satisfactory discussions of the prooemium, the *prokatastasis*, or introductory statement of the case, and the narration; they may be excerpts from a longer version. Books 3 and 4, however, are of considerable interest, for they lay out in detail a theory of rhetorical invention that differs in a number of ways from earlier accounts, and

---

[15] Scholia to Aeschines and Demosthenes have now been edited by Dilts.

[16] See my *Greek Rhetoric under Christian Emperors*, 95.

they are useful in understanding composition as practiced by later Greek writers.

Book 3 discusses the "proof" as a part of an oration.[17] The author begins with what he calls *prokataskeuē*, or "preparation" for the proof, which takes the form of a proposition and partition of the argument, placed early in a speech. He then says that the "headings" of stasis theory (meaning those described in the work of Hermogenes) need either confirmation or rebuttal, which is accomplished by "epicheiremes." Many writers have discussed these, but not clearly; he will describe as exactly as possible the invention of an epicheireme to confirm a heading, the *ergasia*, or "working," that confirms the epicheireme, and the invention of an enthymeme to confirm the ergasia (p. 133 Rabe). What we have here is a variation on the "five-part argument" first described in Cicero's *On Invention* (1.61) and discussed above in chapter 6. The enthymeme, to Aristotle one of the two forms of logical reasoning in persuasive discourse, over the course of several centuries has been converted into a subsidiary part of a formal compositional unit used by declaimers, to whom a technique of amplification was often of more interest than actual persuasion of an audience. Yet the later Greek rhetoricians might reasonably claim that the result was, because of its fullness, more logical and more satisfying, at least to an academic mind, than the simple tools of rhetorical proof offered by Aristotle. Greek rhetoricians of the second and third centuries, to be discussed in the next section of this chapter—Anonymous Seguerianus and Apsines, for example—generally follow the Aristotelian tradition of distinguishing external and artistic proof and dividing the latter into matters of ethos, logos, and pathos. They call the instrument of logical proof "epicheireme" and subdivide it into example and enthymeme, though their definitions of enthymeme differ considerably. "Topics" are to them the sources of enthymemes. In contrast, the Hermogenic *On Invention* does not discuss the three means of persuasion at all but relates argument to stasis theory.

According to the author of *On Invention*, if the stasis of a speech is determined by the first speaker in a deliberative debate or a trial, simple statement and proof is enough. A fuller form of argument, however, is required if a speaker responds to an opponent's "headings." The parts of this fuller statement are (1) the opponent's *prōtasis*, or premise, restated; (2) the opponent's *hypophora*, or reason; (3) the speaker's *antiprōtasis*, or response to the premise; (4) the speaker's *lysis* or *anthypophora*, his supporting reason. An example is offered from a deliberative declamation: "Perhaps some such statement as this will come from my opponents, that it is difficult to dig a

---

[17] The standard modern edition by Rabe changes the order of some passages as found in the manuscripts to a more logical sequence of subjects; see my *Greek Rhetoric under Christian Emperors*, 88–89. Rabe's sequence will be followed here.

canal through the Chersonese; it is not difficult to refute their view, for it is an easy thing to dig a canal." There will then be need of an epicheireme to support the claim. The author is aware that nothing is really proved by the argument. As he says, "It is an ornament of discourse and often nothing more" (p. 134 Rabe). The procedure does, however, encourage a student to articulate his argument clearly in the way that insistence on "topic sentences" is a tool in the teaching of composition in modern times.

In Rabe's arrangement of the text the next subject discussed is *enstasis*. *Enstasis* is the point in the argument where the heading emerges. If a speaker declares "It was permitted for me to kill my son," he is declaring the stasis on which he hopes to rely. If the opponent says, "It was not permitted," he is employing *enstasis*. If he adds a second line of defense, "And even if it were permitted, it was not right to do it in the presence of his mother," he is employing *antiparastasis*. Since debate was not a part of declamation, this exchange will not literally take place but will be implicit in such expressions as "my opponent claims that . . . but I say. . . ." A declaimer could, of course, invent anything he wanted as the position of the imaginary opponent.

A detailed description (pp. 140–54 Rabe) is provided of the sequence to be used in a fully developed argument—lysis, epicheireme, ergasia, and enthymeme—but it can be easily seen in an amplification of the argument about digging a canal in the Chersonese: The opponent's proposition is, "It will be difficult to dig through the Chersonese." The student's proper response to this is lysis, or rebuttal, from *enstasis*, defining the stasis:[18] "It will not be difficult." Then comes the epicheireme, or supporting reason: "for we shall dig earth and digging is child's play," followed by the ergasia, or "working" of the argument, in this case by supplying an example: "Even the king of the Persians, when forced, once dug through Athos." Finally, there is the enthymeme: "Yet he dug through a mountain and we shall dig through earth." Quintilian had noted (10.1.2) that already in his time one of the meanings of "enthymeme" was "the conclusion of an argument drawn from consequences or differences, although there is little agreement on the subject." Epicheiremes, in the Hermogenic system, are drawn from the circumstances of the speakers, the speeches, the facts, the courts, the case, and from "life" (p. 140 Rabe), and are divided into place, time, manner, person, cause, and act. These are "topics," though not called that here. An ergasia, supporting an epicheireme, is derived from comparison, example, the lesser, the greater, the equal, and the opposite, which are also topics. An enthymeme is the supporting statement to an ergasia and clinches the argument. It should be characterized by *drimytēs*, or "sharpness," which

[18] *Lysis* and *enstasis* are used by Aristotle to mean "refutation" and "objection" repectively; see *On Rhetoric* 2.25.1.

is one of Hermogenes "ideas" of style. Enthymemes are said to be derived from the same sources as epicheiremes and assume the same form as ergasiae. It is possible to add an epenthymeme, or additional supporting statement: "And yet he [the king of Persia] did so in order to conquer, we in order that we not suffer in being conquered" (p. 152 Rabe).

Instead of arguing by the system of epicheiremes and enthymemes just described, it is possible to use the technique of "from beginning to end," referred to in Hermogenes' *On Staseis*. This has its own "topic" of proof, called *hypodiairesis*, or "subdivision," which amplifies significant words (pp. 154–58 Rabe). For example, "Then he killed his three sons," subjected to *hypodiairesis*, becomes "Then, not in a moment of passion but after a time of thought, he did not inform on but killed, not one son but three, not someone else's but his own." At the end of book 3 the author discusses some variants on this, how an opponent can counter it, and how to meet arguments in stasis of definition and reasoning by means of *diaskeuē*, or elaboration, which the author equates with *diatyposis*, or vivid description.

In book 4 aspects of style are treated in terms of their contribution to invention, with discussion of figures, tropes, characters of style, and how to treat "figured problems" in declamation. Two general categories of style are recognized, determined by the nature of the epicheiremes and ergasia. If these are "political," the style should be *strongylos*, compact or tense, containing the "idea" of *drimytēs*, or sharpness, which is achieved by antithesis and a periodic style. An antithesis, by multiplication of its parts, can be worked into a *pneuma*, literally "a breath," which is the author's term for a long, complex sentence. A *pneuma* may be periodic if grammatical completion is postponed until the end, but a *periodos* in itself is shorter, with from one to four cola. (A unit of up to six syllables is a "comma"; a longer unit up to the length of a line of hexameter is a "colon.") The author shows how to construct a period in which the "turning" is in each of the grammatical cases. If a *pneuma* exceeds the ability of a speaker to deliver it in one breath, it becomes a *tasis*.

That the primary goal of the treatise was to prepare students for declamation is evident throughout, but nowhere more clearly than in the discussion of "figured problems," which concludes *On Invention*. We also know about these problems from a handbook of rhetoric wrongly attributed to Dionysius of Halicarnassus and from discussion in Apsines. Figured problems are part of the declaimers' search for novelty. In the simplest form, a speaker argues against his apparent personal interest, as when a declaimer takes on the unhistorical role of Pericles imagined as arguing in favor of the Athenians' handing him over to the Spartans as a hostage. The author claims (p. 208 Rabe) to have invented a new kind of figured problem in which a speaker speaks in his own self-interest without appearing to do so. An example is an adaptation of the story of Oedipus. There is a rumor that a father-in-law has seduced his daughter-in-law. An oracle declares that a child who is about to be born to the daughter-in-law will be the murderer of its father. The father-in-law is the true father, and not wanting to be killed, favors having the child exposed but pretends to be acting in the interests of his son. The son is aware that he is not himself the child's father: he opposes abandoning the child in some remote place where it will die, pretending that it is because of his love for it, but actually he wants it to grow up and kill his father (the child's true father). Since it is unseemly for a son to accuse his father of adultery, the son must use "emphasis," a rhetorical term common in later Greek to describe something that means more than it says to those who understand. "Imagine, O father," he can say, "that the child is your own. You are killing that which you begot. . . ." The audience for the declamation would know the full hypothesis and enjoy the effect.

The fourth treatise in the rhetorical corpus of Hermogenes is a genuine and important work, *On Ideas of Style*. "Idea" is reminiscent of Platonic forms, transcendent concepts imitated in particular contexts; the concepts represent a development of the "characters" and "virtues" of style as discussed by Dionysius of Halicarnassus, and versions of them can be found elsewhere in rhetorical handbooks of the second century, for example, the treatise wrongly ascribed to Aelius Aristides. Hermogenes worked out the ideas into a full system, much as he worked out stasis theory. His work had great influence on teaching and composition throughout the Byzantine period and had significant use in the Renaissance, when it was translated into Latin and influenced composition in western European literatures, including English.[19]

On Ideas begins with a rather diffuse introduction, in which the following points emerge. Understanding the ideas of style is necessary for an orator and is the basis of literary criticism. Natural ability is important in a student, but without critical guidelines it can lead to disaster in practice, whereas an average student can achieve success by study and practice. Ideas are general qualities, not characteristics of single authors, but in most writers some one idea predominates and gives his writings their peculiar flavor. The ideas are combined in a variety of ways to make style poetical, panegyrical, deliberative, judicial, or something else. The great master of these combinations was Demosthenes. Previous accounts of the ideas are confused; criticism of Demosthenes in particular has suffered from lack of attention to them. In contrast to other works in the corpus, *On Ideas* is chiefly a work of criticism; it does not apply its theory to contemporary declamation.

The seven basic ideas are then identified (pp. 217–18 Rabe) as *saphēneia* (clarity), *megethos* (grandeur), *kallos* (beauty), *gorgotēs* (rapidity), *ēthos*

---

[19] Wooten's translation, *Hermogenes' On Types of Style*, includes an introduction and notes; on the influence of the treatise in the West, see Patterson, *Hermogenes and the Renaissance*.

(character), *alētheia* (sincerity), and *deinotēs* (force). Most have subdivisions, making a total of thirteen. Although Hermogenes treats them in groups that can be regarded as the plain, the grand, the middle, and the mixed, he does not make this point and apparently thought that those traditional concepts were of little use in teaching. He approaches the ideas in terms of what he calls (p. 218 Rabe) the "elements" of speech, listed as *ennoia* (thought), *methodos* (approach, but subsequently identified with figures of thought), *lexis* (initially style in general, but subsequently word choice), *schēmata* (figures of speech), *kōla* (clauses), *synthesis* (word order), *anapausis* (cadence), and rhythm. Application of these concepts can be seen in the discussion of the first idea, clarity. It is a product of two qualities, correctness and good judgment. The thought should be clear and familiar; the method is an orderly presentation of the bare subject, avoiding figures of thought; the diction employs common words; figures of speech are avoided; the cola are short and divided into commata; the composition is simple; the pauses are appropriate; the rhythm is iambic or trochac. Clarity is thus the standard of the simplest and most natural form of expression; all other ideas are departures from it. In the rest of book 1 Hermogenes proceeds to discuss forms of grandeur and beauty. Book 2 continues with the other ideas, leading to force, which is "the correct mixture of all the aforesaid forms of speech and their opposites" (pp. 368–69 Rabe). It is here that the greatness of Demosthenes is most evident. *On Ideas* concludes with a long chapter on civic oratory, defined in the traditional terms of deliberative, judicial, and panegyrical (epideictic). For successful public speaking the most important idea is clarity when combined with character, sincerity, and rapidity, but other ideas ought to be found as well. Deliberative rhetoric especially needs grandeur and force, whereas judicial seeks ideas associated with character. The best panegyrical style is Platonic. All poetry is regarded as a part of panegyrical rhetoric, and Homer and Hesiod are discussed in terms of thought, method, and the other elements. Hermogenes then turns to discussion of the Attic orators. He is familiar with a canon of ten, to which he adds Critias (p. 403 Rabe). Finally, he discusses dialogues and history, also as forms of panegyric. His canons are Atticist and classicizing, but he does include two writers of his own century, Nicostratus and Aelius Aristides, as worthy of inclusion among the classics. At the very end he returns to the greatest models, Homer, Plato, and above all Demosthenes.

One reason for the appeal of Hermogenes' work on style in the following centuries is that he often employs categories congenial to Neoplatonism, which after A.D. 200 became the dominant philosophical movement in the Greek world. For example, in discussing *ennoia* (thought) as a feature of solemnity (a subdivision of grandeur) (pp. 243–47 Rabe), he distinguishes four types that are suggestive of levels of being as understood by Neoplatonists: things said of the gods as divine, for example in Plato's *Timaeus*;

thoughts about divine things, such as the universe; thoughts about divine things manifested in human nature and society, such as justice, and great and glorious human events, such as the Battle of Marathon. Plato is cited as an example of the method of solemnity and also for his use of long vowels to secure solemn diction.

On Ideas contains references to a projected addition, *On the Method of Deinotēs*, and an epilogue indicates that this will immediately follow. The fifth place in the Hermogenic corpus is indeed filled by a short treatise with that title, discussing thirty-seven miscellaneous devices of style, and is of relatively little interest. It is not generally thought to be by Hermogenes; perhaps some editor filled a void with a collection of material from other sources.

Hermogenes seems to have regarded his treatises on stasis, invention, and style as together constituting an "art of rhetoric" (see p. 378 Rabe). Medieval manuscripts of his works often bear the general title "Art of Rhetoric," suggesting coverage of the entire subject. There are rather few references to Hermogenes in writings dating from the second to the fourth century; in the fifth century, however, Syrianus, head of the Neoplatonic school in Athens, wrote important commentaries to *On Staseis* and *On Ideas*, and Hermogenes began to emerge as the most important authority on rhetoric, overshadowing Aristotle, Dionysius of Halicarnassus, and other later writers. Only Aphthonius' treatise on progymnasmata gained a place beside Hermogenes' works in the standard rhetorical corpus.

Prolegomena

Teachers of rhetoric sometimes began a course of lectures with an introduction discussing the nature of the subject and its connection with other disciplines, and versions of these lectures were often prefixed to published treatises. The earliest extant introduction to rhetoric is the first chapter of Aristotle's *On Rhetoric*, which relates rhetoric to dialectic, criticizes previous treatments of the subject, and lists some ways in which rhetoric is useful, before offering a definition of rhetoric, at the beginning of the second chapter. The first book of Cicero's *On Invention* begins with a preface on the relationship between rhetoric and philosophy, and the second book has a preface that gives a short historical account of the development of rhetoric. Quintilian begins his *Institutio* with elementary and grammatical education, but when he turns to rhetoric, in the second half of book 2, he discusses definitions of rhetoric (2.15), its utility (2.16), whether it is an "art" (2.17), the other arts contributing to it (1.18), whether nature or theory is more important (2.19), whether rhetoric is a "virtue" (2.20), and what its materials are. He continues in book 3 with a survey of writers on rhetoric and with other introductory questions.

By the fourth and fifth centuries Greek writers on rhetoric were regularly prefixing introductions, called "prolegomena," to the commentaries they wrote on parts of the Hermogenic corpus. These prolegomena show the influence of Neoplatonic philosophy, take traditional form, and continue to be found throughout the Byzantine period in manuscripts that contain rhetorical treatises and commentaries on them. Among the earliest of the later Greek writers to whom prolegomena are attributed are Sopatros and Marcellinus, each of whom wrote commentaries to Hermogenes' *On Staseis*, as did the Neoplatonist philosopher Syrianus.

Sopatros seems to have been a teacher of rhetoric in Athens in the later fourth century. He wrote a number of works on rhetoric, of which the best preserved are a long treatise entitled *Divisions of Questions*, which contains examples, with pedagogical instruction, of eighty-one themes for declamation arranged by stasis,[20] and *Hypomnēma*, a commentary on Hermogenes' *On Staseis*.[21] This commentary has a prolegomenon that illustrates well how Neoplatonic philosophy reached out to embrace rhetoric as an introductory logical discipline. Sopatros begins by describing his subject as a logical art, and then defines and divides *logos* and *technē*. Two species of *logos* are identified, *prosphorikos*, or expository, which produces discourse and reasoning; and *endiathetos*, or "internal," by which we are rational when silent or asleep. Expository *logos* is in turn divided into grammatical and rhetorical; rhetorical is divided further into two arts, that which produces beauty (the art of the ideas of style and the figures) and that which teaches, which is accomplished either through the emotions or through demonstration. An orator engages in three acts: *noēsis*, or thought; *heuresis*, or invention; *diathesis*, or arrangement. *Noēsis* is consideration of the proposed treatment of the case and can be medical, philosophical, or political. Political *noēsis* is equated with rhetorical stasis.

Sopatros then turns to the questions of whether rhetoric is an art, a form of knowledge, or a result of experience; how it came into existence; and what its utility is. In so doing he takes up issues discussed by Plato and Aristotle, who were the two great authorities for Neoplatonists. Like them, he draws an analogy between rhetoric and medicine, which analogy continues to be common in later prolegomena. Rhetoric is not knowledge, he says, because it deals with particulars rather than universals; it is not mere knack or experience (*empeiria*), as Socrates claimed in *Gorgias*, because it involves an understanding of causes and forms; it is a *technē*, or art. Deliberative and judicial rhetoric combine theoretical and practical qualities, as does medicine, but panegyric (epideictic) is purely theoretical, since it does not aim at action.

---

[20] Text in Walz, *Rhetores Graeci*, vol. 8, pp. 1–385; see Innes and Winterbottom, *Sopatros the Rhetor*.

[21] Text in Walz, *Rhetores Graeci*, vol. 5, pp. 1–211.

The next question discussed is the origin of rhetoric. According to Homer and Plato, Sopatros says, rhetoric existed among gods and heroes. Rhetoric was dangerous to practice under tyrannts, though Phalaris had acquired his tyranny by a persuasive speech. Corax in Sicily was the first teacher of rhetoric; Tisias was his student; Gorgias brought the art to Athens and was followed by Antiphon, Thucydides, and Isocrates. Rhetoric most flourished in the time of Demosthenes but declined under Macedonian rule, only to revive in the time of Hadrian and Antoninus Pius (the time of the Second Sophistic). Cicero lived earlier and well understood the art (an unusual reference among Greek rhetoricians). Famous rhetoricians of modern times include Minucianus and Hermogenes; however, they neglected to define rhetoric and to explain in what sense it is an art, which Sopatros seeks to do. Reference is made to a commentary on Minucianus by the Neoplatonist philosopher Porphyry and to debates as to whether rhetoric is limited to judicial and deliberative matters. Here a division found in Quintilian and ultimately derived from Hellenistic literary criticism is introduced: the art, the artist, and the artifact. Sopatros defines an "artist" as a man who knows how to speak well, but he thinks it does not logically follow that an orator must be a good man, which would apply best to a philosopher. He prefers to think of the rhetorical artist as a political orator, knowledgable in political affairs, who can argue on either side of a question in accordance with probability. Definitions of rhetoric are then considered. That which Sopatros prefers is one he attributes to Lollianus and which is elsewhere attributed to Dionysius of Halicarnassus: "an artistic faculty of persuasive speech on a political subject having as its goal to speak well" (vol. 5, p. 17 Walz).

The function of Sopatros' prolegomenon is to place the study of rhetoric, as seen in Hermogenes' *On Staseis*, into a system of knowledge as understood by Neoplatonists. The references to Porphyry are evidence that the latter, a student of Plotinus in the third century and a leading figure in the development of Neoplatonism, had begun this effort at synthesis, definition, and division. Neoplatonists did not, however, develop a new system of rhetoric; as in the case of dialectic, they took over earlier teaching, set it in a new theoretical framework, and wrote commentaries on authoritative texts. The usual method, as practiced by Sopatros in his commentary to *On Staseis*, was to give a lemma, or quotation of a few words from Hermogenes, and then to explain the passage, to identify allusions, to give examples from the classics, to note controversies or divergent authorities, and sometimes to offer criticism. Sopatros and others are mindful of the general philosophical education to which study of rhetoric contributed. Not only could a student there learn the process of definition and division and the contents of rhetorical theory, but the commentaries encouraged verbal skills and they included some philosophical material, for example, reference to Plato's theory of ideas. Sopatros shows little interest in applying rhetoric to speech on contemporary issues; it is for him an academic discipline of intellectual value in itself.

Syrianus became head of the Neoplatonic School in Athens about A.D. 431 and wrote commentaries on Homer, Plato, Aristotle, and Hermogenes' treatises *On Staseis* and *On Ideas*. The only ones to have survived are the commentaries on Aristotle's *Metaphysics* and on the two works of Hermogenes.[22] Instead of writing prolegomena he worked discussion of the issues as we see them in Sopatros' prolegomenon into the body of his commentary, but there are short introductions to each work. That to Hermogenes' *On Ideas* is worth quoting in part, since it reveals the attitude toward Hermogenes in the fifth century by an intellectual leader of the time:

> Almost all the treatises which have come to us from the technical writer Hermogenes are remarkable and filled with political wisdom of a practical sort. I have in mind his work *On Staseis*, on which many others, both sophists and Platonic philosophers, have thought it not unworthy to write commentaries, and his work *On the Method of Deinotēs* and his *Notes for Public Speaking* [= *On Invention*], which he himself mentions, but more than any of the other works his treatise *On Ideas* is worthy of admiration, for it is the best on the subject and the most worked out in accordance with the art and in no way failing in the perfect critical control of discourse. Since, however, much of the contents is not easy for everyone to understand and since up to now I have not met with a commentary on it, I thought it necessary, my dearest boy Alexander, to put together some brief notes to the best of my ability for the more accurate reading of the book. (vol. 2, pp. 1–2 Rabe)

The commentary takes the form of lemmata and notes. In the first of these Syrianus supplies a definition of "idea," which is lacking in Hermognes' text: "An idea is a quality of speech, harmonious with the person and subjects involved, in terms of thought, diction, and the whole interconnection of the harmony. A species (*eidos*) differs from an idea in the same way that a genus differs from a species and the whole from the part. Species encompass ideas, and ideas are subordinate to species. It is impossible for the judicial, deliberative, and panegyrical species of speech to exist apart from a mixture of many ideas" (vol. 2, pp. 2–3 Rabe).

A third extant commentary to Hermogenes' *On Staseis* bears the name of Marcellinus; it is a work of late antiquity but cannot be dated with any certainty. Byzantine scholars regarded Marcellinus' commentary as of comparable authority with those of Sopatros and Syrianus and preserved it in a work containing portions of their commentaries. This composite commentary (vol. 4, pp. 1–864 Walz) has an anonymous prolegomenon, the end of

---

[22] Text in Rabe, *Syriani in Hermogenem*.

which can be identified as the work of Marcellinus, and it seems likely that the prolegomenon as a whole is a revision by a later editor of Marcellinus' original introduction.[23]

This prolegomenon treats the same subjects as did Sopatros, but integrates additional philosophical concepts not found there into the study of rhetoric. For example, the history of rhetoric is considered in terms of five "peristatic," or circumstantial, headings: person, place, time, manner, and cause. Since rhetoric in the historical period was caused by democracy, a description is given of the different kinds of constitution: monarchy, aristocracy, democracy, and their vitiated forms—tyranny, oligarchy, and ochlocracy. The author then turns to the definition of rhetoric. Socrates' definition of rhetoric in the *Gorgias* is reviewed at length, its inconsistency with the treatment in *Phaedrus* noted, and the conclusion reached that Plato's criticism of rhetoric fits sycophancy but does not apply to "our rhetoric," that taught by Neoplatonists. The definition that the author ultimately accepts is the same as that found in Sopatros. The three species of rhetoric are associated with the three Platonic faculties of the soul, deliberative with the appetitive, judicial with the passionate, and panegyrical with the rational. Thus epideictic rhetoric is elevated to the noblest form, the status it in fact enjoyed in the view of the great sophists and their audiences from the second century to the end of the Byzantine period. The prolegomenon ends with the question why Hermogenes did not define rhetoric. The importance of the question for the Neoplatonists was the awkward fact that Plato in *Gorgias* rejected the claim of rhetoric to be an art. According to the author of this prolegomenon, the true reason Hermogenes did not define rhetoric is that he was its ally in its state of danger, attacked by Plato. He did not wish to reply directly to Plato, but approached the subject obliquely, showing that rhetoric is a system that in fact fulfills the definition of art.

A fourth commentary to *On Staseis* is that by George of Alexandria, probably written in the fifth century.[24] It is diffuse and repetitious, but the author had a good knowledge of classical literature. Other commentaries were written between the fourth and sixth century, and parts of them may be included without identification in commentaries of the Byzantine period.[25] Byzantine commentaries on the Aphthonian-Hermogenic corpus are numerous; some are attributed to known scholars, including John Doxapatres in the eleventh century and Maximus Planudes in the thirteenth, and others are anonymous. They regularly include prolegomena. Hugo Rabe's *Prolegomenon Sylloge* is a collection of thirty-three of these. He identified two traditions, both in existence by the fifth century. One tradition organizes

[23] Text in Rabe, *Prolegomenon Sylloge*, 258–96.

[24] Some portions are printed in Walz, *Rhetores Graeci*, vol. 7, no. 1, pp. 655–64 and 690–95; a fuller text, unprinted, exists in the Bibliotèque Nationale in Paris, *Parisinus Graecus* 2919.

[25] For further information, see my *Greek Rhetoric under Christian Emperors*, 115–16.

the material around four questions derived from Aristotelian logic: Does rhetoric exist? What is its definition? What are its qualities? What is its end or purpose? The prolegomenon to Marcellinus' commentary belongs essentially to this tradition. A second tradition is organized around a series of ten questions that include and expand on the four questions. A good example is the fourth in Rabe's collection, which he attributed to an unknown rhetorician of the late fourth or early fifth century living in Asia Minor.

The ten questions are as follows: Did rhetoric come from the gods and exist among them? Did rhetoric exist among the early Greek heroes? How did rhetoric develop in the historical period in Greece? How did it flower in Athens? What is the definition, end, and function of rhetoric? What are its species? How many rhetorics are there? What kinds of delivery are there? What kinds of political constitutions exist? How should rhetoric be taught?

The answers to the first two questions are "yes." The answer to the third is an account of the "invention" of rhetoric in Sicily by Corax and Tisias (stories about them given here and in other prolegomena had been developed over the centuries beyond what Aristotle may have said in his *Synagōgē Technōn* and are of little historical value). Gorgias then brought rhetoric to Athens, where it flowered in the work of the ten Attic orators. The definition of rhetoric, its end, and its function resembles what we have seen in Sopatros and Marcellinus. The species of rhetoric are deliberative, judicial, and epideictic. There are five "rhetorics," each an antistrophos to something else: the first and highest to philosophy; the second to politics; the third to dialectic; the fourth to sycophancy; the fifth to pure flattery. There are three kinds of delivery: *syntonos*, which is a strong, rapid, and rough explosion of breath with an impression of anger, most useful in judicial oratory; *aneimenos*, its opposite, is soft, gentle and mellifluous, apparently to be used in reading poetry aloud or perhaps in epideictic oratory; and *mesos*, suitable for reading a law or letter or giving a lecture. Four kinds of constitution are identified: monarchy, aristocracy, oligarchy, and democracy. The Attic orators lived under democracy, the Lacedaimonians under aristocracy, "but we now fortunately live in a kingdom with faith and orthodoxy" (p. 41 Rabe). Thus the author was a Christian.

The answer to the tenth question, how to teach rhetoric, is a valuable insight into the work of a rhetorician in late antiquity. Seven methods are outlined. First, teaching by allegory, which by this time had become the common method of finding higher meaning in classical poetry. Though the beginnings of allegorical interpretation go back to the sixth century B.C., it was greatly developed by the Hellenistic Stoics and enthusiastically adopted by the Neoplatonists. It was also used in the exegesis of the Christian scriptures, especially to reconcile the Old and New Testaments.[26] The second

---

[26] On allegorical interpretation, see Kennedy, ed., *Cambridge History of Literary Criticism,* esp. 85–86, 209–15, and 320–28.

method of teaching is by preface, when a teacher explains stasis headings and enthymemes and gives a synopsis of a work that is going to be studied. The third is by art, when the teacher gives a running commentary on a text. The fourth is by history, identifying the historical background and participants in a speech read by or to the students. The fifth is by figure, naming each figure of speech used in the text. The sixth is by idea, identifying the Hermogenic ideas of style found in the text. The seventh is by clarification, when the teacher paraphrases the thought of the text. Many of these techniques had been practiced earlier and are noted by Quintilian (2.5.7). All except allegory can be illustrated from the medieval scholia to the speeches of Demosthenes, which originated in lectures on the text by a teacher in late antiquity.

Of the other prolegomena in Rabe's collection, the most interesting is that by Phoebammon, probably written in the sixth century. It is specifically an introduction to Hermogenes' *On Ideas* and reveals the existence of opposition to the concept of ideas. Phoebammon quotes the critics extensively without identifying any by name. Apparently they rejected the concept of both characters and ideas of style, taking their start from Porphyry's analogy "as soul to body, so thought to speech," and argued that since bodies are innumerable it is not possible to generalize about a specific number of characters or ideas. If two styles are similar, this results from chance. Most of the arguments antedate Hermogenes; Quintilian (12.10.66–67) had also had reservations about the theory of characters of style, suggesting that there were actually innumerable kinds. It is not clear whether the criticisms quoted by Phoebammon represent an extreme form of Platonism grounded in the demand made in the *Phaedrus* that discourse be like a living body, or whether that premise is borrowed from the Neoplatonists for controversial purposes only, since the critics seem to reject the whole Platonic theory of ideas. Phoebammon does not appear to believe in the transcendent existence of the ideas of style; they are to him only convenient symbols. His reply to the critics is largely on the practical ground that the ideas are useful teaching devices; the critics, he claims, are lazy and unwilling to undertake the hard work needed to attain excellence in style.

In addition to prolegomena to the study of rhetoric, Neoplatonists wrote introductions to the study of philosophy that follow a similar method.[27] The rhetorical texts studied in the schools were those of the Attic orators, especially Demosthenes; the philosophical texts were the dialogues of Plato and treatises of Aristotle, on which the Neoplatonists wrote extensive commentaries. The only extant commentaries on Aristotle's *On Rhetoric* are two written in the twelfth century, one longer anonymous commentary and one shorter one attributed to an otherwise unknown Stephanus. Both seek to integrate Aristotle's thought with the teaching of Hermo-

---

[27] See Westerink, *Anonymous Progelomena*, and Wildberg, "Neoplatonic Introductions."

genes.[28] There are, however, important commentaries written in late antiquity on the two dialogues of Plato most directly concerned with rhetoric, that by Hermeias of Alexandria, a student of Syrianus in the fifth century, on the *Phaedrus*, and that by Olympiodorus, head of the Alexandrian philosophical school in the sixth century, on the *Gorgias*. Both show knowledge of the Hermogenic corpus and integrate the study of rhetoric into a philosophical system.[29]

Other Greek Rhetorical Treatises

In addition to the Aphthonian-Hermogenic corpus, several other Greek rhetorical handbooks survive from the imperial period. In most cases scholars are still dependent on the version of the text found in Christian Walz's early-nineteenth-century edition of the *Rhetores Graeci* or on the late-nineteenth-century revisions by Leonard Spengel and Caspar Hammer; a few were reedited in the Teubner series in the early twentieth century. There are no English translations except in the case of the *Dionysius Rhetoric*, Menander Rhetor, and Minucianus.

The Anonymous Seguerianus, named for Seguier de St. Brisson who discovered the work in a Paris manuscript in 1843, is a handbook on the four parts of the oration—prooemium, narration, proof, and epilogue—probably an epitome of a larger work written in the late second century.[30] An unusual feature is that each part is considered in terms of invention, arrangement, and style. In contrast to the Hermogenic treatise *On Invention*, this handbook follows a more Aristotelian approach to proof: the means of persuasion are divided into nonartistic and artistic, and the latter are divided into the use of ethos, logos, and pathos; the instrument of logical proof is the epicheireme, which is subdivided into the paradigm and the enthymeme. Topics are the source of enthymemes. Stasis theory is ignored. There are frequent references to theories of the Apollodoreans on the parts of an oration, apparently still a vital force.[31] The author counteracts or supplements these views with citation of three other sources: Nicocles; Alexander, son of Numenius; and Harpocration. Rather little is known about Nicocles. Alexander was an official under Hadrian and must have lived in the mid–second century. He wrote what was apparently the best-known treatise on figures of speech after that of Caecilius; an epitome of it survives, and signs of its influence are clear in most subsequent discussions of figures. He also wrote a general handbook of rhetoric, on which the anonymous author draws. The references to it and to Nicocles' work indicate that both treated proof along

---

[28] For discussion, see my *Greek Rhetoric under Christian Emperors*, 318–20.
[29] For discussion, see my *Greek Rhetoric under Christian Emperors*, 126–32.
[30] Greek text in Spengel, vol. 1, pp. 427–60, and Spengel-Hammer, 352–98.
[31] On Apollodorus and his school, see the discussion in chapter 8 above.

Aristotelian lines. Harpocration wrote works on Hyperides, Herodotus, and Xenophon, a treatise on ideas of style, and an art of rhetoric. He is not, however, the Harpocration who wrote *Lexicon of the Ten Orators*. In discussing stasis theory he is said to have attacked Hermogenes (vol. 7, pp. 349–50).

What is known as *Aristides Rhetoric* is a collection of several works, preserved with genuine works of the great sophist Aelius Aristides but not written by him.[32] The first book, entitled "On Political Discourse," expounds an account of twelve ideas of style similar, but not identical, to those discussed by Hermogenes and not so well arranged and described. There follows discussion of some other aspects of style, a summary of the twenty-ninth oration of Aristides, and a paraphrase of portions of the *Iliad* and the *Odyssey*. The second book is entitled "On the Simple Style," of which the historian Xenophon is taken as the model.

What is called the *Dionysius Rhetoric* is also a collection of miscellaneous material, described in the manuscripts as the *Art of Rhetoric* by Dionysius of Halicarnassus but certainly not his work.[33] Probably it dates from the second half of the second century or the early third century, and the different parts are likely to be the work of different writers. The first seven chapters are a handbook of epideictic rhetoric, anticipating what is found in fuller form in the later works of Menander and the earliest surviving account of the new rhetorical genres that had been developed by second-century sophists and rhetoricians. Many are derived from classical and Hellenistic poetic forms, but by the first century poetry was in decline and its social functions were taken over by epideictic prose, declaimed in public by sophists. Although the progymnasmata taught a student how to write simple encomia, traditional rhetorical handbooks were largely concerned with judicial oratory and had relatively little to say about epideictic. Handbooks like that in the *Dionysius Rhetoric* or that of Menander provided students with rules and topics for these new forms.

The epideictic genres described in the *Dionysius Rhetoric* begin with panegyric, by which is meant an encomiastic speech at a festival of the gods; as we have seen, the term "panegyric" later comes to be used of epideictic rhetoric generally. A second genre is *gamēlion*, a speech at a marriage, often making use of the old "thesis" "Should a man marry?" Third is genethliac, a speech on a birthday. The birthdays of teachers, students, and their friends were celebrated in rhetorical schools. Fourth is *epithalamion*, a speech to a bride and groom on arrival at their new home. Fifth is *prosphonetic*, an ingratiating address to a ruler. Sixth is *epitaphios*, or funeral oration, either public or private. And last is athletic *protreptic*, or speech of exhortation to

---

[32] Greek text in Spengel, vol. 2, pp. 459–554.
[33] Translation of chaps. 1–7 in Russell and Wilson, *Menander Rhetor*, 362–81.

an athlete before the games. Examples of some of these genres can be found among the orations of major sophists of the empire. Dio's *Olympic Discourse*, for example, is a panegryic speech, the tenth oration of Aristides is a birthday speech, there is an epithalamion by the fourth-century orator Himerius, and the prosphonetic is exemplied on a grand scale by Dio's and Aristides' addresses to emperors.

As described in the *Dionysius Rhetoric* each genre is a collection of variations on commonplaces prescribed in considerable detail. A panegyric speech, for example, is to begin with praise of the god in whose honor the festival is held, listing his or her attributes. Then comes praise of the city where the festival is located: its site, origin, founder, history, size, beauty, power, public buildings, rivers, and legends. The next theme is the festival itself, its origin, legends, and history. Other festivals may be compared unfavorably to it. Then comes the program of the festival: topics are suggested for a program including music and the recitation of literature or declamation and a program that is purely athletic. The prize for the winner is then described and praised and can also be compared to other prizes. Finally, there is to be praise of the emperor or others in charge. Although extant speeches do not conform rigidly to these requirements, they often follow similar patterns, and a student or would-be sophist could here find possible subject matter nicely organized and could then concentrate on choice of topics and, what was most valued, diction, composition, maxims, and delivery. The eighth and ninth chapters of the *Dionysius Rhetoric* discuss "figured declamations," a form also described in the Hermogenic treatise *On Invention*, as noted earlier in this chapter. The collection concludes with a section on common mistakes in declamation and advice on characterization and style.

The best example of a traditional rhetorical handbook from this period is the work of Valerius Apsines of Gadara, a sophist in Athens in the first half of the third century.[34] Prooemium; *prokatastasis*, or preparation for the proof; narration; proof; and epilogue are discussed. There is no sign of the influence of Hermogenes. The treatment of proof is Aristotelian, as in the Anonymous Seguerianus, rather than resembling that found in the Hermogenic *On Invention*, and stasis theory is omitted on the ground that previous writers have adequately discussed it. The section on the epilogue has an extended discussion of pity, unusual in a Greek handbook. To the end of the treatise is appended a short essay entitled "On Figured Problems," similar to that in the *Dionysius Rhetoric*.

Commentators on Hermogenes frequently cited Minucianus as a writer on stasis theory whose views Hermogenes was combating. Ever since Hermagoras first formulated stasis theory there had been acrimonious disputes

---

[34] Greek text in Walz, *Rhetores Graeci*, vol. 9, pp. 467–542, and Spengel, *Rhetores Graeci*, vol. 1, pp. 331–414.

among rhetoricians about details. Minucianus was a famous Athenian orator one generation older than Hermogenes. None of his speeches or writings on rhetoric survives, but it seems clear from citations of it that his work on stasis was a major authority from his own time until belatedly eclipsed by that of Hermogenes in the fourth century.[35] Minucianus' influence may have been partly due to the fact that his son, grandson, and great-grandson were all well-known orators or sophists in Athens. A short work entitled *On Epicheiremes* that bears Minucianus' name as author may be by his great-grandson, Minucianus the Younger, a rhetorician in the mid–third century.[36]

The third-century Neoplatonist Porphyry has been mentioned as contributing to the incorporation of rhetoric into a general scheme of liberal education preparatory to study of philosophy. He had been a student of Plotinus, founder of Neoplatonism, and earlier of Cassius Longinus, who taught rhetoric in Athens before he moved to the court of Queen Zenobia of Palmyra about A.D. 268. Longinus then became involved in her opposition to the emperor Aurelian and was put to death when Aurelian captured the city. Porphyry describes Longinus as a "philologist" with a deep interest in philosophy (*Life of Plotinus* 14). The titles of several grammar and literary works by Longinus are known, and a fragmentary rhetorical handbook survives under his name.[37] The famous treatise *On the Sublime* was long attributed to him but is almost certainly a much earlier work by someone else.

Longinus' *Art of Rhetoric* belongs to the Aristotelian tradition also seen in the work of the Anonymous Seguerianus and the handbook by Apsines, untouched by the influence of Hermogenes. Neither stasis nor ideas of style is mentioned. Four parts of rhetoric are discussed, including delivery but not memory, generally ignored by rhetoricians of the time. What is most unusual about the work, however, is that Longinus, almost alone among rhetoricians of the empire, seems to believe that rhetoric is or should be a practical art of persuasion: the able student should be provided with the tools to become a perfect orator, not a declaimer; clarity and grace are the two qualities of style most to be sought; the function of style is to make a speech persuasive; the same is true of delivery.

Two treatises on epideictic rhetoric are attributed to Menander of Laodicea; he may have lived about the end of the third or the beginning of the fourth century but is otherwise unknown. These are among the few late

---

[35] The outline of Minucianus' stasis theory can be reconstructed from the references in the commentators: he identified thirteen headings rather than the fourteen of Hermogenes and thought stasis was determined by the defendant, whereas Hermogenes claimed it was sometimes the plaintiff, sometimes the defendant. See my *Greek Rhetoric under Christian Rulers*, 76–77.

[36] Translation by Meador, "Minucian."

[37] Texts in Spengel, *Rhetores Graeci*, vol. 1, pp. 299–328; Spengel-Hammer, 179–216; and Prickard, *Libellus de Sublimitate* (unnumbered pages at the end of the volume).

Greek rhetorical works easily accessible in English[38] and useful not only in understanding the epideictic genres practiced in the schools at the time but also in analyzing compositional techniques in epideictic passages of Greek literature more generally. Menander discusses about thirty different genres, to which he gives technical names, though many are very similar to each other, and lists the topics to be employed and the order in which they should be arranged. There is also what he calls a *lalia* (2.4), a personal, almost conversational encomium that lacks the formal structure of other genres. The genres include those mentioned earlier in this chapter in the discussion of Nicolaus' account of encomia, and a number of others. The first treatise describes prose hymns to the gods and encomia of cities or places; the second treatise deals with speeches addressed to individuals. Menander's work was studied throughout the Byzantine period, and Latin translations were made in the Renaissance.[39]

Discussions of style in works on rhetoric regularly have something to say about figures of speech, but there are also a number of monographic works on figures in Greek. These name, define, and exemplify a large number of figures in ways that could be memorized by students. The influential treatise by Caecilius of Calacte, written in the Augustan period, is lost; that of Alexander, son of Numenius, written in the second century survives in an epitome.[40] A treatise by Tiberius entitled *On the Figures of Demosthenes* was probably written in the late third or early fourth century. One of the most systematic works was that by Phoebammon, mentioned earlier as the author of a prolegomenon to Hermogenes' *On Ideas*. What survives is apparently an abridgment by a later rhetorician who added some Christian examples of figures.[41] Phoebammon begins by asking four questions: What is the utility of figures? Why are they so called? Do they exist by nature or by art? Are they of one sort or more and what are the differences? In reply, figures are said to be useful in "preserving the qualities of the ancients" and in avoiding satiety, since a hearer is pleased by them. The definitions given by Caecilius and earlier authorities are rejected in favor of the "perfect" definition: "a figure is an alteration in thought or diction, for the better, occurring without a trope," that is, without departing from the proper meaning of a word, as a metaphor does. This definition is in fact that of Alexander (vol. 3, p. 11 Spengel), who is not mentioned, and Phoebammon's account, especially of figures of thought, shows Alexander's influence. Its unusual feature is that the two traditional species of figures of speech and figures of thought are each subdivided into four headings, suggestive of the method of Hermogenes: figures resulting from omission of something; from the addition of

---

[38] See Russell and Wilson, *Menander Rhetor.*
[39] See Harsting, "The Golden Method of Menander."
[40] Text in Spengel, *Rhetores Graeci*, vol. 3, pp. 1–40.
[41] Text in Spengel, *Rhetores Graeci*, vol. 3, pp. 41–56.

something; from inversion of order, and from alteration. These categories were known to Quintilian (9.3.27), and, therefore, were not invented by Phoebammon, but they do not appear in any other Greek treatise. Possibly they originated with grammarians as descriptions of figures of speech and Phoebammon then applied them also to figures of thought, which they do not fit very well, but the scheme is not followed out rigidly.

Among other treatises on figures the most interesting is perhaps an anonymous work by a Christian writer who expressly based his discussion on the Hermogenic treatises *On Invention* and *On Method*.[42] Examples are chiefly drawn from Homer and Demosthenes, but the funeral oration for Basil, by Gregory of Nazianzus, is cited once.

[42] Text in Spengel, *Rhetores Graeci*, vol. 2, pp. 110–60.

The Second Sophistic

In the second quarter of the third century, Philostratus of Lemnos wrote the work in two books called *Lives of the Sophists,* which is the source of the term "second sophistic."[1] "Ancient" sophistry, he says, was founded by Gorgias and flourished for about a century; other ancient sophists briefly discussed are Protagoras, Hippias, Prodicus, Polus, Thrasymachus, Antiphon, Critias, and Isocrates. The speeches of these older sophists, according to Philostratus, were concerned with such themes as courage, justice, heroes, gods, and the nature of the universe, and they aimed at demonstrating the probability of an argument. A "second" sophistic began with the orator Aeschines when exiled from Athens in 330 B.C. These younger sophists were declaimers, more interested in the artistic treatment of a subject than in persuading an audience of some thesis. From Aeschines, however, Philostratus jumps abruptly to an account of sophists of the first and second centuries after Christ. In modern usage, "second sophistic" refers to a cultural and literary movement in Greek society that began in the first century and greatly flourished in the second. The military and political disruptions of the third century adversely affected all aspects of cultural life, but in the fourth century sophistry again became a major influence throughout the Greek world. In the ideological contest between Christianity and paganism for the hearts and minds of Greeks, the sophists as a group were influential teachers of the old religion and old values, but even as early as the second century a Christianized version of sophistry had begun to emerge; it gained strength with the official toleration of Christianity in the fourth century and continued through the fifth and into the sixth. A sophistic tradition can then be traced throughout the Byzantine period and was transplanted to Renaissance Italy by Greek scholars in the fifteenth century.

Within the Second Sophistic Philostratus distinguishes a philosophical tradition, using oratory as a form for expounding philosophical ideas, and a more purely sophistic tradition in schools of declamation, but many sophists were active in both areas. Most taught declamation, often holding chairs of rhetoric in Greek cities; some pleaded cases in the courts of law; major sophists were sometimes sent on embassies to Rome or elsewhere to plead local interests with the emperors or governors, and some were sent by emperors as ambassadors to troubled cities. The most famous sophists traveled

---

[1] Translation by Wright in the Loeb Classical Library. For discussion, see Anderson, *Philostratus.*

widely, giving demonstrations of their skill in theaters or at religious festivals, became friends with powerful Romans, including emperors; and acquired a fame comparable to that of movie stars, athletes, and musical performers today.

Although the sophists of the Roman Empire performed some of the same functions in society as did the sophists of the fifth and fourth centuries B.C., there are striking differences between the two groups. The older sophists were the radicals of their time: they introduced new methods of teaching, questioned traditional values, and encouraged their students to do the same. The later sophists were conservatives, even reactionaries: they introduced no innovations in education, they did not generally encourage original thought on the part of their students, when they criticized contemporary society it was generally for its failures to live up to past standards of conduct, and the philosophy they voiced was usually a combination of Platonic and Stoic beliefs.

The doctrine of imitation of classical models was basic to the literary and rhetorical standards and teachings of these later sophists. The canon of the ten Attic orators was firmly established in the schools by the second century, and the Atticism movement that began with Dionysius of Halicarnassus and others in the Augustan period remained a powerful force, aided by the publication of dictionaries and lexica of Attic Greek. An analogous movement existed in the art and architecture of the time. Sophists, however, differed considerably among themselves in the degree to which they observed strict Attic standards of language and style. The home ground of the Second Sophistic was Asia Minor, and it was there that the most famous sophists were born and had their schools. A tradition of Asianism continued, though that term was rarely used to describe it. Philostratus, for example, says (2.14) that Athenodorus, teaching in Athens, "both Atticized and spoke in an ornate style," and (2.18) that Onomarchus, living on the island of Andros near the coast of Asia Minor, "contracted, like an eye disease, the Ionian *idea* of style which flourished especially in Ephesus." Since no Asian orator of the past had achieved classic status, Ionian sophists often turned to Gorgias for inspiration. The Gorgianic style can even be found in the Christian sermons of Melito, bishop of Sardis in the second century. Philostratus quotes a short passage, reminiscent of Gorgias, from a declamation by Onomarchus about a man who, like Pygmalion, fell in love with a statue:

O loveliness living in an unliving body, who of the gods fashioned you? Some goddess of Persuasion, or Grace, or Eros himself, the father of loveliness? Truly, you have everything: the form of your face, the flower of your flesh, the glance of your eyes, your gracious smile, blushing cheek, hints that you hear! You even have voice, always about to speak. In a moment you will say something, but only when I am gone, unloving sorcerer, unfaithful to your faithful lover. You have given me not a word. Therefore, on you I shall lay the curse that most causes fair ones to shudder: I pray you may grow old. (2.18)

In discussing sophistry Philostratus was interested only in its artistic side, and in this respect he probably reflects the reaction of an average spectator: how splendid the sophist sounded, how clever his maxims were, how excited his audience became! In Greek, as in Latin, the artificiality of declamation in the schools of rhetoric encouraged striving for effect, epigrammatic conceit, and use of poetic metaphors and rhythms. Appropriateness of style to subject, however, continued to be expected; when a sophist delivered a major speech on an important public occasion, his style was likely to be more disciplined and restrained.

Many speeches by major sophists of the Roman Empire survive and can be read today. Some provide valuable historical information or are important for understanding Greek religion and society.[2] Though the sophists admired and tried to imitate Demosthenes, they rarely attained his force and dramatic power; their work as a whole is more reminiscent of Isocrates: wordy, smooth, and bland in thought, though sometimes impassioned in style. It is possible, with patience, to acquire some appreciation of speeches of the Second Sophistic as works of art. The sophists were the great performers and entertainers of their time; their speeches can be approached in the way that listeners today appreciate musical compositions, whether classical or popular. A sophist characteristically structured his work around the development of a small number of themes, on which he played variations like a virtuoso performer, introducing such progymnasmatic forms as myths, narratives, comparison, and ecphrases. Sound and rhythm were as important as sense; reminiscences of classical writers, including poets, often strike the ear, only to be given some original turn; beautiful images are presented to the mind and are woven into changing visual patterns.[3]

Yet the sophists often had an important message, and the content of their speeches deserves serious attention. That message, for which Isocrates was again their best model, was the expression of the traditional values of Hellenic culture in an age dominated by the realities of Roman rule and later by the threat of Christianity. Their noblest themes, voiced on great public occasions but often implicit also in declamations, were the beauties of Greek religion, mythology, literature, and art; the historical achievements of classical Greece, including the defeat of the Persian invasions; the idealism of Greek philosophy, especially that of Plato; the moral excellence of great Greeks of the past; and, taken as a whole, what it meant to be a Greek. Though they could celebrate and flatter Roman emperors or governors, and

---

[2] See Bowersock, *Greek Sophists in the Roman Empire*.
[3] See Cassin, ed., *Le plaisir de parler: Etudes de sophistique comparée*.

though they avoided direct criticism of Roman institutions or Christian-ity, the total effect of their work was to define a distinct culture that be-longed to them and their audiences by inheritance as Greeks. This culture, as they saw it, was intellectually and morally superior, though politically, economically, and militarily subservient to the rule of Rome; it had richness of historical experience, sophistication, and beauty lacking to the vulgar, anti-intellectual perversities of the Christians. There is a persistent note of nostalgia in the work of the sophists. It is no surprise that there is no Latin oratory concerned with the great cultural themes of the Greek sophists; the closest counterpart is Pliny's *Panegyricus*, which is a very Roman work.

The greatest Greek writer of the first and early second centuries after Christ was Plutarch. He was not a sophist, but his extensive writings, the *Lives* and the *Moralia*, sound several of the themes that were later taken up by sophists, including the historical, philosophical, and cultural achieve-ments of classical Greece. The most important Greek writer of the mid–second century is the satirist Lucian. He began as a sophist, and his works include some declamations, but he reacted against the affectations of soph-ists and satirizes them in a lecture called in the Loeb Library translation *A Professor of Public Speaking*.[4] The earliest of the sophists discussed by Phi-lostratus whose works are preserved is Dio of Prusa in Bithynia.

Dio Chrysostom

Eighty surviving orations are attributed to Dio, most of which are genu-inely his works.[5] By the third century he had become known as "Chrysosto-mos," or "the Golden Tongued," an epithet later also given to the Christian orator John of Antioch. Dio was born in Prusa around A.D. 40 and was thus a contemporary of Plutarch and Quintilian. He was a member of a promi-nent family with business interests in the province of Bithynia in northwest-ern Asia Minor; he certainly declaimed and at some periods in his career had private students, but he may never have taught rhetoric on a regular basis. Some of his educational ideas can be found in oration 18, which is a letter to an unnamed adult whose studies seem to have been neglected. Dio ex-plains that he would outline a different course for a boy or for one who intended to plead in the courts; there is thus no attention to the theory of rhetoric, and the objective is a general literary background for cultured speech, a knowledge of character, a sense of style, and a few models for particular occasions. Dio is clearly anxious not to discourage the addressee by making the course too difficult. He suggests a reading list that starts with

[4] See my *Art of Rhetoric in the Roman World*, 585–90.
[5] Translations by Cohoon and Crosby in the Loeb Classical Library; text and English com-mentary on orations 7, 12, and 36 by Russell; for further discussion and bibliography, see my *Art of Rhetoric in the Roman World*, 566–82, and C. P. Jones, *The Roman World of Dio Chrysostom*.

the comic poet Menander and includes Euripides, Homer, and major Attic historians and orators. At the end he recommends a few orators "a little before our time," since their abilities are more reasonably attainable by a modern student than are those of the great figures of the distant past.

Around A.D. 80 Dio went to Rome, probably on provincial business, and was nearly ruined there through his connections with an important person who fell from favor and was executed by Domitian in 82.[6] Dio himself was exiled from Italy and his home province of Bithynia. He went first to Greece to consult the Delphic oracle about what he should do. The reply was that he should keep on doing what he was doing until he came to the end of the earth. This he interpreted to mean that he should follow the life of a wandering Cynic philosopher, going from place to place with few possessions, earning his way as a servant, and talking about philosophy.[7] His route took him around Greece and then far to the north through eastern Europe. At the time of Domitian's death, Dio was in a Roman army camp near the Danube. Philostratus describes (1.7) how, on receipt of the news, he stripped off his rags "like Odysseus fighting the suitors," jumped on an altar, and delivered an invective against tyranny and an exhortation to the troops to responsible action. Under Nerva and Trajan he was allowed to resume a leading position at home in Bithynia, visited Rome, addressed the four speeches of his *On Kingship* to Trajan, and seems even to have become a friend of the emperor.

Synesius of Cyrene, a Greek writer of the early fifth century, admired Dio, wrote a playful *Encomium of Baldness* in reply to Dio's *Encomium of Hair*, and has left an essay on Dio that makes a sharp distinction between his career before and after exile. According to Synesius, Dio began as a sophist strongly opposed to philosophy. He mentions a speech entitled *Against the Philosophers* and several sophistic speeches, including *Eulogy of the Gnat*. The effect of exile, however, Synesius says, was to convince Dio that the rewards of life that he had been pursuing—power, wealth, fame, and pleasure—were idle and to turn him in the direction of philosophy, which he expressed in oratorical form. This conversion may be somewhat exaggerated, but it seems likely that Dio's declamatory works were written early in his career and that most of his major orations on serious themes, as well as some works in dialogue form, date from the time of his exile or later. Dio was not an original philosopher; he draws on Platonic, Stoic, and Cynic sources to discuss ethics and aspects of metaphysics with ethical significance. In this sense he resembles his contemporary Plutarch, but he was less of a scholar than Plutarch, not much interested in history, and more inter-

---

[6] Usually thought to be Flavius Sabinus, but perhaps more likely Arrecinus Clemens; see Brian W. Jones, "The Exile of Dio."

[7] Probably no sharp conversion from rhetoric to philosophy should be envisioned; see Moles, "Career and Conversion of Dio."

ested in persuading an audience to improve the quality of their lives. Several of his speeches, probably dating from his exile, are diatribes drawing on the life and teachings of Diogenes the Cynic. Examples include the sixth oration, on tyranny; the eighth, on virtues; the ninth, which describes Diogenes' teaching at the Isthmian games; and the tenth; on servants. Stoicism furnishes the inspiration for the fourteenth and fifteenth speeches, on slavery and freedom, and the twenty-first develops the Stoic paradox that only the wise man is always happy.

Toward the end of his life, when he had returned to Bithynia, Dio was active in public life there.[8] His speeches from that period are the only surviving examples of what might be called the day-to-day deliberative oratory of the Roman Empire. Oration 45 is especially interesting in this respect. It was delivered in the assembly in Prusa early in the reign of Trajan to defend the role Dio had played in negotiations between the city and the emperor. There is no pathos and little ornamentation. After explaining his earlier conduct, Dio goes on to propose a program for the beautification and political development of the region. We last hear of Dio in letters of Pliny the Younger (10.81–82), about A.D. 111, when the latter was governor of the province and Dio was meeting opposition in trying to complete a program of public works in his native city.

Dio's finest speeches include the four in his *On Kingship*; the *Euboeic Discourse*,[9] which is a parable about a man shipwrecked on the island of Euboea and saved by simple but virtuous peasants whose way of life is charmingly told; the *Trojan Discourse*, a tour de force arguing that the Trojans actually won the Trojan War; and his speech at the Olympic games (oration 12).[10] The latter is a particularly good example of a sophistic speech on important cultural themes in the grand manner and deserves some description here. It was apparently delivered at the first Olympic festival after Dio's return from exile, which would date it to A.D. 97; what is true in the case of Pliny's *Panegyricus*, carefully revised and expanded for publication, may be true of Dio's *Olympicus* and other major works. Sophists regularly attended and spoke at the great athletic festivals of Greece; the earliest known example is Gorgias' speech at Olympia.

The *Olympicus* consists of prooemion, proposition, division of the question, proof, and epilogue. Aristotle had suggested (*On Rhetoric* 3.14.1) that an epideictic orator should begin with some theme unrelated to the main subject of the speech, develop it in a showy way, and then link it to what follows. He instanced the opening of Isocrates' *Helen*, which starts with an attack on eristics. A common topic of all prooemia is the speaker himself, his lack of skill, or the difficulty of his task. Dio accords with these conventions

[8] See Sheppard, "Dio Chrysostom, the Bithynian Years."
[9] Translation by Hadas, *Hunters of Euboea.*
[10] For further discussion, see my *Art of Rhetoric in the Roman World*, 571–81.

in his introduction (1–20), which does not reveal the subject he will discuss, and develops a bird metaphor: Dio is the owl, the philosopher-bird, reticent of speech, with no special cause to plead, and resembling Socrates, a bird who attracted other birds to himself. Showy sophists, he says, are like peacocks. Toward the end of the prooemion Dio mentions his exile and says that his speech will wander as he has, but this is deliberate self-deprecation, for the structure of the speech shows careful planning.

The introduction is then linked to a proposition (21–26) by a rhetorical question: What should he speak about? He suggests that he might describe the lands and people he saw in exile, or he might discuss the nature and power of divinity, a topic suggested by the great temple of Zeus at Olympia with its famous statue of the god by Phidias, by then over five hundred years old. He also asks if he should not invoke the muses, as Hesiod did, and he quotes the first eight lines of *Works and Days*. He uses the invocation to lead to his main subject, which is the question of how the human conception of deity, including the contributions of poets and sculptors, has been created.

The division of the question (27–46), based on Platonic and Stoic writers, identifies two main sources of human understanding of divinity, those that are inborn, involving direct perception of the order and beauty of the universe, and those that are acquired. The latter are divided into three: the conception presented by the poets, that enjoined by lawgivers, and that envisioned in the fine arts. As he turns to this last source Dio inserts a brief exhortation to attention (43): he has at last come to the real subject of his speech.

The proof extends from sections 47 to 83 and is primarily a demonstration of the contribution of Phidias, a sculptor in the fifth century B.C., to the Hellenic conception of Zeus, with comparisons to the contributions of poets. In a dramatic passage, Phidias is imagined before a tribunal of Greeks, where he is questioned about his statue (49–54): "Has he achieved a suitable representation of the god?" To this Phidias is made to reply (55–83) that he has achieved as much as possible in his difficult medium. Various qualities of Zeus that Phidias tried to portray are discussed. The passage is one of the better pieces of art criticism from antiquity and may have some originality. Phidias was a frequent character in declamation; here Dio composes a prosopopoeia, which he sets within his own speech, framing philosophy and religion within oratory.

The short epilogue (84–85) recapitulates the questions Dio has discussed and ends with a brief prosopopoeia in which Zeus gives moral advice to the Greeks: they carry out their rites beautifully, but they neglect themselves. Zeus is made to quote Homer, who was a major contributor to his own conceptualization. Although there is no immediate course of action recommended, Dio is clearly seeking to persuade by enhancing understanding of religion. The speech is, in fact, a pagan sermon, preaching the faith of Hellenism, its gods, its poetry, its art, and its culture as a whole. This theme became the noblest subject of oratory from this time to the end of pagan antiquity.

Polemon and Herodes Atticus

Philostratus gives impressionistic accounts of thirty-six major sophists of the second century. He is not very systematic nor probably entirely trustworthy, and often he fails to give details that the historian of rhetoric would like, but a fascinating picture of the society of the times emerges and numerous incidents are vividly recounted. Among the sophists to whom he gives special attention are Polemon (1.25) and Herodes Atticus (2.1). Two declamations by Polemon and one by Herodes survive.

Polemon was born in Laodicea in Asia Minor around A.D. 90. He studied rhetoric in Smyrna with Scopilian, to whom Philostratus also devotes a chapter, and Stoic philosophy with Timocrates.[11] This seems to have resulted in a quarrel with Scopilian. Students often studied with several different teachers, and teachers competed acrimoniously with each other for the best students. He also claimed to have studied with Dio Chrysostom. Beginning around A.D. 110, he had his own school in Smyrna, was the leading sophist there for a generation, and attracted students from all over the Greek world. As a result of his fame he became a major political leader in Smyrna, pleaded cases in the law courts, spoke in the assembly, and was sent on embassies to the emperors Trajan and Hadrian. Polemon was a special favorite of the emperor Hadrian, the most philhellene of Roman emperors and the one most interested in sophistry, and he seems to have functioned at times as Hadrian's personal spokesman in the East. All sorts of honors were poured on him, including the right to travel at public expense, honorary membership in the Museum at Alexandria, and enormous sums of money in return for his rhetorical or political services.

Philostratus, utilizing the concept of the ideas of style, gives the following account of Polemon's eloquence:

> Polemon's style (*idea*) was hot, combative, and sharply echoing, like the trump at the Olympic games. His Demosthenic cast of thought gives it distinction, and there is gravity which is not dull but shining and inspired, as though delivered from an oracle's seat. Those who say that he handled invective the best of the sophists but defense less well fail to

---

[11] For a detailed account of Polemon's career, see Willy Stegman's article "Antonius Polemon," in *Paulys Realencyclopädie der classischen Alterntumswissenschaft*, vol. 21, cols. 1320–57.

understand the man, for several of his declamations refute this claim as not true, especially the speech in which Demosthenes swears he did not accept a bribe of fifty talents. In establishing this difficult defense he is equal to the demands of the argument by his abundance [*peribolē*, one of the "ideas" of style] and art.

The subjects of Polemon's declamations mentioned by Philostratus are mostly prosopopoeiae on deliberative or judicial themes from real or imagined historical incidents, but like other great sophists Polemon was invited to speak on important public occasions. For example, he gave the speech at the dedication of the temple of Olympian Zeus in Athens. Clearly he was a great showman, with a dramatic sense. Philostratus describes Polemon's delivery on the basis of a report by Herodes Atticus. Because of arthritis, he was carried to the auditorium on a litter. A theme of declamation was then proposed for him, probably by the host or by some important person in the audience or by popular demand; he would have had a repertory that included most well-known themes, but in treating any he would have wanted to show his originality in ex tempore composition. Once the theme was determined, according to Herodes, Polemon withdrew for a short time to meditate on it. He then returned and took a seat in front of the audience. He spoke in a clear, ringing voice, dispassionately at first, but gradually with more excitement, leaping from his chair as he came to the climax of his argument and stamping the ground "like the horse in Homer." At the end of a rhythmic phrase he would smile, as if to show how easy it was. Polemon's two surviving declamations are in the person of fathers of two heroes killed at the battle of Marathon who dispute the honor of delivering a funeral oration over the dead.[12]

Philostratus' account of the death and burial of Polemon at Laodicea is the most bizarre anecdote in *Lives of the Sophists*. At the age of fifty-six, after much painful rheumatic suffering, the great sophist had returned to Laodicea. Feeling his death approaching, he demanded of his family that he be buried while still alive. As he was being shut up in the tomb, he exhorted the workmen, "Hurry, hurry, lest the sun see me reduced to silence!" And to his weeping family, as the cover was put on the sarcophagus, he cried out his last words, "Give me a body and I shall declaim!"

Herodes Atticus was the wealthiest Greek of his time, the most famous private philanthropist of antiquity (builder of both the Odeon and the stadium at Athens), the intimate friend of emperors, and the holder of numerous high offices, including a Roman consulship in A.D. 143. That he was also a sophist of professional standing, in the view of some of his contemporaries and successors perhaps the greatest sophist of his age, is a good indication

---

[12] As Russell notes, *Greek Declamation*, 81 and 111, these are "short, dense, and sober" pieces, not quite what one would expect from the descriptions of Polemon's style.

of the enormous appeal of the sophistic movement to the upper classes of the second century. Although he probably never taught rhetoric, he may sometimes have had advanced students in his entourage. His activities as a sophist took the form of declamations and occasional epideictic speeches on important occasions. Philostratus greatly admired him and devotes his longest essay (2.1) to him. As befitted an Athenian, he favored a relatively simple style, for which his favorite classical model was Critias, one of the few native Athenians among the sophists of the fifth century B.C. One of his declamations survives, a deliberative speech entitled *On the Constitution*, based on a speech by Thrasymachus known from Dionysius of Halicarnassus' essay *On Isaeus*. It is so classical that scholars once thought it was a genuine work of the fifth century B.C.

Aelius Aristides

The only second-century sophist to have been accepted by later grammarians and rhetoricians into the canon of the Attic orators was Aristides.[13] Philostratus, who devotes a chapter to him (2.9), says that since he lacked ability at ex tempore oratory he became a careful workman who sought purity of language based on study of the classics; that his strengths were his learning, his force, and his ability to portray character; that he was the most disciplined of all the sophists; and that he did not seek to please the crowd. These qualities, together with the cultural and moral values displayed in the speeches, were what made his works especially suitable for study by students in late antiquity and the Byzantine period; that in turn is the principal reason why so many of them are preserved. His not entirely attractive personality emerges from his work and descriptions of him; he was sometimes testy with audiences that did not appreciate him, and throughout much of his life he suffered from debilitating psychosomatic illness. His *Sacred Discourses* contain a revealing account of his suffering, his dreams, and his cure through the agency of the god Aesclepius.[14] Most of his life was passed in Asia Minor, where he was born in Mysia about A.D. 117; he lived and taught principally in Smyrna but traveled to Egypt, Greece, and Rome, and died in 189.

Numerous orations by Aristides have survived, all written in pure Attic Greek.[15] These include prose hymns to the gods to be used as prologues at sophistic displays, a considerable number of declamations based on events in Greek history, *Sacred Discourses*, an encomium of Rome,

[13] The most important study of Aristides is Boulanger, *Aelius Aristide*.

[14] See Behr, *Aristides and the Sacred Tales*.

[15] Translation by Behr, *The Complete Works*; translation of a selection of speeches by Behr in the Loeb Classical Library; for the Roman and Panathenaic discourses, see Oliver, "The Ruling Power" and "The Civilizing Power."

Panathenaicus,[16] a prose monody for Smyrna after its destruction in an earthquake, treatises entitled *On Rhetoric* and *On the Four*, and other works.

Roman Discourse, or *Encomium on Rome*, was probably delivered on the second of two visits to Rome during the reign of Antoninus Pius.[17] Aristides says it was an offering of thanks for reaching Rome safely. He does not seem to have come as an ambassador, but he had friends in the capital and was probably invited to visit them in acknowledgement of his great reputation among intellectuals in the East. The speech is entirely encomiastic and consists largely of comparisons between Rome and previous great cities, to Rome's advantage, but as such it provided Romans with a vision of Hellenism as understood in the East and for Greek readers stressed the advantages Rome had bestowed on them, especially the peace it had brought and the way it had shared its citizenship. This expression of loyalty to Rome by a famous Greek may have been appreciated by the regime. Though somewhat informative to the historian of the empire and beautifully finished in diction and composition, the speech lacks the significance of Pliny's *Panegyric* and Dio's *On Kingship*, for Aristides does not seek to influence future policy as they did. Probably he did not think it necessary or desirable. Pliny and Dio had spoken when the memories of Nero and Domitian were still very much alive; Nerva and Trajan had brought much better times, but there was apprehension as to how long this could be maintained and a need to stress the importance of enlightened leadership. Aristides visited Rome after fifty years of rule by emperors who admired Greek culture and who enjoyed wide support all over the empire. He probably had little understanding of problems that were beginning to emerge and were to engulf the empire in war and tyranny by the end of the century.

At the end of the first century B.C. the Hellenistic philosophical schools were largely moribund except for an eclectic form of Stoicism that sought to teach public and private morality and provided what philosophical background could be found for the official pagan religion, largely through allegorizing the gods. In the following two centuries the vacuum in philosophical thought began to be filled by a renaissance of Platonism. Most sophists admired the dialogues of Plato for their literary art and their philosophical idealism, and their expositions of Platonism in a popular form probably contributed to the emergence of Neoplatonism in the third century, but the increasing influence of philosophers, most conspicuous in Marcus Aurelius' abandonment of rhetoric for philosophy, was also a threat to the sophists' control of formal education. Plato's hostility to rhetoric was a challenge for the sophists, as it was later to the Neoplatonists. The most extensive surviving efforts to answer Plato are the work of Aristides. His long oration, really

---

[16] See Day, *The Glory of Athens*.

[17] The speech has usually been dated to the first visit in 143, but good reasons for dating it in 155 are advanced by Klein, "Zu Datierung des Romrede."

a treatise, *On Rhetoric*, replies to *Gorgias* and seeks to show that rhetoric is an important, legitimate art and that what Socrates says against rhetoric could equally be objected to philosophy. Aristides treats the subject very seriously, claiming that he has a responsibility to defend rhetoric as one would a parent and invoking the aid of Hermes, Apollo, and the muses. Although he often draws on Plato's works in other speeches and admires him as a writer, he cannot accept Plato's views of rhetoric and his criticism of the great statesmen of the fifth century B.C. His equally long treatise *On the Four* is his answer to Socrates' criticism of Miltiades, Cimon, Themistocles, and Pericles. Aristides' replies to Plato were taken seriously by Neoplatonists; according to the Byzantine encyclopedia *Souda*, Porphyry wrote a reply to Aristides' *On Rhetoric*. This has not survived. To a modern reader, these and other works of Aristides are likely to seem bland, wordy, and superficial, lacking even the historical interest of somewhat similar works of Isocrates. That Aristides came to be regarded as the greatest of the later sophists is indicative of what counted as high rhetorical art in his time and of the intellectual exhaustion of the period.

Sophistry from the Late Second to the Early Fourth Century

Philostratus' *Lives* ends with discussion of several sophists of the late second and early third centuries. These include (1.24) Antipater the Syrian, who had been one of his own teachers, was the tutor of the emperor Caracalla, and held a consulship and governorship of Bithynia under Septimius Severus; as well as two sophists who wrote works extant today. Julius Pollux (2.12) was the teacher of the future emperor Commodus and is the object of bitter satire in Lucian's *Professor of Public Speaking*. An abridged version of his *Onomasticon* survives. It is a thesaurus of Attic Greek, arranged by subject in a way useful to a student of rhetoric: for example, it lists fifty-two terms for praising a king and thirty-three to abuse a tax collector. Claudius Aelianus (2.31) was a learned Roman who chose to write in Greek. Although Philostratus praises his style, his surviving works use a strange mixture of dialects and fail to observe the standards of rhetorical composition of the time. They include a treatise entitled *On Animals* in seventeen books, collecting miscellaneous facts and anecdotes and seeking to show that animals have human virtues and vices; a *Varied History*, which is a miscellaneous collection of anecdotes about famous people that might be useful to a student of rhetoric; and two fragmentary religious treatises. A sophistic writer of the reign of Commodus not mentioned by Philostratus is Maximus of Tyre. He is known today from his *Dialexeis*, a collection of forty-one philosophical lectures, including, for example, "Whether Socrates Did Rightly in Not Answering His Critics." The form is that of the diatribe, the thought is unoriginal and derived from Plato and the Cynics, and the manner is that of a sophist.

The third century proved to be the worst period in the long history of Rome: a time of barbarian invasions deep into the empire, administrative collapse, wars between claimants for the throne, military autocracies, civil unrest, natural disasters, and economic chaos. Schools of rhetoric in the cities of the empire continued as best they could. Apsines and Cassius Longinus, among writers on rhetoric discussed in the previous chapter, were both active in this period; sophists continued to declaim, though opportunities to travel and acquire fame throughout the cities of the empire were reduced.[18] Neither in Greek nor in Latin was there literary composition of artistic merit. Only in philosophy was there significant achievement, for this is the period in which Plotinus and his successors, including Porphyry, created the complex, mystical, sometimes even magical, system of Neoplatonism with its doctrine of the transcendent One and its hierarchies of being, an otherworldy philosophy that found converts in the disillusioned and depressed. It is also the period in which Christianity, despite persecution, greatly advanced the construction of a systematic theology, incorporating into it features of Platonism and Stoicism, and developed methods of biblical exegesis that included some features of rhetorical theory. This will be discussed in the next chapter.

The Sophistic Renaissance of the Fourth Century

With the accession to the throne of Diocletian in A.D. 284 and to a greater extent after the accession of Constantine in 306, strong emperors began to restore order to society. Both in Greek and in Latin, the fourth century is a period of intellectual and literary renascence, which continued on into the fifth century and in which sophists played a major role. Many of their works survive, information about them can be found in the writings of contemporary historians, and a vivid picture of activities in rhetorical schools, especially those of Athens, emerges from a description of them by Eunapius. He was born in Sardis around A.D. 346. At the age of sixteen he went to Athens to study rhetoric and philosophy; he remained there for five years and then returned to Sardis to teach rhetoric until his death about 414. Eunapius is an entertaining writer but a maddening historical source because of his casual attitude toward detail. The sophists appealed to him particularly because of their efforts to preserve the old eloquence of Greece at a time when everything else, he felt, was slipping into decay. He means in particular the

[18] An example of sophistic oratory of the mid–third century is oration 35 in the works of Aristides. It is a *basilicos logos*, or encomium, by an unknown speaker, probably addressing Philip the Arab, emperor in A.D. 244–49. It imitates Xenophon's *Agesilaus* and Isocrates' *Evagoras*, shows the influence of Dio's *On Kingship* and Aristides' encomium of Rome, and accords with the rules for epideictic oratory found in rhetoric handbooks. See de Blois, "The *Eis Basileia* of Pseudo-Aristides."

victory of Christianity over paganism. The title of his work, in contrast to Philostratus' *Lives of the Sophists*, is *Lives of the Philosophers and Sophists*, for he saw sophistry as a philosophical movement embracing Hellenic wisdom and eloquence in a Neoplatonic synthesis, and his work shows almost no interest in rhetorical theory.[19] Information in Eunapius' work about the schools of Athens can be supplemented by Libanius' account of his studies there, found in the latter's autobiographical first oration, and by some other contemporary sources.

From the fourth to the sixth century Athens was the greatest educational center of the ancient world. It owed this eminence to the fame of the philosophers and sophists who taught there and the ability of the students they attracted from all over the Roman Empire. The schools in Athens did not make up a university in the modern sense: although teachers gave lectures and students studied texts and practiced exercises in rhetoric and dialectic, there were no examinations and no academic degrees were conferred. The Neoplatonic philosophical school consisted of its scholarch, a number of senior scholars, and a group of advanced students. It owned property and had an endowment from gifts. The rhetorical schools consisted of the separate schools of sophists and their students, housed in the sophist's home, which usually had a large room for lectures and declamations and a library. One such house, complete with auditorium, has been excavated on the north slope of the Acropolis. Although there were only three official sophists, there were at any given time several other private schools of rhetoric. Rivalry among teachers and between students of different teachers was sharp. Students coming to Athens to study with one sophist were sometimes kidnapped by the students of another and forced to join his school. Libanius says (1.16) that an oath of loyalty to the teacher was required of all students. Student riots were frequent; the whole atmosphere of the city encouraged jealousy, ambition, and notoriety. The prospect of the excitement was for many young men an inducement to study there (1.19).

Prohaeresius

The leading official sophist in Athens in the early fourth century was Julian of Caesarea. His death, around A.D. 330, produced considerable excitement among the sophists who vied for his chair. A chair carried a stipend, exemption from certain taxes and duties, and other privileges. Eunapius' report (pp. 487–90 in Wright's Loeb edition), confused as it is, can be reduced to the following succession of events. From among the many appli-

[19] Translation of Eunapius by Wright together with his translation of Philostratus in the Loeb Classical Library. The following discussion of fourth-century schools and sophists is based on my *Greek Rhetoric under Christian Emperors*, 133–79, which provides additional information and bibliography.

cants for the chair, the city council elected six finalists to participate in a contest of declamation before the governor of the province, who was to make the final choice. The strongest contenders in the final stage were Hephaestion and Prohaeresius (also spelled Proaeresius). Hephaestion declined to compete against Prohaeresius, but the other candidates bribed the governor and drove Prohaeresius out of town. With the arrival of a new governor and the endorsement of the emperor, Constantius II, Prohaeresius was able to return. The new governor then assembled the sophists for the final contest and, to the horror of most of them, announced that he would propose a theme for an ex tempore declamation and that Prohaeresius was invited to compete. The ability to speak on a theme extemporaneously was admired by the public, but Prohaeresius was unusual in having greatly cultivated it; other sophists were fond of quoting a remark of Aelius Aristides, "We are not those who vomit but those who polish." As the governor was about to propose a theme, Prohaeresius saw two of his enemies in the back of the auditorium and, confident in his own great abilities to speak ex tempore, dramatically called on the governor to ask them to propose the theme. Unfortunately we are not told what the theme was, but from Eunapius' account it is clear that it was a judicial problem like those found in Hermogenes' *On Staseis* and involved stasis of definition. It was difficult, because it allowed little opportunity for adornment and thus taxed the competitors' ingenuity.[20] Prohaeresius put on his usual virtuoso performance and clearly gained the appointment; Eunapius, in his casual way, fails to say that, but he subsequently (p. 495) mentions the three official sophists as being Epiphanius the Syrian, Diophantus the Arabian, and Prohaeresius the Armenian.

In A.D. 313 the emperor Constantine issued the Edict of Milan which, for the first time, extended religious toleration to Christians. He became a Christian himself, and all his successors except Julian adhered to the new religion. Until the fifth century, when Christianity had become widely accepted, most sophists clung to the old religion. When a teacher of rhetoric became a Christian, he generally gave up his school; the most famous example is Saint Augustine. A few sophists, however, managed to reconcile their secular occupation with Christian faith; Malchion in the third century seems to have done so (Eusebius, *Church History* 7.29). Prohaeresius is the most famous example of a fourth-century sophist who was a Christian. When Julian the Apostate was emperor (A.D. 360–63), as part of his program to restore paganism, he prohibited the teaching of grammar and rhetoric by Christians but offered an exemption to Prohaeresius, whom he had known

---

[20] There is a fictional account of the contest in the seventh chapter of Gore Vidal's novel *Julian*, in which the theme is imagined to be "Which side of a woman is the most pleasing, front or back?" That is not a possible theme for declamation, though it was an occasional subject for dialectical disputation in sophisticated private society. Vidal's novel is based on readings of the Greek sources and gives a vivid account of the schools, but many of the details are unhistorical.

as a student. There is an extant letter from Julian to Prohaeresius (*Epistle* 14) in which the emperor compliments the sophist's eloquence and compares him to Pericles. Prohaeresius refused the exemption and stopped teaching rhetoric during Julian's reign. It is a pity that none of Prohaeresius' speeches are preserved, since it would be interesting to see how he handled the pagan elements traditional in sophistic oratory; probably he treated them as allegories, and it is unlikely that he introduced Christian themes. Eunapius refers to a speech on a gift of grain to Athens as a personal favor to Prohaeresius by the Christian emperor Constans, in which speech the sophist introduced the story of the goddess Demeter's visit among humans to give them the original gift of grain. His declamations on historical themes seem to have been best remembered, and in these he could largely avoid religious ideas. On Prohaeresius' death, his fellow sophist Diophantus delivered a funeral oration, which refers to his use of historical themes: it concluded, "O Marathon and Salamis, now have you been silenced. What a trumpet for your trophies have you lost!" (Eunapius, p. 494).

Himerius

The only Athenian sophist of this period whose oratory is preserved is Himerius. He was born in Bithynia about A.D. 320, studied in Athens, taught rhetoric in Constantinople from 343 to 352, and then returned to teach in Athens from 352 to 361. In the latter year, Julian became emperor; he had probably briefly been Himerius' student in Athens, and the sophist, an enthusiastic supporter of the old religion who was distressed at the growing stength of Christianity, went to join his court. After Julian's death in 363 Himerius probably remained in Asia Minor and may have visited Egypt. When Prohaeresius died in 369, Himerius returned to Athens and may have been given his chair. His latest datable speeches were written in 383.[21]

Eunapius did not personally know Himerius but had read his speeches and says (p. 517) that they "had the ring of political oratory." This suggests that he most often dealt with judicial themes, represented by the first seven speeches in our texts, most preserved only in part.[22] One, for example, is a speech in the person of Hyperides speaking on behalf of Demosthenes, another a speech for Demosthenes against Aeschines, a third an accusation against Epicurus for impiety. The remaining speeches are panegyrics in a variety of forms. The serious work of declamation was carried on in the schools in the morning, but after the baths and dinner sophists brought

---

[21] On this revised chronology of Himerius' career, see Barnes, "Himerius and the Fourth Century."

[22] We have, in whole or in excerpts made by Photius in the ninth century, thirty-two speeches out of an original seventy-five. The standard edition is Colonna, *Himerii Declamationes et Orationes*; there is no English translation.

students together for social meetings that furnished the occasion for speeches on birthdays, weddings, or departures from school. Leading sophists, including Himerius, also spoke in the theater on official occasions, such as festivals or the arrival of an important visitor to the city. Himerius' works include examples of this public as well as private epideictic rhetoric.

Oration 48 is a *prosphōnētikos* addressed to Hermogenes, governor of Achaea, who was visiting Athens from Corinth, the capital of the province. It is an example of Himerius' art in its fully developed form. He begins abruptly with a myth:

> They longed once for Philoctetes as well, after the plague, did the Greeks, and much to the gods did they pray. He, as his suffering abated, taking his bow into his hands, sought to know whether he could still shoot his target-lovers. Now that same Philoctetes did Odysseus summon to battle, arriving and giving token of his art,—that Odysseus who also activates almost the whole poem of Homer, making possible for it to be strummed with verse and music; for the latter busies himself in his poem a little with Achilles, the son of Thetis, describing his battle on the Scamander and his race [with Hector], but Odysseus is everywhere in the epic and with him for the most part the poet is found to take pains. For the victory of Philoctetes and for whatever this Philoctetes accomplished at Troy with his bow, Odysseus took the credit among the Greeks.
>
> You, my friend, order us, taking up not the bow of Heracles but the songs of the muses, to shoot for the Greeks. Behold, I obey you in this too. But O that I had moved my lyre long ago, since I desired to address you in the midst of the Greeks, but now I wish to denounce with you, my children [his Athenian audience], the Attic Cupids, because stilling their songs for a long time they allowed him [the governor] to be tended by the Ephyrian [i.e., Corinthian] Cupids.

Himerius builds his speech with progymnasmatic forms. The *mythos* of Philoctetes is followed by a *psogos*, or invective, against "Attic Cupids" for delaying the coming of the leader of the muses, who is Apollo but becomes an image for the governor. That is followed by an *ekphrasis*, a description of winter, the season through which they have been waiting; a *chreia* about Anacreon; a *synkrisis* of Anacreon and Himerius, and a second *psogos*, against the governor for not coming earlier. The image of the governor as leader of the muses is continued. In one of many rhetorical questions, Himerius asks, "Did not the god [i.e., the emperor] send you to Greece in order that speeches may flower their ancient flower?" Himerius then declares that he knows why the governor's arrival was delayed, and an elaborate *mythos* ensues about the Nile, with an *ekphrasis* of Egypt in time of flood. The long wait for the Nile flood makes it even more wonderful when it does come, and that cannot be until the proper festival. Possibly we should associate Hermogenes' visit with the Thargelia, the festival of Apollo in early summer. Then comes another *mythos*, drawn from the early Greek poet Alcaeus, about Apollo's journey in the winter to the land of the Hyperboreans, with his return in the summer and an *ekphrasis* of singing birds.

The complaint that the governor has not previously come has now been turned into a compliment about how good it is to have him, and Himerius is ready to move on to the governor's virtues. Or almost ready, for first we are treated to a Neoplatonic excursus on the soul, reminiscent of Plato's *Phaedrus*. Then at last Himerius describes the governor's education, career, and virtues as was traditional in panegyric. Even so, he breaks up the narrative with a *chreia* about Pythagoras and a *mythos* about Dionysus, inspired by the governor's travels.

The speech as a whole is a remarkable tour de force in a highly developed art form. Beauty is sought in every possible way—in content, description, and sound. Himerius should probably be imagined delivering it in an elevated chanting tone, with carefully planned gestures. His audience would have been made up of connoisseurs, who appreciated the allusions, the figures, the enthymemes, and the rhythms. The speech is to the fourth century after Christ what the poems of Pindar were to the early classical period. Modern readers generally have more taste for Pindar than for Himerius, but the primary reason for that may be the freshness with which Pindar seems to strike his lyre and the oppressive weight of a thousand years of literary history, which mutes our ears to the bell-like tones of Himerius.

As known to Photius in the ninth century, some speeches of Himerius were accompanied by *prothēoriai*, introductory remarks made by the sophist to explain to his students the treatment he will follow. Photius quotes two of these, which are valuable indications of how Himerius viewed his art. Oration 9 is an epithalamium, a prose marriage hymn, addressed to Himerius' student Severus. The *prothēoria* runs as follows:

> It might perhaps seem to someone beside the point to lay down rules about marriage speeches, for where Hymen and choruses and the freedom of poetic license are present, what occasion is there for rules of art? But since the man of learning must do nothing artless even in such speeches, it is worthwhile saying a little about them also. Now let the best rule for epithalamia be to look to the poets for the style, to the needs of the occasion for the contents, to the subject for the rhythm. If the speech aims at all of these things, the composition will exhibit considerable clarity. Of its four parts, the first contains the beginning of the speech, presenting by means of polished enthymemes the thought from which the speaker takes his demonstration; in the second part we render the institution of marriage, naturally common though it is, pleasurable by the novelty of the epicheiremes and the figures of thought, sweetly intermingling

moreover some obscure allusions which will not escape an audience keen for these things. The third part contains the encomium of those who marry, which, when brought forward in an inquiry about the praiseworthy, quickly fits the occasion. The speech ends with a description of the bride in which the speech attains as well a poetic grace, taking its rhythm from the subject.

Himerius aims at an aesthetic experience and is utilizing a version of the "ideas" of style; that word does not occur here but does in the *protheōria* to the tenth speech.[23]

Himerius' sixty-eighth speech is a short protreptic to students to seek *poikilia* in composition. *Poikilia* is described as the variegated play of thought, style, allusion, and rhythm and is compared to the figures on the shield of Achilles and to the transformations of Proteus. Proteus is a good image for a sophist, but not the only one. In Plato's *Republic* (596d) Glaucon ironically calls the demiurge, or creator of the world, a "wonderous sophist," and Himerius here imitates him by calling the Neoplatonic creator and disposer of all things "the great sophist in the sky." Sophistic creations are a microcosm of the universe.

Libanius

Smyrna, Ephesus, and other cities of the Ionian coast had been the most important centers of sophistry in the second century, but by the fourth were eclipsed by Athens, Nicomedia, Constantinople, and Antioch. Much information about rhetoric in Antioch is available in the vast writings of Libanius, who was a native of the city and held a chair of sophistry there from 354 until his death about 394. Antioch was a very different place from ivory-towered Athens. It was the leading administrative, military, and commercial center of the Levant; teachers and students did not dominate society there as in Athens, and Libanius' orations had more relevance for the real world than did those of Athenian sophists.

We have more detailed information about the career, works, and personality of Libanius than about any other Greek of antiquity. The corpus of his preserved works comprises fifty-one declamations; ninety-six progymnasmata; sixty-four orations; the *Hypotheses*, or introductions, to the speeches of Demosthenes; and about sixteen hundred letters. He wrote excellent Attic Greek and represents the fading tradition of pagan classical culture of his age in its purest form. He knew personally all the leading figures of public life, including the emperors, and he had opinions of his own, which he argued forcefully. He was tolerant, humane, and often personable, despite the hypochondria from which he suffered and even cultivated in imita-

[23] For translation of that *protheōria*, see Walden, *Universities of Ancient Greece*, 238–39.

tion of Aristides. He was also wordy and repetitive, and often tiresome, artificial, and unimaginative. Despite his opposition to Christianity, his works, like those of Aristides, became classics in the Byzantine schools. Study of them over the next thousand years contributed to an understanding of classicism in the high style and a sense of the importance of oratory. To his contemporaries and later readers he seemed to show that great oratory was possible under the rule of emperors.

Within the scope of this book it is not possible to provide any comprehensive account of Libanius' career as a teacher or of his writings.[24] His autobiographical first oration is the best starting point for a study of his activities.[25] Perhaps his finest speech is *Antiochus* (oration 11), an encomium of his native city given at the local Olympic games there in the summer of 360.[26] It opens with a prooemium, in which Libanius says he has postponed speaking the praises of Antioch until his eloquence matured and that he will show that the ancient and modern preeminence of the city are due to the same factors. He then takes these up one by one, including the physical situation, the inhabitants and their histories, the harmony of the classes and their virtues, the city's size, its military importance, the eloquence of its sophists, the patriotism of its citizens. Toward the end (196–250) there is an unusually detailed ekphrasis of the city as he knew it, including its streets, buildings, and commerce. Like Himerius, Libanius incorporates progymnasmatic forms into his oratory, but he is less fond of myths and ornamentation than Himerius and more given to narrative and to arguing theses. The speech ends with a summation and declaration that his debt to his city has been repaid to the best of his ability. It is possible that one objective of the speech was to counteract the increasing importance of Christian Constantinople, a city Libanius never liked, by showing that there was a greater city in the East. More generally, Libanius is describing his ideal of a Greek polis with the hope that his fellow citizens will be persuaded to try to achieve that ideal, much as Pericles' Funeral Oration in Thucydides' *History* describes an ideal Athens.

Libanius welcomed the accession of Julian and his program for the restoration of paganism but was initially reserved with Julian: he did not want to give the impression of tainting his own position with the qualities of a flatterer (1.118–23). Preparations for a Persian war brought Julian to Antioch for an extended stay; while there he apparently came to understand Libanius' situation and requested a speech. The encomiastic *Prosphoneticus* (oration 13) was the answer. On Julian's death in battle Libanius composed

---

[24] Some greater detail, with bibliography, can be found in my *Greek Rhetoric under Christian Emperors*, 150–63.

[25] See Norman, *Libanius' Autobiography*. Representative speeches and letters are translated by Norman in the Loeb Classical Library.

[26] Translation by Downey, "Libanius' Oration in Praise of Antioch."

in his honor both an emotional *Monody* (oration 17) and a formal funeral oration (oration 18), in which Julian is presented as the Hellenic ideal, "a paragon of such virtue, both moral and political, whereby the way to personal salvation is revealed and the state and society purged of grossness and error and brought to perfection." A later speech that deals directly with Christianity is *For the Temples*, addressed to the emperor Theodosius around 386. It is a spirited attack on the pillaging and destruction of pagan temples, especially those in country districts, by Christian monks. Libanius claims that this is illegal and against the interest of the state. Animal sacrifice had been prohibited by this time, but sacrifice of incense and perfume was still legal, and the temples remained open. Libanius does not attack Christianity as such, only its extremists, and of course he addresses the emperor with great deference, especially at the beginning. Toward the end, however, comes a striking passage (51–54) in which he seems almost to dare the emperor to take the ultimate step of prohibiting pagan worship. Five years later it was done. Libanius consistently tried to arrest and reverse changes rather than to introduce new social and political principles as the basis of reform. *On the Temples* is unusual in its presentation of powerful, sustained thought. More often his political speeches proceed argument, by argument with little organization into a greater whole. The result is that they often lack internal dynamics: they reach no stirring climaxes, as had those of Demosthenes. One reason is doubtless that none of them is a product of open, spirited debate. *On the Temples* was probably sent in written form to the emperor, not delivered in person and certainly not part of a debate on the issue.

Libanius spoke on public issues throughout most of his life, but he was at the same time teaching students: he directed their reading of Greek literature and taught both progymnasmata and declamation. The reading course was based on Homer, Hesiod and other poets, Demosthenes, Lysias and other orators, Herodotus, Thucydides, and other historians (*Epistle* 1036). Many progymnasmata and declamations, given as models for the students to imitate, have been preserved. They were admired for centuries and make interesting reading today. His style in these exercises is less poetic and less sententious than that of many sophists. Some of the declamations have a *protheōriai* that reveals how Libanius viewed the theme. For example, the third is a speech for Menelaus asking the Trojans to give up Helen, and the fourth is a similar speech for Odysseus. In the *protheōria* he says that the characterization and style are to be based on what Homer says about the oratory of these two heroes, and similar arguments are to be used in both but differently treated because of the difference in characterization. The sixth declamation, for Orestes on the charge of murdering his mother, has a long *protheōria* about the characterization and style required: Orestes should not try to soothe the jury by mildness of manner, because that will undermine the sense of outrage that is the best justification for his action. Some of the themes may have had contemporary relevance: in declamation 22, for example, the violation of sanctuary from arrest at an altar. A version of a defense of Socrates at his trial could be read as a defense of Julian.

In addition to prosopopoeiae of historical characters there are declamations in which character types are imagined as the speaker. The most famous of these is the twenty-sixth. A misanthrope appears before the city council and asks to be required to drink hemlock. His problem is that he has been trapped into a marriage with a garrulous woman and can no longer bear his life. This unlikely situation is made probable by effective presentation of the character of the speaker. He describes the steps by which his natural fears were allayed as he was led into the marriage by a friend, and he vividly presents the streams of words emanating from his loquacious bride. The first half of the speech is a narrative of the speaker's situation, the second an answer to objections that might be raised to his request. The speech may have inspired Ben Jonson's comedy, *The Silent Woman*.

Themistius

Although Themistius did not teach rhetoric and regarded himself as a philosopher and political orator, and although he consistently took the side of philosophy in its dispute with rhetoric, he also argues in his twenty-first oration that a philosopher should use the methods of the sophists, he composed and delivered epideictic speeches, and his speeches as a whole show the influence of sophistic forms. He was born in Paphlagonia in 317 and became a professor of philosophy in Constantinople in 345. Though himself a pagan, he couched his thought in terms acceptable to many Christians. His political theory was permanently influential in the Greek world. It may be summarized as the belief that a philosophical ruler must be born to his task and will rule by divine right; he will learn from professional philosophers but lives in a world of action; he should understand government and protect his subjects; though he will share moral qualities with others, he should be distinguished by *philanthrōpia*, a godlike love of humanity. The ideal king is the personification of the law (see, e.g., oration 5.64).[27] Themistius was a practical philosopher, who sought to make the political and ethical views of Plato and Aristotle understood in his own age. The metaphysical, mystical thought of Neoplatonism had little interest for him. His extant works include paraphrases of Aristotle's logical and scientific works, which were doubtless useful to his own work as they were to later students.

[27] For further discussion of Themistius, with bibliography, see my *Greek Rhetoric under Christian Emperors*, 32–35 and 165.

Some thirty-seven orations attributed to Themistius have survived. The first is an encomium of the emperor Constantius, delivered in his presence in A.D. 350. It does not observe some usual conventions of panegyric, for at the outset Themistius tells the emperor that he admires his soul, not his possessions, and though he affects to believe that Constantius is virtuous, he also lectures him sternly. A professor of philosophy, like a Christian bishop, could venture to take a much stronger moral stance than could a professional sophist. "There is no advantage," Themistius says, "to having your crown on straight, but your character dragging in the mud, and your scepter of gold, but your soul more worthless than lead, and to clothe your body in fine and colorful raiment, while exhibiting a mind bare of virtue, and to hit birds when you shoot them, but to miss wisdom when you take counsel, accustomed to sit easily on a horse, but more easily to fall from justice" (1.12).[28]

In 355 Constantius appointed Themistius to the senate of Constantinople. He was active there until his death around 388. Nineteen of his orations are encomia of emperors, delivered in the senate or elsewhere, usually on imperial commission; others are protreptics to philosophy or diatribes on moral theses, for example, oration 30, "Should One Work the Soil?"

Synesius

Another philosopher-orator who did not hesitate to lecture an emperor was Synesius of Cyrene.[29] His *Discourse on Kingship* was addressed to the twenty-one-year-old Arcadius, who sat uneasily on the Eastern throne, and it is partially modeled on Dio Chrysostom's speeches to Trajan. Synesius here encourages the young emperor to look beyond his corrupt court, to beware of flattery, to avoid the influence of barbarians serving the Romans for pay, to lead his army in person, and to make direct contact with his people. Synesius was born around 370, studied Neoplatonic philosophy in Alexandria, visited Athens and Constantinople, and married a Christian. In 410 he was elected bishop of Cyrene, a position he accepted reluctantly on the conditions that he would not renounce such Platonic beliefs as the preexistence of the soul and would not have to divorce his wife. He is one of the most attractive personalities and one of the finest orators of late antiquity.

One might hesitate to call Synesius a sophist at all if it were not for the existence of his charming *Encomium of Baldness*, written as noted earlier in response to Dio Chrysostom's *Encomium of Hair*, and his apologetic work

[28] Translated by Downey, "Themistius' First Oration." This is the only complete speech of Themistius available in English translation.

[29] For further discussion, with bibliography, see my *Greek Rhetoric under Christian Emperors*, 22–23 and 35–44, and Bregman, *Synesius*. For translations, see FitzGerald, *Letters* and *Essays*.

entitled *Dio*. Gorgias had described his *Encomium of Helen* as a *paignia*, a playful piece, and we have met other references to verbal exercises on trivial themes. The genre is sometimes called "adoxography," or writings about what is "unworthy."[30] Synesius' *Encomium* is much more playful than Dio's: Dio had described admiring his hair in a mirror; Synesius describes his premature baldness in mock heroic terms and musters examples of the advantages of baldness from mythology, history, and nature, with numerous references to classical writers.[31] The sphere, in Platonism, is the perfect form, and all that can be said in praise of a sphere can be said in praise of a bald head! But Synesius greatly admired Dio and takes him as his model of the philosopher-sophist. His work entitled *Dio* is an encomium of classical learning that puts the highest value on philosophical truth but insists that it can be effectively expounded only in a literary form, with both rational argument and stylistic ornament: "If our human nature is a variable quality also, it will certainly weary of a life of contemplation, to the point of foregoing its greatness and of descending; for we are not mind undefiled, but mind in the soul of a living creature; and for our own sakes therefore we must seek after the more human forms of literature, providing a home for our nature when it descends"(section 6).[32] Although he criticizes empty sophists and gives a vivid description of one of their performances (section 11), he also vigorously attacks Christian monks who took an oath of silence. At the end Synesius denies that he is a teacher, for a teacher tends to become jealous of knowledge, but he also describes how he gave readings from poetry and philosophy and tried to invent something new and to add explanations of the readings in lectures: "And as many 'characters' of style as exist, and however divine, in every one of my imitations of these my own personal note must be added. It is thus that the highest string, itself awaiting the rhythm, reechoes to the melody that is being played"(16).

In the last years of Synesius' life, Cyrene, a Greek enclave on the North African coast, was under constant threat of attack by barbarians from the desert. As bishop, he assumed responsibility for military and political leadership as well as spiritual. What is called his *Second Katastasis* may have been given during deliberations in the city council or may be a letter sent to Roman officials to seek help against the barbarians. It ends with a passage that powerfully conveys the experience of living in those dangerous times:

> How many times shall I call upon God and turn to him? How often shall I press my hands upon the railings? But necessity is a mighty thing and all-powerful. I long to give my eyes a sleep uninterrupted by the sound of the trumpet of alarm. How much longer shall I guard the intervals between the turrets? I am weary of picketing the night patrols, guard-

[30] For a survey, see Pease, "Things without Honor."
[31] New translation by Kendall, *Synesius, In Praise of Baldness*.
[32] FitzGerald, *Essays*, vol. 1, p. 160.

ing others and guarded myself in turn, I who used to hold many a vigil, waiting for the omens from the stars, am now worn out watching for the onset of the enemy. We sleep for a span measured by the water clock, and the alarm bell often breaks in upon the position allotted me for slumber. And if I close my eyes for a moment, oh, what sombre dreams![33]

The "University" of Constantinople

When, late in the third century, Diocletian established an Eastern capital at Nicomedia, he made special provision for education there in grammar, rhetoric, and philosophy, not only in Greek but in Latin. One of those appointed to teach Latin rhetoric was Lactantius, to be discussed in the next chapter. Beginning in 324 a grander Eastern capital was founded in Constantinople, built near the site of ancient Byzantium, and within a few years there were schools of grammar, rhetoric, and philosophy there as well. Both Himerius and Libanius taught for a while in Constantinople. In 370 the Eastern and Western emperors issued regulations for students coming to Constantinople or Rome to study (Theodosian Code 14.9.1). They were required to have a travel permit from their home towns, a birth certificate, and letters of recommendation. When they arrived they were to register with the master of tax assessment, whose office kept an eye on them. Ordinarily, they could expect to stay until they were twenty-one years old, but if they failed to study they could be sent home.

On February 27, 425, Theodosius II issued an edict that has often been described as creating the "University" of Constantinople (Theodosian Code 14.9.3; see also 15.1.53). Certainly it organized education there in a way never seen before. Professors who did not hold official appointments were restricted to teaching in private homes. Conversely, those with official appointments were to teach in the "auditorium of the capitol" and not give private instruction. Each professor was to have his own classroom. Thirty-one official appointments were to be made: ten professors of Latin grammar, three of Latin rhetoric, ten of Greek grammar, five of Greek rhetoric (sophists), two of law,[34] and one of philosophy. Appointments of the faculty were to be made by the senate. After twenty years of teaching, including service elsewhere, a professor could retire as a Count of the First Order. No word for "university" occurs in the edicts, nothing is said about a library, and there is no provision for anything like examinations or degrees. Information about the history of the "university" is very slight; it had probably collapsed by the eighth century, but something like it was later revived.[35]

---

[33] FitzGerald, *Essays*, vol. 2, p. 367.

[34] The study of law was professionalized in later antiquity, and a law school had existed in Beirut since the third century. Law had to be studied in Latin.

[35] See my *Greek Rhetoric under Christian Emperors*, 165–67, 273–75, 274, 278, 305, and 315–16.

The School of Gaza

In the late fifth and early sixth centuries, Gaza in Palestine was the home of a classicizing, Christian school of rhetoric.[36] Among those who taught there was Zosimus—whose life of Demosthenes and commentary on his speeches is probably the main source for medieval scholia on Demosthenes—as well as Procopius and Choricius.

Procopius of Gaza (who should not be confused with the historian Procopius of Caesarea) lived from about 465 to 527 and is chiefly famous for his ability at ekphrasis. He wrote commentaries on the Old Testament and declamations, called *Dialexeis*, some of which seem to have some connection with a rose festival in the spring. The second, for example, describes a walk in the countryside, where Procopius is reminded of Plato's *Phaedrus*, and ends with an encomium of the rose. Four other declamations are prosopopoeiae: of a shepherd and a merchant at the arrival of spring, of what Aphrodite said when she caught her foot on a thorn while seeking Adonis, and of what Phoenix said when Agamemnon sent him to plead with Achilles for Briseis. It does not seem possible to take the pagan elements in these works as allegory; apparently Greek mythology in Gaza was viewed as innocent aesthetic fiction. There are also two ekphrases of works of art, one of a picture of Phaedra and Hippolytus, one of a remarkable clock in Gaza. These are preserved in a manuscript with earlier descriptions of paintings by Philostratus the Elder and Callistratus and constitute a minor sophistic genre that aims at reproducing in words the experience of looking at works of art. Finally, there is an encomium of the emperor Anastasius on the occasion of the dedication of a statue of him in Gaza. Procopius addresses the statue as though it were the ruler himself.

Choricius was Procopius' successor and was active in the years 520–40. His extant works include three encomia, two funeral orations, an epithalamium, twelve declamations, and twenty-eight short speeches that were used to awaken the interest of an audience to which the sophist was going to deliver a panegyric or declamation. Some are connected with festivals, others are more like philosophical diatribes. One of the funeral orations is in memory of Procopius. Excellence in a sophist is said to consist in the ability to astound an audience in the theater and to initiate the young into the rites of learning. Procopius never tolerated from his students non-Attic diction, irrelevant thought, poor rhythm, or composition that offended the ear. The speech includes a lament in which Procopius is imagined in his usual way of life, feeding the flock of his young students, gathering the leaders of the city to hear his speeches, playing with his sister's children, and giving wedding speeches. There follows a consolation, which reaches a climax in the argu-

---

[36] For further information and bibliography, see my *Greek Rhetoric under Christian Emperors*, 169–77.

ment that Demosthenes too had to die, and at the same age (sixty-two) as Procopius, but Demosthenes left Athens in crisis, while Procopius has sailed into a safe harbor. Choricius' declamations resemble the prosopopoeiae of Libanius. Several are contrasting pairs: Polydamas and Priam; a young hero and an old father. All but one have a *protheōria*, concentrating on the presentation of character and appropriate argument but not discussing style.

The Decline of the Schools

The educational system of late antiquity, including the schools of sophists, declined markedly during the reign of Justinian (A.D. 527–65).[37] The influences at work seem to have been Christian opposition to paganism, the emperor's desire to secure greater centralization of control, and severe financial constraints on the payment of public teachers. According to Procopius of Caesarea (*Secret History* 26.5–6), Justinian terminated stipends to teachers and confiscated municipal funds used for the purpose. A rescript of 529 ordered that the governor of Achaea was to allow no one to teach philosophy or law in Athens, ending a tradition that had begun with Plato nine hundred years before. Private rhetorical schools perhaps continued in Athens until the Slavic invasion of Greece in 579. Under Justinian official sophists were appointed only in Constantinople, Alexandria, and Rome, but the situation in Rome was tenuous, and we have little knowledge about Greek sophists in Rome except for the visits there of some of the famous men who have been mentioned earlier. Melior Felix, in 534, is the last known sophist in Rome, though Justinian made a brief effort to reestablish higher education in the city in 554. The period from the late sixth to the eighth century is the "Dark Ages" in the East, a time of historical turmoil, the anti-intellectual "iconoclastic movement" in the Greek church, and the loss of many works of classical literature, but there is nevertheless some evidence for study of classical rhetoric in a few cities and for public address in a sophistic style.[38] In the ninth century, concurrent with the beginnings of the Carolingian renaissance in the West, a new age of learning and oratory dawned in the Byzantine Empire.[39]

[37] See my *Greek Rhetoric under Christian Emperors*, 177–79.
[38] See my *Greek Rhetoric under Christian Emperors*, 265–78.
[39] See my *Greek Rhetoric under Christian Emperors*, 278–320, and Conley, *Rhetoric* 63–69.

Christianity and Classical Rhetoric

Greco-Roman paganism, like polytheism in other parts of the world, had its origins in animistic beliefs, the personification of benign and maleficent natural forces as anthropomorphic gods. The practice of religion took the form of sacrifices to appease, or gain favor from, the gods, on extraordinary occasions human sacrifices but usually animal sacrifices or offerings of food and incense. These actions were performed by priests and accompanied by formulaic words, but pagan priests did not preach to the people. Religious beliefs and morality were primarily taught and learned from literature, including the Homeric poems and Greek drama, later from the lectures and writings of philosophers, especially the Stoics, who incorporated traditional religion into their doctrines by means of allegorical interpretation. As seen in the last chapter, in later antiquity the speeches of sophists often directly or indirectly reinforced traditional religious belief. Parallel to the official cults of Greek and Roman cities, there existed, especially among Romans, a private religion of household and agricultural gods, and there were also mystery religions, of which the most famous were Orphism, the Eleusinian Mysteries, and the cult of the Great Mother. Individuals could be initiated into these mysteries and obtain a knowledge (*gnōsis*) that was thought to insure survival of the soul after death. Greco-Roman religion was tolerant and easily absorbed new gods and new cults, such as Isis from Egypt and Mithra from Persia, often identifying foreign gods with traditional Greek divinities.

Judaism originated in polytheism and the belief that among the many gods there was one special god of the Israelites. It developed into a monotheism that was centered on the divine word, enunciated in an authoritative sacred text. Judaism and its derivatives, Christianity and Islam, are speech-based religions to a much greater extent than Greco-Roman paganism. The stages of creation as described in the first chapter of Genesis (after the initial creation of heaven and earth) result from God's speech: "God *said*, 'Let there be light. . . .'" Throughout the Old Testament, God speaks directly to patriarchs and prophets, and they in turn convey his message by speech to the people, much as the early Greek bard regarded himself as inspired by, and owing his words to, the muses. The fourth chapter of Exodus, in which Aaron emerges as the "orator" of the Jews, is an important description of Hebrew rhetoric. In terms of invention it relies heavily on proclamation based on the divine authority of the speaker, but it supports this with logical argument. Note the examples and enthymemes used even in the Ten Commandments to gain persuasion: "I am the Lord your God, *who brought you out of the house of Egypt. . . .*" or "You shall not take the

257

name of the Lord your God in vain; *for the Lord will not hold him guiltless who takes his name in vain.*" The rhetoric of the Old Testament also includes features of style. The psalmists and prophets employed a rich imagery, largely drawn from nature and pastoral agriculture, later taken over by Christian preachers: the shepherd and his flock, the vine and its branches, and so on. The Book of Proverbs, drawing in part on Egyptian wisdom literature, contains rhetorical precepts, for example, "The wise of heart is called a man of discernment, and pleasant speech increases persuasiveness. . . . Pleasant words are like a honeycomb, sweetness to the soul and health to the body" (Proverbs 16:21–24).[1] By Hellenistic times Jewish worship included reading from the law and the prophets and preaching by a rabbi, who interpreted the sacred texts and applied their message to the life of the congregation. In the New Testament both Jesus and Paul are described as preaching in synagogues. This is the origin of the Christian homily. In Greek, *homilia* originally meant "conversation," but it became the term for a simple sermon based on the interpretation of Scripture and was later used for all preaching except epideictic sermons. From it comes "homiletics," meaning the study of preaching. By Hellenistic times, Jews were also studying Greek grammar, rhetoric, and philosophy, and in a few instances (e.g., Caecilius of Calacte) even teaching classical rhetoric.

Christian rhetoric is a complex subject; it owes much to Jewish traditions, but New Testament writers chose Greek as their vehicle of communication with the world and in so doing tacitly accepted some conventions of Greek rhetoric. When early Christians spoke, wrote, heard, or read religious discourse in Greek, even if relatively uneducated, they had expectations of the form the message would take and of what would be persuasive. This was complicated, however, by the extent to which writers observed or disregarded the conventions of classical literary genres: oratory, biography, historiography, or the literary epistle. Some of the New Testament authors, including Paul, Luke, and the author of the Epistle to the Hebrews, were well educated, were familiar with some Greek literature, and used devices of classical rhetoric freely. Greek rhetorical schools existed throughout Palestine, Syria, and Asia Minor, the birthplace of Christianity. Other New Testament writers, Mark in particular, were much less familiar with Greek rhetoric or less sympathetic to it. Mark's Gospel is the clearest example of what may be called "radical Christian rhetoric," a cast of thought that prefers authoritative proclamation to rational argument. Matthew's Gospel takes a middle ground; it is strongly Jewish in focus, but passages in Matthew that parallel language in Mark often convert proclamations into enthymemes, that is, they add supporting reasons. In recent years, scholars have made an increasing use of classical rhetoric as a tool for understanding the New Tes-

---

[1] This passage was the inspiration for Judah Messer Leon, who, in the fifteenth century, wrote *The Book of the Honeycomb's Flow* (edited and translated by Rabinowitz), in which he analyzed the Old Testament in terms of classical rhetoric.

tament, and an extensive bibliography of the subject now exists.[2] One fundamental discovery has been the extent to which the Greek concept of *pistis*, the "means of persuasion" as taught in the rhetorical schools, underlies and helped to form the Christian concept of *pistis*, meaning "faith."[3] Here only a brief outline can be offered of the history of the reaction to, and reception of, classical rhetoric by Christian speakers and writers. A major source is *Ecclesiastical History*, written by Eusebius in the fourth century.[4]

Deliberative, judicial, and epideictic speeches are quoted in the Gospels, Acts of the Apostles, and Revelations, utilizing in various degrees what was taught in schools of rhetoric or found in the works of Greek historians, and some of the Epistles of Paul closely resemble speeches. There is, however, also a bias against rhetoric in the New Testament. In Mark 13:11, Jesus tells his disciples to take no thought of what they are to say if brought to trial, "but say whatever is given you in that hour, for it is not you who speak but the Holy Spirit." A famous passage is in the second chapter of Paul's First Epistle to the Corinthians, where he seems to reject the whole of classical rhetoric: "I did not come proclaiming to you the testimony of God in lofty words of wisdom; for I decided to know nothing among you except Jesus Christ and him crucified. . . . Yet among the mature we do impart wisdom, although it is not a wisdom of this age or the rulers of this age, who are doomed to pass away. But we impart a secret and hidden wisdom of God, which was decreed before the ages for our glorification." Paul is trying to counteract the influence of Apollos or others who had been preaching in Corinth and whose eloquence had undermined his influence there, but he himself is a master of many techniques of persuasion.[5] Corinth was a prosperous and sophisticated Greek city; it is not surprising that eloquence should have an appeal there.

Unlike Judaism, Christianity had missionary zeal—one reason it awakened Roman opposition. From the second century we have a considerable number of "apologetic" works in both Greek and Latin, in the form of speeches, letters, or dialogues, which were addressed to audiences educated in rhetoric and sought to explain Christianity and to defend it against slanders heaped upon it by its opponents. Charges included the allegation that Christians met at dawn to kill small children, drink their blood, and eat their flesh. Among the more famous of these works in Greek are the *Apology* of Justin Martyr, addressed to the emperor Antoninus Pius; the *Apology* of

---

[2] For an introduction to method, see Kennedy, *New Testament Interpretation through Rhetorical Criticism*; more recent bibliography is listed in the surveys by Watson, "The New Testament and Greco-Roman Rhetoric." See also, Robbins, *Jesus the Teacher* and *Patterns of Persuasion*; Warner, ed. *The Bible as Rhetoric*; Watson, *Invention, Arrangement, and Style*; and Watson, ed. *Persuasive Artistry*.

[3] See Kinneavy, *Origins*.

[4] Translation by Lake and Oulton in the Loeb Classical Library.

[5] See Kennedy, *New Testament Interpretation*, esp. 141–56, and " 'Truth' and 'Rhetoric' in the Pauline Epistles."

Athenagoras, which uses references to Greek philosophers and poets to support the claims that Christian worship and teaching were innocent, reasonable, and moral; and Tatian's *Oration to the Greeks*. The latter work, written around A.D. 167, is an odd mixture of sophistic cleverness and Christian piety, using figures of speech and quotations from Greek poets. The Greek apologists were contemporary with the great sophists of the second century, they utilized Attic Greek rather than the Koine of the previous generations of Christians, and their works often resemble compositions of the sophists in style, though not in form or content. In Latin, the most impressive apologetic works are those of Tertullian (c. 160–225), a native of Carthage who had practiced as an advocate and taught rhetoric in Rome before his conversion. His *Apologeticus*, a fiery invective in the style of Roman declamation, is addressed to the governors of Roman provinces and seeks to refute the arguments against Christianity in judicial terms. A topos much employed by the apologists is to grant that there is some truth in Greek philosophy, but to claim that it was derived indirectly from Moses. Plato, for example, is alleged to have learned much from Jews in Egypt.

By the end of the second century something approximating a canon of the Old and New Testaments existed. These sacred works were regarded as containing all that needed be known to secure salvation, but they required interpretation; in particular, many things in the Old Testament, if taken literally, seemed inconsistent with the teaching of the New Testament. The most important figure in the early development of Christian exegesis was Origen (c. 184–254), who taught in Alexandria and in Caesarea in Palestine. Origen regarded the Bible as inspired in every respect and arranged by God in a series of levels (*On First Principles* 4.1.11). The "corporeal" level is the literal meaning of the text; a second level is the moral meaning, in which the text provides a typology for the life of human beings; the highest level is the spiritual or theological meaning, for example, discovering in the text reference to the incarnation or resurrection of Christ. The spiritual level is always present but veiled, and its elucidation is the chief objective of the exegete or preacher. This can only be done by allegorical interpretation. Techniques of allegorical interpretation of the Homeric poems had been developed much earlier by the Stoics and had been applied to the Old Testament by the Jewish philosopher Philo in the first century. Origen and his successors adapted allegory to the special needs of Christianity at about the time that Neoplatonists were beginning to employ allegory in reading Greek poetry and philosophy.

Christian Panegyric

In the third century some Christians deliberately adopted sophistic genres in addressing educated Christian audiences. The earliest extant example of the use of the structure and topics of classical epideictic oratory to create

Christian panegyric is apparently the farewell speech of Gregory Thaumaturgus to Origen in 238. Its introduction in particular is that of a student of the sophists practicing panegyric, and throughout the speech there is no mention of Christ. The fourth century was the great age of Christian panegyric in Greek, made possible by the official toleration of Christianity after 313 and the conversion of Constantine and his successors. Speeches by Eusebius, bishop of Caesarea, show stages in this development. The earliest of his panegyrics, quoted in full in *Ecclesiastical History* 10.4, was delivered on the occasion of the rebuilding of a church in Tyre in 316 or 317 and honors Paulinus, bishop of Tyre, who had directed the effort. Though an eloquent speech, with much amplification, use of figures, and an extended ekphrasis of the church, in other ways it is far from being a panegyric in the sophistic sense. The style is more biblical than classical, and what Eusebius primarily celebrates is the victory of Christianity over its enemies, and the visible and material church at Tyre is made a symbol for the invisible and spiritual Church. A version of a speech given by Eusebius on the occasion of the thirtieth anniversary of Constantine's accession, July 25, 336, survives, combined with another given at the Holy Sepulcher in Jerusalem the previous year.[6] In the prooemium Eusebius distinguishes between his role as a Christian orator and that of a secular encomiast, but the style is more classical than the speech at Tyre, including references to Homer, and he develops topics of Constantine's virtues and actions. Finally, Eusebius' *Life of Constantine* is a panegyrical biography in four books.[7] It includes topics that would be found in a sophistic funeral oration, including an account of the emperor's parents, his life and virtues, and his death. There is a synkrisis of Constantine with Cyrus and Alexander the Great (1.7–8), an ekphrasis of the Holy Sepulcher (3.34–39), and a description of Constantine as an orator (4.29). Appended to the *Life* is an example of Constantine's oratory, *To the Assembly of the Saints.* Constantine urges his audience to attend to the truth of what he says rather than to his language, and he prays that the Holy Spirit will furnish him with words, but the speech acknowledges the importance of Platonic thought and contains much logical argument, including epicheiremes as described in the Hermogenic *On Invention.*[8]

Gregory of Nazianzus

The most important figure in the synthesis of Greek rhetoric and Christianity is Gregory of Nazianzus, rightly regarded as the greatest Greek orator since Demosthenes. His speeches became the preeminent model of Christian eloquence throughout the Byzantine period. In form and style they resemble speeches of the sophists but greatly surpass them in the power of

[6] See Drake, *In Praise of Constantine.*
[7] Translation by Richardson, *Life of Constantine.*
[8] For further discussion, see my *Greek Rhetoric under Christian Emperors*, 194–97.

thought and intensity of conviction. The Christian orator had an important new message for the world; he had something to say that the sophists could not match in their nostalgia for the fading Hellenic tradition.

Gregory was born in Cappadocia around A.D. 330. After studying grammar there, rhetoric in Caesarea, and philosophy in Alexandria, about 350 he came to Athens, where he continued studing rhetoric for nine years with Prohaeresius and Himerius. He was joined there by a fellow Cappadocian named Basil, who was an equally important figure in fourth-century Christianity and an orator of note but more hostile to rhetoric than Gregory.[9] Basil's brother was Gregory of Nyssa, the third of the "Cappadocian Fathers"; his panegyrics and funeral orations utilize techniques taught by sophists, but he is most important as a profound theologian deeply indebted to Plato and later Greek philosophy. Gregory of Nazianzus describes his experiences in Athens in an autobiographical poem, in his funeral oration for Basil, and in other works. After Basil's departure, he taught rhetoric briefly in Athens and probably also on his return to Cappadocia, but he then abandoned rhetoric as a career, was baptized, and was ordained into the clergy. He became bishop of Constantinople, at the time the highest position in the Greek Church, and attained great fame as a preacher in defense of orthodoxy against heresy, but he was ill suited by temperament for ecclesiastical politics and eventually retired to his family's country estate in Cappadocia, where he wrote letters and poetry, may have edited his speeches into their present form, and died around 390.

Gregory's surviving works include 45 orations, 244 letters, and a considerable amount of poetry. In his encomium of Saint Cyprian he classifies Christian speeches into three groups: moral edification, teaching of dogma, and celebration of great lives. His *Apologeticus* (oration 2) describes his ideal of the Christian preacher, which draws on the view of the orator found in Isocrates and the sophists and on the description of the philosophical orator in Plato's *Phaedrus*. All of his speeches show the influence of his extensive rhetorical training.[10]

Gregory's masterpiece is the funeral oration for his friend Basil (oration 43): "the grandest subject that has ever fallen to the lot of an orator," as he puts it in the opening lines.[11] Basil died in 379 when Gregory was in Constantinople; the speech was not given at the actual funeral but at some later memorial service, and its length indicates that the published version, like

[9] See my *Greek Rhetoric under Christian Emperors*, 239–40. Basil is the author of a series of sermons and of a treatise, *To the Young on How They Should Benefit from Greek Writings*; it acknowledges the utility of studying secular literature but advises careful choice and warns against pagan mythology. Text and commentary by Wilson, *Saint Basil*; translation by Deferrari in the Loeb Classical Library edition of Basil's letters, vol. 4, 249–348.

[10] For further discussion and bibliography, see my *Greek Rhetoric under Christian Emperors*, 215–39, and Ruether, *Gregory of Nazianzus*.

[11] Translation by McCauley, *Funeral Orations*, 27–99.

that of Pliny's *Panegyricus*, is amplified beyond what was actually said. Gregory follows the rules for an *epitaphios* as found in Menander Rhetor (2.11) but omits the consolation and adds an account of Basil's death and funeral, which, in Menander's system, is more usual in a monody delivered immediately after death. The treatment of the traditional headings varies with the degree to which they seemed important for a Christian. Progymnasmatic forms are introduced to amplify or ornament the thought, the most elaborate being a synkrisis of Basil with patriarchs, prophets, and apostles. Greek culture is treated with respect, even reverence, there are repeated references or allusions to Greek literature, and the grand sophistic style is employed throughout, but with biblical allusions and imagery also woven in, and much is said of Basil's eloquence: "an orator among orators, even before he studied with rhetoricians, a philosopher among philosophers even before he learned the doctrines of philosophers. . . . Eloquence was his byword, from which he culled enough to make it an assistance to him in Christian philosophy, since power of this kind is needed to set forth the objects of our contemplation" (43.13). There is an extended section on Basil's education, including the time he and Gregory spent together in Athens, "which has been to me, if to anyone, a city truly golden and the patroness of all that is good" (43.14). It is in Pindar (*Olympian* 6.1), not in the Bible, that Gregory finds the best words to describe their friendship, "a well-built chamber with pillars of gold" (43.20). In the course of this section Gregory utilizes three separate synkriseis: the sacred with the secular, himself and Basil with Orestes and Pylades, and Basil's moral discipline with that of Minos and Rhadamanthus. Later, in discussion of Basil's bishopric, there is a synkrisis of the emperor Valens and the Persian king Xerxes that allows Gregory to bring in one of the favorite topoi of Isocrates and the later sophists, a reference to the Persian invasion of Greece when the invaders "walked" over the sea and "sailed" over the land. The most emotional part is the narrative of Basil's death near the end and the ekphrasis of his funeral, which is followed by a short epilogue, recapitulating Basil's virtues and then returning to the opening theme of Gregory's effort to praise him, with a final prayer to Basil in heaven as a saint. The speech as a whole is an eloquent tribute to the theological, intellectual, and moral virtues of its subject, but rather hostile to Basil's work as a statesman of the Church, and in its emphasis on Basil as preacher neglects the two aspects of his career that had the greatest historical significance: his organization of Eastern monasticism and his reform of the liturgy.

Other Major Figures of the Fourth Century

Theological controversy was bitter within the Church between the orthodox (that is, those who eventually won) and heretics (those who eventually lost). All the weapons of rhetoric were used by both sides in life-and-death

263

battles, to which extant texts give great attention. Among the important sources are descriptions and records of what was said at councils of the Church, for here one can see something of rhetoric in actual debate.[12] The most important debate in the fourth century was that between the orthodox and the Arians on the question of the nature of Christ in relation to God the Father. Gregory and Basil were both strongly on the orthodox side; its greatest champion was Athanasius, bishop of Alexandria, a skilled but unscrupulous dialectician whose invectives are not pleasant reading and whose homilies are ill arranged and saccharin. Athanasius saw rhetoric as a form of lying, cultivated by heretics. The writings of the Arians were largely destroyed, but we do have some homilies by Asterius, an Arian called a "many-headed sophist" by Athanasius and who wrote in a flamboyant Asian style with biblical imagery. Athanasius' most famous work is his *Life of Saint Anthony*; though it shows some influence of classical panegyric, it is also antirhetorical, even anti-intellectual, in its unqualified praise for the illiterate holy man who chose to live as a hermit in the Egyptian desert.[13] A final important figure in the melding of classical rhetoric into Christianity is John Chrysostom (c. 349–407). He had studied rhetoric with Libanius in Antioch, and it is he more than anyone else who raised the homily, a simple sermon explicating a biblical text, to the level of high rhetorical artistry.[14]

The Latin Fathers

Of the major Latin Fathers of the Church, five were teachers of rhetoric before their conversion to Christianity: Tertullian in the second century, Cyprian in the third, and Arnobius, Lactantius, and Augustine in the fourth. Not surprisingly, they regarded rhetoric as a useful tool for Christians and use techniques they had once taught to persuade their readers of Christian truth. All engaged in spirited dispute with pagans and heretics. Like Romans generally, they were, however, rather distrustful of philosophical studies, which could lead to heresy. Tertullian speaks with respect of Demosthenes and Cicero (*Apologeticus* 11 and 15–16); he says that Christians should study rhetoric but not teach it (*On Idolatry* 10). His own Latin is reminiscent of Tacitus or the schools of declamation. Cyprian, a generation later, writes a more Ciceronian Latin but, with his paganism, put off all interest in literature and never quotes classical authors. Arnobius, in contrast, avoids scriptural quotation and seeks to refute the pagans by quoting their own

---

[12] For discussion of rhetoric in the councils of Nicea (A.D. 325), Ephesus (431), and Chalcedon (451), see my *Greek Rhetoric under Christian Emperors*, 200–207 and 258–64.

[13] For further discussion and bibliography, see my *Greek Rhetoric under Christian Emperors*, 208–15.

[14] For discussion and bibliography, see my *Greek Rhetoric under Christian Emperors*, 241–54.

texts against them. His student Lactantius has earned the title "the Christian Cicero," from his fine prose style and his great admiration for Cicero. The Latin Father with the most ambivalent attitude toward rhetoric was Jerome (c. 337–97), whose Latin translation of the Bible became the standard version in the West. In his long letter to the virgin Eustachium (*Epistles* 22), he describes how he tried to reject secular learning and fasted, but then read Cicero. If he tried to read the Hebrew prophets, their style revolted him. He became ill, and preparations were made for his funeral. He dreamed he was in heaven before the judgment seat, being examined about the condition of his soul. In reply to his claim that he was a Christian, the judge replied "You lie; you are a Ciceronian; for 'where your treasure is there will your heart be also'" (Matthew 6:21). Jerome promised to mend his ways, but it is doubtful if he kept the promise strictly.

These authors wrote apologetic treatises or published attacks on pagans and heretics, and Jerome composed commentaries on the Scriptures; none of them adopted the epideictic forms of Greek sophists. We have already noted that there was rather little Latin imitation of the Greek Second Sophistic except for Pliny's *Panegyric of Trajan*. In the fourth century the custom of giving thanks to an emperor or other high official for an administrative appointment continued, or was resumed, in imitation of Pliny. Eleven such speeches survive. The earliest surviving Christian panegyrics in Latin are by Ambrose, bishop of Milan from 375 to 397. These are funeral orations for the emperors Valentinian II and Theodosius; though they are eloquent works, with some of the characteristics of the secular genre, they are also very Christian. Ambrose uses the occasion to develop his view of the emperor as a son of the Church, serving Christ, and subject to the advice of a bishop. Ambrose's other sermons show him as a powerful homiletic preacher, indebted to the exegetical method of Origen. It was hearing Ambrose use allegorical interpretation that first made it possible for Augustine to accept the Scriptures with full faith (*Confessions* 5.14.24).

Saint Augustine

Augustine was born in 354 at Thagaste, about two hundred miles southwest of Carthage on the edge of the African desert. His mother, Monica, was a devout Christian, but Augustine himself did not accept Christianity until he was thirty years old. In his *Confessions*, surely the greatest work of Latin literature from late antiquity, he describes his education and career in vivid detail. After elementary education at Thagaste he began studying rhetoric in the larger town of Madaura and later studied for three years in Carthage. His goal at this time was to become a pleader in the law courts, but as he looks back at that period in his life he reprimands himself severely and questions the value of rhetorical studies.[15] In the course of his studies he came upon Cicero's dialogue *Hortensius*, an exhortation to philosophy now lost. This led him to study of philosophy and religion. The Christian Scriptures initially repelled him; his whole education had been the cultivation of literary taste, and he found the Bible in the Latin translation then available "unworthy compared to the dignity of Cicero" (3.5.9). He explored Manichaeism, a version of Zoroastrian dualism, and Academic skepticism as expounded by Cicero, without becoming satisfied. Meanwhile, to support himself he had become a teacher of rhetoric, first in Thagaste, then in Carthage. In 383 he decided to go to Rome to teach; he would earn better fees, and student discipline, a great problem in Carthage, was better there. When the great pagan orator Symmachus was asked to nominate a candidate for the chair of rhetoric in Milan, the administrative capital of the Western empire, Augustine applied. Symmachus listened to him declaim and gave him the nomination. He taught rhetoric in Milan for two academic years. Meanwhile, his quest for religious truth lead him more and more in the direction of accepting Christianity. In the fall of 386 he quietly resigned his chair of rhetoric, giving poor health as the reason, and retired with a group of friends to a country villa for meditation and conversation. From this resulted a series of philosophical dialogues in Ciceronian style. In the spring of 387 he returned to Milan to be baptized. In the following years he went to Ostia, to Rome, to Carthage, and home to Thagaste. In 391 he was ordained a priest at Hippo in North Africa and was bishop of Hippo from 395 until his death in 430.

In 411 Augustine was one of the participants in a church conference at Carthage, called by the emperor to resolve a bitter dispute between the Catholic leaders in North Africa and the heretical group known as Donatists, who might be described as "puritans." This is worth notice because it is the first public meeting in history of which we have a verbatim account, reporting what was actually said.[16] Under the direction of an official appointed by the emperor, stenographers took down every word. Their notes were immediately transcribed, and every speaker was required to read over, and sign his name to, the record, acknowledging that these were the words he used. Only corrections in grammar and syntax were permitted. The conference lasted three days, and we have the record of the first two and part of the third, a valuable document for study of applied rhetoric in this period; there is also an analytical table of contents and, preserved separately, Augustine's *Breviculus*, his personal summary of the meeting. One issue was whether the meeting should be regarded as deliberative or judicial as each side tried to dominate discussion. Much of what was said relates to the

---

[15] On Augustine's "antirhetoric," see Boyle, "Augustine in the Garden of Zeus."

[16] Latin text and French translation by Lancel, *Conférence de Carthage*; discussion by Frend, *The Donatist Church*.

credentials, or lack of them, of the Donatist bishops. The language of the speakers is extremely convoluted, difficult Latin—what seems to have passed for eloquence in some circles at this time, seen also in some contemporary writings. Augustine's *Breviculus* is, however, in his usual elegant Ciceronian style.

A full understanding of Augustine's evolving view of rhetoric would require discussion of his early dialogues, especially *On Order* and *On the Teacher*, as well as many passages in the *Confessions*, and would require comparison of his theories with the actual practice in his numerous sermons, commentaries, and controversial writings. There is a considerable body of scholarship on these subjects.[17] The most important of Augustine's works for the history of rhetoric is, however, *On Christian Doctrine* (or *On Christian Learning*).[18] The discussion here will be restricted to that work, which is the only extensive discussion of rhetoric from a Christian point of view by an ancient writer and which had, and continues to have, great influence. The first two-thirds (through 3.25.35) was written in 397, the rest in 426–27. It is thus a mature work, representing Augustine's view after a lifetime of study and preaching.

In the prologue Augustine says he is writing precepts—thus a handbook—for treating the Scriptures that will be useful to teachers and anticipates possible objections to his work: a preacher or teacher should not rely solely on divine assistance; that is a form of pride that leads to the extreme position of not reading the Scriptures at all. Book 1 then begins with the statement that there are two needs: that of discovering (*inveniendi*) what is to be understood in the Bible and of expounding (*proferendi*) what has been learned there. These roughly correspond to "invention," based on exegesis, discussed in books 1 through 3, and style (*elocutio*) as understood in rhetoric, discussed in book 4. All Christian learning concerns either natural objects, which Augustine calls "things" (*res*), or signs (*signa*). Book 1 discusses "things": some things—Father, Son, and Holy Spirit—are to be enjoyed; some—these, it eventually emerges, include rhetoric and other secular knowledge—are to be used; some—those whom we love—are to be enjoyed and used. Already in book 1 Augustine's basic principle of scriptural exegesis is clearly stated: whoever "thinks that he understands the divine scriptures or any part of them so that it does not build the double love of God and of

[17] Among valuable contributions are Parsons, "Vocabulary and Rhetoric of the Letters"; Bogan, "Vocabulary and Style of the Soliloquies and Dialogues"; Finaert, *Saint Augustin rhéteur*; Marrou, *Saint Augustin*; Murphy, *Rhetoric in the Middle Ages*, 43–64; Brown, *Augustine of Hippo* and *Power and Persuasion*; Eden, *Poetic and Legal Fiction*, 112–41; Cameron, *Rhetoric of Empire*, esp. 42–47, 66–67, and 157. Additional bibliography in Horner, *Historical Rhetoric*, and Murphy, *Rhetoric in the Middle Ages*.

[18] The best English translation is by Robertson, *On Christian Doctrine*; cf. Kennedy, *Classical Rhetoric*, 153–60.

our neighbor does not understand it at all" (1.36.40). This requires the interpretation of "signs" as found in Scripture, the subject of books 2 and 3.

Signs are natural or conventional, literal or figurative, and known, unknown, or ambiguous. Many things in the Bible are covered with a "dense mist": God did this to conquer human pride; for what is too easily understood frequently seems worthless, and figurative language can teach and delight the reader (2.6.7). This is the common Christian explanation of obscurity in the Scriptures. Interpretation of signs found in the Bible, according to Augustine, requires knowledge of languages, natural objects, numbers, music, history, science, and the arts and crafts. What about pagan literature and philosophy? Should the Christian study these? Augustine's answer is "yes, within certain limits." Sophistic reasoning (*sophismata*) is to be rejected, but it is God's intent that human beings should use logical argument based on definition and division (2.32.50). Although the rules of eloquence can be used to make falsehoods credible, they can also be used for true purposes; to conciliate an audience by expressions of charity, to narrate facts clearly, or to interest or refresh an audience by varied style is to use principles ordained by God, not to make up some human art (2.36.54). Just as the Israelites had the right to take valuable objects ("Egyptian gold") with them when they fled from Egypt, so the Christian has a right to take and use rhetoric and other secular knowledge (2.40.60).

Book 3 discusses ambiguous signs. It could be regarded as the Christian counterpart of that part of rhetorical stasis theory concerned with the letter versus the intent of a law, for the Scriptures are in fact law. When literal interpretation causes ambiguity, Augustine believes the text must be understood figuratively. Literal interpretation, especially of the Old Testament, can be dangerous and misleading, but Augustine is not concerned that something true but unintended may be read into a passage. God foresaw whatever is found in the passage and more; the context needs to be considered, and the best guide is the rule of faith—love of God and love of neighbor (3.28.39). Educated readers will recognize in the Scriptures many rhetorical tropes, of which several are named: allegory, enigma, parabola, metaphor, and irony or antiphrasis (3.29.40–41). Book 3 concludes with a discussion of the seven "rules" of Tyconius for the explication of obscurities in Scripture. They are "topics," some of them what Aristotle would call "specific topics" (e.g., "the Lord and his Body"), others "common topics" (e.g., "species and genus"). Augustine discusses the fifth rule, "Of Times," in terms of the rhetorical trope synecdoche (3.35.50).

In book 4, Augustine turns to preaching and teaching what has been found in Scripture. The book falls into six parts: introduction (sections 1–5, as numbered in Robertson's translation), a description of the eloquence of the Bible (6–26), discussion of Cicero's concept of the "duties of the orator" as they apply to preaching (27–33), a similar discussion of the three kinds of style (33–58), the role of character in persuasion (59–63), and a brief conclusion (64). The rules of rhetoric, he says, should be learned elsewhere, but he does briefly summarize them in a passage that identifies the functions of the four traditional parts of an oration (4.2.3). Rhetoric should be studied by the young, but more is gained by imitation of good models than from knowledge of rule. This includes reading ecclesiastical literature—no specific models are recommended—listening to preachers, writing, and practice speaking.

Earlier in his life Augustine had found the Bible lacking in literary qualities, but by the time of book 4 of *On Christian Doctrine* he has changed his mind, perhaps in part because of Jerome's new translation. He gives special attention to tropes, figures, and periodic style in the writings of Paul and Amos; in the latter text, "words were not devised by human industry, but were poured forth from the divine mind both wisely and eloquently, not in such a way that wisdom was directed toward eloquence, but in such a way that eloquence did not abandon wisdom" (4.7.21). The style of Scripture is always appropriate (4.6.9); its preeminent quality, which should also be the quality sought by a preacher, is *evidentia*, "vivid clarity." This is in agreement with Aristotle's view of the virtue of style in *On Rhetoric* 3.2.1, but Augustine shows no direct knowledge of Aristotle. His only ackowledged source on rhetoric is Cicero. From Cicero—"a certain eloquent man"—he takes the concept of the three "duties of the orator": to teach, to delight, and to move. Augustine thinks that it is necessary to delight a listener in order to retain him as listener; it is necessary to move him in order to impel him to do what is right (4.12.27). As Cicero had done in *Orator*, Augustine relates the three duties to the three kinds of style: teaching to the plain style, delighting to the middle style, and moving to the grand style (4.17.34). Examples are cited from the Bible, Cyprian, and Ambrose. The styles should be mingled, but a speech is said to be in the style that predominates (4.22.51). Augustine, in common with most Latin writers, shows no knowledge of Hermogenes' "ideas" of style. He concludes the discussion of style by saying, "It is the universal office of eloquence in any of these styles to speak in a manner leading to persuasion; and the end of eloquence is persuasion, by speech, of what you intend. In any of these three styles an eloquent man speaks in a manner suitable to persuasion, but if he does not persuade he has not attained the end of eloquence" (4.25.55).

Augustine's view of the importance of moral character in rhetoric is significantly different from what Aristotle, Cicero, or Quintilian had to say about rhetorical ethos. The private life of the speaker—his works as a Christian and the consistency between his teaching and his actions—has, he thinks, greater weight in persuasion than any verbal eloquence. Under certain circumstances, however, a bad man may be a good orator (4.29.62). Quintilian would have been surprised. What Augustine has in mind is the situation in which a hypocrite has written a sermon that preaches true doctrine but would be unpersuasive to an audience that knew him; it can be persuasive if the sermon is then read aloud by a man known to be virtuous. It became common in later antiquity for priests of little rhetorical ability to read sermons published by others, including those of Augustine.

By the time Augustine wrote *On Christian Doctrine*, the Roman Empire was nominally Christianized except for some die-hard intellectuals and some country folk (*pagani* means "those in the country"). He thus does not discuss missionary preaching, which was important in the early Church and for those going out among the barbarians of northern Europe. Nor does he discuss epideictic preaching: no advice is given about funeral oratory or other speeches for special occasions. The preaching and teaching he describes is essentially homiletic—the explanation of Scriptural texts—to be addressed to catechumens (those preparing for baptism in the Church) or Christian congregations that may be ignorant, indifferent, or in danger of heresy. The function of Christian eloquence in Augustine's system is to explain belief and convert it into works, to move the faithful to the Christian life. It is to be a popular eloquence, addressed to all sorts and conditions of people. Augustine does not distinguish Christian rhetoric from classical, Jewish, or other rhetorics; to him, eloquence is eloquence in any tradition. He does not identify the distinctive imagery Christianity borrowed from the Old Testament. What is Christian about Christian rhetoric is content and values. This means, of course, that Christian rhetoric has its own special topics, which he groups together under the one great heading of love of God and of neighbor. Although he does not discuss the arrangement and unity of a speech, it is clear that to him the Bible and the Christian message have that one great theme of love. Saint Paul preached the crucified and risen Christ and the judgment to come for those who did not believe. Though Augustine discussed such matters elsewhere, it is remarkable how small a part these and other theological "doctrines" play in *De Doctrina Christiana*, nor does Augustine recommend to Christian preachers the powerful rhetorical weapon they have most favored throughout history: the promise of heaven and the threat of eternal damnation.

The Survival of Classical Rhetoric from
Late Antiquity to the Middle Ages

There is no single point when classical civilization ends and the Middle Ages begins, nor when the history of classical rhetoric ends. Beginning in the fifth century after Christ in the West and in the sixth century in the East, there was a deterioration of the conditions of civic life that had created and sustained the study and uses of rhetoric throughout antiquity in courts of law and deliberative assemblies. Schools of rhetoric continued to exist, more in the East than in the West, but they were fewer and were only partially replaced by study of rhetoric in some monasteries. The acceptance of classical rhetoric by such influential Christians as Gregory of Nazianzus and Augustine in the fourth century significantly contributed to continuation of the tradition, though the functions of the study of rhetoric in the Church were transferred from preparation for public address in law courts and assemblies to knowledge useful in interpreting the Bible, in preaching, and in ecclesiastical disputation. Furthermore, these functions were largely performed by a relatively small number of bishops and other ecclesiastical officials, not by ordinary priests or monks. In both the Greek East and the Latin West "rhetoric" continued to mean classical rhetoric as it had been formulated by the fourth century: in the East the Hermogenic tradition, in the West a reductive version of the Ciceronian.

The Decline in the East

As described in previous chapters, during the fifth century the Hermogenic corpus continued to be studied in the East as the basic rhetorical textbook, complemented by prolegomena; Aphthonius on progymnasmata; study of the Attic orators, especially Demosthenes; and occasional reading of other authorities, especially Dionysius of Halicarnassus, Apsines, and handbooks of figures of speech. Plato's *Gorgias* and *Phaedrus* were studied in philosophical schools; Aristotle's *On Rhetoric* was little read. Declamation was still being practiced in the sixth century at the school of Gaza and probably in Constantinople and some other places. The death of Justinian in A.D. 565 is sometimes taken as the dividing point between late antiquity and the early Byzantine Middle Ages; though an Eastern "Roman" empire survived, political conditions were very difficult for the next two centuries, and the Eastern Church lost much of its enthusiasm for secular learning. The emperor Leo III (717–41) is alleged to have burned both the professors and the library of whatever remained of the "University" of Constantinople; this is probably not literally true, but is symbolic of attitudes of the time. Many works of classical literature were permanently lost through the destruction of libraries and through lack of interest in making new copies of deteriorating manuscripts. Nevertheless, we occasionally hear of individuals who were educated in rhetoric.[1] One was Maximus the Confessor; the account of his trial for treason and heresy in 653 shows him drawing on the rhetoric of the classical tradition in opposition to a nonartistic rhetoric of intimidation and brute force that prevailed at the time. After an apparent lapse of two centuries, secular panegyric reemerged in the early ninth century, as best seen in the funeral orations of Theodore the Studite for his mother and uncle. His contemporary, John of Sardis, is the earliest Byzantine author known to have revived the tradition of writing commentaries on rhetorical handbooks. His prolegomenon and commentary to Aphthonius' treatise on progymnasmata survive, and he probably also wrote a commentary on stasis. The apparent goal of such works was to help students learn to express themselves in Attic Greek, the high style, a knowledge of which became the mark of an educated person in the ninth century and later. A Greek intellectual renaissance begins in the second half of the ninth century, contemporary with the Carolingian Age in western Europe. The leading figure is Photius, the learned Patriarch of Constantinople from 856 to 886. Although Byzantine civilization adapted classical rhetoric to its own needs, and in the process created a highly artificial, often tortured prose style for learned and official communication that was regarded as Attic but was no longer comprehensible to the masses, it never developed a distinctive theory of rhetoric: it continued to rely on the Aphthonian-Hermogenic texts and to imitate late classical models of panegyric until the fall of Constantinople to the Turks in 1453. Scholars from the East, George of Trebizond in particular, then brought their knowledge of Greek rhetoric to Renaissance Italy.

In the early nineteenth century, Christian Walz collected most Greek treatises on rhetoric surviving from antiquity and many Byzantine commentaries and discussions into a work in nine volumes entitled *Rhetores Graeci*, published between 1832 and 1836; this has remained a standard work and was reprinted in 1968; the more important later Greek treatises were reedited by Leonard Spengel in three volumes between 1853 and 1856 under the same title, and the first volume of Spengel's collection was edited again by Caspar Hammer in 1894. In the early twentieth century Hugo Rabe reedited the *Prolegomena*, the Hermogenic corpus, and several important other works. The editions of Walz, Spengel, Hammer, and Rabe, together with a few other publications, are the basis of scholarly study today of later Greek and Byzantine rhetoric. There are other medieval Greek manuscripts con-

---

[1] See discussion in my *Greek Rhetoric under Christian Emperors*, 267–78.

taining discussions of rhetoric, mostly commentaries, that have never been edited and printed. The relatively few works that have been translated into English are identified in the notes in the previous chapters.

The Decline in the West

In the West, the schools of rhetoric flourished through the fourth century; we get some glimpse of them in the writings of Ausonius. He taught rhetoric in Bordeaux, gave an account of other teachers there in a poem called *The Professors of Bordeaux*, applied his knowledge in numerous works in verse and prose (including panegyrics), and later held a series of offices in Rome, which climaxed in a consulship in A.D. 379.[2] The fourth century is probably the time of the collections known as the *Declamations of Quintilian* and of some of the handbooks of rhetoric to be discussed later in this chapter. Panegyric is also represented by the collection known as the *Panegyrici Latini,* by panegyrical poems of Claudian, and by fragmentary speeches of Symmachus. The latter was the most famous Latin orator of the fourth century and the most vigorous defender of paganism; a vast collection of his letters survives, as well as *Relationes*, which is a collection of official communications to the emperor on behalf of the Roman senate.[3] In 394 a rhetorician actually became emperor of the West, though briefly. Eugenius, a teacher of rhetoric who had become a prominent official in Rome, acquired the title through the influence of Arbogast the Frank; he was defeated by the Eastern emperor Theodosius in 396 and beheaded. The cultural gap between the Eastern and Western empire widened in the fourth century; an important factor was the declining knowledge of Greek in the West. There are very few signs among late Latin writers on rhetoric of familiarity with the works of Hermogenes or other Greek rhetoricians; theirs was largely a Latin, and in particular a Ciceronian, tradition. In the *Confessions* (1.13.20) Augustine describes how much he hated studying Greek as a boy, and he never seems to have acquired much fluency in it.

Rome was sacked by the Visigoths in 410; they withdrew but continued to dominate much of northern Italy, Gaul, and Spain. The Vandals moved through Spain and into North Africa, leaving devastation in their wake. This is, however, the time of Augustine's treatise *On Christian Doctrine*, and influential writings on rhetoric by Martianus Capella and Macrobius date from the same period. In 476, the young emperor Romulus Augustulus was deposed, marking the political end of the Western empire; Italy was then ruled by an Ostrogothic king, with his capital at Ravenna. The civil administration, however, remained much as it had been and was open to Romans. Latin remained the official language. In the sixth century, Boethius and

[2] Translations by Evelyn-White in the Loeb Classical Library.
[3] Translation by Barrow, *Prefect and Emperor*.

Cassiodorus attained high rank in the Ostrogothic court, the last great survivors of classical learning. Boethius, most famous for *The Consolation of Philosophy*, wrote an erudite treatise on rhetorical topics and a commentary on Cicero's *Topics*, as well as other learned works. He was executed in 524. Cassiodorus, a leading orator in the classical style at the Ostrogothic court, retired in midcentury to a monastery in southern Italy, where he wrote *Institutes of Divine and Secular Letters*, an encyclopedia containing a compendium of classical rhetoric. Some study of rhetoric survived in Gaul and elsewhere through the sixth century; the seventh was the cultural low point in the West, but Isidore of Seville compiled his encyclopedia of the liberal arts early in the century and the Venerable Bede, living in Britain around 700, wrote a short treatise on tropes and figures of speech in the Bible. Charlemagne's victories at the end of the eighth century inaugurated a revival of learning, to which the writings on rhetoric of Alcuin and Rabanus Maurus contributed. Classical grammar and rhetoric were intensively studied in French and English cathedral schools of the eleventh and twelfth centuries, but rhetoric was overshadowed by dialectic in medieval universities until the Renaissance brought a rediscovery of major works on rhetoric by Cicero and Quintilian and of Greek writings. Meanwhile, distinctive medieval rhetorical theories of letter writing (the *dictamen*), preaching, and verse composition had developed in Italy, France, and England.

Latin Grammarians of Later Antiquity

The dividing line between the disciplines of grammar and rhetoric was a flexible one in antiquity, especially on matters relating to style.[4] Grammarians taught the poets but in so doing introduced students to tropes and figures. The most famous of all Latin grammarians was Donatus, who was teaching in Rome in the middle of the fourth century. His *Ars Minor* became the basic Latin grammar of the Middle Ages, but is limited to discussion of the parts of speech; the third book of his longer *Ars Grammatica*, however, discusses the faults and virtues of style and, under the title *Barbarismus*, was a basic source on tropes and figures of speech for later students. Donatus defined a "barbarism" as a grammatical error in the use of a single word and a "solecism" as an error in the use of words in a context, but what would otherwise be a barbarism can in poetry be a "metaplasm," or ornament of style, and what would otherwise be a solecism can in poetry be *scemata* (from Greek *schēmata*), or figures. Figures are divided into those of speech (*scemata lexeos*), which are a proper subject for a grammarian and are discussed in detail, and figures of thought (*scemata sensum*), which are used in oratory and left to the rhetorician. Donatus wrote a commentary on the comedies of Terence, which survives, and a commentary on the poems

---

[4] See Schenkeveld, "Figures and Tropes."

of Virgil, which does not, but much of the latter was incorporated into the extant commentary by Servius later in the century. The best example of the application of grammatical and rhetorical theory to literary criticism is the *Saturnalia* of Macrobius, probably written in the 430s. It is in dialogue form and largely devoted to discussion of Virgil's knowledge of religion, philosophy, and rhetoric. This work was much studied in the Middle Ages and contributed to the view that not only was Virgil the greatest poet, but he should also be considered a great orator.

The "Minor" Latin Rhetoricians

In 1863 Karl Halm collected much of the surviving technical writing on rhetoric in Latin from the Roman Empire (except for such major works as those of Quintilian and Boethius) and the early medieval period in a volume entitled *Rhetores Latini Minores*. This has remained an authoritative collection, though there are now better modern editions of the more important works. A brief survey of the contents of Halm's collection will provide an introduction to rhetoric as taught in late antiquity and the early Middle Ages.

The first five works in Halm's collection are handbooks of figures which identify the figures by their Greek names, provide a Latin translation, and give an example. One of the handbooks is in verse, presumably making it easier to memorize. Most of the larger treatises on rhetoric in the collection also include an account of figures. The study of figures of speech was basic to rhetoric and has remained so. The student of classical rhetoric was expected to be able to recognize them in reading poets and prose writers, to name them, and to use them in his own compositions. The use of tropes, figures of speech, and figures of thought is what, more than anything else, made prose seem artistic. Although the handbooks classify figures by types, they cannot be said to offer any theory of figures as a phenomenon of language, nothing like the complex theories of twentieth-century literary critics, nor even the often-perceptive remarks of such Greek critics as Demetrius or Longinus; they show no understanding of the importance of figures in conveying emotion or of their use in argumentation. Figures were thought of purely as devices of ornamentation and study of them, and of rhetoric as a whole, was a matter of memorizing technical terms and definitions.

The importance of rote memorization and recitation is seen clearly in the sixth treatise in Halm's collection, which is the *Ars Rhetorica* of Fortunatianus, written in the fourth or perhaps the fifth century.[5] It takes the form of

---

[5] There is now a good edition, with Italian commentary, by Calboli Montefusco. She has shown that the author's name was Consultus Fortunatianus, not C. Chirius Fortunatianus, as given by Halm. English translation of the first four pages of book 1 in Miller et al., *Readings in Medieval Rhetoric*, 25–32.

a catechism, that is, short questions and answers to be memorized by the student. The first question is "What is rhetoric?" to which the answer is "The science of speaking well" (Quintilian's definition, though not so identified). All five parts of rhetoric are included, though invention is treated in greater detail than the others. Books 1 and 2 consist of questions and answers about invention, including stasis theory and topics; book 3 has questions and answers about arrangement, style, memory, and delivery. Cicero's orations are often cited for examples. The discussion of invention is based on the system of Hermagoras, but apparently known through intermediate sources. Cicero's treatise *On Invention* is one; the commentary on it by Marcomannus, discussed below, is another. A new feature of Fortunatianus' handbook, found also in some other late Latin handbooks, is the concept of *ductus* (1.5–7), the overall method of approach in a speech, which is divided into simple, subtle, figured, oblique, and mixed. The discussion of style (3.3–12) is surprisingly short; despite use of Greek sources it takes no account of the theory of "ideas" that had been developed in Greek, but it does have an unusual classification of "characters" of style. They are first divided into Greek terms that mean "quantity, quality, and length." Quantity refers to the traditional grand, plain, and middle styles; quality is divided into dramatic, narrative, and mixed; length into long, short, and middle.

Taking the works in Halm's collection as a whole, it is clear that Cicero's youthful treatise *On Invention* was emerging by the fourth century as the major authority on its subject, overshadowing Cicero's mature works on rhetoric or the treatise of Quintilian, even though these works were still easily available at the time. The reason is not difficult to grasp. *On Invention* combined Ciceronian authority with the kind of succinct, dry exposition of theory that could be reduced to lists and be memorized. Students, and most teachers as well, were not interested in, and probably often not capable of understanding, longer and more complex discussions of rhetoric. But even *On Invention* seemed difficult and in need of explanation. The earliest commentary was perhaps that of Marcomannus, the first Roman writer to bear a Germanic name. His work, now lost, was a source for Julius Victor, Fortunatianus, and Sulpitius Victor. He was probably a teacher of rhetoric in the third century, who relied heavily on earlier Greek sources that transmitted a version of Hermagoras' stasis theory. They may have included an anonymous Greek handbook on rhetoric of the second or third century that is partially preserved in a papyrus from Oxyrhynchus in Egypt.[6] Other commentaries followed, gradually making *On Invention* the major authority for those parts of rhetoric it discusses. The longest treatise (number 8) in Halm's collection is a detailed commentary to *On Invention* written by Vic-

---

[6] See Haslam, "Rhetorical Treatise."

torinus in the fourth century. He also wrote lost Latin translations of Greek philosophical works, a grammar, and commentaries on parts of the Bible. Victorinus knew Marcomannus' commentary and in one passage says it is wrong (p. 173 Halm). In Halm's collection Victorinus' work is followed by an anonymous commentary on parts of book 1 of *On Invention* (number 9); the twenty-second and twenty-third treatises in the collection are also parts of commentaries on the first book of *On Invention*, the latter written by Grillius in the fifth century. These are the earliest of a long series of such commentaries that continued to be written until the fifteenth century.[7] Much of the discussion naturally relates to explaining stasis theory. It is remarkable how important stasis theory remained in the study of rhetoric in late antiquity and the Middle Ages, second in importance only to figures of speech and sometimes overshadowing even that. It is true that the determination of the stasis of a case remained useful for anyone addressing a judge or jury, and some kind of legal process, whether secular or ecclesiastical, never entirely disappeared; there are examples of the application of stasis theory in the scanty evidence for trials well into the Middle Ages. An excellent instance is the account of the treason trial of Praetextatus, bishop of Rouen, as described by Gregory of Tours in the late sixth century.[8] Perhaps more important, however, was the belief that stasis theory was a useful way to introduce a student to logical argument. This could be preparation for dialectic by those who might go on to philosophical studies, but stasis theory had the attraction of something that was complex and technical, but not too complex for its technical terminology to be memorized. It was a good discipline for students' minds, whether or not they ever made use of it. The number of such students certainly declined radically; until the mid–fifth century literacy was common, and formal education was available in most cities and towns. Thereafter, rhetoric was studied only by the few, primarily those preparing for a career in the Church.

The seventh work in Halm's collection is a short treatise on stasis theory, perhaps drawing directly on Hermagoras' original work. It is found in manuscripts appended to Fortunatianus' handbook, carries the name of Saint Augustine as its author, and is followed by a longer handbook on dialectic, also attributed to Augustine. In his *Retractationes* (1.6) Augustine mentions having written treatments of five of the liberal arts—dialectic, rhetoric, geometry, arthmetic, and "philosophy"—when he was teaching rhetoric in Milan, but he says the texts are lost. The little work on rhetoric under his name is not likely to be genuine.[9]

[7] See Ward, "From Antiquity to the Renaissance."

[8] Gregory, *History of the Franks* 5.18. For discussion, see Kennedy, "Forms and Functions."

[9] See discussion and translation by Dieter and Kurth, "The *De Rhetorica* of Aurelius Augustinus," and translation in Miller et al., *Readings in Medieval Rhetoric*, 6–24.

The tenth and eleventh treatises in Halm's collection are short rhetorical handbooks primarily concerned with stasis theory by Sulpitius Victor and Julius Severianus, also dating from the fourth or fifth century. The twelfth treatise, the *Art of Rhetoric* of Julius Victor, is a more substantial work, and although its sources include Hermagoras (at least indirectly), Marcomannus, and the treatise of Aquila Romanus on figures (number 2 in Halm), it also draws on Cicero's dialogue *On the Orator* and *Orator*, and many passages are excerpts or paraphrases from Quintilian. It is also unusual in devoting chapters at the end to criticism of declamation, echoing Quintilian's views; to *sermocinatio*, or conversational speech; and to letter writing.

Texts numbered 13, 14, and 15 in Halm's collection are the sections on rhetoric from the three great encyclopedias of the liberal arts that became basic reference works of the Middle Ages: that by Martianus Capella in the early fifth century, Cassiodorus in the middle of the sixth, and Isidore of Seville at the beginning of the seventh. A concept of *enkyklios paideia*, or comprehensive education, can be traced back to Isocrates and the early Greek sophists. The earliest known Latin encyclopedia, which included a section on rhetoric, was the work of Cato the Elder in the second century B.C. Cicero's friend Varro wrote an encyclopedia, as did Celsus in the first century after Christ. Celsus' discussion of rhetoric is mentioned repeatedly by Quintilian and cited by some later writers. The concept of the "liberal arts," or arts that should be studied by one who is free (*liber*) from other duties or the need to work, owes much to Cicero. Schools of grammar and rhetoric provided elementary and secondary education. For those who went on to some study of philosophy, dialectic was basic. A compendium of knowledge of these three subjects—grammar, rhetoric, and dialectic—is provided in the encyclopedias of Martianus, Cassiodorus, and Isidore. They became the "trivium" of the liberal arts course, or training in verbal skills, of medieval schools and universities but were not known by that term in antiquity, nor did any one school or person teach all three, as was later common. The "quadrivium" of medieval schools—the quantitative arts of arithmetic, geometry, astronomy (more often called astrology), and music—did not form a curriculum in antiquity. Roman children studied arithmetic, and Cicero and Quintilian recommend a knowledge of geometry, astronomy, and music for students of rhetoric, but a prospective student had to find a special teacher or do independent study based on published handbooks. Study of geometry, astronomy, and music was commoner in Greek-speaking than in Latin-speaking areas. Some other subjects, including agriculture, medicine, and architecture, were sometimes included among the liberal arts and discussed in encyclopedias; the only surviving part of Celsus' encyclopedia is his account of medicine.

Martianus Capella

Martianus' encyclopedia was written in Carthage about the same time that Augustine was completing *On Christian Doctrine*. Its title is *On the Marriage of Philology and Mercury*.[10] The first two books are a heavy-handed allegory in which seven bridesmaids at the wedding of these figures represent the liberal arts. This is written in a difficult, dense, and affected prose style, learned in schools of grammar and rhetoric at the time and used for literary composition when a writer wanted to show off his learning. There follow separate books on grammar, dialectic, and rhetoric (in that order), and the four quantitative arts. Putting rhetoric after dialectic seems to reflect a philosophical prejudice against it as less important. The discussion of rhetoric in book 5 begins in the allegorical style but then switches to a rather dry, pedantic, and sometimes confused account of invention, style, memory, delivery, and arrangement (in that order), illustrated with examples from Cicero's orations. Clearly these were studied in the schools at the time. There are also references to traditional themes of declamation. The main sources of the rhetorical doctrine are Cicero's *On Invention*, Victorinus' commentary on it, and another commentary that was also used by Fortunatianus and has been attributed to Marcomannus.[11] Medieval scholars liked Martianus' work because of its allegory and despite its paganism; there are nearly 250 manuscripts, many from the Carolingian period, and allegorical representations of the liberal arts are common in medieval art.

Cassiodorus

After withdrawing from public life at the Ostrogothic court around 550, Cassiodorus founded a monastery in the "toe" of Italy. Here he placed unusual emphasis on collecting, editing, copying, and commenting on texts, and here he wrote his *Institutiones* or "Introduction" to divine and human readings.[12] It contains (2.2.1–17) a short survey of rhetoric based on Fortunatianus, Victorinus, and Martianus, with some reference to Cicero's *On Invention* and *On the Orator*, Quintilian, and Augustine. The purpose as described in 2.27.1 is to provide the monks with some knowledge of rhetoric to use in interpreting the Bible. Since the monks did not preach, there was no need to discuss sermons and no need to discuss delivery, but there is a short section on memory. Although Cassiodorus mentions figures of speech as important in biblical interpretation, and although in an analysis of the Psalms in book 1 he makes use of rhetoric, the actual account of rhetoric in book 2, concerned primarily with stasis theory, argumentation, and the parts

[10] Translation by Stahl, *Martianus Capella*, vol. 2.
[11] See Stahl et al., *Martianus Capella*, vol. 1, pp. 115–21.
[12] Translation by Leslie Jones, *Divine and Human Readings*.

279

of an oration, makes no attempt to find these in Scripture. The work was in almost every medieval library; it had the advantage over Martianus' encyclopedia of being Christian, but its account of rhetoric is much less satisfactory. Probably readers who knew only this work drew the conclusion that rhetoric was one of those arcane subjects understood in the classical past, and therefore respected by the learned, but of little relevance to their lives.

Isidore of Seville

The same conclusion might be drawn from the encyclopedia called *Etymologies*, written by Isidore of Seville about fifty years later.[13] This is a much more ambitious work, collecting everything Isidore knew about the classical past, including the liberal arts, but what Isidore had to say about rhetoric (2.1–22) is a series of extracts from earlier sources, with little organization and little understanding. Invention and style are discusssed; arrangement is given four sentences; memory and delivery are ignored. A chapter on law, inserted between discussion of the syllogism and that of style, suggests that Isidore thought rhetorical invention had some utility in judicial processes, though what this might be is not explained.

None of the later Latin treatises give much attention to memory and delivery; this probably indicates that rhetoric was less and less regarded as preparation for public speaking, which was less and less important for most people. Christian writers on rhetoric thought of rhetoric either as a logical discipline—thus their continuing interest in stasis theory—or as useful in interpreting the Scriptures, not as preparation for preaching, an art that declined parallel with the decline of public address. The acceptance of Cicero's *On Invention* as the major authority on rhetoric also contributed to the view that stasis theory and argumentation were the essential parts of rhetoric. *Rhetoric for Herennius*, used in later centuries to complement *On Invention*, gives an excellent account of memory and delivery but was little read at this time.

Other Late Latin Works on Rhetoric

One writer who did use *Rhetoric for Herennius* and regarded it as a genuine work by Cicero was Rufinus of Antioch, the fifth-century author of the treatise *On the Meters of Comic Poets and the Rhythms of Orators*. This treatise is printed in its entirety in Heinrich Keil's *Grammatici Latini*, together with other late antique works on meter. The section on rhetorical periods and rhythms also appears as number 23 in Halm's collection.[14] Rufinus was a competent scholar who relies principally on Cicero's discus-

---

[13] There is a French translation by André, *Etymologies*; a portion of the section on rhetoric is translated into English in Miller et al., *Readings in Medieval Rhetoric*, 79–95.

[14] Translation in Miller et al., *Readings in Medieval Rhetoric*, 37–51.

~~sions of prose~~ rhythm but also quotes several other authorities, including Quintilian.

The only Latin handbook of progymnasmata is a simplified version of the one attributed to Hermogenes, made by the grammarian Priscian about A.D. 500 (number 17 in Halm).[15] Familiarity with the Hermogenic corpus was rare among Latin writers, but Priscian taught in Constantinople and thus was quite familiar with it. From Quintilian's account of school exercises (1.9), it is clear that versions of progymnasmata (Priscian calls them *praeexercitamina*) had long been taught by Latin grammarians. Moreover, in *suasoriae* as taught in schools of rhetoric a student was expected to memorize and deliver a speech that was a more advanced version of one of the grammatical exercises, impersonating a character and praising or blaming someone or something or offering advice to a mythological or historical figure. These exercises continued to be practiced in late antiquity. The eighteenth work in Halm's collection is a series of chapters by Emporius "the Orator" giving advice for such exercises, probably written early in the fifth century. *Ethopoeiae, loci communes, encomia,* and *suasoriae* are each briefly discussed.[16] Emporius largely avoids mythological themes, probably because of Christian distaste for them, but includes legendary figures from the Homeric poems and Virgil's *Aeneid*. Number 20 in Halm's collection also relates to declamation. It consists of excerpts from some late Latin treatise by an unknown author that gives a brief account of stasis theory as it might be used in declamation, followed by advice about encomia. There are then short chapters on historiography and epistolography. The author clearly regards the writing of history as a form of encomium, and letters also utilize topics of praise and blame. There is no indication here that letter writing was an exercise in the schools, but the common use of the epistolary form for what in other circumstances might have been an epideictic or deliberative speech suggests that such exercises may sometimes have been practiced.

Bede and Alcuin

The remaining two works in Halm's collection are medieval: the earlier (number 24) is a handbook of figures and tropes written in Britain in the early eighth century by the Venerable Bede.[17] It is based on Donatus' account of figures but draws its examples solely from the Bible and is intended to show that the Bible surpasses all other writings in artistic composition as well as in all other ways. Bede's major work, *The Ecclesiastical History of the English People*, gives excellent glimpses of public address in the early medie-

[15] Translation in Miller et al., *Readings in Medieval Rhetoric*, 52–68.

[16] Translation of the section on ethopoeia in Miller et al., *Readings in Medieval Rhetoric*, 33–36.

[17] Translation by Tannenhaus, "Bede's *De Schematibus et Tropis*," in Miller et al. *Readings in Medieval Rhetoric*, 96–122.

val period, including missionary preaching (e.g., 1.25 and 5.19) and versions of the speeches given at the Synod of Whitby in 664 on the date of the observance of Easter (3.25).[18] These speeches show considerable skill in argumentation and are important evidence that oratory continued to have some role in society even in the "darkest" of what are often called the Dark Ages.

The remaining work in Halm's collection (number 16) is the *Dialogue of Charlemagne and Alcuin concerning Rhetoric and the Virtues*, written by Alcuin (in Latin, Albinus) in 794.[19] Alcuin was a Briton whom Charlemagne came to know and placed in charge of the palace school at Aachen in 781 as part of an effort to improve literacy. In 795 Charlemagne issued an edict, "On Cultivating Letters," which encouraged churches and monasteries to provide instruction in grammar and rhetoric primarily so that a larger number of persons would be able to read the Scriptures. This could be said to mark the beginning of the rebirth of classical studies that characterizes the "Carolingian" Age and led to the formation of cathedral schools and eventually universities. The dialogue form as used by Alcuin is more reminiscent of the question and answer catechism found in the work by Fortunatianus than it is of a Ciceronian dialogue. Definitions and divisions of each of the five parts of rhetoric are briefly set out. The sources are primarily Cicero's *On Invention* and, for subjects not discussed there, the rhetorical handbook of Julius Victor. Because of the reliance on Cicero's work, focus is almost exclusively on judicial rhetoric. Whether or not this interested Charlemagne is not known, but the following centuries saw the beginnings of the jury system in medieval Europe and with it some increased opportunity for the use of judicial rhetoric. Alcuin did not discuss preaching, but his student Rabanus Maurus subsequently wrote a major treatise on the subject, *On the Education of Clerics*, which draws heavily on Augustine and contributed to the revival of preaching in the following centuries. An encomium of the Holy Cross by Rabanus also shows an effort to revive Christian panegyric.

Boethius

The most important late Latin works on rhetoric not included in Halm's collection are those by Boethius, written in the early sixth century. Boethius was probably the most learned Roman of his time, thoroughly conversant with Greek, and the major figure in transmitting Aristotle's logical works to the medieval West, where they became the basis for scholastic philosophy. He also wrote theological works and treatises on the quadrivium. At the same time, he was a leading statesman-orator at the Ostrogothic court: con-

[18] Translation by Colgrave and Mynors, *Bede's Ecclesiastical History*.
[19] Translation by Howell, *Rhetoric of Alcuin*.

sul in 510, head of the civil service from 520 to 522. His imprisonment and execution (in 524) resulted from accusations of conspiracy with the Eastern emperor against the Ostrogothic kingdom; in prison, he wrote his most famous work, *On the Consolation of Philosophy.*

Boethius' most important discussion of rhetoric is to be found in the fourth book of *De Topicis Differentiis, On Topical "Differentiae."*[20] This work is not a handbook but a treatise addressed to scholars, and the objective of the fourth book is to demonstrate that rhetorical topics can be subsumed under the same headings as dialectical topics. Boethius explains the difference between dialectic and rhetoric quite clearly. Dialectic examines theses, that is general propositions; rhetoric investigates and discusses hypotheses or specific cases, though dialectic may occasionally use specific instances and rhetoric may occasionally discuss a thesis on which the hypothesis depends. Dialectic takes the form of question and answer, rhetoric uses continuous discourse; dialectic uses complete syllogisms, rhetoric uses enthymemes (in the Aristotelian sense); dialectic elicits a decision from an opponent, rhetoric from a judge. The outline of rhetoric that follows is Ciceronian; despite Boethius' familiarity with other writings of Aristotle he does not refer to *On Rhetoric* and probably knew it only indirectly, but he applies Aristotelian logic to rhetorical definitions and divisions. He takes a broader, more theoretical view of his subject than do late Latin rhetoricians, providing few examples, and the result is an abstract description of the discipline of rhetoric, its parts, and its topics rather than a handbook of rhetorical practice. He promises to discuss the genus of the art, its species, matter, parts, instrument, parts of the instrument, work, function of the speaker, end, questions, and topics. There is no tradition of discussing these matters, he says, for ancient authors have written about particulars rather than the art as a whole. This is not entirely true; Aristotle, Cicero, and Quintilian discuss these concepts, and something is said about them also in Greek prolegomena. The latter were part of the effort of Neoplatonists to make rhetoric propaedeutic to philosophy; Aristotle had regarded rhetoric as a "counterpart" to dialectic; Boethius' position seems to be that rhetoric is subsumed under dialectic and represents a special case of dialectic when applied to political questions.[21]

Boethius defines rhetoric as "a faculty" divided into three species—judicial, demonstrative, and deliberative—and five parts—invention, arrangement, style, memory, and delivery. He divides the oration into six parts—exordium, narration, partition, proof, refutation, and peroration. Only invention is discussed in what follows, but occasional remarks keep the whole

[20] Translation by Stump, *De Topicis Differentiis.* What is called Boethius' *Speculatio de Cognatione Rhetoricae* is apparently a version of part of book 4 of this longer work. There is a translation of the *Speculatio* in Miller et al., *Readings in Medieval Rhetoric,* 69–76.

[21] See Leff, "Boethius' *De Differentiis Topicis.*"

in view, as when he says that the end of rhetoric is sometimes within the orator, when he has spoken in a way appropriate for persuasion, sometimes in the audience, when it has been persuaded. Rhetoric is inherent in its species, and the species in its cases. The parts of cases are called *status* (i.e., *staseis*), which can also be called *constitutiones* (the term used in Cicero's *On Invention*) or *quaestiones*. The discussion of topics is based on Cicero's *Topics*, on which Boethius had written a commentary that survives,[22] and also on Themistius' work on the subject. Toward the end, the difference between rhetoric and dialectic is stated in a different way: dialectic discovers arguments from qualities, such as genus, similarity, and contrarity; rhetoric from things that take on a quality, from the thing that is the genus or is similar or is contrary.

A THOUSAND years separated Boethius from Socrates' discussions with Gorgias and Phaedrus on the nature of rhetoric. Those thousand years had seen the formulation, development, and impoverishment of the classical system of civic rhetoric. Boethius, at the end of antiquity, again asks and suggests answers to fundamental questions about the nature of rhetoric. His answers were accepted by medieval scholars: *De Topicis Differentiis* was the text adopted for teaching rhetoric at the University of Paris in its statutes of 1215, the first curriculum of higher education in Europe. Between the fifteenth and the seventeenth centuries scholars reopened the debate and found somewhat different answers, which have deeply affected our understanding of rhetoric today. An answer, to which Isocrates, Cicero, and Quintilian might have agreed and which is seriously considered today, is that the method of dialectic and the discourses of philosophy, religion, literature, history, economics, and even science are subsumed under the genus of rhetoric.

[22] Translated by Stump, *In Ciceronis Topica*.

This Bibliography includes basic reference works on classical rhetoric and books and articles referred to in the notes by author and short title, except for translations in the Loeb Classical Library. The latter were long published by William Heineman Ltd. in London jointly with Harvard University Press in Cambridge, Massachusetts, but now exclusively by Harvard University Press. They are easily located in library catalogues under both the name of the Greek or Latin author and the name of the translator. Other translations identified in the notes are listed here under the name of the translator.

Achard, Guy, ed. and trans. *Rhétorique à Herennius*. Paris: Les Belles Lettres, 1989.

Adamietz, Joachim, ed. and comm. *M. F. Quintiliani Institutionis Oratoriae Liber III*. Munich: Wilhelm Fink, 1966.

Anderson, Graham. *Philostratus: Biography and Belles Lettres in the Third Century A.D.* London: Croom Helm, 1986.

André, Jacques, ed. and trans. *Isidore de Seville, Etymologies*. Paris: Les Belles Lettres, 1981.

Austin, R. G., ed. and comm. *Quintiliani Institutionis Oratoriae Liber XII*. Oxford: Clarendon Press, 1948.

Baldwin, Charles S. *Medieval Rhetoric and Poetic (to 1400) Interpreted from Representative Works*. New York: Macmillan, 1928.

Barnes, T. D. "Himerius and the Fourth Century." *Classical Philology* 72 (1987):206–25.

_____. "Synesius in Constantinople." *Greek, Roman, and Byzantine Studies* 26 (1986):93–112.

Barrow, R. H. *Prefect and Emperor: The "Relationes" of Symmachus, A.D. 384*. Oxford: Clarendon Press, 1973.

Behr, Charles A. *Aelius Aristides and the Sacred Tales*. Amsterdam: Hakkert, 1968.

_____, trans. *P. Aelius Aristides, The Complete Works*. 2 vols. Leiden: Brill, 1981 86.

Benario, Herbert W., trans. *Tacitus: Agricola, Germany, Dialogue on Orators*. Indianapolis: Bobbs-Merrill, 1967.

Bird, Otto A. *Cultures in Conflict: An Essay in the Philosophy of the Humanities*. Notre Dame: University of Notre Dame Press, 1976.

Blinn, Sharon B., and Mary Garrett. "Aristotelian *Topoi* as a Cross-Cultural Analytical Tool." *Philosophy and Rhetoric* 26 (1993):93–112.

Blois, Lukas de. "The *Eis Basileia* of Pseudo-Aristides." *Greek, Roman, and Byzantine Studies* 26 (1986):279–88.

Bogan, Mary Inez. "The Vocabulary and Style of the Soliloquies and Dialogues of Saint Augustine." *Catholic University of America Patristic Studies* 42 (1935).

Bonner, S. F. *Roman Declamation in the Late Republic and Early Empire*. Berkeley: University of California Press, 1949.

Boulanger, André. *Aelius Aristide et la sophistique dans la province d'Asie au IIe siècle de notre ère*. Paris: E. de Boccard, 1923.

Bowersock, Glen W. *Greek Sophists in the Roman Empire*. Oxford: Clarendon Press, 1969.

Boyle, Marjorie O'Rourke. "Augustine in the Garden of Zeus: Lust, Love, and Language." *Harvard Theological Review* 83 (1990):117–39.

Brandes, Paul D. *A History of Aristotle's "Rhetoric."* Metuchen, N.J.: Scarecrow Press, 1989.

Bregman, Jay. *Synesius of Cyrene*. Berkeley: University of California Press, 1982.

Brown, Peter. *Augustine of Hippo: A Biography*. Berkeley: University of California Press, 1969.

———. *Power and Persuasion in Late Antiquity*. Madison: University of Wisconsin Press, 1992.

Buffière, Félix., ed. and trans. *Héraclite, Allégories d'Homère*. Paris: Les Belles Lettres, 1989.

Burkert, Walter. "Aristoteles im Theater: Zur Datierum des 3. Buch der *Rhetorik* und der *Poetik*." *Museum Helveticum* 32 (1975):67–72.

Butler, H. E., trans. *The Apologia and Florida of Apuleius of Madaura*. Oxford: Clarendon Press, 1909.

Butts, James R. "The Progymnasmata of Theon: A New Text with Translation and Commentary." Dissertation. Claremont Graduate School, 1987.

Cahn, Michael. "The Rhetoric of Rhetoric: Six Tropes of Disciplinary Self-Constitution." In *The Recovery of Rhetoric*, edited by R. H. Roberts and J. M. M. Good, 61–84. Charlottesville: University Press of Virginia, 1993.

Cairns, Francis. *Generic Composition in Greek and Latin Poetry*. Edinburgh: University Press, 1972.

Calboli, Gualtiero, ed. and comm. *Rhetorica ad C. Herennium*. Bologna: Riccardo Pàtron, 1969.

Calboli Montefusco, Lucia. *La dottrina degli Status nella retorica greca e romana*. Bologna: Dipartimento di Filologia Classica et Medioevale, 1984.

———, ed. and comm. *Consulti Fortunatiani Ars Rhetorica*. Bologna: Pàtron Editore, 1979.

Cameron, Averil. *Christianity and the Rhetoric of Empire: The Develpment of Christian Discourse*. Berkeley: University of California Press, 1991.

Carawan, Edwin. "The *Tetralogies* and Athenian Homicide Trials." *American Journal of Philology* 114 (1993):235–70.

Cassin, Barbara, ed. *Le plaisir de parler: Etudes de sophistique comparée*. Paris: Edition de Minuit, 1986.

Cole, Thomas. *The Origins of Rhetoric in Ancient Greece*. Baltimore: Johns Hopkins University Press, 1991.

———. "Who Was Corax?" *Illinois Classical Studies* 16 (1991):65–84.

Colgrave, Bertram, and R. A. B. Mynors, trans. *Bede's Ecclesiastical History of the English People*. Oxford: Clarendon Press, 1969.

Colonna, Aristides, ed. *Himerii Declamationes et Orationes*. Rome: Typis Publicae Officinae Polygraphicae, 1951.

Colpi, Bruno. *Die Paideia des Themistocles: Ein Beitrag zur Geschichte der Bildung in 4. Jr. n. Chr.* Frankfurt: Lang, 1987.

Colson, F. H., ed. and comm. *Quintilian's Institutio Oratoria, Book I*. Cambridge, Cambridge University Press, 1924.

Conley, Thomas M. "Logical Hylomorphism and Aristotle's *Koinoi Topoi*." *Central States Speech Journal* 29 (1978):92–97.

———. *Rhetoric in the European Traditon*. New York: Longman, 1990.

Connor, W. Robert, ed. *Greek Orations*. Ann Arbor: University of Michigan Press, 1966.

Consigny, Scott. "The Styles of Gorgias." *Rhetoric Society Quarterly* 22 (1992):43–53.

Cope, E. M., and J. E. Sandys, eds. *Aristotle's Rhetoric with a Commentary*. 3 vols. Cambridge: Cambridge University Press, 1877.

Cousin, Jean, ed. and trans. *Quintilien, Institution oratoire*. 7 vols. Paris: Les Belles Lettres, 1975–80.

Craig, Christopher P. *Form as Argument in Cicero's Speeches: A Study of Dilemma*. Atlanta: Scholars Press, 1993.

Day, J. W. *The Glory of Athens: The Popular Tradition as Reflected in the Panathenaicus of Aelius Aristides*. Chicago: Ares, 1980.

Delanois, Marcel. "Du plan logique au plan psychologique chez Démosthène." *Les Etudes Classiques* 19 (1951):177–89.

Derrida, Jacques. "Plato's Pharmacy." In *Dissemination*, translated by Barbara Johnson, 63–171. Chicago: University of Chicago Press, 1981.

Dieter, Otto A. L., and William C. Kurth, trans. "The *De Rhetorica* of Aurelius Augustinus." *Speech Monographs* 35 (1968):90–108.

Dilts, M. R., ed. *Scholia Demosthenica*. 2 vols. Leipzig: Teubner, 1983.

———, ed. *Scholia in Aeschinem*. Leipzig: Teubner, 1992.

Dodds, E. R., ed. and comm. *Plato, Gorgias*. Oxford: Clarendon Press, 1959.

Donnelly, Francis X. *Cicero's Milo: A Rhetorical Commentary*. New York: Fordham University Press, 1934.

Douglas, A. E., ed. and comm. *M. Tullii Ciceronis Brutus*. Oxford: Clarendon Press, 1966.

Dover, K. J. *Greek Homosexuality*. Cambridge: Harvard University Press, 1978.

———. *Lysias and the Corpus Lysiacum*. Berkeley: University of California Press, 1968.

Downey, Glanville, trans. "Libanius' Oration in Praise of Antioch." *Proceedings of the American Philosophical Society* 103 (1959):652–86.

———, trans. "Themistius' First Oration." *Greek, Roman, and Byzantine Studies* 1 (1958):49–69.

Drake, Harold Allen. *In Praise of Constantine: A Historical Study and New Translation of Eusebius' Triennial Oration*. Berkeley: University of California Press, 1976.

Eden, Kathy. *Poetic and Legal Fiction in the Aristotelian Tradition*. Princeton: Princeton University Press, 1986.

Fairweather, Janet. *Seneca the Elder*. Cambridge: Cambridge University Press, 1981.

Fantham, Elaine. "The Growth of Literature and Criticism at Rome." In *The Cambridge History of Literary Criticism I: Classical Criticism*, edited by George A. Kennedy, 220–44; "Latin Criticism of the Early Empire," 274–96. Cambridge: Cambridge University Press, 1989.

Ferrari, G. R. F. *Listening to the Cicadas: A Study of Plato's Phaedrus*. Cambridge: Cambridge University Press, 1987.

Finaert, Joesph. *Saint Augustin rhéteur*. Paris: Les Belles Lettres, 1939.

Finley, John H. "The Origins of Thucydides' Style." *Harvard Studies in Classical Philology* 50 (1939):35–84. Reprinted in *Three Essays on Thucydides*. Cambridge: Harvard University Press, 1967.

FitzGerald, Augustine, trans. *The Essays and Hymns of Synesius of Cyrene*. 2 vols. London: Oxford University Press, 1930.

————, trans. *The Letters of Synesius of Cyrene*. London: Oxford University Press, 1926.

Fortenbaugh, William W. "Aristotle On Persuasion through Character." *Rhetorica* 10 (1992):207–44.

————. "Theophrastus on Delivery." *Rutgers University Studies in Classical Humanities* 2 (1985):269–85.

Fortenbaugh, William W., and David C. Mirhady, eds. "Peripatetic Rhetoric after Aristotle." *Rutgers University Studies in Classical Humanities* Vol. 6. New Brunswick: Rutgers University Press, 1993.

Fortenbaugh, William W. et al., eds. *Theophrastus of Eresus: Sources for His Life, Writings, Thought and Influence*. 2 vols. Leiden: Brill, 1992.

Frend, W. H. C. *The Donatist Church*. Oxford: Clarendon Press, 1952.

Fuhrmann, Manfred, ed. *Anaximenis Ars Rhetorica*. Leipzig: Teubner, 1966.

Gaines, Robert N. "Philodemus on the Three Activities of Rhetorical Invention." *Rhetorica* 3 (1985):155–63.

————. "Qualities of Rhetorical Expression in Philodemus." *Transactions of the American Philological Association* 112 (1982):71–81.

Geffcken, Katherine A. *Comedy in the Pro Caelio*. Leiden: Brill, 1973.

Goodwin, William W., ed. and comm. *Demosthenes, On the Crown*. Cambridge: Cambridge University Press, 1904.

Gotoff, Harold C. *Cicero's Caesarian Speeches: A Stylistic Commentary*. Chapel Hill: University of North Carolina Press, 1993.

————. *Cicero's Elegant Style: An Analysis of the Pro Archia*. Urbana: University of Illinois Press, 1979.

Granatelli, Rossella. *Apollodori Pergameni ac Theodori Gadarei Testimonia et Fragmenta*. Rome: Bretschneider, 1991.

Grant, Michael, trans. *Cicero, Murder Trials*. Harmondsworth, Eng.: Penguin, 1975.

————, trans. *Cicero, Selected Political Speeches*. Harmondsworth, Eng.: Penguin, 1969.

Grimaldi, W. M. A. *Aristotle, "Rhetoric": A Commentary*. 2 vols. New York: Fordham University Press, 1980–88.

Grube, G. M. A. "Theodorus of Gadara." *American Journal of Philology* 80 (1959):337–65.

————, trans. and comm. *A Greek Critic: Demetrius On Style*. Toronto: University of Toronto Press, 1961.

Guthrie, W. K. C. *A History of Greek Philosophy*. 6 vols. Cambridge: Cambridge University Press, 1962–81.

Hadas, Moses, trans. *The Hunters of Euboea*. Garden City, N.Y., Doubleday, 1953.

Halm, Carolus, ed. *Rhetores Latini Minores*. Leipzig: Teubner, 1863. Reprint, Dubuque, Iowa: Wm. C. Brown (no date); Frankfurt: Minerva, 1964.

Hardy, E. G. "The Speech of Claudius on the Adlection of Gallic Senators." *Journal of Philology* 32 (1913):79–95.

Harsting, Pernille. "The Golden Method of Menander Rhetor: The Translations and the Reception of the *Peri Epideiktikōn* in the Italian Renaissance." *Analecta Romana Instituti Danici* 20 (1992):139–57.

Haslam, Michael. "3708, Rhetorical Treatise." *Oxyrhynchus Papiri* 53 (1986):60–88.

Havelock, Eric A. *The Literate Revolution in Greece and Its Cultural Consequences.* Princeton: Princeton University Press, 1982.

Hendrickson, G. L. "Literary Sources in Cicero's *Brutus* and the Technique of Citation in Dialogue." *American Journal of Philology* 27 (1906):184–99.

Horner, Winifred, ed. *Historical Rhetoric: An Annotated Bibliography of Selected Sources in English.* Boston: G. K. Hall, 1980.

Howell, Wilbur Samuel, trans. *The Rhetoric of Alcuin and Charlemagne.* Princeton: Princeton University Press, 1941.

Hubbell, H. M., trans. "The *Rhetorica* of Philodemus." *Transactions of the Connecticut Academy of Arts and Sciences* 23 (1920):243–382.

Innes, Doreen C. "Philodemus." In *Cambridge History of Literary Criticism.* Vol. 1. Edited by George A. Kennedy, 215–19; "Augustan Critics," 245–73. Cambridge: Cambridge University Press, 1989.

Innes, Doreen C., and Michael Winterbottom. *Sopatros the Rhetor: Studies in the Text of the Diairesis Zētēmatōn.* London: Institute of Classical Studies of the University, 1988.

Jaeger, Werner. *Demosthenes: The Origin and Development of His Policy.* Berkeley: University of California Press, 1938.

Janko, Richard. *Aristotle on Comedy: Towards a Reconstruction of Poetics II.* Berkeley: University of California Press, 1984.

Jones, Brian W. "Domitian and the Exile of Dio of Prusa." *La Parola del Passato* 45 (1990):348–57.

Jones, C. P. *The Roman World of Dio Chrysostom.* Cambridge: Harvard University Press, 1978.

Jones, Leslie Weber, trans. *An Introduction to Divine and Human Readings by Cassiodorus Senator.* New York: Columbia University Press, 1946.

Kendall, G. H., trans. *Synesius, In Praise of Baldness.* Vancouver: Pharmakon Press, 1985.

Kennedy, George A. *The Art of Persuasion in Greece.* Princeton: Princeton University Press, 1963.

_____. *The Art of Rhetoric in the Roman World.* Princeton: Princeton University Press, 1972.

_____. *Classical Rhetoric and Its Christian and Secular Tradition from Ancient to Modern Times.* Chapel Hill: University of North Carolina Press, 1980.

_____. "Encolpius and Agamemnon in Petronius." *American Journal of Philology* 99 (1978):171–78.

_____. "Forms and Functions of Latin Speech," *Medieval and Renaissance Studies.* Vol. 10. Chapel Hill: University of North Carolina Press, 1984, 45–73.

_____. *Greek Rhetoric under Christian Emperors.* Princeton: Princeton University Press, 1983.

Kennedy, George A. *New Testament Interpretation through Rhetorical Criticism.* Chapel Hill: University of North Carolina Press, 1984.

———. *Quintilian.* New York: Twayne Publishers, 1969.

———. "'Truth' and 'Rhetoric' in the Pauline Epistles." In *The Bible as Rhetoric: Studies in Biblical Persuasion and Credibility,* edited by Martin Warner, 195–202. London: Routledge, 1990.

———, trans. *Aristotle On Rhetoric: A Theory of Civic Discourse.* New York: Oxford University Press, 1991.

———, ed. *The Cambridge History of Literary Criticism.* Vol. 1: *Classical Criticism.* Cambridge: Cambridge University Press, 1989.

Kimball, Bruce A. *Orators and Philosophers: A History of the Idea of Liberal Education.* New York: Teachers College Press, 1986.

Kinneavy, James L. *Greek Rhetorical Origins of Christian Faith.* New York: Oxford University Press, 1987.

Kirby, John T. *The Rhetoric of Cicero's Pro Cluentio.* Amsterdam: J. C. Gieben, 1990.

Klein, R. "Zu Datierung der Romrede des Aelius Aristides." *Historia* 30 (1981):337–50.

Kumaniechi, Kazimer, ed. *Cicero, De oratore.* Leipzig: Teubner, 1969.

Kustas, George L. *Diatribe in Ancient Rhetorical Theory.* Berkeley: Center for Hermeneutical and Modern Culture, 1976.

Lancel, Serge, ed. *Actes de la Conférence de Carthage en 411.* 3 vols. Paris: Edition de Cerf, 1972.

Lausberg, Heinrich. *Handbuch der literarischen Rhetorik.* 2 vols. Munich: Max Huebler, 1960.

Leeman, Anton. *Orationis Ratio: The Stylistic Theories and Practice of the Roman Orators, Historians, and Philosophers.* 2 vols. Amsterdam: Hakkert, 1963.

Leeman, Anton, Harm Pinkster, et al. *De Oratore Libri III: Kommentar.* 3 vols. to date. Heildeberg: Winter, 1981–.

Leff, Michael C. "Boethius' *De Differentiis Topicis,* Book IV." In *Medieval Eloquence: Studies in the Theory and Practice of Medieval Rhetoric,* edited by James J. Murphy, 3–14. Berkeley: University of California Press, 1978.

———. "The Topics of Argumentative Invention in Latin Rhetorical Theory from Cicero to Boethius." *Rhetorica* 1 (1983):23–44.

Little, Charles E. *Quintilian the School Master.* 2 vols. Nashville: George Peabody College for Teachers, 1951.

Longo Auricchio, Francisca, ed. and trans. "*Philodemou Peri Rhētorikēs,* Libros Primum et Secundum." *Ricerche sui papiri Ercolanesi.* Vol. 3. Naples: Giannini Editore, 1977.

Loraux, Nicole. *The Invention of Athens: The Funeral Oration in the Classical City,* translated by Alan Sheridan. Cambridge: Harvard University Press, 1986.

McCauley, Leo P., trans. *Funeral Orations by Saint Gregory Nazianzen and Saint Ambrose.* Washington: Catholic University of American Press, 1968.

MacMullen, Ramsey. "Hellenizing the Romans (Second Century B.C.)." *Historia* 40 (1991):419–38.

Malcovati, Enrica, ed. *Oratorum Romanorum Fragmenta.* Pavia, It.: G. B. Paravia, 1953.

Malherbe, Abraham J. "Ancient Epistolary Theorists." *Ohio Journal of Religious Studies* 5 (1977):3–77.

_____. *Moral Exhortation: A Greco-Roman Sourcebook*. Philadelphia: Westminster Press, 1986.

Marrou, Henri-Irenée. *A History of Education in Antiquity*, translated by George Lamb. New York: Sheed and Ward, 1956.

_____. *Saint Augustin et la fin de la culture antique*. 2d ed. Paris: E. de Boccard, 1949.

Martin, Richard P. *The Language of Heroes: Speech and Performance in the Iliad*. Ithaca, N.Y.: Cornell University Press, 1989.

Matson, Patricia P., Philip Rollinson, and Marion Sousa, eds. *Readings from Classical Rhetoric*. Carbondale: Southern Illinois University Press, 1990.

Matthes, Dieter. "Hermagoras von Temnos 1904–1955." *Lustrum* 3 (1958):58–214.

May, James M. *Trials of Character: The Eloquence of Ciceronian Ethos*. Chapel Hill: University of North Carolina Press, 1988.

Meador, Prentice A., Jr. "Minucian, *On Epicheiremes*: An Introduction and a Translation." *Speech Monographs* 31 (1964):54–63.

Miller, Joseph M., Michael H. Prosser, and Thomas W. Benson, eds. *Readings in Medieval Rhetoric*. Bloomington: Indiana University Press, 1973.

Moles, J. L. "The Career and Conversion of Dio Chrysostom." *Journal of Hellenic Studies* 98 (1978):79–100.

Montague, Holly W. "Advocacy and Politics: The Paradox of Cicero's *Pro Ligario*." *American Journal of Philology* 113 (1992):559–74.

Morford, Mark P. O. "*Iubes Esse Liberos*: Pliny's *Panegyricus* and Liberty." *American Journal of Philology* 113 (1992):575–93.

Murgia, Charles E. "Pliny's Letters and the *Dialogus*." *Harvard Studies in Classical Philology* 89 (1985):171–206.

Murphy, James J. *Rhetoric in the Middle Ages: A History of Rhetorical Theory from Saint Augustine to the Renaissance*. Berkeley: University of California Press, 1974.

_____. "*Topos* and *Figura*: Historical Cause and Effect?" In *De Ortu Grammaticae: Studies in Medieval Grammar and Linguistic Theory in Memory of Jan Pinborg* (*Studies in the History of the Language Sciences* 43), 239–53. Amsterdam: Benjamins, 1990.

Nadeau, Raymond, trans. "The *Progymnasmata* of Aphthonius." *Speech Monographs* 19 (1952) 264–85.

_____. "Hermogenes' *On Stases*: A Translation with an Introduction and Notes." *Speech Monographs* 31 (1964):361–424.

Navarre, Octave. *Essai sur la rhétorique grecque avant d'Aristote*. Paris: Hachette, 1900.

Nelson, W. F. "Topoi: Evidence of Human Conceptual Behavior." *Philosophy and Rhetoric* 2 (1969):1–11.

Norden, Eduard. *Antike Kunstprose vom VI. Jahrhunderts vor Christus bis in die Zeit der Renaissance*. 2 vols. Leipzig: Teubner, 1909. Reprint, Stuttgart: Teubner, 1958.

Norman, A. F., ed. and comm. *Libanius' Autobiography*. London: Oxford University Press, 1965.

Ochs, Donovan J. "Aristotle's Concept of Formal Topics." *Speech Monographs* 36 (1969):419–25.

O'Donnell, James J. *Cassiodorus*. Berkeley: University of California Press, 1979.

Oliver, James H., trans "The Civilizing Power: A Study of the Panathenaic Discourse of Aelius Aristides against the Background of Literature and Cultural Conflict." *Transactions of the American Philosophical Society* 58, 1 (1968).

————, trans. "The Ruling Power: A Study of the Roman Empire in the Second Century after Christ through the Roman Oration of Aelius Aristides." *Transactions of the American Philosophical Society* 43, 4 (1953).

O'Neil, Edward N. "The Chreia in Greco-Roman Literature and Education." In *The Institute for Antiquity and Christianity Report 1972–80*, edited by Marvin W. Meyer, 19–22. Claremont, Calif., Claremont Graduate School, 1981.

Ong, Walter J. *Orality and Literacy: The Technologizing of the Word*. London: Methuen, 1982.

O'Sullivan, Neil. *Alcidamas, Aristophanes, and the Beginnings of Greek Stylistic Theory*. Hermes Einzelschriften 60. Stuttgart: Franz Steiner, 1992.

Parsons, Wilfrid. "A Study of the Vocabulary and Rhetoric of the Letters of Saint Augustine." *Catholic University of America Patristic Studies* 3 (1923).

Patterson, Annabel M. *Hermogenes and the Renaissance: Seven Ideas of Style*. Princeton: Princeton University Press, 1970.

Pease, Arthur Stanley. "Things without Honor." *Classical Philology* 21 (1926):27–42.

Peterson, William, ed. and comm. *M. Fabi Quintiliani Institutionis Oratoriae Liber Decimus*. Oxford: Clarendon Press, 1891.

Prickard, Arthur O., ed. *Libellus de Sublimitate Dionysio Longine fere Adscriptus Accedunt Exercepta Quaedam e Cassii Longini Operibus*. Oxford: Clarendon Press, 1906.

Pritchett, W. Kendrick, trans. *Dionysius of Halicarnassus: On Thucydides*. Berkeley: University of California Press, 1975.

Rabe, Hugo, ed. *Hermogenis Opera*. Leipzig: Teubner, 1913.

————, ed. *Prolegomenon Sylloge*. Leipzig: Teubner, 1931.

Rabinowitz, Isaac, ed. and trans. *The Book of the Honeycomb's Flow by Judah Messer Leon*. Ithaca, N.Y.: Cornell University Press, 1983.

Radermacher, Ludwig, ed. *Artium Scriptores (Reste der voraristotelischen Rhetorik)*. Oesterreichische Akademie der Wissenschaften, Philosophisch-historische Klasse, *Sitzungsberichte* 227, 3. Vienna: Rudolf M. Rohrer, 1951.

Raedt, H. de. "Plan psychologique de la première *Philippique* de Démosthène." *Les Etudes Classiques* 19 (1951):227–29.

Richardson, Ernest Cushing, trans. "Eusebius' *Life of Constantine*." In A *Select Library of Nicene and Post-Nicene Fathers of the Church*, edited by Philip Schall and Henry Wace, 471–559. Second series. Vol. 1. Grand Rapids, Mich.: Eerdmanns, 1955.

Rist, John M. *The Mind of Aristotle: A Study in Philosophical Growth*. Toronto: University of Toronto Press, 1977.

Robbins, Vernon K. *Jesus the Teacher: A Socio-Rhetorical Interpretation of Mark*. Philadelphia: Fortress Press, 1984.

————, and Burton L. Mack. *Patterns of Persuasion in the Gospels*. Sonoma, Calif., Polebridge, 1989.

Roberts, W. Rhys, ed. and trans. *Demetrius, On Style*. Cambridge: Cambridge University Press, 1902.

———, ed. and trans. *Dionysius of Halicrnassus, On Literary Composition*. Cambridge: Cambridge University Press, 1910.

———, ed. and trans. *Dionysius of Halicarnassus, Three Literary Letters*. Cambridge: Cambridge University Press, 1901.

Robertson, D. W., Jr., trans. *Saint Augustine On Christian Doctrine*. Indianapolis: Bobbs-Merrill, 1958.

Romilly, Jacqueline de. *Magic and Rhetoric in Ancient Greece*. Cambridge: Harvard University Press, 1975.

Roques, Denis. *Synésius de Cyrène et la Cyrénaique du bas empire*. Paris: CNRS, 1988.

Rowe, Galen. "The Many Facets of *Hybris* in Demosthenes, *Against Meidias*." *American Journal of Philology* 114 (1993):397–406.

Ruether, Rosemary Radford. *Gregory of Nazianzus: Rhetor and Philosopher*. Oxford: Clarendon Press, 1969.

Russell, D. A. "Greek Criticism of the Empire." In *The Cambridge History of Literary Criticism I: Classical Criticism*, edited by George A. Kennedy, 297–329. Cambridge: Cambridge University Press, 1989.

———. *Greek Declamation*. Cambridge: Cambridge University Press, 1983.

Russell, D. A., ed. and comm. *Dio Chrysostom, Orations VII, XII, and XXXVI*. Cambridge: Cambridge University Press, 1992.

Russell, D. A., and N. G. Wilson, eds. and trans. *Menander Rhetor*. Oxford: Clarendon Press, 1981.

Russell, D. A., and Michael Winterbottom, eds. *Ancient Literary Criticism: The Principal Texts in New Translations*. Oxford: Clarendon Press, 1972.

Sandys, J. E., ed. and comm. *M. Tulli Ciceronis ad Brutum Orator*. Cambridge: Cambridge University Press, 1885.

Saunders, A. N. W., trans. *Greek Political Oratory*. Harmondsworth, Eng.: Penguin, 1970.

Schenkeveld, Dirk M. "Figures and Tropes: A Border-Case between Grammar and Rhetoric." In *Rhetorik zwischen den Wissenschaften*, edited by Gert Ueding, 149–57. Tübingen, Ger.: Max Miemeter Verlag, 1991.

Schiappa, Edward. "Did Plato Coin *Rhētorikē*?" *American Journal of Philology* 111 (1990):457–70.

———. *Protagoras and Logos*. Columbia: University of South Carolina Press, 1991.

Sealey, Raphael. *Demosthenes and His Time: A Study in Defeat*. New York: Oxford University Press, 1993.

Sheppard, A. R. R. "Dio Chrysostom, the Bithynian Years." *L'Antiquité Classique* 53 (1984):157–73.

Sinclair, Patrick. "A Study in the Sociology of Rhetoric: The *Sententia* in *Rhetorica ad Herennium*." *American Journal of Philology* 114 (1993):561–80.

Solmsen, Friedrich. "The Aristotelian Tradition in Ancient Rhetoric." *American Journal of Philology* 62 (1941):35–50, 169–90.

———. "The Gift of Speech in Homer and Hesiod." *Transactions of the American Philological Association* 85 (1954):1–15.

Solmsen, Friedrich. *Intellectual Experiments of the Greek Enlightenment*. Princeton: Princeton University Press, 1975.

Spengel, Leonard, ed. *Rhetores Graeci*. 3 vols. Leipzig: Teubner, 1853–56. Reprint, Frankfurt: Minerva, 1966.

Spengel, Leonard, and Caspar Hammer, eds. *Rhetores Graeci*. Vol. 1. Leipzig: Teubner, 1894.

Sprague, Rosamond Kent, ed. *The Older Sophists*. Columbia: University of South Carolina Press, 1972.

Squires, Simon, ed. and trans. *Commentaries on Five Speeches of Cicero by Asconius*. Bristol, Eng.: Bristol Classical Press, 1990.

Stahl, William Harris, and Richard Johnson, with E. L. Burge. *Martianus Capella and the Seven Liberal Arts*. 2 vols. New York: Columbia University Press, 1971.

Stowers, Stanley K. *The Diatribe and Paul's Letter to the Romans*. Chico, Calif.: Scholars Press, 1981.

Stump, Eleonore, trans. and comm. *Boethius's De Topicis Differentiis*. Ithaca, N.Y.: Cornell University Press, 1978.

————, trans. and comm. *Boethius's In Ciceronis Topica*. Ithaca, N.Y.: Cornell University Press, 1988.

Sussman, Lewis A. *The Elder Seneca*. Leiden: Brill, 1978.

————. *The Major Declamations Ascribed to Quintilian: A Translation*. Frankfurt: Peter Lang, 1987.

Untersteiner, Mario. *The Sophists*, translated by Kathleen Freeman. Oxford: Basil Blackwell, 1954.

Usener, Hermann, and Ludwig Radermacher, eds. *Dionysii Halicarnasei Quae Exstant*. 6 vols. Leipzig: Teubner, 1899. Reprint, 1965.

Van den Hout, M. P. J., ed. *M. Cornelii Frontonis Epistulae*. Leiden: Brill, 1954.

Walden, John W. H. *The Universities of Ancient Greece*. New York: Scribners, 1909.

Walz, Christian, ed. *Rhetores Graeci*. 9 vols. London and elsewhere, 1832–36; Reprint, Osnabrück, Ger.: Zeller, 1968.

Ward, John O. "From Antiquity to the Renaissance: Glosses and Commentaries on Cicero's *Rhetorica*." In *Medieval Eloquence: Studies in the Theory and Practice of Medieval Rhetoric*, edited by James J. Murphy, 25–67. Berkeley: University of California Press, 1978.

Warner, Martin, ed. *The Bible as Rhetoric: Studies in Biblical Persuasion and Credibility*. London: Routledge, 1990.

Watson, Duane Frederick. *Invention, Arrangement, and Style: Rhetorical Criticism of Jude and 2 Peter*. Atlanta: Scholars Press, 1988.

————. "The New Testament and Greco-Roman Rhetoric." *Journal of the Episcopal Theological Seminary* 31 (1988):465–72 and 33 (1990):513–24.

————, ed. *Persuasive Artistry: Studies in New Testament Rhetoric in Honor of George A. Kennedy*. Sheffield, Eng.: Academic Press, 1991.

Westerink, L. G. *Anonymous Prolegomena to Platonic Philosophy*. Amsterdam: Hakkert, 1967.

Wildberg, Christian. "Three Neoplatonic Introductions to Philosophy: Ammonius, David, and Elias." *Hermathena* 149 (1990):33–51.

Williams, James G. "Parable and Chreia: From Q to Narrative Gospel." *Semeia* 43 (1988):85–114.

Wilson, Nigel, ed. and comm. *Saint Basil on the Value of Greek Literature*. London: Duckworth, 1975.

Winterbottom, Michael. "Quintilian and the *Vir Bonus*." *Journal of Roman Studies* 54 (1964):90–97.

_____. *M. Fabi Quintiliani Institutionis Oratoriae Libri Duodecem*. 2 vols. Oxford: Clarendon Press, 1970.

Wisse, Jakob. *Ethos and Pathos from Aristotle to Cicero*. Amsterdam: Hakkert, 1989.

Wooten, Cecil. "The Ambassador's Speech: A Particularly Hellenistic Genre of Oratory." *Quarterly Journal of Speech* 59 (1973):209–12.

_____. *Cicero's Philippics and Their Demosthenic Model: The Rhetoric of Crisis*. Chapel Hill: University of North Carolina Press, 1983.

_____. "Le développement du style asiatique pendant l'époque hellénistique." *Revue des Etudes Grecques* 88 (1975):94–104.

_____., trans. *Hermogenes' On Types of Style*. Chapel Hill: University of North Carolina Press, 1987.

Index